NEW YORK JEW

ALFRED KAZIN

NEW
YORK
JEW

VINTAGE BOOKS
A Division of Random House
New York

FIRST VINTAGE BOOKS EDITION, MAY 1979

Copyright © 1978 by Alfred Kazin
All rights reserved under International and Pan-American
Copyright Conventions. Published in the United States
by Random House, Inc., New York, and in Canada
by Random House of Canada Limited, Toronto.
Originally published by Alfred A. Knopf, Inc., in May 1978.

*Grateful acknowledgment is made to the following for per-
mission to reprint previously published material:*
Harcourt Brace Jovanovich, Inc.: Excerpts from COMPLETE
POEMS 1923–1962, *by E. E. Cummings. Harcourt Brace
Jovanovich, 1972.*
Hill & Wang: Excerpt from "The Distant Runners" from
COLLECTED AND NEW POEMS, 1924–1963, *by
Mark Van Doren. Copyright © 1963 by Mark Van Doren.
Reprinted by permission of Hill & Wang (now a
division of Farrar, Straus & Giroux).*
*Houghton Mifflin Company: Excerpts from "Permit Me Voyage"
from* THE COLLECTED POEMS OF JAMES AGEE,
edited by Robert Fitzgerald. Houghton Mifflin Company, 1968.
Liveright Publishing Corporation: Excerpt from THE
COMPLETE POEMS AND SELECTED LETTERS
AND PROSE OF HART CRANE, *edited by Brom Weber.
Reprinted with permission of Liveright Publishing Corporation.
Copyright 1933, © 1958, 1966 by Liveright Publishing
Corporation.*

Library of Congress Cataloging in Publication Data
Kazin, Alfred, 1915-
New York Jew.
Includes index.
1. Kazin, Alfred, 1915   2. Critics—
United States—Biography.   3.   American literature
—20th century—History and criticism.   4.   New
York (City)—Intellectual life.   I.   Title.
PS29.K38A36   1979   810'.9   [B]   78-23501
ISBN 0-394-72867-X pbk.

Manufactured in the United States of America

FOR CATHRAEL KAZIN

CONTENTS

NEW YORK JEW

Chapter I

WORDS

Anything can happen now that we've slid over this bridge, I thought, anything at all.
—The Great Gatsby

One dreamlike week in 1942 I published my first book, *On Native Grounds*, became an editor of *The New Republic*, and with my wife, Natasha, moved into a little apartment on Twenty-fourth Street and Lexington. Its casement windows looked out on a shop that sold everything you could possibly need for your horse. From across the street the shop seemed to gleam with silver rein buckles, brightly polished saddles and bridles. In front of the shop stood a prancing, thoroughly affable wooden horse painted bright yellow.

I had never lived in Manhattan before. In those first few weeks of my "arrival" in the big city I went between my home, my publishers at Lexington and Twenty-eighth and *The New Republic* at Forty-ninth and Madison in a dizzy exaltation mixed with the direst suspicion of what might happen next. Riding away from the office at the "violet hour" in the sudden opulence of wartime, when the incomparable autumn light of New York still hung over the buildings that would soon be shadowed by the faint wartime brownout, I could feel, when the taxi skidded around the circular passageway under the ramp of Grand Central into Fourth Avenue, sensations

of personal deliverance that came and went like the
light between the arches. I was stupefied by the advance
interest in my book, which would soon give me a considerable boost at *The New Republic*; I loved working
in the center of New York and living in Manhattan.
Riding home at the rush hour, I could taste all the wild
distraction of New York in wartime like a first martini.
But I missed my long solitary days in the Forty-second
Street Library, I was expecting at every moment to be
called into the Army, and I was not prepared for so
much good fortune.

I had begun my book in our single room in Brooklyn
Heights soon after our wedding at City Hall. It was
1938. We were twenty-three, we had known each other
two weeks, Natasha was taking her doctorate in bacteri-
ology at Bellevue, and we were both in a terrible rush to
get away from everything we had grown up with. Beginning my book in a mood of great husbandly contentment, I soon knew that thanks to an idle suggestion from
Carl Van Doren, who liked my first reviews and literary
essays, I had found my natural subject. Van Doren
wondered why there had never been a study of the
"new" American writing in the twentieth century that
would also be a historical explanation of its emergence.

For almost five years I had worked toward the book
in the great open reading room, 315, of the New York
Public Library, often in great all-day bouts of reading
that began when the place opened at nine in the morning
and that ended only at ten at night. With my friend
Richard Hofstadter, who was writing *Social Darwinism
in American Thought* for his doctorate at Columbia, I
would snatch my lunch in the Automat across the street
from the Library, run up Fifth Avenue in the "brownout" for exercise, find a pool parlor off Times Square
for a hurried game of Ping-Pong, then return to the

great yellow tables in 315, somehow always smelling of fresh varnish and piled with our books, on which we had left little notes saying "BACK SOON, DO NOT DISTURB." We spent an afternoon every week in the Trans-Lux Newsreel Theatre on Broadway and solemnly congratulated each other the day we were privileged to look at lines of heavy tanks lumbering off the Detroit assembly lines like new automobiles. War, blessed war, had come to the rescue of my generation, and nothing would ever be the same.

I had written my book at the kitchen table in Brooklyn Heights; on Forty-first Street near the El in Long Island City; at Provincetown in the summer of 1940; and the last summer at Yaddo in Saratoga, where, as I saw Natasha walking away down Union Avenue to her train, I was blinded by my tears and the grief that was to come. For almost five years I had lived in a state of scholarly innocence, of unexpected intellectual assurance that floated my book home on the radical confidence of the 1930s. I had gone back and forth between the subway and 315, between Bryant Park and 315, between the Automat's coffee spigot and 315, between Natasha's influenza lab at Bellevue and 315.

There it was, as soon as you walked up the great marble steps off Fifth Avenue. "ON THE DIFFUSION OF EDUCATION AMONG THE PEOPLE REST THE PRESERVATION AND PERPETUATION OF OUR FREE INSTITUTIONS." It said that to you as you entered the great hall, in gold letters on the pylons facing the Fifth Avenue entrance. The entrance also read: "THE LIBRARY IS OPEN EVERY DAY OF THE YEAR 9 A.M.–10 P.M., MONDAY–SATURDAY. 1–10 SUNDAY."

Year after year I seemed to have nothing more delightful to do than to sit much of the day and many an evening at one of those great golden tables acquainting

myself with every side of my subject. Whenever I was
free to read, the great Library seemed free to receive
me. Anything I had heard of and wanted to see, the
blessed place owned: first editions of American novels
out of those germinal decades after the Civil War that
led to my theme of the "modern"; old catalogues from
long-departed Chicago publishers who had been young
men in the 1890s trying to support a little realism; yellowing, crumbling, but intact sets of the old *Masses*
(1911–1918), which was to the Stalinist *New Masses*
what St. Francis is to the Inquisition; the old *Delineator*,
under the brief editorship of the disgraceful failed
novelist Theodore Dreiser, which cravenly opposed the
vile sexual immorality that had wrecked *Sister Carrie*;
the *Smart Set*, which was "not for the boneheads," said
Mencken and Nathan when they took it over in 1914;
The Chap-Book, which was published in Chicago in
the yellow nineties, yellow especially in Chicago, and
whose honesty about the local scene explained why so
many strong novels would soon come out of Chicago;
forgotten pamphlets by genteel lady hacks of 1900 still
attacking Henry James for *his* un-American immorality
in permitting a splendid American type like Daisy Miller
to walk in the Colosseum at night with a greaser; every
possible item bearing on Randolph Bourne, Eugene
Victor Debs, Max Eastman, Art Young and the many
other Socialists and writers collared by the government
for opposing what Dos Passos would call "Mr. Wilson's
War"; the endless medical advice by Upton Sinclair on
how rice cured his headaches and on how to avoid the
death by drink suffered by armies of American writers;
the opinions on practically everything by James Hune-
ker, Henry Mencken, Willard Huntington Wright, Irving
Babbitt, Paul Elmer More, Edmund Wilson, R. P.

Blackmur, Allen Tate, their followers and their followers' followers.

So between 1938 and 1942 I would many a morning and evening make my way across Fifth Avenue to the main door under the inscription "BUT ABOVE ALL THINGS TRUTH BEARETH AWAY THE VICTORY," past the great hall with its tantalizing display of Renaissance maps, incunabula, letters by Dickens; and since I was too intent on 315 to wait for the elevator, would dash up those steps whose exhilaratingly smooth marble was so much a part of the lordly building designed in 1898 by Carrère & Hastings, past the enormous wall painting "Blind Milton Dictating *Paradise Lost* to His Daughters," through the third-floor halls lined with the many prints of old New York fires and firemen collected by Isaac Newton Phelps Stokes for his iconography of New York City, and finally arrive at the great catalogue room lined wall to wall with trays of endlessly thumbed cards.

I was my own staff researcher, a totally unaffiliated free lance and occasional evening college instructor who was educating himself in the mind of modern America by writing, in the middle of the Great Depression, a wildly ambitious literary and intellectual history. 315 was my intellectual armory. My privacy was complete. No one behind the information desk ever asked me *why* I needed to look at the yellowing, crumbling, fast-fading material about insurgent young Chicago and San Francisco publishing houses in 1897. No one suggested that I might manage whatever-it-was-I-was-doing with something more readily available than the very first issue of *Poetry* in 1912; *The New Republic* in 1914; muckraking *Collier's* in the Theodore Roosevelt era; material showing President Nicholas Murray Butler's displeasure

with Professor Charles A. Beard's *An Economic In-
terpretation of the Constitution of the United States*;
Professor Beard's resignation from Columbia when
President Butler sharply discouraged objections to "Mr.
Wilson's War"; the attacks of John S. Sumner's anti-vice
league on Theodore Dreiser's *The "Genius"*; Alfred A.
Knopf persuading cowardly booksellers to show the
new American and European novelists he was publish-
ing; Eugene O'Neill's experiences living a season on the
Provincetown dunes near the old Peaked Hill Bar Coast
Guard station facing the Atlantic.

As one of "the people" in the New York Public Library, I could get the story of Mrs. Frank Doubleday
getting Mr. Frank Doubleday to suppress Doubleday,
Page & Co.'s edition of *Sister Carrie*; Frank Norris's
efforts as an editor at Doubleday to sneak out review
copies of that wicked book; the 1918 propaganda by
"literary" people that H. L. Mencken was "pro-Ger-
man," attacks so personal that by 1940 Mencken was
defending Hitler; the founding of new magazines, publishing houses, experimental theaters by "new people"
who were radicals, sexual and political, even in the ivy-
dead American universities. . . . I came to know what
Edmund Wilson thought of his classmate Scot Fitzgerald when they were both at Princeton and how that
dogged libertarian John Dos Passos was so horrified
by the Communist execution of anarchists and Socialists
during the Spanish Civil War—and his friend Hemingway's indifference to these murders—that Dos Passos
turned sharp right.

"There's my Middle West," Fitzgerald crooned in
the last slow movement of *The Great Gatsby*. Years
before I saw Chicago, I learned what hope, élan, intellectual freshness came with those pioneer realists out of
the Middle West who said there was no American lit-

erature but the one *they* were rushing to create. My subject had to do with the "modern" as democracy; with America itself as the modern; with the end of the nineteenth century as the great preparation: in lonely small towns, prairie villages, isolated colleges, dusty law offices, national magazines, and provincial "academies" where no one suspected that the obedient-looking young reporters, law clerks, librarians, teachers would turn out to be Willa Cather, Robert Frost, Sinclair Lewis, Wallace Stevens, Marianne Moore. The new literature was being created inside an old century—proud, stormy, yet elegant. The elegance was still in those great halls of the Library; up those marble stairs; always surrounded by pictures of the mid-century reservoir that had been replaced by the Library, the old fire fighters in their red wagons, the traditional view from the Battery. These put me right back into the turn of the century that saw the building of the Library—and the intellectual insurgence and radical hope that bedrocked my book. Even the spacious twin reading rooms, each two blocks long, gave me a sense of the powerful amenity that I craved for my own life, a world of power in which my own people had moved about as strangers.

It fascinated me, in those days of our easy radicalism before the war—and only the war—ended the Great Depression, to do my reading and thinking in that asylum and church of the unemployed; of crazy ideologists and equally crazy Bible students doggedly writing "YOU LIE!" in the reference books on the open shelves; of puzzle fans searching every encyclopedia; of commission salesmen secretly tearing address lists out of city directories.

Whatever happened to the little man with one slice of hair across his bald head, like General MacArthur's, the little man who was always there every day I ever went in between 1938 and 1942, poring with a faint smile over a large six-column Bible in Hebrew, Greek, Latin, English, French, German? Or the bony, ugly, screeching madwoman who reminded me of Maxim Gorky's "Boless," the anguished old maid who had a professional scribe take down passionate letters to a lover and then asked the scribe to make up letters from the lover to her? She invariably accused the man reading next to her of trying to pick her up. She would cry out with a madly contented smile—"This is a library, Buster! A place to read in! Get it, Buster?"

Street philosophers, fanatics, advertising agents, the homeless—passing faces in the crowd. I liked reading and working out my ideas in the midst of that endless crowd walking in and out of 315 looking for *something*; that Depression crowd so pent up, searching for puzzle contests, beauty contests, clues to buried treasure off Sandy Hook; seeking lost and dead rich relatives in old New York books of genealogy and Pittsburgh telephone books. Reading in the midst of this jumpy Depression crowd, I, too, was seeking fame and fortune by sitting at the end of a long golden table next to the sets of American authors on the open shelves. I could feel on my skin the worry of all those people; I could hear day and evening those restless hungry footsteps; I was entangled in the hunger of all those aimless, bewildered, panicky seekers for "opportunity." I must have looked as mad to them as they did to me: jumping up with excitement and walking about the great halls as I discovered that just for the asking I could obtain all the books anyone would ever want to read by William Dean Howells, Henry James, Stephen Crane, Joseph Kirkland, Robert Herrick, Ed Howe, Henry Blake Fuller, Frank Norris, Theodore Dreiser, Jack London. I could read the mind behind each book. I felt connected with

knows his prayers and will teach them to my father, will as a matter of course join the other pieceworkers when they cry out as they put on their prayer shawls, "How Goodly Are Your Tents, O Jacob, Your Habitations, O Israel!"

How young he looks to me, how puzzled, crammed and laden with burdens. I must save him. It is all up to me. It will always be up to me. The Jews are my unconscious. In Russia the great Pobedonostsev, head of the Russian Synod and friend to Dostoevsky, disposed of the noxious Russian Jews in one sentence: "One-third will die, one-third will leave the country, and the last third will be completely assimilated within the Russian people." But if Russia segregated and tortured the proscribed Jews, America gives some arrivals a little joy. Already a father and with another child on the way, my patriarch "takes it into his head" to organize miserable pieceworkers by himself. I can just hear my pregnant—certainly more "practical"—grandmother telling him off. He works harder, harder; he is tearing at my heart; those first lockouts and picket lines in winter will kill him yet! I see him forever trudging about, pack on back, pack and back, like those "Jew peddlers" you can still see in New York pushing a cart full of second-hand clothes and ringing a bell—"I cash old clóthes! I cash old clóthes!" I would like to save him, he is so young and looks so baffled and walled in by this strange land.

He dies, twenty-five, maybe twenty-six. His body is flung in with thousands of other immigrant Jews who perished those first years on the East Side. My father will never be able to find his father's grave. The terrified widow gives birth to a posthumous child, who is of course named Abraham after his dead father. Alone now with her two sons in oceanic New York, my grandmother somehow makes her way back to Minsk, puts my father into the orphan asylum, finds work as a maid, then marrying again and starting a new family, seems not to have had much contact with my father. He wound up in one of the agricultural schools set up by the philanthropist Baron de Hirsch to put young Jews on the land, then came to America on his own when he was nineteen. My Uncle Abraham will never be able to prove that he was born here. My grandmother must have left in a terrible hurry. My father will never get over the shock of his father's death, the sudden return to Russia, the orphan asylum, and the long absence from his mother. The older I get, the more orphaned he will seem to me, and in some way more my son than my father. Returning here alone as a timid young workman of nineteen, he somehow became "Charlie." His Hebrew name, which I loved for him but which only my mother ever used, was Gedaliah, "God Is Great," after the guardian of the Jews exempt from the Babylonian captivity who was "treacherously murdered," say all the books, on a day of mourning that is still commemorated by fasting among the most pious Jews.

Gedaliah became "Charlie" and an unreachably lonely, self-centered, always "peculiar" man who was not like other Jewish fathers, not a hustler and a bustler, not "regular," not active for his children. In the midst of our tumultuous Jewish neighborhood, he was grimly alone. He became a great man for walking about instead of talking, for walking alone. He liked to feel himself near an exit, and he certainly knew how to make an exit quickly, silently, disapprovingly. He slid out the front door just as soon after supper as he could. I never suspected him of really going anywhere. He just wanted to get away from where he was currently at, to make his getaway. He was a man notably lacking in curiosity about other people, and preferred to hug his solitude in lonely city walks and to sit out an afternoon in the Eastern Parkway branch of the Brooklyn Public Library.

But as a boy I idolized him for the connection with America-at-large that he had made as a painter on the Union Pacific Railroad. He had gone West with the railroad, had been offered a homestead, had seen the great country that my illiterate housebound mother would never know. I lovingly enlarged every morsel of our walks to museums, parks, libraries; our working-class solidarity, father and son, as he described great labor struggles and the struggle for Socialism—in my childhood the only Jewish religion that could take him out of himself. I saw him break down when Eugene V. Debs died, when Robert M. La Follette lost the Presidency, when Sacco and Vanzetti went to the chair.

Later, when I began to write about him, I could feel the pulse of our every walk together in the Brooklyn Botanic Garden. As a Jew segregated in the Pale, he would never have been allowed into St. Petersburg. "Nice!" he allowed. "But you should have seen the Czar's Summer Palace!" What beautiful myths and obstinate delusions these despised Russian Jews lived on! My wonderful Aunt Nechama for seventy years believed in the sainthood of Prince Peter Kropotkin. Russia would live by his teaching, then "the whole world." But it was always bliss when my father returned from work with the New York *World* and the *Jewish Daily Forward*. *"Forward! You have nothing to lose but your chains! You have a world to win!"*

Standing with him at the kitchen sink, I keep pouring the harsh abrasive Gold Dust Twins washing powder into his hands as he gruntingly peels and scrubs the paint off. Sitting with him at Lewisohn Stadium waiting to hear our favorite late-nineteenth-century Russian heartthrobs, I am intoxicated by the blue, still light summer evening. Blaze. I would always have a sense of grace in the protracted summer light, "gold-beaten out to ages." At fifteen I felt such delight to be at an open-air concert with my father that I treasured his silences as part of the glittering lights on the stage, the long school shades drawn down in the City College across the street that I would be entering the next year, the slow vibration from side to side of all those emotional music lovers humming the slow movement of Tchaikov-sky's Fifth along with the orchestra. Afterward, we ate watermelon in the Bickford's at 137th and Broadway, rode the open top of a Fifth Avenue bus. I was proud of my father then and especially in those quiet woman-less weeks when my mother went off to Iowa to tend to a cousin who had gone off her head. My father and I, happily letting the household go to hell, ate in cafeterias. I took pleasure in every instance of our companionship, even in the never to be gotten over fact that when I was with him in the paint store a lady had banteringly called him "good-looking." (We had proudly reported this to my mother, who seemed unimpressed.) When I began to write about him, my memories of good times were slight yet haunting. I seemed to have made him up from the beginning. He had been my first guide to the Russian past, to the Jewish working class, to Gedaliah the guard-ian of the Jews exempt from the Babylonian captivity, the Jewish Workers Bund of Russia and Poland, the Workmen's Circle, the Brotherhood of Painters and Decorators, the Wobblies he met out West, William Jennings Bryan, Big Bill Haywood, the *Appeal to Rea-son*, the New York *Call*, and, always and above all, the sainthood of Eugene Victor Debs: "While there is a lower class, I am in it. . . . While there is a soul in prison, I am not free." I made my father up in the image of the dispossessed, the excluded, the oppressed working class, until neither of us was young any more and Jews were no longer in the working class.

Thinking about the mystery of my father's powerlessness, my unfatherly father's frequent references to the shock of his father's death and his long absence from his mother, I used to think of him as "the orphan"—something I certainly was not. I felt myself engulfed in my parents' marriage; trapped in their loneliness with each other; attached by destiny to mother, father, my baby sister, to the cousin who lived with us, and all *her* friends. I was attentive to every minute shade of feeling and temperament in everyone around me, the moodiness I called their Russianness; was full of my commanding, endlessly resourceful work slave of a mother, my reclusive, ungiving father. I could not imagine a life in which they had no place. To be free of so much belonging! To have had, as my father said, "no family"! But he was an orphan, and I was not; he became a house painter just moderately accomplished at this trade, and my sister and I became writers. When he read me on my childhood, it occurred to him that since both his children were writers, he would write something for publication about *his* childhood. His first and last effort was a few pages in a notebook, "Trials and Tribulations of an Immigrant." When I typed it out for him—he wanted it sent to a magazine—I put in some periods, which he never did, and conventionalized the spelling. The original read as follows:

After graduation from the Baron de Hirsch school of agriculture in Minsk I decided that Russia holds no future for me   The pogroms at that time made painful reading I was dreaming about America but how could I come to America when I did not have any money so I decided to have a talk with the director of the school he should give me a loan   I left Russia in April 1906   I arrived the following month at Ellis Island   The Hebrew Immigrant Aid Society took me off the boat   I had an adress of an aunt   While eating supper it was Friday evening at my table there was a man sitting near me   I mention that I have an adress of an aunt in New York   I showed him the adress and he told me that my aunt lives only one block away   At that time quite a few men came to the immigrant aid society for their meals especially the sabbath meals the men that used to come for their meals were very poore

in the fall of 1906 there was an exciting campaign William R Hearst was running for governor on the democratic ticket against Charles E. Hughs who investigated the New York state insurance scandal Mr Hearst published even a jewish newspaper to catch the jewish votes on the east side thousands of people used to congregate around the Jewish Daily Forward to hear the speakers at that time there was a Jewish committee who sent Jewish immigrants all over the country especially to Texas Instead they sent me to Albany   They gave me a job in a Potash factory near the Hudson river   I was working on a machine that covered the cans filled with potash   in the fall of 1907 we went through a little depression and the factory where I was working closed down so I decided to go further west.

I came to Chicago   I tried hard to get a job till somebody told me that I can get a job in the stock yards   you could smell of the stock yards for blocks away   I got a job in one of the packing houses to pick up the skins of Cattle filled with salt and shake them free of salt   it was very hard work and I quit after a week

I couldn't get another job so I decided to go further west   I arrived in Omaha Nebrasca   I met a man that recommended me a job with the Union Pacific railroad they were painting a bridge in Omaha and so I became

a painter although I did not know how to paint but I
have learned it   the bridge job lasted about six months
then they sent me with a gang to paint stations & bridges
on the road as far as Wyoming till one day I was painting
a roof on a ice house in grand Island Nebrasca a small
village on the Union Pacific   the rope that held two
ladders on both sides of the roof gave way and I fell
about thirty feet to the ground but I was lucky there were
telegraph wires near the ice house that broke my fall
and except for a few minor injuries I was not badly hurt

an ambulance took me to a Catholic hospital in the
village the doctors and sisters were surprised that a Jew
should work for a living all the Jews they knew were
business men or professionals   when I recovered I went
back to work   the men that worked with me were a
bunch of sweeds and Norvegians   We used to get our
pay once a month and on payday they used to get drunk
and for a couple of days they didn't work til they spent
their money   after a while I got tired of traveling and I
asked to be transfered to the Union Pacific shops in
Omaha to paint box cars   I remember one day Eugene
V. Debs spoke in one of the largest parks   I was impressed by his eloquence and an old man standing near
me said that Mr Debs reminds him of Abraham Lincoln
also a great orator.

In the spring of 1910 I decided to go back to Chicago
and to remain a painter   I got fired from a couple of
jobs but as I became more experienced I could hold a
job and later I joined the Union of the brotherhood of
painters and that was the best move I ever made

at that time in Chicago there was Jane Adams Hulle
House in Chicago where a whole lot of immigrants used
to take English courses and American history I also
tooke some courses but it was hard to work by the day
and take lessons in the evening and my education ended
right there   I also used to attend lectures and debates on
Sundays downtown one of the most interesting debates

used to take place between Clarence Darrow the brilliant
lawyer and Arthur Morrow Lewis the socialist on religion
and socialism it was very interesting indeed

in 1912 i decided to go east as I did not hear from my
mother for six years

Communists made up an important part of the clien-
tele in Room 315 during the thirties. But with each
passing year Stalin's purges, betrayals, and assassinations
seemed to dishearten still another of those over-illumi-
nated friends who had so often disapproved of my in-
discriminate reading and had spent their afternoons in
315 doggedly relating Chaucer to dialectical materialism. My friend Hofstadter, passionately involved in the
history of American intellect, had, like me, given up on
Stalin and Stalinists from the moment we had learned
of the G.P.U.'s "executions" of left dissidents in Spain
and had heard Earl Browder in Madison Square Garden
proclaim, with his bureaucratic little smirk, that Trotsky,
Bukharin, Zinoviev were Nazi agents. Doctrinaires, unresting polemicists, ideologists of one idea, professional
apologists for a horrible tyranny and soon to be Hitler's
apologists as well as Stalin's when together Russia and
Germany crushed Poland in 1939, Communists were
obdurate fanatics with the mind-set of secret policemen.
But Communists would always be around, first as Communists, then as professional anti-Communists.

Hofstadter and I were in quest of, forever fascinated
by, what Lewis Mumford had called "the brown decades" of the nineteenth century—the years of crude
expansion and technical innovation in which *our* America had settled into shape. There was something about
the end of the century—the explosive American money-
making that would drive so many Americans mad; the
piling up of new immigrant masses in the great American cities; the stark boldness and plainness of Brooklyn

Bridge; the quivering truthfulness of Dickinson; the lonely realism of Eakins—that fascinated us. The background was America the powerhouse and our own fear of it. Hofstadter, the half-Jew and once-Lutheran choirboy, liked to mock my fascination with Henry Adams by quoting Adams's insane hatred of Jews, especially immigrant Jews: "God tried drowning out the world once, but it did no kind of good, and there are said to be four-hundred-and-fifty-thousand Jews now doing Kosher in New York alone. God himself owned failure."

But we were both in the spell of what had caught and frightened Adams. America, as even its most provincial visionaries had known, would soon be the greatest power instrument in history—we all went to make up that instrument. America was the perfect subject for history. It condensed so much into two centuries that here man was already "in sight of his own end" and fascinated by his capacity for self-destruction.

This was a comfortable thought to the gloomily skeptical humorist in Hofstadter. He was a derisive critic and parodist of every American Utopia and its wild prophets, a natural oppositionist to fashion and its satirist, a creature suspended between gloom and fun, between disdain for the expected and mad parody. He was filled with divided loyalties and powerfully disturbed emotions that never showed. The crazily promising yet undependable American scene gripped him absolutely. Like Mencken, he could not imagine a society more interesting; Mencken was a favorite resource in his many glooms. We had been formed by the Great Depression, but Hofstadter was a secret conservative in a radical period. The times caught up with him. He was secret in many things, in some strange no man's land between his Yiddish-speaking Polish father and his dead Lutheran mother. There were terrible fears for his life, even fiercer ambitions, that he seemed to hold together by the will to write, to succeed and to hold out, to dominate *himself*. I loved him. Even when he was dying of leukemia in 1970, he kept inching away at the first unfinished volume—*America at 1750*—of the big narrative history that was his greatest dream as a writer. The manuscript was still at his bed when he died. "I've never had the slightest trouble with my *will*."

We never met when we were twenty. He had just married the brilliantly temperamental and sometimes overpowering Felice Swados. She had a graduate degree in philosophy, wanted to be a novelist, and had no sooner become another lowly woman researcher on *Time* than she set out to write its medicine column. She came from a medical family.

Dick was sitting in the single room on Montague Street in Brooklyn Heights that was their first New York "apartment," and he looked marvelous, fresh, the all-American collegian just in from Buffalo with that unmistakable flat accent. He was talking with a crisp laughing intelligence that refreshed me, and he was soon telling Jewish jokes, jokes about Jews, doing impersonations of Jews in the style of the raucous comedian Lou Holtz. Dick also specialized in playing our favorite non-hero, F.D.R., who was as despised on the left for not doing enough as he was hated on the right for doing all too much.

We were obsessed by Roosevelt, he was so much the wily slippery confidence man unable for very long to satisfy "people of principle." But his real fault was that we did not know where his bantering elusive sense of superiority came from, what he had done to deserve so much power. Dick, unlike other historians of our generation, was afraid of power, thought it naturally something that led to excess and made one heartless. Even

when he became famous, he stiffly held off from all
public leaders. Dick wanted to study power, not share
in it; he meant to keep subtlety at any price. Roosevelt
the aristo-politician, forever mischievous, condescending, knew how to say "my old friend" in eleven languages. He reduced everything into one-sentence paragraphs, and with this seductive simplicity was directly in
touch with millions.

Dick was directly afraid of power—including his
wife's power over him. Felice was probably the first to
recognize just how brilliant he was, and fought him on
it. I understood her driving rages, was all too familiar
with her energy, her ambition, the unappeasable frustra-
tion that poured out its wrath on her husband's head.
More vivid to me than anyone else in that driven herd of
Jews arriving at the pierhead was the figure of a young
woman standing with her back to me in Alfred Stieglitz's
great photograph of 1907, "The Steerage." I dimly
knew that Stieglitz had taken the photograph going *to*
Europe. The figures in the photographs were returning,
but no matter. The woman is wearing a long wide skirt,
and she has draped herself head and back with a long
white towel with a double-striped border that puts her
at the center of the picture. Though she is surrounded on
every side, the others are looking down or just away in
mid-ocean reverie. Nobody is looking at her. This sur-
prises me very much; I cannot take my eyes off her and
I cannot understand why so many men, wearing derbies,
caps (one is even in a straw hat), can be so dreamily
looking down without being as *fixed* by her as I am.

She is my mother—in that picture and for that year.
She had better not turn around and let me see her face.
The woman I know—have I ever known another so
well?—is bent to the service of some undecipherable
tyranny. I can more easily picture her even before her

marriage as distinctly unbeautiful, obsessive, madly
anxious, undefeatably active. She is obsessed with her
failure to *change* anything. In none of her photographs
does she ever smile. There is a certain suspicion. Even
when she allows herself a nap—the Yiddish phrase is
"to catch a little dream"—she complains of never being
able to dream at all. Illiterate and a nervous stammerer,
she is nevertheless as resourceful and intuitive as the
world was before it learned to read. But she will never
accomplish anything except *us*, she will never know
when to stop, she will never lose some abysmal loneliness in the New World. She will never be happy or make
her husband happy. Yet with pride I picture her at
eighteen, not afraid to set out. She is the ugly duckling
in a family of just too many girls. She arrives with a beloved older brother who will unwillingly return on the
pleas of a wife too pious and fearful to cross the heathen
ocean, a wife too pious to flee the Nazis and who will be
shot by them right on her doorstep.

My mother at eighteen wears a pince-nez, a long
black skirt, a severe black shirtwaist, and every day except the Sabbath goes back and forth between her room
on Orchard Street and the Triangle Shirtwaist factory.
"If you don't come in on Sunday, don't come in on
Monday." One day her left hand is caught in the sewing
machine; a needle goes straight down the palm, severing
a large vein. They sew her up so clumsily that a tuft of
flesh always lies folded over the palm. But though she is
already bent over the machine as she will be for life, she
knows beyond anything else that we exist in this world in
order to be married. A Jewish girl unmarried is "alone
in the world," a condition horrid, unnatural, a little
death. In from the West comes my father, who hasn't
heard from his mother in six years. In comes my mother,
whose beloved handsome older brother has returned to

comfort his pious, fearful wife. My father and mother meet in an East Side boarding house; they are from neighboring provinces in Russia; they marry. On the Saturday night they marry, knowing hardly anyone, my mother goes out and brings back some food to their room, and finds my father sobbing.

The Hofstadters—Felice openly laughing—would listen with rapture to my tales of an anarchist uncle and aunt who had five sons but disdained "bourgeois marriage," yet separated because my aunt had been reading Marx; of the baker widow in our tenement who invariably left a great round onion roll for me to find when I left for school in the morning. In Buffalo, Jews who made it into the middle class called themselves "white" and poor Jewish workers "black." My family was definitely black. Felice would grin at me as she read aloud letters she was writing her friends in Northampton and Cambridge about me and my pent-up mother. Like her political passion for sailors and other proletarian types in Brooklyn Heights, who were always hilariously crawling in through the window to take potluck with the Hofstadters, this was what she liked to call her Marxist directness. With the many medical men in her family, she fancied herself a doctor of souls torn by the free-enterprise system. She explained her friends to themselves as easily as she explained the bankruptcy of philosophy under capitalist culture.

Felice's hearty sense of her own powers tended to put Dick into shadow. He was certainly not to emerge as a historian until he had doggedly looked after her in her sudden, shocking, fatal illness at the end of the war. He began to write *The American Political Tradition* on a pad in her darkened sickroom; he could not see the first words, but he finished the book. I on my side also felt endlessly challenged by Felice. She was on *Time*, she was in the great world and knew it. What authority she radiated over us! What clinical powers! She was large, assured, eager, scathing yet flirtatious, an elusive minx under the baby bangs that rustled on her forehead while she patiently explained the laws of her social development underlying famous novels and systems of philosophy. She made me long for so much daily excitement from a woman in my own life. She would have been shocked if I had told her. Not her ideas impressed me, not even her bountiful and coy figure. It was her pride, her belief in mastery.

The young woman who in 1942 is also twenty-seven, to whom I have been married for four years, and who now walks into Room 315 to pick me up for dinner before we both return to work, is dark, looks as "Russian" as her name, is slight, intensely gentle and reserved, and very good to look at. Natasha, my wife, has olive skin, a heart-shaped face that regularly tears me to bits, is loving yet removed. In my obsession to possess her all the way, I am regularly defeated. I will keep looking for her long after we have parted. She is a girl of precise delicate movements at the microscope; perhaps her heart is hidden from herself as well as from me. She has a crazy mother from whom her father is always in flight and a brilliant young brother who will die of his mother's insatiable bitterness. She is very careful not to show too much. The day after our wedding, I joyously came home to find her on the floor, almost unconscious after a swooping visit from her mother.

In this surpassing silence of the heart we live like two friends, always *sympathisch*, spiritually close. In these first years she has made everything possible for me. I have never felt so easy, so loving, so sure of my work. Natasha's long black hair is coiled in a Russian woman-doctor's bun at the very top of her head to leave her free for science. This leaves her neck free and glistening. I can never get enough of the back of Natasha's neck. At Bellevue, in her white lab coat, she wears delicate little glasses. As she bends over the microscope studying influenza strains for her thesis she makes such a tenderly appealing figure that I drop *The Princess Casamassima* to rush across the dusty lab and hug her. The white mice, alarmed by my unscientific attitude, race round and round their cages.

Natasha wears the brown stockings worn by all progressive girls in the thirties (we boycott the silk produced by Imperialist Japan) and walks slightly pigeontoed. There is a schoolgirl's hesitation and modesty in her walk, especially when she clutches her briefcase tightly but somewhat timidly. We work all the time. Sundays alone we take off. Before Pearl Harbor we take excursion steamers up and down the coast to the Atlantic Highlands and to Point Judith, in Rhode Island. We tramp the bridges that in those days always had a lane for walkers—on Brooklyn Bridge it was the "central promenade"—and one birthday walk all around Manhattan Island. Sunday morning, the BMT subway station at Whitehall is empty and echoes silence along all its blue and white tiles as we wait for a train that may never come. The vacancy of the BMT this crazy Sunday morning makes me cringe. Why am I emptily pursuing New York Sunday after Sunday, Natasha grimly trotting after me like a good Chinese wife? What am I looking for in all this mad prowling? Walking is thinking; thinking is moving, moving *out*. Natasha is stuck with this "dynamo," as she wonderingly puts it, who stammeringly cannot stop reading, noting, collecting material, walking, writing, pushing at the world to let him in.

Natasha makes all things possible. The first happy

years are consumed by work, my work. I live in a romantic cloud, never admitting that anything is ever wrong, that I can ever want anything else. Natasha and I love each other, will go on loving for years after our marriage has collapsed. We were the last Puritans. Any bluntness between husbands and wives was unknown to me. "Failure"—nothingness—losing—had so long been the background of my life, of everyone related to me, that Natasha's growing uneasiness about her work at Bellevue made me cringe. There suddenly, unbelievably, seemed no way of bridging a gap. What are we doing Sunday after Sunday homelessly tramping about? What are we doing in the New Jersey hills this Sunday of all Sundays when we hear from a passing car radio that Costa Rica has just declared war on Japan? *Costa Rica?* We did not learn of Pearl Harbor till we had returned in the evening, then rushed to Times Square to buy the first papers, to watch the crowds, to stare at the shocking news bulletins racing around the Times tower.

It was frozen cold that December night. A few mildly drunk sailors were trying to whoop it up, but the crowd was silent, numb, waiting. The next day a liberated Roosevelt went before Congress, asked for a declaration of war. Would I get to finish my book? Planes were overhead patrolling the coastline. At three in the afternoon New York had its first air-raid alarm. On Fifth Avenue an ambulance happened at the same time to be screaming its way through traffic. People rushed out of offices and the Library to see New York under fire.

I would be allowed to finish my book. It was published, I was invited to join *The New Republic*, we moved to Lexington and Twenty-fourth, and soon everything was different as the view from our casement windows. We were in the heart of the city, and the battle had just begun. Working on my history of modern

American writing, I had not known many writers. I had reviewed many books, but did not think of myself as a challenge to other writers. When my book, my first gread *deed*, opened up so many things for me, I was amazed at suddenly coming out well. I felt like a man afraid of heights who finds himself looking over the side of a roof. As the reviews began to come in, the sudden invitations, the florid compliments and passionate attacks, I would take any train to Washington to lose myself in the commotion of war. I was desperate to get overseas. I could not bear so much examination, the loss of my old solitude when I had had the whole day long to read and write in. Above all, I could not bear having to justify myself to the many writers around *The New Republic* who seemed even more amazed by my book than I was. But more often I would find myself following women down the street, excited by the whirl of New York in midtown, the smell of wartime money, the high lean tower of the RCA Building, the flashing reflections of St. Patrick's in the glass doors of department stores across the way. I was excited by the women in the bus every morning, the women in the morning light, the proud, the fashionable women of midtown, the breasts and hot purple mouths of the women in Saks, the blazing femaleness in those department-store windows, on the streets and at every counter—women hot- and cold-looking at once, so that I longed for them from my office window and dreamed about them all night. I now dreamed continually of women I had seen in midtown and had followed. I was strict as ever and ashamed—but not so ashamed that I did not go on dreaming and waiting.

In 1942 *The New Republic* was still being published in New York. But even in its glossy offices in the building high over Hattie Carnegie's at Forty-ninth and Madison, it bore little resemblance to the "journal of opinion" that from the original brownstone, far off on West Twenty-first Street near the docks, had been such an intellectual force in American life. Although many famous names were still on the masthead, the magazine was entirely in the hands of Bruce Bliven, who put it out with the help of Betty Huling, the loud-swearing, fiercely competent copy editor, and two young men. The other young man was Thomas Sancton, a sensitive newspaperman from New Orleans who was awed and horrified by New York. After passionate editorials on the outrages being committed against black soldiers in the Deep South, he published even more bitterly felt laments on the inhumanity of the terrible big city. Between Malcolm Cowley, the last literary editor with independent authority, and myself (Bliven hired me because he had never heard of me; he was always under attack from literary intellectuals), there had been a whole succession of angrily frustrated editors of the book section. My immediate predecessor was Nigel Dennis, who had quit after a more than usually violent disagreement with the boss.

As I did not know in 1942, Edmund Wilson had been fired years before by the owner—the daughter of the millionaire William C. Whitney and the widow of Willard Straight—after an unsuccessful effort to oust Bliven. "I'm a terrible conspirator," Wilson confessed unnecessarily when he told me the story at Wellfleet on Cape Cod in 1960. Before the farcical in-office *Putsch*, there had been a bitter dispute after the command had gone out from the owner, now married to an Englishman and living in England, to reverse its between-wars isolationism and to support the war. The first editors of *The New Republic*, founded in 1914 on the last wave of the Progressive movement, had identified so enthusiastically with Woodrow Wilson that they never recovered from Versailles and grimly held to the isolationism then usual with American "progressives." Edmund Wilson saw Pearl Harbor as a plot by Roosevelt. The old *New Republic* editors were now being asked to support the war, but Wilson seemed to see this more as a war against Bruce Bliven than against Hitler. Many of the original editors were persuaded to leave their names on the masthead but to stay away except for an occasional office lunch. The magazine was left entirely to Bliven, who dominated but showed no joy. He felt inferior to the *New Republic* tradition.

Bliven had been managing editor of a New York daily before he had been hired by Herbert Croly in the twenties to lend his practical talents to a magazine famous for intellectual stars like Walter Lippmann and Edmund Wilson. By 1942 his long war with the old *New Republic* intellectuals left a personal bitterness that could be heard at every office lunch. Bliven was a stout round man who looked to me very much like the Oliver Hardy of Laurel and Hardy. Like Oliver Hardy, he assumed an anxious geniality that often collapsed into bitter self-control. The literary side of the magazine worried him because certain damned intellectuals had put things over on him. He brooded on the memory of Edmund Wilson, his great enemy on the old staff. No one told me why Wilson had left. His name could be mentioned only if Bliven brought it up. I did not know this. "What do I think of Edmund Wilson? I think, damn it to hell, that Edmund Wilson is the best critic in the English-speaking world!"

Bliven was suspicious of literary men who mocked the war-swollen American ego. Allen Tate, stung by my criticisms of his self-proclaimed "reactionary" criticism, challenged me to publish *More Sonnets at Christmas*.

Tate, not yet a Catholic, had in the thirties written two dense and imploring *Sonnets at Christmas* lamenting his physical oddity, "dull critter of enormous head," and his anguish, "punished by crimes of which I would be quit," over a "stinking lie" he had told at ten "that got a black boy whipped."

More Sonnets at Christmas showed Tate no longer wailing a dead Christ but well on the way to accepting His resurrection. More resolute than he had been ten years earlier, he strikes out against the pride of war and the delusions of total victory—"The Huns gelded and feeding in a ring"—and the liberal delusion that the current war would ease the path to social progress. Henry Wallace, who was to become editor of *The New Republic* after F.D.R. yanked him from the Vice-Presidency, had in his confidant dreaminess explained that "the century on which we are entering can be and must be the century of the common man." One of Wallace's rumored "war aims" was a quart of milk to every Hottentot. Tate scorned "well-milked Chinese, Negroes who cannot sing." He intimated a definite contempt.

> The American people fully armed
> With assurance policies, righteous and harmed,
> Battle the world of which they're not at all. . . .

Deriding his past weakness, Tate now saw the boy who at ten had "told a stinking lie/That got a black boy whipped" as growing into a typical American youth untouched by guilt, asleep to his spiritual nothingness, "whose only fear/Is of an enemy in remote oceans/Unstalked by Christ: these are the better notions."

Tate's lines were more difficult in structure than in meaning; they were often simply evasive, as if to hide his ill-concealed longing for absolutism. His poetry had a way of saying things in opposition to an unseen critic. Like Tate himself, they seemed to say and unsay things in the same breath. The cool clear authority behind his critical essays became in his poems a form of public agony. He was obsessed by Eliot, but he could never seem to attain Eliot's honestly suffering tone. There was something unacknowledged and unexpressed in Tate's poetry. But Tate was famous for thinking the whole modern world an infamy. His new Christmas sonnets said that the new world war was just another power play. The war had nothing but more evil to contribute to the secret grief at the heart of modern life. All things were in a state of contradiction. All wars were boyish and fought by boys. But some of these boys, in *our* new Roman Empire, were "pro-consuls of the air."

Since *The New Republic* was running on its cover BEWARE A STATIC WAR! Bliven was not likely to enjoy Tate's barbed offering to us of *More Sonnets at Christmas*. He would not publish them. "If I don't understand these poems," he summed up one late wintry afternoon, after a hopeless argument into which I had dragged Malcolm Cowley for support, "how in hell do you expect our readers to understand them?" This picture of our audience surprised me. I insisted on a free hand in the literary department and Tate's sonnets were published. But there was no understanding between "the front of the book" and "the back of the book." The major purpose of the time, as one *New Republic* cover put it, was to "turn the war into a global New Deal." Since Roosevelt had happily substituted "Dr. Win-the-War" for "Dr. New Deal," this was the kind of self-hypnosis that was soon to put Henry Wallace into the editor's chair. The "century of the common man" was just a starter. Wallace liked to call Christ "the greatest liberal of all when He put life before things—when He said to seek the Kingdom of Heaven first and things would take care of themselves."

The "front of the book" was politics, the war—the real world. The "back of the book" was literature, the arts, "a lot of intellectuals." The contrast between Bliven's anxieties and his loudly crusading editorials for a "global New Deal" soon made *The New Republic* futile to me. Furtive whispering and impolite laughter could be heard from cubicle to cubicle. In mine I saw a procession of young Village poets and philosophers—Delmore Schwartz, William Barrett, Isaac Rosenfeld, Weldon Kees—for whom the only real magazine was *Partisan Review*. They looked on the "N.R." as a source of cash, but despised it with all the righteous fury that we were likely to feel for a magazine that seemed to think of the Soviet-American alliance as a progressive war, a people's war, a lovable war. Stalin was now everyone's "Uncle Joe." He was not ours.

Since the managing editor from New Orleans wrote against "New York intellectuals" and Bliven expected their scorn, the magazine famous for bringing together Randolph Bourne, Walter Lippmann, Herbert Croly, Edmund Wilson, Francis Hackett, Robert Morss Lovett, Philip Littell, and Malcolm Cowley was clearly different from what it had been. It was still printed on the crumbly butcher paper that seemed indispensable to minority causes in the United States, but it never had more—it often had less—than thirty thousand subscribers. These were the faithful behind *The New Republic* and *The Nation*. Bliven's anxious leadership reflected the end of a period. There was no illumination in the "front of the book" and no hope in the "back of the book."

There were explosive days when Delmore Schwartz

happened in and out of the elevator. Delmore never just came in. He spilled out in a reedy voice, a headlong rush of words, that seemed to engage every muscle in his face as he twisted and spat in the rage of his opinions. On the days when Delmore erupted in the office to get a book for review and to berate me for something I had just published, he conversed in a style of great bitterness that nevertheless tried to be classical and impersonal in its reasoning. Since he could write without rage and always with a great show of reasoning, a certain classical outlook—he had been trained in philosophy—was the style of his terribly proper, intellectual poems and profound early stories. The contrast was even physical. He moved heavily, his head turning with some uneasiness. He seemed to see his life as a clash between gravity, heaviness, depression, and poetry, which was the absolute, the truth, elusive as "the tip of snow on the windowsill."

I would look at his amazingly wide, stone-white, sweaty brow, knotted with intellectual indignation as with ropes. I would grow properly frightened, Delmore was such a prophecy of the last literary generation to believe in the authority of culture, the logic of tradition. There was this belief, which not even Hitler would destroy in some of us, that there *was* a reason behind all frightfulness. Of course, every political season the reason changed. Once it was "imperialism." When the killing began, it was "human nature," or the devil in us. Delmore was already the poet on the cross of culture, every muscle contorted; Brooklyn's best, nailed down. But from his cross he shrieked the most brilliant things, the most scathing things, excitedly analyzing a passage by "my king, James Joyce," and, like a mad shuttlecock, flying at anyone who saw less beauty in his favorite texts than he did.

Delmore talked with his whole face. The hopeless intensity of every feeling was there the last time I saw him. It was a few years before his terrible death, in 1966, in a sleazy Broadway hotel, after which his body lay around Bellevue unknown and unclaimed. He was railing against his friend Saul Bellow. Bellow was returning the fund he had collected for Delmore's treatment. Delmore did not think he needed treatment. He thought of the fund as his personal property. He was in a squalid box of a room on Greenwich Street near the river. It was a room that only long practice in disaster could have discovered. He was buried up to his fine eyes in accusations of "betrayal," unbearably sicker than in the forties, not so much talking as accusing, erupting, plotting, demanding, suffering. Everything was vehement and tragic at once. You could not leave him without hating yourself.

His face could be marvelous even in his most manic flights. It had a way of withdrawing into lonely thought that somehow transcended every angry occasion. His body nobly represented him even when he was throwing words at people he did not trust. Although he was bitterly witty in his mysterious fashion—"Europe is still the biggest thing in North America"—storming up against people with the same passionate logic with which he argued for or against certain books, his face was as remarkable in a relaxed moment as the first time I had seen him, in a train going up to Boston. I had been struck by the immense intellectual devotion in it, the fine distraction, the obstinate love behind the familiarly Jewish-frantic manner.

In those days he looked what he was—obsessive, unable to let go on anyone or about anything, but more gifted than anyone else, not petty, full of the excited discoveries he was then making as a teacher of composition at Harvard. He looked, as a friend said, "our poet." No writer of my generation, typically lamented by a Communist poet as "caught between the wars, with all the street lights out," knew so well from the inside what literature was and what a poet should aim at. He looked proud. He still had a young authority. He had come on the scene in his early twenties with stories and poems that astonished everyone by being impeccably formally *right* in the prevailing Eliot tradition—emotional ingenuity tuned to perfect pitch by gravity of manner. Although he talked fast and masticated his words, he could grow marvelously possessed between gulps of argument and boyish smiles. There was the unmistakable look of the poet speaking from his own depths. He stood for something, and he knew it.

The single most beautiful thing he was ever to write, the classic story of the Jewish son unable to escape the history represented by his family, was the highly charged personal fantasy "In Dreams Begin Responsibilities." The narrator imagines himself in the darkness of a movie theater watching his father walk down the quiet shaded streets of Brooklyn to court his mother. The light is bad, the film is patchy, and from time to time the young writer, watching his own unhappy destiny being prepared in the bad temper of his father and the quarrels of his parents-to-be, cries out from the darkness of the theater against the ill-fated marriage. At one point he stands up and tells the figures on the screen not to marry. "Don't do it! It's not too late to change your minds, both of you. Nothing good will come of it, only remorse, hatred, scandal, and two children whose characters are monstrous."

"In Dreams Begin Responsibilities" was straight, beautiful, haunting. It was a little masterpiece that used up a man's whole life even before he had lived it. It was

the greatest fable I was ever to read of "our experience."
It was the one work of Delmore Schwartz's life that had
the power of a dream, and it remains with me as if I had
dreamed it myself. Delmore was never again to bring
out with such precision what it was to be a marked man,
under a curse and wolfishly alone. We used to laugh at
the story that Delmore's mother had appropriated his
name from a delicatessen, though "Delmore" was more
innocently pretentious than Lionel, Clifton, Clifford,
Hilton, Leslie, Walt Whitman. But with his terrible belief in working things out intellectually, Delmore saw
in his mother's innocent cultural pretension "a wound
like circumcision." He would be a clown with an urgent
message to deliver. Delmore's tortured personal epics,
Shenandoah and *Genesis*, showed him struggling with
ridiculous names for himself like Shenandoah Fish and
Hershey Green. The friends he put into his stories were
also cruelly tagged by fate. Poor Shenandoah, poor
Hershey, poor Rudyard Bell, Edmund Kish, Ferdinand
Harrap, Francis French, and Mortimer London, poor
Algernon. Poor Von Humboldt Fleisher, a final sacrifice
to his famous self-laceration! Such names piled on each
other became funnier than Groucho's J. Worthington
Silverstein. Delmore could not laugh anything off. He
pacticed "irony" as if this famous literary strategy of
the time was a Jew's only defense. Of course he could
not see the joke. He was the drama.

"A poet shouldn't be that unhappy," Auden said with
derision, looking at the photograph on Delmore's book,
Summer Knowledge. The eyes looked almost blind in
their sick milky introspection; the face that had once
moved me by its independent devotion was now furrowed and creased with unimaginable pain. Less than
ever now was he looking *at* anything. But anyone who
understood Delmore's mind knew that he was finally

drowning in his own blood. He was hopelessly caught up in the logical web, still trying to prove the injustice that was everywhere being practiced against him. *This* was his lifelong dilemma. The worse things got, the more actively, frantically, outragedly he *argued* against them. He was a terrifying and terrified rationalist, a prisoner of his superb intellectual training. The great philosophers and poets were always in his mind, training him into a victim of the logic he loved more than himself. He would never come to believe in the "absurd" that filled the decade in which he died. His end was "absurd" enough to please the exuberant chaos around him, but it was absurd in Delmore's own desperate style.

He had surely predicted it. He was, more than the rest of us, expert in anguish. Even when impaled on his favorite theme, betrayal, he lacked the saving grace of madness. He was the prisoner of culture, and could never be distracted from its supposed truth. He would never lose himself in that dream of a totally other world that becomes to the eye of genius the only real world. Delmore could be maddening, but he never relaxed in the full madness of art. He would never lose his faith in the rationality of the world.

1943. Now began the nightmare that would bring everything else into question, that will haunt me to my last breath. The Nazis had organized the killing of every Jew within their grasp. Three months before Pearl Harbor, Charles Lindbergh at an America First rally had threatened the "Jewish *race*." "Instead of agitating for war, the Jewish groups in this country should be opposing it in every possible way, for they will be among the first to feel its consequences." Even Edmund Wilson, another isolationist, was to write in later years that while Jews "had even stronger reasons for fighting [Hitler] than had their ancestors for resisting the Greeks and the Romans," this was illogical, since "the extermination of six million Jews was already very far advanced by the time the United States took action." By "taking action" Wilson meant Pearl Harbor, which he attributed to a conspiracy by Roosevelt.

The systematic murder of Europe's Jews had not yet begun by the time we entered the war. But by the end of 1942 and especially the terrible spring of 1943, when the Warsaw ghetto was destroyed after its last desperate attack on the Nazis, it was clear to me what was not clear to "progressives" with their whimpers for a "global New Deal." The Nazis planned what even Edmund Wilson called the "extermination" of every Jew on earth. But to everyone but us—and by no means all of us— this was unreal. In the second battle for Kharkov, the Germans were reported to have given up a tactical advantage in order to round up Jews. Meanwhile Hitler's recent ally Stalin destroyed every democrat and Socialist who could oppose *his* Poland after the war. Henryk Erlich and Victor Alter, leaders of the Jewish Workers Bund of Poland, had fled to Russia and gladly joined the Anti-Fascist People's Committee, organized by the Russians after the Germans attacked them in 1941. Erlich and Alter were arrested and shot, charged with "urging Soviet troops not to resist the Nazis, and urging an immediate peace treaty with Nazi Germany."

Even in death the Jews were an "anomaly," a contradiction to the great "unifying" tendencies of modern life and revolution. Though prime objects of Hitler's hatred, they were a side issue for everyone else. There had never been any real room for them in the secular thought of the Enlightenment; there was no room for them in Communist images of a "final conflict" that would resolve all the divisions of humanity by obliterating the "class enemy"; there was especially no room for them on an earth dominated by the revolutionary zeal of the Nazis. By the overwhelming logic of totalitarianism, all things and all people not absorbable into the sacred "movement" would have to be destroyed. By the overwhelming movement toward total domination that the Nazis had set up in Germany and now all over Europe under the slogan of revolution—an "organic" revolution that assimilated into the New Order all existing institutions— the Jews could not be included. They had to die.

The Jews, anywhere, had to die. They were "the enemy." They were "unassimilable." The Jews had been ruled out of existence by the Nazis and could not be admitted into the thought of those who were fighting Hitler. In a world increasingly conceived as the struggle of "modern" revolutionary forces, the Jews seemed to be entirely a people of the past, living in the past. Revolutions exist in order to perpetuate revolution. The Jews could not be fitted into Nazi or Communist schemes; they did not belong; they could not be explained. So now their organized destruction could not be accounted for. The indifference of the Vatican extended even to priests and nuns who had been born Jews. The Allies would not bomb the railroad tracks leading to Auschwitz, support Jewish self-defense behind the Nazi lines, open their doors to the masses of refugees. Roosevelt could not pay attention to the "Jewish problem." He could not take it all in—Churchill did—and was afraid of disturbing American "opinion." The Jews were not a factor in Allied plans for the postwar scene.

The Jews were just a people *accused*, as of old; a people whose only mission was to feel guilty. Without any suspension, any possibility of salvation even through conversion, a whole people in the control of the most powerful state in Europe was condemned by the infamy that it had been guilty throughout history and should, in its totality, be made a sacrifice.

Jews were supposed to bear witness, to give meaning to their historic existence as Jews, to lift the curse from the word "Jew" and turn it into a blessing. Some who were not living the atrocity now sought to live it, to live the passion suffered by their brothers and sisters. A tremor went through those not yet lined up for "extermination." I did not know then how *many* Jews were scratching with their fingernails the low ceilings of the gas chambers into which they had been herded, family by family, hand in hand with their children. I did not know then that the dead, by families, would *the morning after* be standing together in death, so tightly wedged together that the *capos* would have to break them apart with hooks. But I did know that there were Jews outside the circle of death who felt that *they* could speak out, that Jews could not be totally pushed to the sidelines in death as they had been in life.

On May 12, 1943, in London, the Polish Jew Shmuel Ziegelboim, who represented the Jewish Workers Bund in the Polish Cabinet in exile, was found dead by his own hand in a London flat. His wife and child had been killed by the Nazis. I had never heard of Shmuel Ziegelboim, and so many Socialists, Jews, and Poles had already died that I might never have thought of him if he had not left a letter that was published in a negligible corner of *The New York Times*.

His letter was addressed to the President of Poland and to Prime Minister Sikorski.

I take the liberty of addressing to you my last words, and through you to the Polish government and to the Polish people, the governments and peoples of the Allied states—to the conscience of the world.

From the latest information received from Poland, it is evident that the Germans, with the most ruthless cruelty, are now murdering the few remaining Jews in Poland. Behind the ghetto's walls the last act of a tragedy unprecedented in history is being performed. The responsibility for this crime of murdering the entire Jewish population of Poland falls in the first instance on the perpetrators, but indirectly it is also a burden on the whole of humanity, the people and the governments of the Allied states which thus far have made no effort toward concrete action for the purpose of curtailing this crime.

By the passive observation of the murder of defenseless millions, and of the maltreatment of children, women and old men, these countries have become the criminals' accomplices. I must also state that although the Polish government has in a high degree contributed to the enlistment of world opinion, it has yet done so insufficiently. It has not done anything that could correspond to the magnitude of the drama being enacted now in Poland. From some 3,500,000 Polish Jews and about 700,000 other Jews deported to Poland from other countries—according to official statistics provided by the underground Bund organization—there remained in April of this year only about 300,000 and this remaining murder still goes on.

I cannot be silent—I cannot live—while remnants of the Jewish people of Poland, of whom I am a representative, are perishing. My comrades in the Warsaw ghetto took weapons in their hands on that last heroic impulse. It was not my destiny to die there together with them, but I belong to them, and in their mass graves. By my death I wish to express my strongest protest against the inactivity with which the world is looking on and permitting the extermination of my people.

I know how little human life is worth today; but as I was unable to do anything during my life, perhaps by my death I shall contribute to breaking down the indifference of those who may now—at the last moment—rescue the few Polish Jews still alive from certain annihilation.

My life belongs to the Jewish people of Poland and I therefore give it to them. I wish that this remaining handful of the original several millions of Polish Jews could live to see the liberation of a new world of freedom, and the justice of true socialism. I believe that such a Poland will arise and that such a world will come.

I trust that the President and the Prime Minister will direct my words to all those for whom they are destined, and that the Polish government will immediately take appropriate action in the fields of diplomacy. I bid my farewell herewith to everybody and everything dear to me and loved by me.

S. Ziegelboim

The *Times* report added: "That was the letter. It suggests that possibly Shmuel Ziegelboim will have accomplished as much in dying as he did in living."

I reprinted Ziegelboim's last message in *The New Republic*. Then I quoted lines from William Blake's "London" that haunted me in these war-tormented years:

> In every cry of every Man,
> In every Infant's cry of fear,
> In every voice, in every ban,
> The mind-forg'd manacles I hear.

Under this I wrote that "something has already been done—by us the bystanders as well as by the Nazi killers—that will never be undone. Hitler will leave hatred of the Jews as his last political trick, as it was his first. The people who have been most indifferent to the massacre of the Jews will be just those who wonder why all the pacts and all the formal justice will have done so little to give them their prewar 'security' again.

"You who want only to live and let live, to have the good life back—and think you can dump three million Jews into the furnace, and sigh in the genuine impotence of your undeniable regret, and then build Europe back again. Where so great a murder has been allowed, no one is safe."

This cry in a "liberal" weekly brought much sighing and handshaking from colleagues. Three well-known writers praised my "courage" in writing so directly about the "Jewish tragedy." But the war in 1943 seemed far from won. The Jews, as the fat German said in the comic skit, could be a nuisance. "You Chews are always talking about you Chews!"

Out of the millions killed by Hitler, it was a modest trade-union official whose protesting came most clearly to me. Perhaps he would not have put it as the Psalmist did:

> I have come into deep waters,
>> and the flood sweeps over me.
> I am weary with my crying;
>> my throat is parched.
> My eyes grow dim
>> with waiting for my God.
> More in number than the hairs of my head
>> are those who hate me without cause;
> mighty are those who would destroy me,
>> those who attack me with lies.
>
> . . . zeal for they house has consumed me. . . .

In my private history of the world I took down every morsel of fact and rumor relating to the murder of my people. I was to discover that the Vatican knew no later than the beginning of 1941 that the Nazis were deporting large numbers of Jews, and this at a time when not even the Jewish agencies were aware that the deportations were part of a general mass annihilation. Vatican diplomats quoted an Italian war correspondent: "Almost all the Roumanian Jews crammed into a railroad train with sealed doors and windows were reported dead on arrival. . . . The real tragic aspect of this anti-Jewish action is the absolute coolness with which the responsible authorities impart orders and the indifference of the officers who attend executions, smoking cigarettes."

There were many protests from individual priests. Several French Catholic priests had been fighting Vichy's submission to the Nazi anti-Jewish policy. Julius Saliège, Archbishop of Toulouse, wrote a pastoral letter in the fall of 1942 that I copied into my notebook:

> There is a Christian morality, there is a human morality, that imposes duties and confers rights. These duties and these rights derive from the very nature of man. They may be violated. No mortal has the power to suppress them. That children, women, fathers, mothers should be treated as a wretched herd, that members of the same family should be separated from one another and embarked for unknown destinations, was a spectacle reserved for our bad time to see.
>
> Why does the right of asylum no longer exist in our churches?
>
> Why are we a vanquished people?
>
> Lord, have pity on us!
>
> Our Lady, pray for France!
>
> These Jews are men, these Jewesses are women; these aliens are men and women. All is not permissible against them, against these men and women, against these fathers and mothers. They belong to mankind. They are our brethren as are so many others. No Christian can forget that.

One day at the end of 1942, I wandered into CBS to see a friend who monitored foreign broadcasts and found him staring open-mouthed at a transcript he had just made. "You've always praised Ezra Pound to me as a master of language," he said bitterly. "Will you kindly put your eyes on this?" The transcript was of Pound's twice-weekly broadcasts on the Italian Fascist radio, which my friend had started taking down the day Pearl Harbor was attacked.

The first thing I saw was a reference to Mrs. Roosevelt consorting with "niggers." I felt amazement more than anything else as I read these pronouncements by one of the original poets and master critics of the twentieth century, *the* writer most responsible for making modernism in literature part of our lives.

> Things often do look simple to me. Roosevelt is more in the hands of the Jews than Wilson was in 1919. (December 7, 1941.)

> Politically and economically the U.S. has had economic and political syphilis for the past 80 years, ever since 1862. And England has had economic syphilis for 240 years. . . . (February 3, 1942.)

> That any Jew in the White House should send American kids to die for the private interests of the scum of the English earth . . . and the dregs of the Levantine . . .

> What I'm getting at with all this. What am I getting at? Which? What? What? Which? (February 26, 1942.)

> My job, as I see it, is to save what's left of America and to help keep up some sort of civilization somewhere or other.

> Ezra Pound speaking from Europe for the American heritage.

F.D.R. is below the biological level at which the concept of honor enters the mind. (March 26, 1942.)

It becomes increasingly difficult to discuss American affairs except on a racial basis.

Don't start a pogrom—an old-style killing of small Jews. That system is no good whatever. Of course, if some man had a stroke of genius, and could start a pogrom up at the top, there might be something to say for it. But on the whole, legal measures are preferable. The 60 kikes who started this war might be sent to St. Helena as a measure of world prophylaxis, and some hyper-kikes or non-Jewish kikes along with them. (April 30, 1942.)

Pound had always worked on me like a whirlwind. The nervous force of his style; his ability to draw the reader into the magic circle made up of Pound's sacred models; above all, his dizzy and dizzying sense of history; his constant adjurations when to read, what to read, how to read, did make his culture heroes shine with the strength of his intellectual passion. He made me think of characters in Dante's *Inferno* who come alive because Dante's vehemence brings them into the light. As a critic, he never explained anything with patience. But he was certainly the passionate teacher, the great transmitter, in images that impressed by their nervous force. He was a magnet to himself, "the poet" who had turned himself into the heir of all the ages. By the yammer of his obsessive mind, he made himself a magnet to others.

Of course Pound was "crazy"! Many poets with Pound's irritable force had been great melancholics, certified madmen, lunatics. I was to know poets who were less "touched" and more self-destructive—Sylvia Plath, Randall Jarrell, John Berryman. Yeats had called

Pound's *Cantos* "nervous obsession, nightmare, stammering and confusion." Opening any Canto, I was excited by Pound's gift for imitation, his perfect instinct for how a great line should sound. Then I would get unnerved by the voice screeching from that forest of Pound's associations with poetry, history, gossip, the Adamses, Chinese ideograms, Greek, Provençal, Italian "touchstones." It was as if Whitman's homely, sleepy American ransacking of the world went frenetic; hot and cold; dirty and sacred; abominable and sublime. At times there was such great faking of sense that his critics became fakes and never complained that he told the same anecdote twice. Perhaps they did not notice. The great epic—"an epic is a poem that includes history"— came at you falling and churning. It was all pieces, driftwood flotsam and jetsam, reading, attributions, quotations, misappropriations steaming at you from the will of the poet's sacred ego. My mind to me a kingdom is. Everything that comes into *my* mind is sacred. Yet my own mind had never been able to turn off Pound's voice. Pound had the mad prophet's gift, straight out of the Bible. I could not escape his voice. The voice was always there, holding me *because* it was crazy. He had the single gift of the great man; he was not remotely like anyone else.

And now that voice was being directed against us. The voice was not like T. S. Eliot saying in *After Strange Gods*—the year Hitler came to power!—that "reasons of race and religion combine to make any large number of free-thinking Jews undesirable." It was the voice of the spoiled infant whose every instinct was sacred to himself. Pound was infatuated with every scrap of feeling turning up in the crevices of his brain.

The voice was probably not influencing anybody. It was not Hitler's. It was not Pound's influence I dreaded.

It was his witchlike instinct for the hate buried in the age, coming to the surface in the Warsaw ghetto and the ovens of Treblinka. Pound had said that poets are the "antennae of the race." His "crazy," all too keen sense of what was buried in the nerve cells of History unnerved me. Pound had always made me uneasy. That had been part of his excitement. His nervous, gibbering, prophetic power showed an ability to link the ages together. He had his mad gift for personalizing history and for making other persons speak as History. I, Ezra Pound, speaking out of the whirlwind of my mind. I, Ezra Pound, speaking from Europe for the American heritage. I tell you how to read, what to think. "Don't start a pogrom—an old-style killing of small Jews. That system is no good whatever. Of course, if some man had a stroke of genius, and could start a pogrom up at the top, there might be something to say for it."

Small Jews. Little Jews. Pound was the voice of the public whirlwind. Even if I had been able to explain Pound to them, my father and mother would never have understood how one man could be possessed by this much belief in himself. That was the trouble with "small Jews." I saw them, all through the terrible war years of the Holocaust and after, in the image of my mother and father—people of the past, living in the past, caught up in a flame of totalitarian revolution that existed solely to keep *itself* aflame. They would never understand this or fully credit it even when they were being rounded up. And soon it would emerge, as our brother Kafka had said, that "not the murderer but the victim is guilty." Pound himself was to say after the war that no man named Ezra could be an anti-Semite. And that he had not known of the gas chambers.

But I did. And I, too, could personalize History. The line-up was always before my eyes. I could imagine my

father and mother, my sister and myself, our original
tenement family of "small Jews," all too clearly—fuel
for the flames, dying by a single flame that burned us
all up at once. Would we, too, die because we could not
understand where our murderers came from? What they
wanted of us?

Years after the war, from her children in Israel, I
heard in detail of how my aunt had refused to flee with
everyone else into the forest. "Maybe it is God's will?"
she had wondered. She was shot on her doorstep.

Chapter II

MIDTOWN AND THE VILLAGE

One of the better experiences at *The New Republic* was the editorial lunch in its private dining room. This had been a famous institution in the paper's early days on West Twenty-first Street, when Herbert Croly and Francis Hackett and Walter Lippmann and Robert Morss Lovett and Edmund Wilson had no doubt had a good deal to say to each other. I had heard about these brilliant occasions and had even read about them in books. In particularly genial moments during the light-hearted twenties, the editors had piled manuscripts along the lazy Susan that was the table's centerpiece and had sent them whirling around to each other.

In 1942 and 1943 the interest of these lunches was the vividness of some famous guest. For some weeks there was the startling reappearance of old *New Republic* editors and contributors. Van Wyck Brooks, white hair *en brosse* and a headmaster's thick white mustache, straddled the back of a chair after lunch, very shy but gamely trying to look at ease. I suspected him of wanting to take off for that literary Arcadia where all writers were unfailingly gentle like himself, exquisitely fragile, and wrote with old-fashioned nib pens in their New

England country houses without having to go out to lunch with editors at Forty-ninth and Madison.

Brooks's writing always had a light charm for me. He had a gift for locating his literary subjects within a moment and place that made some of his books vibrate with the sense of his own moment and place in American literature. By the 1940s, he was more and more a portraitist of writers, not the powerfully radical critic who had once explained the new modern generation to itself. Brooks had written the great polemic of the new insurgent literature in *America's Coming-of-Age*. As an editor of *The Freeman*, of *The Dial*, he had been the impassioned social intelligence who had first called attention to the split in American consciousness between lowbrow and highbrow, between the acquisitive society and its overlay of intellectual gentility. Brooks's intuition of many unconscious contradictions in American life had given him a resolute tone and purpose in *America's Coming-of-Age* and had finally led him to *The Ordeal of Mark Twain*.

The Ordeal was Brooks's strongest, most fervent, most incisive book. Despite the attacks by the professional Westerner Bernard De Voto, who until he learned better could never understand that the harmony Mark Twain sought for his books was not present in his own life, *The Ordeal of Mark Twain* proved itself over the years. Even De Voto, as editor of Mark Twain's apoplectic last writings on American plutocracy and grandiose moral hypocrisy, admitted Brooks's original charge that Mark Twain had been hamstrung by the genteel world he married into.

But Brooks could not endure controversy and was to go through a prolonged nervous ordeal of his own that left him unweariedly conciliatory to every item in the difficult past. He now became nostalgic and evasively charming about those just conflicts he had located in American culture and in the heart of Mark Twain. What sickened Brooks was his sense of some insoluble American problem. It clung to him like an incubus. Unlike his sturdier and more expansive friend Lewis Mumford, who addressed himself on a large scale to every social problem with the confidence of a Victorian prophet, Brooks knew nothing but literature. Mumford had worked up for himself a great competence in the history of technology and architecture. He occupied himself brilliantly with every social malady and aesthetic disfigurement in the New York that obsessed him as the exciting and disturbing world center it was. Brooks's breakdown in the late twenties owed something to his lack of sufficient mental interests, to his long intellectual introspection, some burning sense of his own mental apostasy. He could bear anything but intellectual fight. Slowly, intuitively, and rather cagily he put himself together again by a full return to a nostalgia incarnated in the American past. He thrived on images of a century that, for him somehow had no conflicts. With his particular feeling for the biographical portrait, for the writer as the easy reflection of his time (and for his idyllic passages), Brooks in *The Flowering of New England* and later books created the most brilliant photograph album of the nineteenth century. For him it was a golden age without social struggle, without killing, war, monopoly, without religious turmoil, without American power lust. His strategy made every writer charming and reduced every book to fitting quotations.

By 1942, Brooks was an immensely successful, rosily optimistic celebrator of America the beautiful. He was to reserve his barbs for Proust, Eliot, and Joyce. The 1930s had encouraged a documentary literature of social investigation and national self-discovery. The war had elevated this into a national self-celebration. "Modernism," like the "Japs," had somehow got us into war by sapping our will to fight. Archibald MacLeish had suggested this in "The Irresponsibles" and Mumford in *Men Must Act*. Hitler's accomplices and stooges in the Vichy regime liked to blame decadents like Proust and Léon Blum for the French defeat in 1940. Brooks like other American writers jealous of the artistic prestige of Eliot, Proust, and Joyce, found it comfortable to believe that the modernist revolution was played out—"the ash of a burned out cigar"—yet still of support to the enemy.

Brooks had all our attention that day at *The New Republic*, but remained as private as a writer in his study. He could give nothing away. To see Van Wyck Brooks at last, but gently slipping away from every public topic and literary issue, was strange, for it made me concentrate on his mustache, his mannered haircut, and his wonderful white linen waistcoat. Henry James had worn just such a waistcoat over his bookish belly. Adam Verver, in *The Golden Bowl*, wore a white linen waistcoat. Brooks had brilliantly turned himself into a period piece, a smooth Edwardian dandy. I wondered if he wore a tie and tweed jacket when he wrote in the morning. Brooks confirmed something I had guessed at in the rugged features of Carl Van Doren, the mustachioed handsomeness of Lewis Mumford, the prematurely white hair over the mildly ravaged face of Lionel Trilling. They had a conscious air; they were the voice of tradition. They came out of their studies with an air ironic, faintly burdened, as if determined to meet the world only halfway.

Looking at my old hero with awe and apprehension was like reading *New England: Indian Summer* again. My favorite of the many sunny scenes in the book

showed William Dean Howells and Henry James in
1872 strolling in the Boston Public Garden. There was
Howells excitedly digging the end of his cane into the
ground as they discussed the prospects of American
fiction. My God, Van Wyck Brooks in 1942 looked
just like Howells! In that dining room high above Madison Avenue, a room overbright with the sharp New
York light, Brooks was all white and portly, like the
stubby Mr. Howells himself, that damnably genial man.

Unlike Stark Young, who was still *The New Republic*'s drama critic but who on his rare appearance at an
office lunch would, in his campy overdone Southern
accent, maliciously undermine the fine liberal professions circulating around the table, Brooks seemed not
superior to *The New Republic* in its anti-intellectual
state, just untouched by it.

Young was openly contemptuous. He was still involved with modernism, as he always had been. As a
young instructor at the University of Texas, he had
written to Henry James asking for the right order in
which to read the Master's many books. James had written back in the greatest detail to the "delightful young
man." Of course Stark Young was a Southern "reactionary," had joined Tate and Ransom in the famous
"I'll Take My Stand" protest of Southern "agrarians"
against industrializing the South. With some cynicism,
he had even concocted one of the most popular romantic
novels about the ante-bellum South, *So Red the Rose*.
But Young only trifled with "views." He was a theater
man who, even when he appeared most confused—a
very large edifice just about to topple—was all theater,
professional camp, and verbal roguishness. So large a
man to be so elfish!

Stark Young was the most eccentrically interesting
writer on New York theater I ever read. Though he

sooner or later wove his way round to some underhand piece of brilliance, he was faithful first to his epicurean mind and wrote every drama piece as if he needed to please only himself. Any review by Stark Young was like an old-fashioned English squire's rambling slightly woozy monologue after dinner, punctuated by hiccoughs as he sat over his walnuts and wine. He said more good things about theater as stylized human behavior, more interesting things about the Broadway commodity he was reviewing, than you would have expected from that great bald Charlus heavily sitting at table in his mansion. Young was an actor, a flirtatiously genial, oily, subtle man, yet a strangely halting speaker and writer; I could never tell how much he was enlarging the stories he liked to tell me about Chaplin, Tallulah, Stanislavsky, the Lunts in order to make himself as big as he looked. He looked, he looked—how much he looked! He seemed as finished, as rounded-out as a character in a novel. I knew him as a performer in conversation, where he played many parts and imitated many other performers. He seemed to keep himself afloat by the comic fixity of his eye even as he grew more and more seductive. He was forty years older than I and had to be content with playing Socrates, the comic gadfly, since I did not seem to understand that he could play Alcibiades, the lover.

Night after night over our modest supper, I talked to Natasha about Young's clownish winks and leers. They were a great puzzle at the time. She listened patiently. How proud I was of *our* virtue, though it was steadily killing me! What virtuous times "we" lived in, though Natasha just listened. The outside world was still more real to me than I was. Everything was still more real than what in a secret poem I called my Lord Heart. My Lord Heart was amazed by other people's happi-

ness. My Lord Heart did not know how to tell Natasha
what Natasha knew as well as William Blake:

> What is it men in women do require?
> The lineaments of Gratified Desire.
> What is it women do in men require?
> The lineaments of Gratified Desire.

Young gave up on me; his flirtatiousness became mechanical, ironic. Still talking to me by the hour, he
stumbled about in his mind the way he did in his pieces.
He got to a particular point by infinite preliminaries. If
one line of rumination did not promise well, he started
another in mid-sentence. Once he awakened from his
monologue to give me—because he liked something I
had written—a first edition of Robert Frost's *North of
Boston* with an unpublished verse letter in it that Frost
had given him when they were young teachers at Amherst. Frost had been rescued by Alexander Meiklejohn
to become Amherst's poet. Not until I met Meiklejohn
at Berkeley in 1963 did I learn that Frost had had
wicked homosexual Stark Young fired from Amherst—
thus sending him at the right time to *The New Republic*.

In Stark Young I glimpsed for the first time the delightful chaos that a Southern writer could be. He was
not always at the ready, like the New York intellectuals
I knew. He was an actor, a great pretender, as full of
manner and malice, stealthy charm, learning and sheer
pretense, as the Southern "aristocrats" he had faked in
So Red the Rose. With so much flashing out of Young
as from a lighthouse, I felt about him, as I did about
my colleague Tom Sancton weeping over attacks on
Negro soldiers in the South, or about Allen Tate in our
most furious disagreements, that Southern writers were
more tragically in conflict with themselves and their

past, moodier and more sympathetic, than other writers I was meeting for the first time.

Tate, with his unconvincing absolutes about the old South's slavery and religion, furiously began every conversation as if I personified the liberal New York Jewish enemy. But the more we saw each other—we both played the violin with more temperament than finesse, and on Saturday afternoons rustily plowed through miles of standard eighteenth-century duets—the more we were joined by disagreement. Tate was a Latinist, a traditionalist yearning for the Church. Eliot's mysterious authority held him prisoner. With nose and eyes planted in his enormous head like candles in a cake, he looked oddly pitiable but still aggressive. When half seas over, he was insulting enough to satisfy his longing for strength. Like all the Southern writers I ever met in New York, he had a homesickness for the South he no longer lived in that made him see everything in New York with derisory eyes—especially Jews. The Southerners I met were generally disturbed by Jews—obsessed, condescending, always just veering off with a smile from some irreversible insult. They were not used to taking Jews seriously. "Ah reserve the right, my dear Alfred," Tate once said, drawing himself up with an air, "to say what Ah think about Joos." One visitor's day at lunch when Max Lerner, as resolutely ready to confront any social evil as a boxer waiting for that first clang of the bell, was bravely denouncing Southern poll taxes, Stark Young, who had been listening with a patronizing smile, leaned across the table to me and, in his richest plantation accent, said dreamily, "Hasn't Max the most beautiful eyes?"

There was no connection between the notables at lunch and the young Village writers angrily waiting for books

to review. Reviewers at *The New Republic* now tended
to be not the old hacks of the thirties but young poets
and novelists belligerently on their way up, and contemptuous of established names.

Through the Chicago writer Isaac Rosenfeld—whose
wife, Vasiliki, was my secretary—I met Saul Bellow,
who was also just in from Chicago, and who carried
around with him a sense of his destiny as a novelist that
excited everyone around him. Bellow was the first writer
of my generation—we had been born ten days apart—
who talked of Lawrence and Joyce, Hemingway and
Fitzgerald, not as books in the library but as fellow
operators in the same business. As I walked him across
Brooklyn Bridge and among my favorite streets in
Brooklyn Heights, he looked my city over with great
detachment. He had the gift—without warning, it would
follow a séance of brooding Jewish introspection—of
making you see the most microscopic event in the street
because *he* happened to be seeing it. In the course of
some startling observations on the future of the war,
the pain of Nazism, the neurotic effects of apartment-
house living on his friends in New York (Chicago was
different; it was a *good* thing to grow up in Chicago),
he thought up some very funny jokes, puns, and double
entendres. It was sometimes difficult to catch the punch
line, he laughed so fast with hearty pleasure at things so
well said. And they were well said, in a voice that already shaped its words with careful public clarity. He
explained, as casually as if he were in a ball park fault-
ing a pitcher, that Fitzgerald was weak, but Dreiser
strong in the right places. He examined Hemingway's
style like a surgeon pondering another surgeon's stitches.
Then, familiarly calling on the D. H. Lawrence we all
loved as our particular brother in arms, he pointed to
the bilious and smoke-dirty sky over the Squibb factory

on Columbia Heights. Like Lawrence, he wanted no
"umbrella" between him and the essential mystery. He
wanted direct contact with everything in the universe
around him.

Bellow had not yet published a novel; he was known
for his stories and evident brilliance only to intellectuals
around *Partisan Review* and the University of Chicago.
Yet walking the unfamiliar Brooklyn streets, he seemed
to be measuring the hidden strength of all things in the
universe, from the industrial grime surrounding Brooklyn Bridge to the prima donnas of the American novel,
from the lasting effects of Hitler to the mass tensions of
New York. He was measuring the world's power to resist
him, he was putting himself up as a contender. Although
he was friendly, unpretentious, and funny, he was ambitious and dedicated in a style I had never seen in an
urban Jewish intellectual; he expected the world to come
to him. He had pledged himself to a great destiny. He
was going to take on more than the rest of us were.

It was bracing to meet with someone exactly my age
and background who looked at life with this loftiness,
this proud sense of vocation. "And being a novelist,"
Lawrence said, "I consider myself superior to the saint,
the scientist, the philosopher, and the poet, who are all
great masters of different bits of man alive, but never
get the whole hog." To be a novelist! To take on anything and everything! As Bellow talked, I had an image
of a wrestler in the old Greek style, an agonist contend-
ing in the games for the prize. Life was dramatically as
well as emotionally a contest to him. In some way I
could not define, he seemed to be always training for it.
And he was wary—eager, sardonic, and wary.

For a man with such a range of interests, Bellow
talked with great austerity. He addressed himself to the
strength of life hidden in people. An anthropologist by

training, he liked to estimate other people's physical
capacity, the thickness of their skins, the strength in
their hands, the force in their chests. He talked like a
Darwinian, calculating the power of survival hidden in
the species. There was nothing idle or shadowy about
his observations; he did not talk for effect. His defini-
tions, epigrams, were of a formal plainness that went
right to the point and stopped. That was the victory he
wanted. There was not the slightest verbal inflation in
anything he said. Yet his observations were direct and
penetrating; they took on the elegance of achieved
thought. When he considered something, his eyes slightly
set as if studying its power to deceive him, one realized
how formidable he was on topics generally exhausted
by ideology or neglected by intellectuals too fine to consider them. Suddenly everything tiresomely grievous
came alive in the focus of this man's unfamiliar
imagination.

Listening to Bellow, I became intellectually happy—
an effect he was soon to have on a great many other
writers of our generation. We were coming through.
There seemed nothing deliberate about Bellow's sense
of destiny. He was proud in a laconic way, like an old
Jew who feels himself closer to God than anybody else.
He could be unbearable in his unresting image of himself, but he was never smug and could be as openly
vulnerable as anyone I ever met. Then he would nail
with quiet ferocity someone who had astonished him
by offering the mildest criticism.

The proud novelist-to-be, like the young Joseph in
the Bible, airily confided his dreams of greatness to his
brothers; he would be quick to divide the world into
allies and enemies. I believed in him as a novelist because, like his strength in being a Jew, *this* was a sealed
treasure undamaged by his many anxieties. Saul was

clearly a man chosen by talent, like those Jewish virtuosos—Heifetz, Rubinstein, Milstein, Horowitz—who
had been shaped into slim and elegant men of the world
by talent alone. Even his conscious good looks were
those of a coming celebrity. But the great thing was
Saul's talent for the literature of direct experience. Every
day, I saw intellectuals clever enough to make the world
over, who indeed had made the world over many times.
Yet Bellow, who had been brought up in the same uto-
pianism and was himself a nimble adept of the University of Chicago style, full of the Great Books and jokes
from Aristophanes, would obviously be first and last a
novelist, a storyteller, creating new myths out of himself and every other intellectual he had ever known,
fought, loved, hated. This loosened the bonds of ideology for the rest of us. It was refreshing to be with a man
who disposed of so many pedantic distinctions. It
seemed to have something to do with his love of Yiddish and Jewish jokes, his affection for big-city low life,
his sense of himself as a *creative* Jew. Saul was the first
Jewish writer I met who seemed as clever about every
side of life as a businessman. He was in touch.

I lived my life among brilliant intellectuals, and would
soon encounter Lionel Trilling, who had very warmly reviewed *On Native Grounds* and one day came into *The
New Republic* office to discuss some possible pieces with
Bliven. Trilling was an intense intellectual admiration
of mine, but we were not fated to have much conversation. Ten years older than I, the first Jew in recorded
history to get tenure in a Columbia English Department
as crowded with three-barreled Anglican names as the
House of Bishops, Trilling in his middle thirties was
fascinating, subtle, and careful. "We have room for only
one Jew," the English chairman had told Clifton Fadi-
man at their graduation, "and we have chosen Mr.

Trilling." Those ten years between us reinforced my impression of Trilling as a writer who had absorbed the casual, more gentlemanly style of the twenties much as Bellow and I had absorbed the social angers of the abrasive lower-class thirties.

Trilling already had his distinguished white hair over a handsome face that seemed to be furrowed, hooded, closed up with constant thought. The life was all within, despite his debonair practiced easiness of manner. With his look of consciously occupying an important place, his already worn face of thought, his brilliant discriminations as we talked, he quietly defended himself from the many things he had left behind. He seemed to feel more than the usual literary connection to things English, and proudly told me that his mother had been born in England. Victorian England would be his intellectual motherland. During the heyday of Marxist criticism, I had been grateful to him for writing against the spirit of the age and for the intense devotion behind his wonderful book on Matthew Arnold. He still believed in culture as a guide to society. In person, there was immense and even cavernous subtlety to the man, along with much timidity, a self-protectiveness as elegant as a fencer's; my first meetings with Trilling were just too awesome. With the deep-sunk colored pouches under his eyes, the cigarette always in hand like an intellectual gesture, an air that combined weariness, vanity, and immense caution, he was already a personage. He seemed intent on not diminishing his career by a single word. At our very first meeting in *The New Republic*, when I brought him into Bliven's office so as to stress the importance of his writing for us, Trilling astonished me by saying, very firmly, that he would not write anything that did not "promote my reputation." Bliven gave every assurance that Trilling would not have to write anything that did not promote his reputation. Although I found so much solemnity about one's reputation hilarious, I was impressed by the tight-lipped seriousness with which Trilling said "my reputation." It seemed to resemble an expensive picture on view. "My reputation" was to be nursed along like money in the bank. It was capital. I had never encountered a Jewish intellectual so conscious of social position, so full of adopted finery in his conversation. "I should scarcely have believed that."

In those early days, as we and Trilling and his wife, Diana, met at *Partisan Review* parties, we were all disaffected radicals. Even the bitterly anti-Stalinist leftists were too conformist and doctrinaire for such individual talents as Bellow and Trilling. There were brilliant WASPS and Yale men in the *Partisan Review* orbit, Dwight Macdonald and Fred Dupee, for whom radical activity had been an extension of their personal restlessness in the twenties, their excited discovery of another America during the Depression. There were scholarly anti-Fascist exiles, Nicola Chiaromonte and Paolo Milano; Irish Catholics, William Barrett, James T. Farrell. Mary McCarthy from Seattle was the star of the magazine. Elizabeth Hardwick from Kentucky wrote extraordinarily sensitive stories and essays. But for the many brilliant Jews around what Edmund Wilson called "Partisansky Review"—Trilling and Bellow, Philip Rahv, William Phillips, Delmore Schwartz, Meyer Schapiro, Harold Rosenberg, Paul Goodman, Irving Howe, Daniel Bell, Sidney Hook, Lionel Abel, Isaac Rosenfeld, Clement Greenberg, Leslie Fiedler—the "movement" had become another theology to be sloughed off like Judaism. Their creativity was to arise out of a historic tension between the whole traditions and systems of ideas. The aim was unlimited freedom of speculation, the union of a free radicalism with modernism. Somehow America in wartime supplied the assurance that this was possible. Fugitives from orthodoxy in religion and radicalism alike, they had been formed by the national culture without always knowing it. Their faith was to be "intellectuals"; around *Partisan Review* it was safer to be an intellectual than a mere writer.

The sudden emergence of Jews as literary figures was certainly due to their improved status in an economy liberated by the war and catapulted by war into domination of the "free world." Immensely subtle and learned authorities on Matthew Arnold, Henry James, James Joyce, Paul Cézanne could hardly be identified with Depression novels out of the tenements like *Jews Without Money, Haunch Paunch and Jowl, Call It Sleep, The Old Bunch.* Speculative by nature, sophisticated in the lore of modern literature and painting, even the novelists and poets among these new writers were intellectuals and university teachers who respected nothing in this world so much as a great new world idea. They put all their zeal for social revolution into the purer and perhaps more lasting revolution of modern literature and art. They would soon be the intellectual style setters, the cultural leaders and gurus of a modernism that would replace the old academic orthodoxies. Kafka might be obliterated in all the German-language countries under the influence of Hitler; Babel and Mandelstam might perish in Stalin's camps; *Finnegans Wake* and Picasso's latest might still be a joke to fat European burghers. But Kafka, Babel, Joyce, Picasso—not to forget Malraux, Sartre, Italo Svevo, Stravinsky, Schönberg —were the gods of this world to those intellectuals who wanted to be both established and advanced, and soon were.

They were still outsiders for all their inside knowledge of the modern. The "accommodation to America" did not keep Jewish intellectuals like the Trillings from criticizing their own liberalism. They saw with the eyes of great twentieth-century masters, Eliot, Yeats, Mann, who were conservative and even aristocratic. To be a Jew and yet not Jewish; to be of course a liberal, yet to see everything that was wrong with the "imagination of liberalism"; to be Freudian and a master of propriety; academic and yet intellectually avant-garde—this produced the tension, the necessary intellectual ordeal, that was soon to make Trilling the particular voice of intellectuals superior to liberalism. Freud said that "being a Jew, I would always be in the opposition." A master of distinctions, Trilling was to perform with particular subtlety as a critic of liberalism and radicalism who could not be tied down to any conservative position. The fascination of his work to the many ex-liberals and post-radicals in his audience was that he made every distinction, touched every base, without finding himself stranded on any. No one could have been more discerning, and less involved.

One night at the Trillings' the conversation came around to Paul Goodman. Goodman in 1942 was still the *enfant terrible*, the homemade avant-garde with a dozen books to his credit who could interest no commercial publisher. He had not yet attained fame as a loving analyst of the young, or as an anarchist setting out community schemes. But he was already A Figure— if only in the Village—with a deep apostolic sense of himself, his bisexual life, his fate, his homelessness, his early orphan roamings on the sidewalks of New York. He seemed to press his self-declared difference as a writer and his boldness as a lover into everything he said and wrote. He was as assertive as Robespierre, Napoleon, Trotsky. Anything I picked up of his always

seemed to me as roughly written as a leaflet. But he
fascinated—or intimidated—because with all his ferocious conceit as novelist, poet, philosopher-at-large,
writing was a way of living to a desperate man whose
theme was love; looking for love. He was open about his
pickups, his hopes and disasters, his love for boys; I was
awed by his hungry searching and the unashamed naïve
egomania with which he celebrated his desires as the
privilege of his gifts as writer and oracle.

That night at the Trillings', still basking in the warmth
of Lionel's review of my book, I had innocently brought
myself and some of my recent essays in a state of respectful homage—and discovered that despite Lionel's
guarded amiability, I was distinctly *persona non grata*
with his wife. Diana had been writing reviews for *The
New Republic* before my accession and, on her most
recent appearance in the paper, had without my knowledge been described in the contributors' box as "the
wife of Lionel Trilling." Despite all my efforts to explain away this stupidity and to make amends, Diana
fixed me with an unforgiving stare that was to last forever. She was a dogged woman and looked it, with a
passion for polemic against all possible dupes of the
Soviet Union that in the McCarthy era and the heyday
of the American Committee for Cultural Freedom was
to make her the scourge of all mistaken ill-thinking
"anti-anti-Communists." She was tirelessly attentive to
the intellectuals—a class that included some writers
(by no means just any writers), and was often referred
to by both Trillings, with great disappointment, as "our
educated classes," our "enlightened" classes. Her favorite literary genre seemed to be the letter to the editor.
Sometimes she wrote in to criticize an unfavorable review of a book for not being unfavorable enough.

With this seething sense of her intellectual-political

righteousness, Diana always seemed more alert to the wrongdoing of other intellectuals than to the beauty of creative art. And I was young, and despite my admiration for her husband's subtle intelligence, distinctly not one of his humble imitators at Columbia. I must have irritated her profoundly. Her anxieties were soon all astir. The evening wore on slowly and heavily, my heart sinking fast at every glacial stare and exasperated grunt from Diana as I beseechingly offered up cultural conversation first to both of them, and on being steadily cold-shouldered by her, to him alone. Did Professor Trilling, uh, care for the novels of Henry Green? Was he as fond as I was of the Glyndebourne Festival recording of *The Marriage of Figaro* I had seen lying atop their phonograph? And what, if I might venture the question, did Professor Trilling think of that famous bad boy Paul Goodman?

To my relief and surprise, Trilling and I found ourselves agreeing, with the little furtive smile of such heavily proper people as ourselves, that we rather *envied* Paul Goodman his "scandalous" reputation. Here we were, two eminently right-thinking, heavily moral literary critics, both in the very flower of life, who had to confess that we rather envied this street gamin, this bohemian, the intense amorousness of his Village life!

Trilling opened up surprisingly on the topic of Goodman, lost his ceremonially guarded air. Smiling happily, he gave rein to some ancient fantasies about tearing off into the wild blue yonder. With a grin he admitted that he had once been fired from Columbia for being a "Marxist and a Freudian." He had actually gone off for a year to teach way out there—he waved his arm—at the University of Wisconsin. I understood him completely. New York was a great adventure for *them*, not for the likes of us. I was beginning to understand why

Freud so much occupied Trilling's mind. What a price
one paid for "culture"! Suddenly "the wife of Lionel
Trilling," as irritated with him as she was contemptuous
of me, tore into both of us as "hopeless romantics."
Paul Goodman?! Paul Goodman?! I hurriedly took my
leave and was never again to see the Trillings at home.

For Trilling I would always be "too Jewish," too full
of my lower-class experience. He would always defend
himself from the things he had left behind. This would
go on and on for thirty years; it was *the* barrier, like
his fondness for the words "scarcely," "modulation,"
"our educated classes." I had scarcely enough modulation. Even when Trilling came to praise a novel of "low
life" like *The Adventures of Augie March* (he drove
Bellow wild by withdrawing his approval in a second
article), the abstract diction Trilling favored, his nerve-
less compromised accents, explained why our friend
Harold Rosenberg muttered: "When I first encountered
the style of Lionel Trilling, I looked for the joke and
discovered there wasn't any":

> The extent of Mr. Bellow's success in these pages may
> be judged from the familiarity of the matter upon which
> he exercises his talents. The life of the slums and the
> near-slums of Chicago or some other great city has estab-
> lished itself over the last thirty years as a canonical sub-
> ject in our literature. It is a good subject; it has its own
> implicit richness; one can almost say that if a writer
> comes to it with honesty and painstakingness, he can
> scarcely fail to make something good of it.
> We have, then, a prose which is articulate to the last
> degree, very fluent and rapid, yet thick with metaphor
> and epithet.
> For all its human richness, it is a novel of specific
> moral, intellectual intention—that intention being, as it
> happens, the demonstration of how to achieve and cele-
> brate human richness—and it must be allowed the reso-

lution and relaxation that comes with the sense of
something learned. . . .

I felt more at home with Bellow's attitude toward experience. He was always peering under the covers of
our vaunted culture, thinking ahead of the general line.
Chicago seemed to explain his self-confidence. New
York was so big and "important" that no novelist had
ever done the whole city as Dreiser had done Chicago.
What made the New York intellectual's life a perpetual
culture show was no help to the novelist. The speculative directness of Bellow and his friend Isaac Rosenfeld,
who addressed experience with every possible question,
seemed to me a product of Chicago itself—the city created, a Chicago novelist said at the end of the nineteenth
century, expressly for the purpose of making money.
Chicago gave people the Midwestern openness, a sense
of being at home in America. It had so clearly been
made that a writer could still take it all on. Even the
lofty Great Books curriculum at Robert Maynard Hutchins's University of Chicago sharpened perspective on
so much contemporary reality.

By now, Chicago had done its best for Saul and Isaac;
they were in New York, but they were not like other
New Yorkers. Isaac had specialized in philosophy and
Saul in anthropology, but far from wishing to become
academics, there was an intellectual playfulness about
them both, a gift for insurrectionary proposals. I saw
them as characters from *The Possessed*—temperamental
provocateurs in some nasty provincial town trying by
the force of their talk to raise a little dust. Chicago had
kept them serious. They expected great things of themselves as creative artists, and showed it by their ease of
speculation. In even, clear Midwestern voices, they
would come out with Nietzschean aphorisms in the

midst of the endless clowning at Isaac's first ramshackle apartment in New York on Christopher Street. At the end of Christopher Street there was a ferry to Hoboken, where we regularly went for oysters and beer at an old Irish pub near the rusty ferry station. I had never known intellectuals so close to my own heart. The issue was always how to break through. Both seemed to have unusual inner freedom.

Bellow really had freedom, was soon to dramatize it in those suffering, advancing, brilliantly exploring voices of his development that are the center of his fiction. Isaac, who looked as Old World as our fathers, was to become a martyr to "ideas." He was short and round, bespectacled, and in public frantically friendly. He was to search all through his short and madly restless life— he died at thirty-eight—for Saul's confident touch. Isaac veered from logical positivism to Orphic romanticism to Wilhelm Reich's orgone box as the apocalypse, from Trotsky to Gandhi to Kafka, from revelation to revelation—a jolly-sounding but increasingly desperate pilgrim searching for the ultimate conviction that would turn all things around for him.

Isaac never became the imaginative writer he wanted to be, the writer his friend Saul Bellow was destined to be. Dividing himself up, as usual, he wrote:

> There is our animal nature, not yet created, in which freedom is the death of us; there is our human nature, in process of creation, where reason, our special part, can be the death of us; and there is the imagination, created, whose reasons and meanings are greater than all the others. Here, then, is life—and . . . freedom.

But Isaac was never sure where imagination was. I could never be sure how serious Isaac was about *writing*. Bellow liked to remember Isaac at eleven or twelve, still

in knee pants, delivering a brilliant talk on Schopenhauer. To be with Isaac was to see that he fondly believed that exposing his mind would minister to every
problem. So Isaac became too busy for writing. He became too busy trying his life out. He lived not like a
writer but like a character in search of a plot. Every
day, he woke up determined to be a new man, to recast
everything, to try a new role, to be attractive, promis-
cuous, and wise. What another man with Isaac's rebel-
lious imagination might have put entirely into his work,
as Norman Mailer was to do after the war, Isaac frantically sought to *make* life. He wanted to cast himself
as a wholly new being—and must often have gone to
his desk, after exhausting himself all day long in private
fantasies and loving entanglements with the many
people who were always around him, astonished that
the words for experience, when he came to use them,
were after the heat of experience so frigid. He would
more and more have the look of someone who had
unaccountably lost his way. But Isaac as a character in
this life drama of his own creating had distinction. He
had gone straight to the *Angst* behind all our lives, and,
like Jacob wrestling with the angel, Isaac said to his
demon, "I will not let thee go before thou bless me."
Every Jew I knew lived with this fear, but Isaac ran to
meet it, to live with it, to argue it away.

He often awoke, he told me, in sheer fright, "scared
shitless." He described for me the cold damp winter
mornings in Chicago when he had candled eggs in his
father's dairy, and I could see him shaking in the dark
store with broken eggs mucking his shoes. He confronted his personal terror—his early death—endlessly
speculative about it, proud of his reckless courage in
writing so many theories over the face of his fear. He
was openly taking it on. After an afternoon with Isaac—

who was an excellent flutist, glad to play for you at any
time; who was never too busy to see anybody; who had
just imitated Smerdyakov murdering old Karamazov
and Ivan Karamazov arguing with the Devil, had just
mimicked his friends with enthusiasm, and had explained how *Moby-Dick* had converted him from logical
positivism—his little *contes* of Jewish irregulars in
Chicago seemed overconscious in effect. He liked to
read unfinished first drafts aloud, watching your face.
Even his fine voice and the beautifully formed letters on
the cheap yellow sheets made this less a reading than an
experiment. When I read his fiction, I could see the
theoretician standing apart from the writer of fiction
and waiting to comment on the action that had been
impatiently sketched in. Unlike Bellow, who could use
every morsel of his experience—even his college training in anthropology would turn up in *Henderson the
Rain King*—Isaac lived his fantasies, and in company.
He settled into the Village with the excitement of a
writer discovering his true subject. His new apartment
on Barrow Street was crowded every night with people
who, once they had boisterously climbed up four flights
and fought their way into the apartment past Isaac's
jittery black hound, Smokey, looked as if they never
planned to find their way out again.

One wall of the Rosenfeld kitchen was lined with
snapshots of these friends. Isaac always greeted people
wildly, as if any visitor liberated him from an intolerable dilemma. He liked a certain confusion around him
as proof that he was welcoming life with open arms.
Since Isaac was usually not yet ready to write, felt that
he had first to solve his "problem," to understand himself, he easily gathered around him many dreamy Village types who also had to talk away their fears before
they could write. Isaac brought all his elfin wit and

desperate charm to this pursuit of his psyche. He gave himself to conversation with the mad energy of a clown and the many bright sayings of a thinker still faithful to Wisdom. In his brilliant wanderings, he regularly came upon and ritually vanquished his lifelong intimate —The Fear. Every side of life was open to this hungry speculation, everything waited for the great beast to be sighted. Thinking aloud in his dark and madly jammed living room, with neurotic Smokey yipping and biting at him with every word, Isaac, like Captain Ahab, was alone in the universe with his prey. Like many an American romantic, he suspected that the universe was waiting for *him* to decide its fate. Everything still hung in the balance. For Isaac, as for me, the old addiction to Socialism produced a critical instrument sharpened on existing institutions but not the slightest idea how to reorganize society.

Isaac, even as a novelist, was more interested in ideas than in manners. His favorite characters were philosophic loners like Ishmael, Raskolnikov, Kafka's K. Society was for the bourgeois intellectual who adjusted to it. It was 1942, the bottom of the war, and we who were not in the war took everything as a political failure. We knew about the death camps before we heard the word "Auschwitz." But though Isaac and I talked Blake and Tolstoy and Nietzsche to each other (what Great Books lectures we gave each other!), none of these marvelous liberators of human conscience, these prophets of the divine energy in man, could solve *my* problem. I had just been turned down by the Army because of my stammer. "What would you do," asked roly-poly Dr. Brill, Freud's worst translator, "if you had to say, 'F-F-F-Fire'?" I did not know what to do with myself, how to tie up with what was happening. I felt in excess, bitterly outside, and envied those friends of mine who, though they went into the Army or the merchant marine or even the Office of War Information screaming at the waste of their genius, managed, I noticed from their careers, to fulfill their fantasies of participation and even of power.

At Isaac's endless Village evenings I sometimes responded to his urgent manifestoes, "existential" before the word was heard from France, about the absurdity of life. Isaac also made a fetish of Indian quietism—Gandhi would yet replace Lenin! It was somehow understood that just as the Bolshevik Revolution was the greatest thing to come out of 1914–1918, so the "Indian Revolution will be the greatest thing to come out of this war." The Indians were teaching men how *not* to make gods out of their love of destruction.

For the first time, already feeling intimations of shipwreck in this crazy New York war scene, I had to furnish my own text, to confront a nothingness around me that smelled of death. Isaac, who woke up every morning "scared shitless," was brave but not convincing. I saw his Greenwich Village life as a heroic choice for him and his *Angst*, a first necessary step toward new possibilities of love. But his measures were mechanical.

The process of getting down to his "animal nature" took hold of Isaac. A scientist experimenting on his own sexual possibilities for lack of someone else, Isaac drove himself wild trying to make his body respond with the prodigality promised by theory. Suddenly he turned away from all social measures to Dr. Wilhelm Reich's philosophy of the orgone. Following Dr. Reich's conviction that some of the orgone energy at large in the universe could be absorbed by an individual sitting inside a wooden box lined with metal to Reich's specifications, Isaac, determined to extract more "genitality" from the universe at large, built himself an orgone box in his bedroom.

Like so many of Isaac's attempts to apply his imaginative vision to life, this orgone box was compromised by his poverty and his many interests. It was too evidently a homemade, bargain-basement orgone box. It looked more like a cardboard closet or stage telephone booth than it did a scientific apparatus by which to recover the sexual energy one had lost to "culture." Isaac's orgone box stood up in the midst of an enormous confusion of bedclothes, review copies, manuscripts, children, and the many people who went in and out of the room as if it were the bathroom. Belligerently sitting inside his orgone box, daring philistines to laugh, Isaac nevertheless looked lost, as if he were waiting in his telephone booth for a call that was not coming through. He was so intent on breaking with every imagined repression and anxiety, on not yielding an inch to the Jewish-Puritan Enemy, that he finally turned all this prayed-for-sexual freedom and power into another imaginary country, like the India in his fiction. This country in which he lived a perfect life was always on the other side of a barrier, a country to which Isaac sought entrance but that was never where he lived. He soon wore himself out trying to break into it from every direction at once. Every issue became one of "our animal nature," on which Isaac felt compelled to make a stand for freedom, openness, genitality. But meanwhile he had a family to support, he worked on trade papers, he was briefly on *The New Republic*, and everything came back to Isaac the prisoner in his cell the orgone box. He never broke out.

There were times, I knew, when he envied his less talented but more openly manic Village friends their concentration on "just living," on public "balling." He would talk wistfully about two friends of his, the brothers Stein, who made a family affair out of their public orgies, shared the same girls, determinedly took no precautions in what they called "Russian roulette." The brothers had an abortion fund against the times that "they" lost. I often met at Isaac's house a tall, dim, lost girl from the Midwest who lived with a young Village intellectual but had such intense personal blackouts that I marveled at her powers of survival. "I have my journal," she said. In some way Isaac envied her openness to pain. The cabin boy Pip in *Moby-Dick*, the epic poem of our savage American loneliness, jumped out of the harpooner's boat in fear. Going mad in the sea, he "touched God's footpedal." One of the brothers Stein eventually threw himself from the roof of a state hospital. The dim sweet girl from the Midwest, always on the verge of going down for the last time, seemed to be summoning other people to go down with her. Isaac was drawn to such friends. They had the final, absolute, terrible courage to be vulnerable. Even when his own fiction missed naturalness and disappointed people dazed by his conversation, Isaac took his literary adventures as a sacrifice to "truth." To have the courage of your "animal nature" was to be a victim of bourgeois America.

Isaac as his own subject eventually drove himself wild. Stuck between his demand for perfect love and his desire to be a writer, he missed out on both. As even the Village desperadoes noticed, Isaac was a "failure." Precocious in everything and understandably worn out, he died at thirty-eight. Even his dying would be a kind of failure. But Isaac's best hope for himself was never to save himself. He really was an Isaac, ready to sacrifice himself on the say-so of one earthly father

after another. Every day, with perfect faith, he awaited
his redeemer. Every day in the frantic Village of the
war years, reducing himself to "perfect sex," orgone
boxes, endless book reviews, and all-night conversations
with his friends, he showed his inability to compromise
with the things of this world.

There were evenings in Barrow Street, while I played
the violin part in Bach's B-Minor Suite to Isaac's flute,
when his musical sense of style would make me gasp.
It was as exquisite as his handwriting. Isaac always
meant to *perform* well. The flute dominates the B-Minor
Suite, and Isaac certainly came in strong. The sound of
those notes reverberating off Isaac's breath like water
drops were of a silvery intensity. It seemed to me that
Isaac expressed himself in perfection at last, wrote his
signature on the air.

Going down the steps of that Barrow Street tenement
and back home from the eccentric winding streets of
the Village, the sound of Isaac's impeccable phrasing
still in my ears, I felt that some promised beauty in my
life waited for me. The Village streets, without the
ruler-sharp order of the New York gridiron, were always
a sudden surprise. Streets crossed that had no business
crossing. Suddenly my buried longing to write not from
a judgment seat but some personal narrative of my own
surprised me in the middle of the Village street. I had
written a book but did not know I was a writer. In the
presence of what Whitman had called "music, the com-
biner," I always felt redirected, and in Barrow Street
had a new instinct. A few Sundays later, when I sat in
Town Hall with Natasha at the New Friends of Music
concert and heard Artur Schnabel playing Schubert, the
subtlety of his phrasing, Schnabel and Schubert dancing
to each other, suddenly made me weep. The stiff old
man with a military haircut sat with a straight German

back in a straight chair. When he began the first four "Impromptus," he seemed for the first time to respond, very slightly, to his own playing. I could see him moving his lips as he shaped certain phrases. There was awe on his face. And all the while the straight back, the strict old man in the straight chair! His marvelous musical mind wove its way from bright to sad and back again, recharging itself over and over.

I felt open, disrupted, ready for anything. I more and more wanted to get away from everything. There was a wild longing in my heart to move on and to be changed. On Saturday afternoons, when Natasha and I emptily ambled along the East River, looked at the factories pasted on the horizon in Queens, sat at concerts among newly arrived German Jews who sniffed at everything as if Town Hall were the only America they could approve, I felt the same exasperation with my steady diet of culture that I felt toward *The New Republic* when it found the war promising the revolution of the "little" man and complained that only Winston Churchill's unnatural reactionary opinions kept the promising alliance with Stalin from making the world new.

In an effort to get overseas as a correspondent, I happily accepted an invitation from *Fortune*. It turned out that everybody else on *Fortune* was overseas or trying to get there. *Fortune* wanted cultural essays on "the American tradition." Henry Luce, proud because his large glossy magazine for the executive class did *not* bring in a profit, spoke of *Fortune* as an intellectual service to American leaders. Announcing that this was "the American Century," Luce complained that "the fundamental trouble with Americans has been, and is, that whereas their nation became in the 20th century the most powerful and the most vital, nation in the world, nevertheless Americans were unable to accommodate themselves spiritually and practically to that fact." He was now looking for the Word equal to American power. *Fortune* before the war, with James Agee, Walker Evans, Dwight Macdonald, Archibald MacLeish, Louis Kronenberger, John Kenneth Galbraith on the staff, had brilliantly reported the ravages to American society during the Depression. It was now on the upbeat reporting the war. Luce's great desire was to play teacher to the American people, to be a Big Influence. He of course believed that his magazines, whose very names summed up all human experience—*Time, Life, Fortune*—were the great educational medium. He was looking for a word to fit the great American deed. He was looking for the theology of the business society, for America as word. America was to be *made* word. Luce, born in China of missionary parents, thought of himself as a zealous Christian with a mission. There were so many intellectuals around Luce, and so many old leftists turned in the opposite direction, that he was encouraged by the high-flown discussions around him to think in Big Terms. He would soon insist on American purpose and leadership. "The American Century" opened the door to the hysterical postwar insistence on national orthodoxy.

Missionaries had gone through long years of exile, sacrifice, often developed strong-minded sons with driving, worldly ambitions. Luce certainly drove along with his innocently pretentious theology. He was a relentlessly impatient man, who insisted that everything *work*. Realizing more influence than many a missionary in China, Luce seemed from our first meeting a man sure that there was a particular destiny for him and that he could realize it. The childhood years away from America romanticized America but had not worked against his ability to plan a great publishing venture, to organize, to dominate, to succeed.

From the time I first met him at the Time Inc. executives' private lunch club on the sixty-fourth floor of the RCA Building, Luce radiated an eagerness to interpret and indoctrinate that was impossible to distinguish from nervous self-assurance. I was astonished; he mumbled and masticated his words as impatiently as he downed his food without looking at it—"Food is just fuel." He had an erratic way of getting to the point by trying every other word that came into his head until he came to the word he wanted. The Boss as intellectual eccentric, alternately diffident and authoritarian, was in contrast to the worried wage slaves, liberals all, who worked for him. He appeared just as "Editor" on the masthead of all his magazines. Luce was my first specimen of the Boss as Artist. He was a tireless organizer and hustler, a proven slave driver, and obviously a multimillionaire. But he came on as an intellectual busybody in the T.R. tradition, a master of honest simplicities who read the people and reached the people. Therefore his ideas were sound. He was an inspirational figure with an enormous temperament who certainly did not look or talk like a mere businessman. He had remarkable eyes, wore his hair very long in the back, had ferociously oversize eyebrows that looked as if they had been planted and watered to intimidate subordinates. Like a true artist or impresario, he seemed able to entertain any intellectual fancy, to leave himself open to every experience. But he was getting it all down as he talked, would use it up in his magazines.

I could not always understand him. He had what I came to think of as the Yale mumble; so many of his fellow Yalies on *Time* and *Fortune* used it that I assumed they imitated him. It was a style of speech in-

formally upper-class, and seemed common to rapid
thinkers who assimilated the abundance of this world
faster than they could say it. I linked it with the 1920s,
a democratic rush of words that showed emancipation
from the formality, dignity, remoteness of father's day.
It showed youth and a happy carelessness. It was Gatsby
welcoming you to a party. But Luce's informality, his
seeming impetuousness in words, were not personal at
all, but the style of a man forever educating himself in
public, educating himself at the lunch table—and then
educating his readers.

Riches and power were not enough for Luce, certainly not enough for America itself. He wanted to
show that America was a "proposition" as well as a
power. He was certain—with the natural authority of
the Editor of all the Luce publications—that America
could explain its principles from the world's great stock
of principles. To this end he had embarked on a "philosophy series" at the back of *Fortune*, with essays by
Whitehead and Russell, Ernst Cassirer, William Ernest
Hocking, Susanne Langer, Robert Maynard Hutchins,
and Sidney Hook. My one effort in this series, on America as portrayed by American writers from Emerson
to Melville, was rejected, and I was happily released
to report on the wartime scene in America. Although
Luce at lunch habitually set the topic as America and
What's Wrong with It, he was not interested in anyone's social complaints. I was to spend an amazing
amount of time arguing with him. When I spoke of the
disillusionment experienced after the Civil War by
Adams's generation and of Adams's feeling, watching
the American procession, that the Emperor Had No
Clothes On, Luce looked puzzled, then shouted: "What
Emperor?" With my fingers crossed, I muttered something about money, money. "America is *not, not* mate-

rialist!" he cried. "*Fortune* was founded not to celebrate American business but to explore it!" He then went on to expound Mortimer Adler's version of the eternal verities. This was Luce at his funniest. So far as any real human ideal was concerned, Time Inc. was dead-cold in its neutrality. Its real emphasis was the personal traits behind every successful and "outstanding" career. So it was with joy that I heard Henry Luce, turned Aristotelian, traditionalist, and classicist, say at lunch— "John Dewey sold philosophy out."

The most vivid impression Luce left with me was that of a man puzzled by the limits he had to set himself. Such was his authority within his editorial factory that he sometimes looked baffled by the lack of "follow-up" to his taste for Big Ideas and for Big Thinkers. It was charming, walking back from lunch with him, to see him right in the middle of Rockefeller Center waving his arms madly. He was back to his pet idea. "Political knowledge and political freedom" were the key to everything. But he talked as if he expected the American Renaissance to begin in his office. Like any publishing mogul, he believed in his own words. He wanted immediate solutions to the greatest possible problems, and he wanted them clear, easily tabulated, and immediately applicable to the magazine business.

Luce believed that *writers* could learn to write about anything. When I joined up in 1943, one could still see the improbably tall figure of John Kenneth Galbraith walking in and out of the office with that smiling air of a wholly different physical being dropping in on this inferior planet Earth. James Agee and Robert Fitzgerald were still on *Time*, as Robert Cantwell and John Hersey had been before them. Where *The New Republic*, by the time I got to it, had been full of tired people made more tired by having to pump up liberal idealism, the old Time-Life Building in Rockefeller Center seemed to me brilliantly alive, full of people in every department who seemed as vivid as they were intelligent.

The whole humming Time-Life Building was somehow a slice of the New York feast at its richest and most intoxicating: a brilliant *center* magnifying everything like the fluorescent tubes in the elevators, which seethed with excessive brightness. At the circular stone counter —the famous "goldfish bowl" in the center of the main concourse where people met to go out to lunch and tourists wearing around their necks admission tickets to the different buildings in Rockefeller Center gapingly followed guides around the concourse—I found myself recharged by the crisp centrality, the splendors of midtown New York embodied for me in that spot where James Agee, in his corduroy suit, always comically limped up bowlegged as if he had just dropped off his horse.

It was impossible to feel *oneself* less than brilliantly informed and interesting in the Time-Life Building, so clear was it that the people going to work in those over-lighted elevators were there because they deserved to be. On the desk of every editor and sub-editor dozens of freshly sharpened pencils, in a special size made for Time Inc., rose up in a container like the very symbols of his office. Star writers like Jim Agee lived in the Village. But every morning the old hands from the twenties came in from Chappaqua and Greenwich and Westport and Princeton as if in tow to their own scuffed leather English attaché cases. I could hear their hearty gruff city-room voices chaffing the secretaries. They glowed with the cheerfulness of their relation to Time Inc. Along the underground concourse, shop windows showed amethysts and Indian turquoises and leather from New Mexico. Even in the midst of the war, travel

posters beckoned you to Quito and Rio. Comfortable
steam for hot towels blew out of the urns in the barber-
shops whose windows were lined with eighteenth-century prints of comic shaving scenes.

And I was part of it all, with music down the corridor
from someone's record player, my unlimited view of
Queens and the delicious backsides of secretaries in-
sinuating their way between the desks, the bliss of
watching Jim Agee at lunch in the Maison de Winter
across the street. This was a French restaurant for the
expense-account trade, all *luxe, calme et volupté*, crack-
ling with thick table linen and the oversize menus defer-
entially placed in your hands by waiters always slightly
bending at the waist. There was constant twilight in the
Maison de Winter, a name precious to me from childhood because of that delicious scarlet woman Lady de
Winter in *The Three Musketeers*. It made an unbelievable background to Agee, the most passionate of all
writers on movies. We had just been to a new movie he
was reviewing for *Time*. He now excitedly poured more
and more brandy into his coffee as he demonstrated the
directorial *rhythm* that D. W. Griffith had captured so
magnificently in *The Birth of a Nation*. Beating out the
Griffith rhythm on the table with his gigantic hands, he
beat it so hard that he turned the table over. The waiters
rushed up with apologies.

Agee was music-mad. When he put a Beethoven record on his turntable, he liked to turn the sound on full
blast and put his ear right next to it. Even more than
Bellow, Agee wanted no umbrella between him and the
sky. He could not save himself from drinking all night,
repeatedly falling in love, lamenting the dead father who
was the aching void behind his God-hunger, from dying
in his forties. He came from a middle-class family in
Knoxville, but he looked like an Appalachian moun-

taineer who had gone to Harvard, become a poet, and was now as cannily sophisticated as he was oversized in every gesture. He had first landed a job on *Fortune* by writing a parody of *Time* at Harvard. He reviewed movies for both *Time* and *The Nation* with the same personal expressiveness he brought to *Let Us Now Praise Famous Men*.

This impassioned documentary of Southern sharecroppers during the Depression had begun as an assignment for *Fortune* that *Fortune* never published. It became a book, a personal testament, a great cry of grief over helpless tenant farmers groveling in the earth. It was a great movie in words. Agee's particular gift was to describe a scene as if he were drinking it up with his eyes. This was the personal stamp and the passion that he brought to every column for *Time* and that made him a great artist in journalism. *Time*'s managing editor T. S. Matthews liked to say that Agee was the house ideal. Agee bore down on every subject with his gifted vehemence. He could concentrate on something immediately before him—like the rhythm in *The Birth of a Nation*, the splintered gashed floor of a sharecropper's porch, the father's cold dead forehead in *A Death in the Family* that "gave his hand the stunning shadow of every blow it had ever received"—with a furious force that brought you immediately into his own frame of vision. Like so many Southern writers I knew, his rhetoric, his open suffering and mountainous declamations in taxis and barrooms were hurled at you along with a great literary shrewdness. His aesthetic insight was dizzying in its cruel gift. What I loved most about him was his gift for intoxication. At any given moment he swelled up to the necessary pitch, he made everything in sight seem equally exciting. Never bored, afraid only of missing some exaltation in the air, he seemed at any time to be all there and primed to go off. He talked with the greatest social sense about movies setting styles of American behavior, then veered off to talk about God with the clamorous cry for absolution that he got into his best poem.

> How from the porches of our sky
> The crested glory is declined:
> And to hear with that translated cry
> The strident soul is overshined:
>
> And how this world of wildness through
> True poets shall walk who herald you:
> Of whom God grant me of your grace
> To be, that shall preserve this race.
>
> Permit me voyage, love, into your hands.

Luce surrounded himself with poets, historians, critics, intellectuals, and near-intellectuals. He was like Catherine the Great, inviting the *philosophers* to her court. But he was no despot. Once you saw with astonishment how much these confident brassy-voiced managing editors solicited your views on American history, God, and the frontier, you realized that Time Inc. was a Hollywood dream factory in which the writers, not the readers, did the dreaming. Many a writer saw himself as an "artist" because he was indulged to think Big Thoughts about the economy that might be just as arresting as Jim Agee's passionate convictions about God and movies, and downstairs Whittaker Chambers's confession box—his office in which other ex-Communists were encouraged to bare their souls to Chambers, the only American in *The Brothers Karamazov*. The Luce organization had a hilarious respect for *writers*. The gift of words was more usable than special knowledge. The idealism all good Americans professed was not so far

from Luce's general idealism. The comfortable profes-
sional-class setting of American discussion at *Fortune*
was a duplicate of the English Departments I was to
teach in after the war. People's "positions" about society
reflected the same word fetishism. Only an occasional
scientist lured into our editorial conferences illustrated
another *way* of thinking. No wonder Luce encouraged
his writers to think Big. The world seemed theirs to
change.

On this subject, no one was more of a dream merchant than tireless Henry Luce. Luce even left all good
liberals on the staff the pleasant sensation of being superior to the Organization. I heard that a walkout had
been threatened when that reactionary danger to the
republic, the boss's own wife, Clare Boothe Luce,
sought to use the file for something she was writing.
But the brilliant poet and translator Robert Fitzgerald
could write an article on the war and the Christian
churches that solemnly avowed the spiritual meaning of
history. The enemies of the Jews were the Church's enemies and Pius XII was a great man indeed.

I was sorry to hear that Edmund Wilson was so hard up
that he had asked for a job on *Time*. It seemed natural,
though. Alongside the hard-nosed old newspapermen—
there were still a few who played Hemingway alongside
patrols in Iceland and Greece—the intellectuals pursued
old chimeras that somehow melted into Luce magazines.

There was a mildly ominous example of this right
next door—my immediate editor, Willi Schlamm.
Schlamm had been editor of the Communist daily in
Vienna, and after his break with Communism had
worked with the great liberal humanist and pacifist Carl
von Ossietzky on the *Weltbühne* and such distinguished
intellectual journals as *Europaische Hefte*. Schlamm was

now one of Luce's principal intellectual advisers. He was rumored to be a force backstage at Time Inc. and was the editor-to-be of a highbrow intellectuals' magazine ("Project X") that Luce was contemplating. Although Schlamm commissioned articles from W. H. Auden and Arthur Koestler, "Project X" never got beyond the drawing board. After some years Luce found that he could do without Schlamm himself. This took Schlamm back to Germany where he became so rabid a propagandist for preventive atomic strike against the Soviet Union that the post-Hitler generation found him unbearable.

If one of the principal war aims was to get to New York, Schlamm had achieved it. New York in 1943 was the beacon, the world city of freedom, openness, hope. Auden was in Brooklyn Heights—"Really, it's all as quiet as the country." I was to meet Marc Chagall wandering about Fifty-seventh Street one Yom Kippur not sure whether it was altogether fitting for him to look in at Pierre Matisse's gallery. Paolo Milano took me over one evening to visit Bertolt Brecht in a dusty flat on Lexington Avenue that he occupied with a shambling eccentric woman whom Brecht ignored with perfect equanimity. Puffing on his usual foul-smelling stogy, Brecht discoursed on his famous alienation effect in a narrowly polemical voice that admitted no qualification or discussion. Unknown to me, Simone Weil was still living on Riverside Drive with her parents. Hannah Arendt and her husband, Heinrich Bluecher, had just barely made their way from Pétain's France and Franco's Spain to West Ninety-fifth Street. Their friend, the great critic Walter Benjamin, had taken his life at the frontier when a Spanish guard turned him back. New York was full of famous conductors who had no orchestra, great pianists who could not get a hearing,

German, French, and Italian intellectuals broadcasting
to their homelands for the Office of War Information.
My "world city" was never more full of talent, brains,
buried treasure. Delmore Schwartz was right. Europe
was still the biggest thing in North America.

For a certain time Schlamm had the ear of Henry
Luce. Schlamm might well have believed that from his
office in the Time-Life Building he at last had the power
and influence to bring back to sound principles an élite
softened by liberalism. Although he was to fizzle out on
both sides of the Atlantic, he never lost the domineering
ambition of his Leninist youth. He was not just another
embittered ex-Communist and professional anti-Communist; he wanted to convert first America, then Germany. No wonder he scared off so many patrons after
making a superb first impression on them.

The impression was certainly there. Schlamm was
fluent in American journalese and even in the "tough"
impatient code of important executives. He was more
attentive to little American details than any other refugee intellectual I met during these years of European
dislocation. But he had kept up all the patronizing
charm of the Viennese café intellectual along with the
cultural solemnity of the Jew brought up under German
culture. Arriving on a Monday morning at the *Fortune*
office, Willi would playfully lay a rose from his garden
at Chappaqua on the desk of each secretary as he
skipped between the desks to his office. As editor of
pieces in which I eloquently celebrated in *Fortune* John
Peter Altgeld's freeing of the Haymarket anarchists and
Henry David Thoreau's commitment to poverty—all in
the American tradition!—Schlamm amused me by the
flattering smoothness with which he proposed the dropping or adding of an occasional word. With double-
edged irony he managed to suggest that both of *us* in-

tellectuals could afford to humor these slight necessities.

This was the period of James Burnham's *The Managerial Revolution*, the first of a series of sharp-witted, thoroughly reactionary political primers by a professor of philosophy who had been a leader of the American Trotskyist movement. Burnham was now reaching American business executives, scientists, and the technocratic élite with the news that they were the leaders of the future. Burnham's analysis was still functionally Marxist. History was nothing but the domination of one class over another. In this eternal power game it was the managers' turn to walk off with the pot. What in Burnham's Lenin-Trotsky period had been allegiance in the name of the working class to an intellectual directorate now became fixed on the "Machiavellians" themselves. Theoreticians deserved to manipulate in the open the power that in the past *they* had assigned to others. Power now belonged to those who could best calculate power.

I was always meeting ex-Communists for whom Lenin's contempt for the masses would remain their intellectual style. No one was so quick to blame "mass culture" for the downfall of his pet ideas as the ex-Communist. "Socialism" had become meaningless to him in the light of totalitarian Russia, but human beings did not deserve anything better. "In France," said Sainte-Beuve, "we remain Catholics after we have ceased to be Christians." To be ex-radical and scornful of democracy was the gospel of intellectuals who had come of age in the Age of Stalin. For Ignazio Silone, George Orwell, Arthur Koestler, W. H. Auden, Stephen Spender, Richard Wright, a god *had* failed. Burnham retained his old Marxist superstition that there was a "predestined" character to History, his Bolshevik scorn for the masses, his need to instruct those in power what they were really up to. A new American Revolution was coming, as open a nightmare of dictatorship by a little group as the Bolshevik Revolution had been secretly so.

I had an intuition about Burnham. This former Catholic, former Trotskyist, and present apostle to the "managers" would think himself from stage to stage, led by the invincibility of his own thinking. At each stage the obvious rightness of his new position would deepen his hopelessness about everything except his own logic. The priesthood of intellectuals must always rise to the top of history. He was a prophet of 1984. I was not likely to forget the conclusion of *The Managerial Revolution*. Burnham drew out to a fine point his account of how a small group, qualified only by its technical hold and managerial skill, was tightening its control over modern society. He indicated that some might find this tragic, but that tragedy required something greater than human beings. So there would be no tragedy in 1984, no tragedy in the managerial revolution, no tragedy to any of these ferocious glaciers moving down on us in the name of History.

Willi Schlamm was to say in *Germany and the East-West Crisis*, a postwar book advocating nuclear war against the Soviet Union, that there was no tragedy in the possible destruction of millions, nothing to repine:

> To resist evil, in spite of what such resistance means in quantitative terms, is either right or it is wrong. If it is right, then I shall resist evil whether such resistance results in physical terror for "only" 100 million people or whether 200 million people will be maimed. The *number* of victims has nothing to do with the moral weight of my decisions. . . . As pain and suffering exist only in the experience of the creature that goes through

pain and suffering, the sum total of *all* conceivable pain
and suffering is all the pain and suffering *one* human
creature can experience. There *is* no more.

Trotsky in his brief moment of power had scornfully
consigned his unsuccessful left-wing opponents to "the
dustbin of History." This was still the either-or, totalist,
Manichean absolutist style that was to lead ex-Communist leaders like Jacques Doriot in France to support the
Nazis, and in America was to give support to McCarthy,
who had no convictions but certainly knew how to use
embittered ex-Leninist "experts on Communism." Ignazio Silone said around this time that "the next war
will be between the Communists and the ex-Communists." Ex-Communists, like Communists, were still organizers, leaders, exhorters; in their own eyes both were
still the only truly "committed" people. Whittaker
Chambers's opinions weighted *Time*'s foreign policy.

What, after all, were so many unresting intellectual
fanatics and snoopers-out of "heresy" doing at Time
Inc.? Henry Luce thought of himself as a maker of national policy and was lending an interested ear to any
overcharged thinker with a mission. Intellectuals, not
just the scientists behind the scenes, now played a prodigious role. They were the polemicists, the phrasemak-
ers, the propagandists in "the battle for men's minds"
that was supposed to tip the balance and decide the
future. Certainly a great shift had occurred among many
who had been liberal or radical before the war. As
Henry Luce said, it was nonsense to believe that the
business of America was business. *The war* demanded
convictions, and no one was likely to have so many on
tap as ex-Communists who had discovered that they had
sold their souls to the devil. They were now the spokesmen of a new orthodoxy. What a brave new world was

this! This war was a battle for men's minds—and minds could be changed from Rockefeller Center.

On every side the chorus now went up that the old liberal civilization was at an end because *man* was vile. "There is a Hitler in each of us." This unpolitical excuse for the Nazis seemed to gratify ex-radicals by confirming their disappointment with human nature. There was a positive acceptance of some "universal" guilt whose real purpose was to make the Holocaust *ordinary*, even to sweep it under the rug. In the Village, Franz Kafka was being turned into the only accurate theologian of our time. In Rockefeller Center it was announced that "the Enlightenment has come to an end." How helpful to some careers it became to say so.

On July 25, 1943, the day Mussolini fell, I was with Luce trying to shake off his objection to a long essay I had written for *Fortune*'s philosophy series on the vision of democracy according to Emerson, Melville, Whitman. Luce thought the American classics "soft in the head." The missionary's son sounded like a freshman Thomist. Before long, his argument against American "error" turned into a defense of Marshal Badoglio, the conqueror of Ethiopia, who had just succeeded Mussolini. Luce warmly supported the Marshal as a force against "disorder." I should not have been surprised. Luce's taste in post-Fascist Italians was as predictable as his taste for "hard" against "soft" philosophies. He automatically plumped for the reactionary old professional soldier who had deserted Mussolini only when absolutely necessary. But crazy as the succession of arguments was that long afternoon in Luce's office— Emerson! Mussolini! Badoglio!—Luce impressively did not take advantage of his position in arguing with a young staffer. He wildly, enthusiastically, argued me around his office. Luce's office seemed as oversized as

Mussolini's, but I was impressed by his willingness to spend the day in argument. At one point he shouted, "Damn it all! I can *prove* what I am saying!" He frantically pressed buttons like a Hollywood producer; assistants and secretaries came running in with files. Flopping his reading glasses over the thickets of his overgrown eyebrows, he irritably read me cables from his correspondents. Driving his glasses back up his furrowed bald front, he looked at me in triumph and barked, "Eh? What do you say to that, eh?"

Funny and direct as Luce was storming around the room that afternoon, his face was sharp and consciously important for all the nervousness of his outward manner. He could not help radiating a sense of power and of respect for what he himself embodied. David and Goliath, I thought as he impatiently ran round and round the circular room. His strong Roman front was furious with concentration and bustling careworn generalship. He was plainly the man in charge of everything. At the moment he was concentrating all his forces on the political virtue of Il Maresciallo Badoglio. But it was not that miserable old Fascist, that butcher of helpless Ethiopians, which interested me. It was the furrow across Henry Luce's forehead like a badge of his authority, and the care he invested in being important. His power had taken him over and had creased him across the front.

Except for those friends of mine who were already in the Army and out of sight, almost all the "old Socialists" I knew in New York seemed to feel that the war was none of their business. "Morally we have to stay out of it." America as the "arsenal of democracy" and Stalin's domination of Eastern Europe were like Hitler, the same order of evil. I could no more share this detach-

ment from the war than I could believe in "the global
New Deal" at *The New Republic* and "the American
Century" at *Fortune*. I saw no alternative to defeating
Hitler; I wanted to live. War made hideous reductions
to the authority of power. The Nazis were being ground
down first in Russia. I hated Stalin, but in 1943 it
seemed to be him or Hitler. The great glacier of the
worst war in history was moving down on us all. If
American soldiers seemed to have no convictions and
fought the war "on imagination alone," the Communist
faithful viewed every victory over the German Army as
proof that Communism was the most rational system
devised by man and Stalin the greatest genius of all
time. The non-Communist left was driven mad by the
need to account for Soviet successes at all. At the opening of the meretricious propaganda film *The North Star*
that Lillian Hellman wrote for Sam Goldwyn, I found
myself watching the preposterous idyllic scenes showing
the tranquil beauty of Soviet life before the war while
listening to outraged shouts of protest from Melvin
Lasky, the future editor of *Encounter*, and postwar
leaders of the Congress for Cultural Freedom.

> We will make this the last war; we will make a free
> world for all men. "The earth belongs to us the people."
> If we fight for it. (Simply but with great force) And we
> will fight for it!
> > [Ends on singing "Motherland."]

It was not Stalin but "that damned Roosevelt" who
seemed to be most in Edmund Wilson's mind when I
first talked with him at this time. Wilson's political opinions—so far as he could express them at all to a stranger
at a time of intellectual discouragement—were those of
Charles A. Beard and the sourest isolationist congressmen. I admired his writing so much that I could never

take his political opinions with the required seriousness, for he seemed to me in equal measure gifted and self-willed.

Wilson summoned me after having read my book on modern American literature. He still had the old-fashioned American progressive's total disapproval of the war. He had long broken with *The New Republic*. He now felt that he was being kept out of magazines. He was soon to have an immense personal revival through his association with *The New Yorker*, and would even become a roving war correspondent. But the afternoon I called on him, he had just come back from *The Nation*, where Freda Kirchwey, to whom the war was a crusade, had turned down some proposal he had made.

Wilson's view of the war was not politically interesting. His politics, veering between personal prejudice and utopian hope, were those of any other American writer hurled from crisis to crisis. It was hardly the political consistency of *To the Finland Station*, published in the aftermath of Stalin's purges and the Nazi-Soviet alliance, that had made this imaginatively conceived history of the great Socialist thinkers so fascinating a gallery of portraits. Wilson had conceived his book when he visited Russia in the thirties. By the time he got Lenin to the Finland Station, it was 1940, and it was more Wilson's usual determination to finish any book he had started than his belief in Lenin's "Socialism" that got him to round out his book in style. Wilson tended to be uneasy and fussy in dealing with political ideas that removed him from the personal and historic context. His greatest interest in any subject was *his* learning it. Socialism was not an idea but an obligation to himself to remove every intellectual obstacle in his exploration of it. He liked to affirm himself a materialist, an atheist, even a behaviorist. My fascination with

Wilson was not based on these professions of ideas. From the time I first read *Axel's Castle*, I felt altogether related to him. He was a basic kind of critic who put you directly in touch with any work he discussed; he was an original, an extraordinary literary artist who wove his essays out of the most intense involvement with his materials.

Meeting him now, I was impressed by a certain seediness, the great bald dome, the lack of small talk, the grumpy concentration on every topic he came to. He had exposed himself to literature as the maximum experience of his life; I felt that he lived *in* literature as he did not anywhere else. It was exactly the communicated depth of this experience that I missed in other literary radicals of the time. This absorption in the actual work in hand, this visible pressure on him of every fresh thought, made him eccentric and cranky, unself-conscious, and a "character." Everything I had guessed from my devoted reading and from hearsay came home to me with unexpected force that day late in 1942.

It was a strange sulphurous afternoon. Wilson and his wife, Mary McCarthy, were staying in a borrowed apartment somewhere in the East Thirties near the Third Avenue El. He seemed at loose ends, uncomfortable with himself as well as with me. When I arrived, he had not yet returned from his visit to *The Nation*; he came in quite sour, curtly indicated that his opposition to the war was making things difficult, and then grumblingly turned his attention to me.

I had already discovered, in my first weeks at *The New Republic*, that Wilson had left there humble admiration of his gifts and fear of a certain implacable thickness in his personality. The copy editor on the staff was a woman who thought him a genius and improbably sexy; she added with bitterness that his character was "hard as a diamond." And the danger Hitler presented at the moment was so obvious that I could see no point to Wilson's isolationism—whatever that meant at the end of 1942!—except in his usual contempt for conventional opinion. It was ridiculous that so gifted a writer should be unable to obtain a review from *The Nation*. But I also felt that Wilson was full of prejudices formed by a more sheltered and complacent America than mine. His isolationism seemed assertive, merely proud. Van Wyck Brooks, in these same years, had been making his "usable past" out of a fiction —American writing as the peaceable kingdom. He had turned the real battleground of ideas—and personalties —into a chummy feast. He allowed the reader to suppose that the best American writers were as afraid of trouble as he himself was. Wilson, in his tougher, more demanding way, seemed to think that the classical republic might be a lost tradition.

A moment would come in London, in April 1945, when stout, ruddy, English-looking Edmund Wilson, in Europe for *The New Yorker*, fêted by the Ministry of Information itself at a grand reception to which all available English writers came to do him honor, would grumble to me, his fellow countryman, how much he distrusted the "Limeys"—they had got us into war again! He was more horrified than ever by the war, for he had seen the ruins in England and was on his way to more ruins in Italy and Greece. Now, at our first encounter in New York, he seemed in his hoarse and abstract political discourse the very type of American crank he had described John Jay Chapman to have been. Chapman was a gifted crank, a heroic crank in the fiercely uncompromising style of his Abolitionist ancestors. He was a critic and scholar who once hired a hall in which to condemn a lynching in Pennsylvania; actually burned off his own hand in remorse for striking a man of whom he was jealous; rejoiced in America's entry into the "Great War"; and repaid a favorite son's death in the war and his own disillusionment by supporting the Ku Klux Klan in its attacks on Jews. The immense historical sense behind Wilson's criticism, architectural in its passionate sense of detail, would always represent for me personal sensibility rather than political acuteness. This flinty old American trust in his own opinions was his flair, his style, his enormous charm for me.

On the afternoon I met him, he dismissed my book to my face, after having summoned me to discuss it. He intimated that anything from the 1890s on was his own special province. The end of the old century was the crisis period that haunted him. It represented his early life within the crisis of an America sinking into the maw of the corporation economy. He was still meditating a book on his period, but the book he eventually wrote, *Patriotic Gore*, was his masterpiece on the Civil War.

At our meeting everything showed him in a state of profound general irritability, but his force impressed me as much as his books had. There was that grumpy, seedy independence, that essential matter-of-fact seriousness. He looked like a man who had been built for thought and nothing else. With his round bald head and that hoarse, heavily breathing voice box coming out of the red face of an overfed fox-hunting squire, Wilson looked apoplectic, stiff, out of breath. But he steadily recomposed every bad-tempered feeling he felt that afternoon into explicit printable phrases. I did not know then that Wilson's mother had turned deaf under the strain of his father's "nervous" illness. In a voice that, like a deaf man's, suggested some despair of ever connecting with the outside world, he nevertheless bent down to his every thought, a watchmaker looking through his lens. Ponderously, with immense effort, he repeatedly made his way to the exact point he wanted to make.

Evidently he saw no need to smooth his way—or mine; he had business in hand. He was naturally, pressingly occupied. I was reminded of the railway president with overcoat over his arm and blueprint rolled up in his hand whose life-size statue used to stand in the old Pennsylvania Station as a monument to the busyness and perpetual alertness of American executives. One felt about Wilson that he got up in the morning thinking, that he went through day in thought, and went to bed, whether or not he had cleared up the matter in hand, with the knowledge that at least he had pursued it all day. Many years later, when I teased him at Wellfleet about wearing a formal white shirt to the beach, he replied, "I have only one way of dressing." At the moment, he seemed to have only one way of discussing a book, whether or not the author was present. He had summoned me to hear his opinion of my book, and I heard it. He was brief and conclusive. He was not much interested in it.

Then the afternoon took a strange turn. Wilson had been merely impatient with my book. Mary McCarthy was much more thorough. She went into my faults with great care. Since her brilliance in putting down friends, enemies, and various idols of the American tribe was already known to me from *Partisan Review* and our first meeting at Provincetown in 1940, I was fascinated by her zeal. She warmed to her topic with positive delight; she looked beautiful in the increasing crispness of her analysis. I thought of my gentle, distinctly unliterary wife. Although Natasha and I were drifting away from

each other, I thought of her with longing in this inhuman setting.

While their intellects were both severe, Wilson expressed himself with comparative hesitancy. Seeing an
opening, I informed him of some musical mistakes he
had made in a story, "Ellen Terhune," that was to become part of *Memoirs of Hecate County*. At this point
Mary McCarthy, taking my word for it in her readiness
to criticize him, warned Wilson that she had alerted
him to the possibility that he had made such mistakes.
He looked rueful. Mary McCarthy's bite and spirit were
now directed toward Wilson, but Wilson himself was
silent. His topic was the book I had written, and when
he had given me his observations and asked me the
questions he had in mind, it was time for me to go
home.

Later, when I came to know him well and to realize
that he was as sensitive as anyone else to criticism, I
realized that in my inexperience I had underestimated
the effect of my writing about him, my presence on
The New Republic after he had departed from it in
rage, his sickened awareness that the war had left him
in a corner—and his conflicts with his wife. He suddenly grasped how unprepared I had been for their
double onslaught, and at the door, grinning, advised me:
"Write about *her* sometime!" When I went down the
stairs in depression, he followed and said he would walk
part of the way with me.

A hard rain came on as we were crossing Third Avenue under the El. Wilson was suddenly talking about
Joyce, worrying over the cabman's shelter scene in
Ulysses. We were standing directly under the El, the
rain bounding off the tracks right on our heads. He was
absorbed in analyzing the scene and did not seem to see

the irony in saying "shelter" over and over at that moment. In a voice that was like no other voice I had ever heard, a voice made even more remarkable by the deep commotion I could hear beneath it, a voice that was like one enormous effort to reach the world, Wilson finally, with all due deliberation, made his point about the cabman's shelter scene in *Ulysses*, looked up at the rain dropping down his face, gave me a friendly pat on the shoulder, and trudged back.

Chapter III

YOU MUST CHANGE YOUR LIFE

One Saturday night late in 1943 I went down, without Natasha, to a party in Greenwich Village at the apartment of a tall, thin, morose, avant-garde composer whose career was entirely "managed" by his resourceful, hunchbacked wife. Isa's face, though perhaps a little too sharp, showed what considerable powers of charm and intelligence she had marshaled against her misfortune. She kept highly polished an alertness about other people's secrets that made her fascinating to me if not always lovable. She lived by "knowing" people, looking into people even when this took the form of looking after them. In her Village circle on Bedford Street, she alone seemed a serene stable entity to be relied on. You always knew where Isa was—she was in their apartment looking after Harold, copying his scores, presenting his songs to influential people in her exquisite thin voice. She was always watchful, elaborately controlled, attentive; occasionally she was breathless in the concentration with which she looked at you.

Isa made a point, for Harold's career, of giving big parties at which she brought together the up-and-coming friends of our age and established names. She silently made herself important to all kinds of famous people. They gladly came to her parties, at which the host sat stiffly apart with a vaguely superior air of boredom about anything that did not relate to the new music. Meanwhile his wife ran up and down their long, loftlike apartment, her unnaturally large sharp triangle of a face glittering with sweat as she brought drinks and tottered in at regular intervals with great platters of food. I recognized at "Isa's"—the parties were always called "Isa's parties," never "Isa's and Harold's"—that one was there because one had become somebody and that one was a somebody because he now moved in the company of other somebodies. It was deeply flattering, especially when one could do nothing for Harold's music, to meet Aaron and Virgil and Lennie, to see Delmore again and relentlessly ambitious Jews on the Harvard faculty like Oscar. I always felt at Isa's that her modest walk-up on Bedford Street represented a connection between New York Jews on the rise, established names in the arts, and rakish Southerners and Californians in the Village that no one but Isa could have made.

Even the women at Isa's had this implicit flattery conferred on them. They had to be "interesting" to get in, and the more "interesting" they were, the more they seemed to wait on Isa for advice, were particularly attentive to her opinion. In the afternoons, when there were no parties, the place was full of people who jostled each other impatiently as if they were competing to see the same therapist. All of Isa's friends were a new type to me, a definite challenge. These Village people were the other side of Isa's more obvious public-relations parties on Saturday nights. On party nights you ran into Virgil Thompson, as bald and smooth as a billiard ball skipping his way from group to group, E. E. Cummings proudly holding up his fine head above so many lesser breeds. In the afternoons—I was there out of fascination with Isa—I saw sitting on the floor people of my own age who apparently did not need to lie about sexual unhappiness, to pretend, to conceal. I was envious of their easy freedom as they sat up like kittens and told Isa everything.

She was the teacher and they the taught. They sat in private little corners with her, she on one of the love seats, the friend on the floor with his face against her doll-like knees. There were also those advanced artists—the composer John Cage, the dancer Merce Cunningham, the writer Paul Goodman—who amazed me by their air of living for art and freedom. In their tautly dedicated faces—and Merce Cunningham's body —they showed a loyalty to their experience of life, to a world all experiment and improvisation, to a boldness beyond speech. All these people of my age whom I met at Isa's impressed me by their aggressive easiness. They seemed in one way or another to be artists in life even more than they were *artists*. And to see them regularly at Isa's, acting as if they never heard of the great war against Hitler and were even contemptuous of it, gave a strange menace and excitement to my own life. I was losing myself, drowning in a world of people who were beautiful, wild, unconsciously cruel in their lack of attachment.

As I walked from the subway at Sheridan Square to Isa's house that crisp early winter evening in 1943, along the still unfamiliar streets of the Village, I felt happy and released. That afternoon, working out my travels in the next few weeks to army camps and naval stations around the country for an article on the political education of American soldiers, "Why We Fight," I had been buoyed up again by the imperial look of New

York I had from my office high in Rockefeller Center, and was now stimulated by the thought of a party in the Village. Like a true native of Brooklyn, I was still a tourist in midtown, Rockefeller Center, Greenwich Village. I had never lived in the Village or anywhere near it. Any Saturday night I happened to see the doorman outside El Chico on Grove Street in his grotesquely overlong "Cossack" coat down to the sidewalk and the frogged buttons about to pop across his big belly, I felt that the purple, red, and green lights flashing into the street were a promise of wickedness. In the crooked streets leading past so many little nineteenth-century houses, I always had a sense of coming into my own, of enjoying some special intimacy with lower Fifth Avenue that made me think of Henry Adams's Esther posing for the mural in the Church of the Ascension on Fifth and Tenth, Mark Twain in his old house on Tenth Street, Dreiser and Millay in Washington Square, Willa Cather on Bank Street. I was strong for history, for the houses where writers had lived; but lately the houses I passed in the Village looked like subtle retreats where, behind their beautiful wooden doors, I could make love. No one from Indiana ever felt the freedom of the Village as much as I did—I who had never lived in it, who could never walk down Eighth Street without expecting that one of the many girls in ballet slippers that year would skip into my life.

So I came into Isa's party that night, up the narrow ancient flight of steps on Bedford Street, in great anticipation and lightness of heart. It was a glittering big party, the first of the holiday season, and as I walked around the room, restless and excited, I saw an oddly contrasting man and young woman who were standing stiffly together in a corner as if they had been quarreling.

The girl's face astonished me. It is a pity that "smit-

ten" is now such a joke. Looking at her, seeing her for
the first time, I did feel that someone was "smiting" me,
that I had been struck. She had the long oval face of
the classic ballerina, a high moon-white cliff of a forehead, already graying coal-black hair that was tied up
behind with a rubber band. But where the face and
body of the classic ballerina seem always to be turned
away in the shy contractions of the "swan" pose, this
girl seemed indifferent to the fact than any man could
read his desires in her face. The face staggered me by
what it suggested of her capacity for giving pleasure.
This was no shy, elusive, self-protecting "swan," arms
all too delicately flung up before her face. Every little
nick in her skin seemed to breathe. And just as up to
the end I could never be near her without feeling the
subtle heat from her skin, so now, under the gray
streaks in the blazing black hair and the crazily towering brow, the long white oval face was luminous, mischievous, alive. Its features subtly rearranged themselves from moment to moment.

She looked me over as I stared at her, then turned
back with dreary patience to her companion, an immensely tall, thin, almost emaciated-looking man with
very thick spectacles. He was a political analyst of
"totalitarian structures," a man famous for knowing his
own worth. At the moment, virtually crouching over
her to make his point, he seemed to be berating her. He
suddenly pointed a finger at her and looked at her with
helpless fury. It was a look I was to see again on the
faces of men who had been having, who were just ending, an affair with Mary Ellen. I knew instantly, looking
at her face as it stonily faced the man's anger, what had
caused so much anger. There was nothing of cupidity in
her face, nothing sly, coy, even flirtatious. It was merely
that no man who was excited by her—and she never

had a lover whom I knew of who was not an intellectual, Jewish or European or both—could help feeling that the sensuousness which she imparted with every click of her tongue, with every commonplace talcum scent you caught from her body as she moved, was also being bestowed upon the world at large. The men who regularly fell in with her probably succumbed to the suggestion of something beautifully lawless and outrageous in the felt emphasis of her walk, in the wide cheekbones that stood out on her face with the same maddening intensity of effect that I would discover in the sweeping curve of her hip.

The man with her tore off in anger, and I went to talk to her. She made not the slightest gesture of interest, but indifferently gave me her number when I asked for it. I talked about her to Isa after the party had emptied out. Isa, enjoying my sudden infatuation more than I did, laughed at me, said she had always known I would "crack." "About time a critic was brought to judgment!" she said. "And especially so horribly overorganized a man as you. . . . Why don't you ever fall in love with me the way the homosexuals do?"

With a vague look of bitterness she told me that the girl was a Californian, had grown up in Hollywood, was married to a young refugee philosopher at U.C.L.A. who was in the Army, and that she, Isa, had so often seen the same look on other men's faces she now saw on mine that she was tired of patching up all the marriages the girl had broken. "Don't admit it even if you do it," she said sourly. "Natasha won't be able to stand it." She stared at me. "And neither will you."

It was odd, I thought later, how everything that had not yet happened was already happening in her mind—and especially in my own. All my life I had lived for the future, had anticipated everything in terms of some overriding idea. Here we were, my fortune-teller and I, counting the full cost of the affair before it had even begun! The anxious rationality of this was all too familiar. I had a sense of rushing toward my fate. I was indeed to feel the tall man's outrage, to see it many times on the same bookish, Jewish face. I was to feel it in strange, hot ways that drove me wild with the unaccountability of loving someone about whose many loves I knew, from the moment I saw her, too much. What with one thing and another, I was to get to know, usually through Mary Ellen herself, just how inconsistent she could be in ways that enraged her intellectual lovers with the meaninglessness that she created.

I knew it, somehow I knew it all from the moment I saw her. It was all to be unsettling, without reason, forever and ever. The bottom could really fall out of things. Everything one had tried desperately long and hard to keep in order suddenly came apart, like the great carton of books I was carrying into our apartment that went smash through my hands the day after Natasha and I married. Everything could fall apart in the sight of a young girl with very wide cheekbones standing at an overcrowded party in Greenwich Village.

I knew when I went home that night that something uncontrollable had started inside me. It was as if I had too swiftly cut myself and knew before the blood began to flow, that a cut had been made.

The next morning I went as usual to my office. It was a brilliantly clear day, and usually it was impossible in that office, overlooking the heaped-up splendor of New York, to feel oneself less than brilliant. It was from working in that building that I knew why every sentence in *Time* had to strike like a rapier, shine like steel. The rows of metal desks glistened in the light. Brilliantly resourceful girls—researchers, who were not allowed to write—walked back and forth on editorial errands to their writers. Early as it was, one writer a cubicle away from me could already be heard chanting to himself from the Bhagavad-Gita. Another was sending out to the hall on his portable phonograph the allegretto from Beethoven's Seventh. The old boys were coming in from Ossining and Greenwich and Stamford with their impressively scuffed English attaché cases, saying witty doomsday things to each other, like characters in a John Cheever story, about the daily disasters of country living. Down in the concourse, where the city mob flowing out into the Fiftieth Street station of the Independent met the tourists with circular tickets around their necks looking with awe at every last wonder in Rockefeller Center, the chromium and steel frames around the window glass glistened more brightly than ever while on the wings of light itself messages sped from the cable center to every corner of the world. And I was part of it all, the Hollywood of the intellectuals, each writer happily in place with his metal desk, his sharpened pencils, his researcher within call, his view of the city. Looking out at my window, I knew that I had been brought to the top of the mountain and shown the kingdom of this world—there was nothing to do but to do it. Mild, unlikely flakes of snow drifted through the air. Christmas was many weeks away, but the people looked as if they had already been worked up to the holiday pitch. On Fifth Avenue long nervous lines were jerkily moving back and forth. The gruffness of the stone, the sharpness of the view, the steely white brilliance of the cold New York spires around me made me dizzy. I was falling through the air, rushing to my doom. I went to the telephone and asked her to have lunch with me that day.

An hour after lunch, we were walking around the

reservoir in Central Park. In the clear, cold afternoon, the path was deserted. But from Central Park West on one side and Fifth Avenue on the other, thousands of windows gleaming in the premature cold winter sun seemed to be shooting off particles of light. Every window was a mirror, the sun was brightly cold. I knew that everyone could see us, that every window struck with light was magnifying our figures on the path. I was excited, hardly knowing what I was saying; but as we came up to the old pump house on the reservoir path, my heart was loud in my ears, and with the wind howling around me I put my hand on her face. In front of those gray rough stones, in the freezing deserted park, we stopped to kiss, and as I looked at the subtle bones slowly working in her face, her body casually poised on one leg like a bird about to take off, I knew that it was decided, that it had been decided for me a long time before. When I kissed her, I dropped into something long drawn out. Suddenly there was time, there would be time to do this right. The strange spaces in her face seemed to give out a curious throbbing stillness. Time, spreading, kept at its center a vein that was pulsing. The ripples in the reservoir went out wider—it was already like being in her, swimming far out in her with effortless strokes. It seemed to me that I was stitched to her. And I knew, more firmly than I had ever known anything, that I wanted it, I wanted her so badly that my heart was clanging in my ears like the wire fence around the reservoir in the wintery wind.

I had to be in Washington the next day, interviewing the general at the Pentagon in charge of Morale Services, and to my surprise she came right to my hotel room. It was the only new hotel that had been built in Washington during the war and, like our lovemaking, it was functional and on the spare side. I could see that the trip down was the adventure for her, an excursion from the Village. Though she was as easy in bed as I had expected, and had funny new words for everything, she was detached. I was impressed mostly by my own sinfulness. I did not want to see her again. That was the price to pay. Later that evening, when I saw her off at Union Station, her face looked lonely in the great crowd massing outside the gate to the New York train, and she kissed me with more affection than I had yet seen in her.

I went back to the hotel and stood weeping over the rumpled bed, I wanted so much to see her in it. In the lobby were uniformed couriers with messages from public relations men in the Pentagon suggesting what to say and which generals to praise in my article "Why We Fight." In an ecstasy of restlessness I walked back to Union Station. Washington was feverish and I had the fever. It was the capital of the Western world now, it was the main place. Circles of power revolved within greater circles of power, like the avenues laid out for the capital.

Union Station seemed to be the center of our happy American disturbance, our busy and prosperous commotion. All day and all night long Union Station pushed out vast masses of people who then grumpily lined up to share a taxi or any vehicle that would get them to their important appointments. Union Station never stopped exploding people out of trains, out through the great hall, out under the classical porticoes at the exits. Out, out! The crowds never left off, the war was great, everybody had a piece of the greatness now. In some way the great marble-white pseudoclassical station, monument to some discarded myth of Imperial Rome in repose, persisted in dwarfing these crowds and mocking all this furious motion. In the enormous men's room, old-fashioned "colored" men were shining up one pair of officer's boots after another indifferently clamped on the footrests, while all around them soldiers in brown army undershirts and shorts were showering, washing, and arguing with the attendants about the quarter they expected for each towel.

The next morning I went to the Pentagon for interviews with the brass, and found myself caught up on wheels that never stopped whirling. Each time I arrived at the Pentagon to interview still another former college dean, foundation executive, advertising man, psychiatrist, or Broadway producer—all in uniform with the Morale Services Division—I could feel the importance of being at the Pentagon itself. I was rolled round and round endless corridors, was led from one ostentatiously courteous escort officer to another, past a dreamlike succession in office doors with important-looking nameplates. I came to rest in front of the spectacularly tall general in charge of Morale Services. The general was another civilian expert—population problems. He was also a great gentleman, aristocratic, shy, who reddened easily and gave out the official line with some hesitation. Though his office was surprisingly small and his manner one of charming mildness, I knew his importance in the scheme of things and my privilege in getting to him. This was the Pentagon in the middle of the war; this was where all the Washington wheels started turning. The importance of a *writer's* being here, watching with hungry envious eyes every human motion radiating out to the war, soon came home to me. Sitting at the general's side was a subtle-looking major; he seemed to be studying the interview and all parties to it with peculiar attentiveness, and his smiling but tense alertness puzzled me until he turned out to be James Gould Cozzens. He was practicing on us, and I was to remember his watchfulness on every page of *Guard of Honor*.

That particular sector of the Pentagon was as crowded with specialty acts as a theatrical agency. One captain, a nephew of the Shuberts, booked camp shows and was as proud of himself as if the only currency anyone needed in this world was free theater tickets. Another, summoning people over like a barker, was a speech expert who bet visitors that after listening to them pronounce ten key words he could guess their place of origin. Another was a brigadier, wearing the jeweled badge of the General Staff, who introduced me to the long-playing record. With a look of manic self-satisfaction he let a record fall slowly to the ground, picked it up, let it fall, picked it up, let it fall. "Can't break!" he said before switching back to his gruff military voice. "Not like your old-fashioned shellac records! Can't break, you know!" He smiled at me with more enthusiasm than I had yet seen in the Pentagon. "Nothing more important to us here than you writers! We need you to get some amazing developments over to the people!" I did not understand why a brigadier general should be pushing phonograph records. The escort officer told me that the general was famous for his stupidity and that Marshall had given strict orders that he was never to be allowed overseas.

A fat, round, constantly smiling Jewish psychiatrist, now a lieutenant colonel, introduced himself as an expert on soldier breakdowns. He had established himself at the Pentagon by starting a political newspaper for troops that dramatically lowered the neuropsychiatric rate. He had been taken out of the medical service to become a prime organizer of orientation courses. Dr.

Rosencrantz beamed at everybody and he beamed all the time. In his first days at the Pentagon, he must have looked out of place among the many slim chic young West Pointers in the more important corridors. By the time I got to him, he looked as if he had successfully psychoanalyzed the government itself. He radiated limitless confidence. His specialty, like that of all brainier Orientation officers, was to keep recruits still torn by the Depression from breaking down and from breaking the Army down. He dealt in case histories by the hundreds, flapped cards at me from a limitless pile. The more "dirty laundry" he fished out of this human vat, the bouncier, happier he seemed to get. Ignoring all embarrassed smiles from his superiors, whom he called the "conformist little nits in this place," he kept his short legs resolutely on his desk and calmly stretched them back again when they fell off.

Dr. Rosencrantz was particularly strong on the importance of having good relations with the Soviets and not burdening oneself with "moral abstractions." "It works, doesn't it?" he said, slapping my back and chewing on an apple or a cigar as he ordered assistants— "God, what *schmucks* the Army gets around here!"—to bring up chart after chart on the decline of psychiatric cases where films and discussion groups on "Why We Fight" were permitted by the local commandant.

The Army was strong on charts. I could never ask Dr. Rosencrantz the simplest question without someone pushing at me many-colored graph charts full of rising and falling columns that showed DISTRIBUTION OF CO-HORT INEFFECTIVES BY SITUATION AND BY DEGREE OF INCAPACITATION . . . Somebody was always reporting in figures to someone else. The theme in this part of the Pentagon was breakdown, the soldier as a patient, the endemic soldier headache as the locus of tension. And then there were the illiterates. There were so many illiterates that by the middle of 1943 special training units were established at the reception centers. "The human material we get is often quite poor."

In my mind I saw a long line of depressed, mentally wounded American migrants out of *The Grapes of Wrath* and *Studs Lonigan*. Their uniforms did not quite fit them, and they did not seem to know where they were shuffling off to as they were caught up in this bewildering system of rules, with its succession of trapdoors for those not sound and quick enough to respond to orders in the required time. For Dr. Rosencrantz, it was a dream of a psychiatrist's war. He was taking inventory of the American system, and he was confident that the thousands of headaches, ulcers, and even self-mutilations could be safely by-passed only by giving so many unhappy soldiers a new social idea. The war was at last exposing America to itself. "This war," he said emphatically, "is really a revolution!" He counseled "good relations with the Russians after the war" as if this were the latest form of therapy for sick GIs. "My idea works, don't it? It works, damn it!" The more he "broke down the figures" for me, relating case history after case history of a soldier brought back to life "by having to consider the political implications of this war, his job in the Army, his whole life," the jollier he became. What he was saying to my eyes and ears was "*I* am having a revolution!"

Meanwhile, there were the official handouts:

> The American soldier is to be not just the best-trained soldier in the world, not just the best-equipped soldier in the world, but the *best-informed soldier in the world*.
>
> The fundamental principle of American information about the war is that we will speak the truth.

A truth need not only be well-rounded, but the utterance of it should be cognizant of the stresses and objectives of the moment. Information which does not inform, counsel, warn, stimulate, remind, instruct, or reiterate for the purpose of training the mind for war, is innocuous and therefore of no value to the military service.

As Oliver Cromwell said, "Give me the man who knows that for which he fights and loves that which he knows."

The next day I went down to Camp Lee in Virginia for my first sight of an army camp where, as they told me in the Pentagon, "they take orientation hard." The general in charge wore his 1917 army campaign hat, a white mustache that bristled though it was severely clipped. He haughtily rolled his own cigarettes and licked the ends round and round into shape while keeping his eyes fastened on me.

He wore an old army shirt, but the pockets on it had zippers that glistened like tinny mirrors. As he unzipped one pocket to take out his cigarette papers, he unzipped the other to take out his little sack of tobacco. He put one end of the drawstring in his mouth and pulled it shut. The synchronization of hands, mouth, zippers, and eyes on me pointed up the atmosphere of performance, the show of authority, he was putting up for a magazine writer. Leathery, patronizing, rough, rejoicing in his power while wearing a buck private's shirt and 1917 hat, he allowed that "I am always glad to see the press."

Camp Lee, like all army and navy installations I would ever visit, had its eager public-relations men fawning on the general. He dismissed them, and pouring out a Scotch for himself, which he later kept dosing with Coca-Cola, he kept his eyes on me as he told me what he had learned about "his" men. "Fairly good ma-

terial," he said, with an air of fatigue, "but not much
go to most of them." He tossed over the results of a
questionnaire. The consensus was that "we are not
fighting to dominate but to keep what we have. We are
fighting to straighten out Europe's messes." There was
great contempt for the Axis. "They will give up as
soon as the fighting gets real tough." More than a quarter of the men thought that war would be over in a
year.

The barracks, icy clean, loomed up before me like a
diagram. Every piece of clothing was hung in relation
to every other piece of clothing. Towel neatly folded,
shirt, another shirt, trousers. Longest garments were in
the center of the rack, graduating each way to the short
towels. As I looked across, the patterned repetition
made me slightly seasick. Even the shelves containing
manuals and books were arranged with the tallest item
in the center, the whole picture graduating down to the
smallest at each end. Now the windows joined in, one
open from the top, the next from the bottom, one open
from the top, the next from the bottom. Top and bottom
succeeded each other down the length of the barracks.
The shoes were lined up just so, the footlockers just so.
A soldier sitting on his blanket writing a letter disturbed
the perfect picture. He looked up at me, ignoring my
public-relations escort, with the look that a man enclosed gives a man standing outside, a look from so far
away that neither he nor I would ever know what it
meant.

I am led past beds, between beds. The repetition of
freshly washed floors, of uniforms, of olive-drab blankets now extends itself to the recreation field where the
soldiers, in full battle dress, are sitting where they usually watch baseball. Orientation is one of the few reliefs

in a soldier's day. All these guys so tensely packed up
in battle dress, with leggings and helmets—their names
labeled across their helmets—are getting the afternoon
off by listening to a news program.

It is school all over again. The captain in front of his
Europe map, Asia map, battle map, his clipboard on his
lectern. What a relief to get away from the *real* Army,
with its drill, its endless jump fences. What a change!
The biggest change of all is that during this recreation
period you can argue with that young captain as he
fumbles around the map of Russia with his pointer and
clears his throat too many times. He doesn't know any
more about far-off places and rushed-through history
than we do!

But it is sweet sitting amid these pines, baseball bats
still scattered over the field, a sergeant comfortably
smoking his pipe as he rests on the ground with his
back against the benches. 1943 has suddenly become
the year of Allied recovery, with victories in North
Africa, the surrender at Stalingrad, the greatest of all
tank battles at Kursk, the new bombing offensives
against Germany. In the great American tradition of
the bull session, anything can be said about anybody.
After the required news talks for the troops, the men
have to vote on what the camp's information officer
proudly describes as "tough policy questions." Should
the Allies make a second front soon? What should our
attitude be toward Russia after the war? Can we trust
Russia to cooperate with us? Should lend-lease to Russia be used to obtain assurances from Russia about the
peace? To crystallize opinion before the voting, there
is an illustrated talk by three soldiers. They declaim by
turns from a script full of resounding affirmations. This
is a war against hunger and want. Against Fascism

wherever it may raise its ugly head. Against war itself.
They quote our President.

"I see one-third of a nation ill-housed, ill-clad, ill-
nourished. Certainly this is no time for any of us to stop
thinking about the social and economic problems which
are the root cause of the social revolutions, today a
supreme factor in the world. For there is nothing mysterious about the foundations of a healthy and strong
democracy.

"In the future days which we seek to make secure, we
look forward to a world founded upon four essential
human freedoms.

"The first is freedom of speech and expression—everywhere in the world.

"The second is freedom of every person to worship
God in his own way—everywhere in the world.

"The third is freedom from want—which, translated
into world terms, means economic understandings which
will secure to every nation a healthy peacetime life for
its inhabitants—everywhere in the world.

"The fourth is freedom from fear, which translated
into world terms, means a world-wide reduction of arma-
ments to such a point and in such a thorough manner
that no nation will be in a position to commit an act of
aggression against any neighbor—anywhere in the world.

"That is no vision of a distant millennium."

In the evening, the famous Tuesday discussion group
of the hospital staff. The program was originated by the
camp psychiatrist and is now run by a pleasantly graying corporal who once taught history. Teacher in this
case *is* teacher, but perhaps I can call him Comrade X.
He certainly knows more about the war than the shyly
unpolitical young doctors and nurses looking up at him
with puzzled frowns, but he doesn't know anything
about *them*. He leads the discussion with a vehemence
and political insistency that leaves most of the twenty-

five doctors, nurses, and orderlies staring at him in amazement.

Silently observing from the back, I enjoyed and suffered this cultural episode. The cool and benign nurses, thoroughly starched into their white uniforms and black hospital capes, stared vaguely as the hot discussion leader made his points by punching the air like a boxer. Much of the time they didn't know where to look. They were just baffled that the young corporal with the thick graying hair could feel so earnestly and talk so fast and cite authorities with so many foreign names. He went on and on, working himself into an angry soliloquy on the need, the historic significance of the second front, the social necessities of the future. Shaking his head as if in despair of all the strength that "political maturity" would require of him in future days, weeks, and months, he stopped at last in exhaustion.

Suddenly a blond young doctor from the Harvard Medical School, hair neatly damped around his ears, got up with an air of polite insolence. Blandly proclaiming his ignorance of the many authorities, place names, and statistics recited by "our young friend from New York," he went on with an innocent look to mock "our friend up front."

"Now," he began with a little smile, leaning both hands on the back of the couch from which two nurses were appreciatively looking up at him, "our friend up front has been saying very eloquently that this war is a revolution. I am sure that we have all been *most* interested to hear that. But"—he shrugged his shoulders with a contempt that made me wince—"I haven't the faintest idea of what he has been talking about.

"Now, Corporal—and don't look so upset, Corporal —*who* is going to make the revolution? Is it you and the people *you* know—in New York? It surely couldn't be me"—he laughed and waved his arm—"or the people in this room!" The audience tittered.

The next day, on the train to Chicago, I kept seeing a white plume of smoke reaching back from the engine, wisps streaking past a dirt-encrusted window in which I saw a face whose calmness shocked me. The plume of smoke kept rushing past the window. The earth fell away. Red barns in Ohio, the November fields brown and cold, looking as if they had been put away for the winter, an occasional bale of yellowing straw rising out of the endless stubble in the fields.

It was Sunday, a cold clear empty-looking Sunday morning despite the train jammed with soldiers, soldiers' wives, and soldiers' babies. I was in the middle of no-where and liked it. While my mind kept crying *Where? Where now*, all night long, bouncing in the upper berth of car 73, I kept reaching out for that body I had as yet just barely encountered in a hotel bed. I was in a state of perfect contradiction, gravely conscious that I had done it at last, and feeling so far-flung that *I* was the smoke racing with the train.

Chicago began as the dark tubular laced-in network of the LaSalle Street station, the Loop shut in by the coiling El overhead. The city then broadened out into the widest coldest seafront streets I had ever seen. Chicago was wild with winter, too big for me, mysteriously laid out. I fell into cold space every time I left the hotel facing the lake. At breakfast, snug within the warmth and old dark wood paneling of the Blackstone, solid rosy-looking Chicago businessmen methodically ate steak and kidneys.

I had to make my way to the lake and the Navy's great training section where, in late November now, every wind tore right through me. Inside the Navy, however, all was busy cheer, endless pots of steaming coffee, solidly black regiments in white leggings marching up and down in training exercises that would never get them on a ship except as stewards' mates. Great Lakes Naval Station was one enormous assembly line producing sailor after sailor like so many planes at Willow Run.

The production figures were stupefying, the distance between man and man even worse. A fresh-faced, charmingly innocent, and enthusiastic redhead lieutenant—"I'm richer than anyone ought to be"—quickly took me in hand, talked to me in anguish about the Negro Problem in America. The Navy did not care for "colored." They served mostly in hospitals, or as stewards' mates. Given a regiment of black troops to train, my lieutenant from Wisconsin, son of a cheese millionaire, had discovered that virtually all were illiterate. In a state of patriotic indignation, he announced to his commanding officer that he would not teach them how to fight until he had taught them how to read. The commanding officer was descended from the man who had set up the Hampton Institute for Negroes—a piece of luck that alone explained the permission the young lieutenant received to set up a literacy school. With superb tact he never set foot inside the classroom, but had arranged for black college graduates, languishing in the Navy as kitchen helpers, to become instructors. He had even written a little reader for his students, called, of course, *Why We Fight*.

This war is the greatest war the world has ever known. The future of many millions of people depends upon its results. If we win it, we shall be able to maintain the Four Freedoms Named By President Roosevelt.

The Four Freedoms are: (1) Freedom From Want

(2) Freedom From Fear (3) Freedom of Speech (4)
Freedom of Worship.

The people of many other lands have never enjoyed
such freedom as ours. We also are fighting that they may
be saved from the men who would make slaves of them.
When we wonder why we are fighting, we should think
of what life would be like if we had no freedom. The
Germans and the Japanese seek to make a world run for
their profit alone.

To them a man is nothing. His home and family are
nothing. He lives merely to serve them. They think of
themselves as kings. We stand in their way and keep
their dream from coming true. Think of your home,
your family, your friends, and be glad you can strike a
blow to defend them.

In groups of sixty at a time, these raw recruits from
the South, after a hard day's training, spent two hours
a night, five nights a week, learning to read and to write.
The walls of the barracks classroom were hung with
graphs and charts. Black arrows pointed up a rise in
Negro literates between the ages of 18 and 27. Other
arrows pointed up a decline in the VD rate. Hand-
printed posters in the largest letters instructed recruits to
WALK IN A PROPER MANNER . . . BE ALERT . . . RE-
CEIVE COMMANDS AND TO PASS ON COMMANDS ONLY
ON ORDERS OF THE COMMANDING OFFICER, OFFICER OF
THE DAY, OFFICER OF THE DECK. The raw recruits, all
too identical in their meek cut-to-the-scalp haircuts,
their black blouses and white leggings, their heads bent
over their readers, were slowly writing out for themselves the lesson of "the greatest war the world has
ever known":

When we wonder why we are fighting, we should think
of what life would be like if we had no freedom.

The young millionaire lieutenant was all on fire.

Sitting with him in his little office, the walls of which were hung with still more charts and graphs, I listened all through one night as he recited with eagerness, with amazement, with passionate indignation, everything he had discovered about the condition of Negroes in the United States. His anger at what his fellow officers didn't know was even stronger than his concern. Did I know what the VD rate was among Negroes in Mississippi compared with that of even the poorest whites in Mississippi? Did I know how few Negroes from the South went beyond the sixth grade? Did I know that even in the Army, which was making an effort to get Negroes into combat, most Negroes were concentrated in the Service and Quartermaster Forces?

I never got to talk to a single Negro recruit, but I certainly listened a lot to my lieutenant. He was the doctor from another world and "his" recruits were his patients. "Thanks to the war," he said. "If I hadn't been commissioned," he said, "none of this would have happened." Thanks to the war, he had discovered the sorrow that was Negro life in America; he pasted it to charts and graphs on every wall near him, and his happiness was the ability of his recruits to read his own reader back to him.

The Germans and the Japanese seek to make a world run for their profit alone. To them a man is nothing. His home and family are nothing.

Thanks to the war, educators in uniform at the Armed Forces Institute were trying to school the millions in the Army and Navy who needed schooling. At the University of Wisconsin they had piled up a great mountain of primers and readers and textbooks going out to soldiers and sailors everywhere in the world. I looked at the books, I studied the correspondence courses men were taking overseas. On the say-so of one uniformed dean after another, I dutifully copied into my notebook H. G. Wells's warning that history had narrowed down to a race between education and catastrophe.

I was looking at all this through a blur, for it would soon be time to go home. In the long punch-drunk nights on trains, I itched and writhed on the scratchy plush seats lined and circled with dried coffee, mucus, vomit. The passenger trains jammed with soldiers' wives and children following after their men were constantly held up by the endless freight trains loaded with arms for war, crisscrossing the country like gigantic cannon. All through the night the broken-down pitiful old passenger trains kept stopping for hours. Even when trains stalled, I could hear in my mind the scrape of metal on metal, the dull self-repeating chugging of wheels.

There were faintly lighted towns that at night flooded me with loneliness as I looked at them through my blurred image in the dirty windows. I was amazed that I was where I was, nowhere in the long dark night, empty except for the gathering information in my mind about "people's education." I was a secret, part of the stolid silence of all those weary people swaying under the harsh lights in the train with every pull and slam of the wheels. Outside, great canvas covers flapped in the wind as the open freight cars loaded with tanks rushed past us. Small towns could be swallowed up so quickly in the intervening darkness. America was endless. In a developing panic I felt I had been thrown out into outer space. I knew no one.

Everything came to a head one glowering winter day at a great army camp and hospital in southern Illinois. Frank Capra had made for the Army a series of *Why We Fight* films—*Prelude to War, The Nazis Strike,*

Divide and Conquer, The Battle of Britain. I was now
to see the last and best, Anatole Litvak's *The Battle of
Russia.* I had seen the earliest films over and over, the
questionnaires put out by the Research Branch of the
Army designed to show the effect of the films on the
captive soldier audience. Did you like it? said the cards
passed out at the Hollywood-like "sneak preview." If
not, why not? Would you like to see the same cast again?
Next time in another story?

Sitting in the dark post theater, we were all of us at
ease; we were at the movies. On the screen, the dear
exciting movie screen, best friend many an American
ever had, jagged arrows leaped across the map to show
the Nazis poised against France in 1940, against England, finally against Russia on June 22, 1941. Loud
thunderclaps of music burst against my brain as I sat
with hundreds of soldiers in the theater. In the excitement and terror of seeing the large swastika map move
across England, I felt together with these men, knew
that with the trustworthy old American movie magic
working on us like a liberating storm, our political souls
were being cleansed and invigorated. We would come
out of the theater knowing what was agreed on all sides
—that it was our privilege to erase the evil in the world
that was Hitler.

Now *The Battle of Russia* comes on, and there it is,
the real thing. This is not the visual Walt Disney dia-
grams of the Union Jack and the Stars and Stripes moving against swastika after swastika, but captured Nazi
films (think of them lining up cameras for this) showing a row of young partisan girls strangling in a row on
a portable gallows. Russian films show the ruins of
Chekhov's house, deliberately burned; Tchaikovsky's
house, deliberately burned.

On the sound track, abysmal mourning, low Slavic

chords, muttering thunder. On the screen, a dead muddy winter scene as old men and women from a village in the Ukraine stoop over the muddy blood-soaked ravines where their people have been left after being shot by the Nazis. The Russian sky behind them is dark and soggy, rain is coming on, and the villagers bend in agony over their dead. Now they are playing broken chords from the *Pathétique*. Nothing I was to see after the war in Russia and East Berlin, with its vast sarcophagi of Russian soldiers, was to bring out the torment of the Russians in the Hitler war as did those scattered shots from captured Nazi newsreels and Soviet sources which I saw on a snow-soaked day at a camp in Illinois. Sitting in the post theater, embracing Russia as my parents had not been allowed to embrace it, I see coming together the divided forces of the Red Army encircling the Germans at Stalingrad. Two long lines of Russian soldiers are running to each other in the snow, hugging each other, bussing each other man to man in the hearty Russian fashion. Stalingrad! Long lines of anti-aircraft guns are lined up in this "beautiful" ballet of war, the katusha rockets whiz brilliantly through the air, soldiers are slithering through the snow toward a ruined apartment house. Doughty, cheeky, round Red Army men, all bundled up in their winter greatcoats, are striding toward victory. The movie makes it plain that victory is on the way. The movies make it easy to sit in southern Illinois and to accept that lovely Russian sacrifice in my behalf. I lose all separateness, feel absolutely at one with the soldiers in that dark theater.

It was a physical shock, walking out of the theater in the gray dripping twilight, watching the men plodding back to their barracks in the last slant of light, to realize how drained I was, how much I had been worked over, appealed to. In the end, as so often happened to

us after a terrific American movie, we were stupefied.
There was no magic bridge between a snowed-on American soldier and the movie he was forced to see about
the sufferings of the Old World. Litvak's heavy concentration of effect—to say nothing of "all those guns in
the picture the Russkies got from us"—did not have
the expected effect on the soldiers marched off to see
The Battle of Russia.

Returning to New York late on a Friday afternoon, I
knew that I could not go home, that I had to see Mary
Ellen. That first night I went to her basement room on
Morton Street, I was shaking as I went down the steps
and rang the bell. When she opened the outside door
and I saw her grin in the feeble light of the hall, I had
the same sense of amazement that I was to have, night
after night now, in that dark little room in the basement
amid her art-magazine reproductions of Rouault Christs,
her cats, the milk bottles on the windowsill, the everlasting smell of plaster of Paris in the bathroom. Among
the burning dark faces of the Rouaults there stood out
on the walls some Japanese prints she loved, spare lines
that set the scene over and again: a few trees, a water-
fall, a clump of bushes, a bearded philosopher dreamily
surveying the scene from a corner. Bent to the rhythm
of the flowering scene, everything expressed that confidence in the perfect ordering of life by art which in the
beginning, so long as we remained in this room, astonished me most. The room was Mary Ellen's work of
art. In that poky damp basement, where she had hardly
room to turn around in under the falling heaps of books,
the everlasting turn and scatter of her cats, she had
somehow made her life, had framed her Japan, with its
clear quiet lines, its grave abstract waters.
    In that room I began to live a dream made up of

Mary Ellen. There was all the voluptuousness I had always dreamed of when the cats came into bed with us and she grinned with delight, her sloe eyes widening, her cheekbones so white as to be almost luminescent in her stretched cheeks. I could never watch her walking around the room with her dancer's stride, her body constantly shifting and stretching, her teeth clicking a harsh tuneless beat, without recognizing that for some reason I had been granted the perfection of my desires. My life had suddenly arranged itself like a dream, as easy, as soundless. And though I could see that it was not my dream alone she was acting out but also her own, that we were assisting each other's fantasies in perfect solitude, I felt as if I had been drugged by the smells of incense, of cat, of plaster in that dark close underground room where every lighted green candle made the room hot without making it lighter. I liked being drugged. In the dream I watched her dancing around the room in her bare feet. Her hands played the air before her as if she were a priestess performing a rite.

And a priestess she was, the priestess who brought so many of us to the mystery of the bed. She made the delights of sex seem the well-practiced gestures of a temple ceremony. This ability to induce delight started from the rhythmical flexibility of her thin, almost emaciated dancer's body. Except for the sweeping curve at her hip, her body did not look anything. Her extraordinary presence lay in the suggestion of her hands and lips, in the tiny jeweled movements of her body—in her smiling confidence, pleasure, ease. Just as kissing her induced the sensation of falling, deepening, so being with her spread such a circle of peace, easiness, perfection that I acquired a respect for sex that I had never known before. I was looking at the candlelight behind her head as I thrust my way ahead in her, and I had never felt anything so keen as the vibration that joined me to her, to the candlelight, to the golden helmet in the Rembrandt portrait that shone up from an open picture book on the floor. Making love in that little room had become one of the true privileges of the human condition. All that I had carried in silence and secrecy so long, all that I had held against the world—all this burst apart as her body, fully stirred, moving in one sinuous line, heaved up at me when she whispered my name.

Afterward, she would talk about the other men with entire naturalness whenever there came into her conversation certain ideas, poems, philosophic systems that she owed to her husband Hans, the young philosophy instructor at U.C.L.A., to the expert on "totalitarian structures" she had been quarreling with the night I met her, to the elderly refugee art historian she had successfully persuaded not to leave his family for her. Her attachments seemed to consist of severe intellectual types. Although she gave herself to me as if no one had ever pleased her so much, I could see that the intellectual challenge from my predecessors was going to be sharp. The way into the temple was some scholarly specialty and distinction, some European knowledge that would excite her. She cared nothing about a "distinguished" career, a man's "famous" book; she did not read much. It was someone's gift for teaching and illuminating her, in immediate action with her alone, that interested her. She would quote lines from Rilke's "Torso of an Archaic Apollo" that her husband had taught her. A statue of Apollo had lost its head, but "his torso glows. . . . Else the curving breast could not thus blind you, nor through the soft turn of the loins could this smile easily have passed into the bright groins where the genitals burned." The headless statue glows; it is a candelabrum restrained but shining, not a fragment and defaced. It glows, this star has shaken the shackles off. It bursts with light, until there is no place that does not see you. *"Du musst dein Leben ändern."* "You must change your life."

She would then make points about the structure of Sanskrit that she owed to a famous philologist I had not connected with her until she quoted him, as she did all her European lover-authorities, with a smile of transcendent self-discovery. She revealed to me many of the new extensions between art history and psychoanalysis that scholarly refugees were bringing over. She became the only link between minds that would have hated each other.

She had the most guileless way of talking about other men and the cultural treasures they had brought her. She even had a way of dreaming out loud about handsome and original scholars like Lionel Trilling and Meyer Schapiro, whose lectures she dropped in on at Columbia, whom she had not met but whose gifts promised intellectual revelations of the kind that excited her most. She never showed jealousy, and she did not understand it in others; the idea of herself possessing anything or anyone baffled her. *Grande amoureuse* as she was, Mary Ellen was peculiarly undemanding in everything relating to clothes, comforts, people. She was so insanely available, so borrowable, that I was never surprised, in later years, to hear of some new lover she had taken, of some old lover I had missed, of a child she had had to abort because the man turned out to be insane, or of her sleeping with one man on the eve of her marriage to someone else. She gave herself away, continually, in little gestures toward death. Her ambition was certainly never to displace anyone's wife, to have money, to live well; it was to have with another those talks about "existential reality" that gave her face the look she had in orgasm; it was to be vibrantly in touch with another's subtlest understanding of life, and so feel that she was really alive. It was nothing for her to go to bed with a man; it was everything for her to give pleasure. By the directness with which she made love, she must have made many a man feel that she was above all grateful for the chance to give love.

There were certainly a great many men in her life and in her mind. Talking about Otto Rank or Erwin Panofsky or Werner Jaeger—each illustrious European scholar's name was a topic fondly associated with some disciple who had been her lover—she would give herself to me with the air of continuing our delightful conversation, but somewhat distractedly, as if she was not sure whom she was with. What frightened me was that she could suddenly matter so little to herself. Piercingly beautiful as she would always seem to me, she was a totally impoverished student, excited by New York, who lived by tutoring a deaf-and-dumb child, was always amazed to go to a good restaurant, and went about all day long and every day in the same thick peasant skirt, pumps with shiny patent-leather bows, a scarf around her head. She always dressed indifferently—I have never known a woman who made so little of clothes. Once, when we met on the steps of the Fifth Avenue Library, I still so happy in my love that I had dressed like a bridegroom, she looked at me with surprise, laughed, and, borrowing some money, ran into a store and came out in a short red coat in which she delightedly pranced down the avenue. I never saw the coat again.

She overlooked everything except being the artist in

touch with her surroundings. The more I came to know her that winter, the more I intimately associated her with charcoal, pastels, Japanese picture books that folded out to make a continuous drawing from page to page, trailing ivy, poems in violet ink on yellow paper written in totally different handwritings, galleries of folk art, primitive art, costume art, cigarettes with Russian paper filters—and above all the scattered, smudged, jagged pages of unfinished poems, unfinished fashion sketches, unfinished sonatas for the violin. There were times, lying with her in bed, when I felt that I was making love not to her but to her sacred objects.

I was taught, she the teacher, sometimes all day and all night. All this answered to my deepest needs. If she woke me at three in the morning to read me a poem she had just begun; if she whisked me away from my work to the new costume museum off Fifth Avenue to see a design that she admired, and then spent days on a fashion sketch that she soon forgot; if our conversations were full of God, Whitehead and Spinoza, Melville and Hawthorne, I felt that she was pressing me to go further, still further. Everything I had done and written now seemed to me tame. The more I thought of the hopes and radical dogmas that had once united Natasha and myself, the more I wanted to bury myself in Mary Ellen's arms in that dark smoky room. The more I admired her for the precariousness of her life, the more grateful I was for the love she gave me. Those violet early mornings after making love, when we would go out for coffee, I had a sense that the world around me was shivery with joy. When I went back to my old apartment to get my things, Natasha's face—not angry, but calm, stolid, full of compassionate contempt—redoubled my fury against the old idealistic life I had known so long, made me feel as if I could run through

Fourteenth Street scattering the shoppers before me.

Looking around her room, Mary Ellen once said, "I will end in a closet." It was this ability to face absolute nothing, the worst, that made me admire her so much. I wanted to get away from the endless connections I lived with; I wanted nothing but the risks she took in her life. Day after day I would watch her draw, dance, write, the straight mane of graying black hair flying off her back, as if I could absorb from the air in which she moved some of the mad courage that excited me. I sensed in Mary Ellen not merely a woman I loved, but a dark punishing wisdom about a world in which everything had fallen to pieces, in which nothing was to be saved. The endless comings and goings of people around her, like the great plume of smoke I kept seeing from all trains during the war, seemed to me the law of our time.

I lost patience with some of her old friends who were always swarming over the apartment I had sublet from Isaac Rosenfeld on Barrow Street, complained about her continued interest in people who reminded me of airless plants floating through the room. She would earnestly explain that the irrational is the heart of life and chide me for trying to "keep the controls on." She was shocked that I lacked the "metaphysical courage" I myself had expounded to her in my analysis of *Moby-Dick*. The Rosenfelds' tumultuous apartment seemed to be made of modishly shallow Russell Wright dishes in different colors, unpainted wooden furniture, gaping sofas, masses of review copies, back issues of *Partisan Review*, *Antioch Review*, the *Journal of Philosophy* forever falling down from the shaky handmade shelves. It still featured up and down every inch of the kitchen wall snapshots of their Village friends. In my excitement and guilt I felt surrounded by cultural accusations from absent Isaac and his many friends. I would never be equal to the orgone box, with its cheap metal slats, neo-Aristotelian critics from the University of Chicago, Count Alfred Korzybski's discoveries in semantics. Isaac, ready to be saved by every new idea, left behind him in Barrow Street an overgrown jungle of bristling ideological challenges, pricklier than the undusted cactuses spearing me in every corner.

In self-defense I took Mary Ellen to visit Alfred Stieglitz at his "shop" at Madison and Fifty-second, An American Place. Stieglitz, now almost eighty, was still belligerently introducing photography as an art and the modern French and American pictures he proclaimed as his own discovery. Surrounded by pictures, he presided from his couch over what he called his "great people," especially his great Americans—his wife, Georgia O'Keeffe, who refused to go abroad like other American painters and alone in New Mexico sought "the great American thing"; John Marin; Marsden Hartley; Charles Demuth; Arthur Dove.

I knew Stieglitz as a very old man who had put away his camera. "The excitement would kill me," he grumbled. His heart was weak, he said. He said it often as he lay back angrily on a couch in the cubicle back of the gallery, defying the pillows to rest him. He liked to talk of the "spiritual" in art. The withered lady aesthetes who surrounded him actually talked of the adored master in the third person. Stieglitz had made them see everything in a new light. His manner was complaining, impatient; his rumpled clothes showed the old artisan from Hoboken who had been trained as an engineer. Now he did not have enough to do and he was surrounded by pictures he usually would refuse to sell. He found most people unworthy of the pictures he loved most.

Receiving us from his bed, he wore a stained woolen vest, like that of an old storekeeper afraid of winter, a dark coat, and shapeless black pants. Silvery sprigs of hair exuded too plentifully from his nose, from his ears, like disused antennae. The pictures all around him promised you entrance to another world. But there was not a hint of ease in this old man, nothing that was pleased with life and himself. He was a cranky, altogether art-crazy old Jewish prophet outstretched— "saving my heart," as he told you over and over—in a Madison Avenue office building. In his cracked truculent old man's voice, with that accent of old New York port towns, crusty as a taxi-driver's, he complained endlessly. Studying Mary Ellen, he grumbled up at her, "You're a beauty," then turned away to bewail his decrepit state.

The gallery was spare, elegant, waxy-smooth. It was hung round and round with the French and Americans whom Stieglitz had been among the first to recognize. There were pictures that he had been sitting on for thirty years like a proprietary hen. I was always hearing from him of the dress manufacturer who wanted one of his beloved Marins but could not have it; Stieglitz felt that the man simply did not have the right feeling for it. Once, he boasted, he pushed the man's check back at him after a weak moment in which he had agreed to sell the picture.

Stieglitz would always remain the biggest item in his own gallery. Picturing himself on the point of death, he remained the proverbially important Jewish son—*he* was the magnet around which even Picasso and Braque collected! From his bed—I never saw him standing or even sitting—he talked and talked against the "picture merchants on Fifty-seventh Street," the salesmen, the sins of the Metropolitan Museum. The everlasting lady followers stood around like courtiers attending a levee.

They talked with the breathlessness that seemed to be the style of conversation at An American Place. They talked between dashes—slowly, in trance-like tones of appreciation, so slowly that they seemed to forget the subject of a sentence by the time they wound their way to its end, and would sigh, shaking their heads in wonder at it all as they lamely concluded, "Wonderful, wonderful. . . ."

I was another slave to Stieglitz's eye. I had become one from the moment I had seen his great photograph "The Steerage" and had imagined my mother as the woman who dominates the composition as she stands on the lower deck draped in an enormous towel, her back always to me. In some way Stieglitz's photographs of old New York possessed my soul, my unconscious past. His was the New York my mother and father had stumbled along as frightened young immigrants. My mother seemed to me frozen forever on that lower deck. In another great composition in black-and-white, horse-cars drawing up at the car barns in winter, my father is the driver in his white brimmed hat and black raincoat with *his* back to me. The snow and the horses' breaths are steaming up like a layer of white air into the center of the picture. New York in winter at the turn of the century, muddy, dirty, black-trodden snow everywhere underfoot, a horsecar with "HARLEM" written on the roof in big spaced letters. There are more horses off on the side, then an umbrella-and-bag store. End of the line. The driver in his black raincoat and white brimmed hat is standing in front of his horses to unbuckle them and to rein the fresh horses who can be seen, blanketed against the cold, off on the side. The curve of the horse-car on its tracks, the curve in the team of horses tamely standing in the white powdery winter air! This is old New York at its wintriest, blackest, dirtiest. The many forms Stieglitz caught also take *my* breath away. My past is there without me.

All the while Stieglitz complained and complained, two white shining sea birds by John Marin gleamed above his head. I looked at Mary Ellen and Stieglitz appreciatively sizing each other up and laughed. A collector of intellectuals, she had finally come across a genius. The lady clique around him talked too much of "Beauty." If he ever got out of bed, it would be to lean out of his seventeenth-floor windows and scream down to Madison Avenue, "Philistines! Philistines!"

But he was too much for her. "Uptown" made her nervous to get back to the Village, and of course I went with her. In the midst of the war, the terrible seas, she had taken up her life on a raft. There was despair in my heart whenever I walked down the four flights in Barrow Street into the gritty back yard, looked up at the useless mocking cold wintry sky. My respect for Mary Ellen's acceptance of everything would fail me. I thought of her white face the night she had looked around her basement room and, shivering, said, "I will end up in a closet."

None of *us* would ever end in a closet, I thought— not the ridiculously proud analyst of "totalitarian structures" I had first met her with; not the uncompromisingly left-wing, soon to be uncompromisingly right-wing Dutch ideologue who was proud of having so long been her Svengali; not even her young husband, who stopping in to see her before he went overseas, seemed as mad for her and as perplexed by her as I. None of *us* would end in a closet; we had too strong a sense of survival. But from the moment I met her, I knew that Mary Ellen could end up in a closet; she might very well end by a knife. She gave herself easily, rapturously, more and more carelessly. It seemed never to occur to her that her interest in ultimate reality might not be shared by everyone who went to bed with her. She was intoxicated by her penniless addiction to every "revelation" that turned up.

I was frightened as I was dazzled by what I had seen in her face that first night; to move in with her was to end the affair. It was understood—it was always in the air—it was part of the excitement of being with her. Everything was provisional. It was not her "infidelity" that troubled me; it was her fanaticism. Like Sartre in one hotel room after another, another wartime philosopher of the great big nothing around us, she made it a fixed principle to stay loose. She wanted to bring life down to its ultimate in disconnection, to make the great refusal—of everything that had been life to me. She needed to be free to move on. There was only a grandmother back in Los Angeles to report to occasionally; completely the orphan, she had taken herself as the only safe measure of the society around her, and saw it as completely unstable. As she once said with a little shrug, "I'm not always in control."

One winter night in 1943, I came back from a tormented visit to Natasha to find Paul Goodman talking to Mary Ellen about God. Her mouth moistly open, she looked like a Buddha positively asleep with rapture. Goodman was a long way off in those war-torn days from the fame he was later to acquire as a therapist to society in general. He was small, eager, and past thirty, still looked like a street fighter stripped for action. His sneakers in all weathers, his tousled hair, his shiny pointed chin—above all, the mound of peanut shells that collected around him on whatever sofa he took up his oracular position—all made him look like a boy. The slightest verbal exchange with another intellectual made him as combative as he was on the handball court, where you could see him lusting and panting to make a drop shot in the corner.

Goodman radiated authority in all branches of learning and in all departments of literature. He did Biblical plays, attempted the haiku, wrote fiction, rough confessional poems, social essays, treatises on language. He was soon to become a leading theorist and sometime practitioner of Gestalt psychotherapy. Patients were encouraged to let their bitterness out in one primal scream. His friends had all to be followers, and he was savage to those strangers to the Village who did not yet know what his authority consisted in. He fascinated me by his tremulous immodesty. But I knew his secret. Despairing, alone, he preached revolution in all departments. His writing was personal scripture to lovers and disciples. Oracle, heal thyself. But Goodman's power over people visibly enlarged him in the moment of contact. It was also mildly poignant. He talked about himself as the "best" playwright, the "best" literary theorist, the "best" poet. But he was soaked in misanthropy and loneliness, the clutch for love from every passer-by at a party, every toughie he picked up on the handball court. Again and again I saw him elevate himself by the sexual force of his conversation, then droop away, spent and exhausted.

No one needed people, sometimes any people, so much as Goodman did. But they had to be mentally his children. What fascinated me in Goodman—what seemed to me his true originality—was that he had transformed himself into his own father. Seeking love angrily, he was an orphan turned professional father. His father had deserted the family when Paul was young; Paul had thrown himself upon the streets and the tumultuous city life. Beginning as a kind of ward of the city, open to every danger and seduction, he filled up the city with his dreams and fantasies of perfect love and unsurpassable wisdom. He was the hurdy-gurdy man, the heart-on-sleeve minstrel in search of love, yet the omnivorous teacher of the city, its daily thaumaturge.

In this daily melancholy creation of himself, Goodman seemed to live only didactically. Everything had to be turned inside out; everything had to be reinterpreted. He was interested in everything, an authority on everything. He had already published, with small experimental presses in the Village, some twenty books—social theory, poetry, fiction, his journals. His writing seemed to be slovenly, a series of personal messages—as a friend said, "too pragmatic." He wrote to save himself, day after day. But the scoffers may have been mistaken. It was obvious that he sincerely believed himself to be a genius.

With people Goodman wished to attract, he showed a winning, humbly speculative, experimental cast of mind that to Mary Ellen, with her love of any general idea, was irresistible. There was the unmistakable feeling that he could try out any new idea on his body or yours. He made a point of dashing things off so as to give you "the man himself"—plain, personal, metaphysical. He specialized in the short, sharp, jabbing, personal style even when he wrote about housing problems; he wanted, he said, to make you feel the grunt, the ache, stab, cramp, of sex. Even in his most self-pitying lyrics he would make a point of writing "hard-on." He would not trifle with the truth. When Trotsky was assassinated in 1940, Goodman published an elegy that reproduced his howls of grief. Reading his many love poems, you felt that what he most wanted was to by-pass words, to make the expected sounds, to leap out of the page itself at the stranger he was writing the poem to attract.

This was the theory. Goodman amazed and somehow unnerved me by a ready omniscience that should have screamed fake, homemade, a contraption, but that to him became as grand as the sky. Jonah, the disconsolate prophet, the totally crisscrossed soul, was in command of everyone else to whom he could explain what ailed him. He honestly felt that nature itself spoke through him. No wonder he drew every experience into himself like a gull snapping up a fish. I always saw him with his eyes harshly bright, his mouth open with excitement, his nose quivering. He talked by instructing, and he talked with such absorption that the only joke his friends permitted themselves was that Paul did not listen even when you praised him. He attacked every writer not limited to small experimental presses in the Village. He said of Edmund Wilson's powerful essay on Dickens, "The Two Scrooges," that it was "seriously dishonest," but of a disciple who had as yet written only four small stories, that he was "the second-best prose writer in New York." Goodman was his own greatest myth. He would never create anything that came near Paul Goodman's idea of Paul Goodman. A year before his death in 1972, he described himself to an audience as "a man of letters in the classic, the old-fashioned sense—like Erasmus and Diderot."

At that late-winter moment in 1943, explaining to her his new idea of God, Goodman seemed to be burning holes in Mary Ellen's skin. I never saw anyone build ideas into such an atmosphere of domination as Goodman did. His sense of himself as great intellectual destiny was now operating on her with such heat that I went sick looking at them both. He looked as animal as a cat. He grew red with rage as he discussed someone else's interpretation of Isaiah, and his eyes dilated with hysteria as he refuted an article in the *Journal of Philosophy*. The more superfine and demonstrative his argument, the more slashing his manner became. I saw that this bisexual could take a woman to bed on the upbeat of an argument about religion, and that he could make an opponent feel not that he had been corrected but that he had been stabbed.

Everything about Goodman was endlessly fascinating to Mary Ellen, who lived ideas with a humbler, private ecstasy. She lighted up with a strange awe as she stood over the more diminutive Goodman. They were lovingly thinking together.

It was only with Goodman that she ever seemed surprised by anything. Even in the cascades of passion, or in the miseries that would occasionally seize her as she walked ceaselessly around the room, softly beating her hands together in despair, everything was expected. She had had so many lovers, she had passed through so many lives, she had holed up in so many rooms; there was no new experience that she was not prepared to take on as coolly as a new lover. But with Goodman there appeared a strange secret numbness in her that was like death. He was so essentially cold to women that there was nothing she could "do" for him, no place where she could touch him; they met and looked at each other like stray polar bears on the same Arctic floe. When he was gone, she would sit all day in a low-slung canvas chair, unable to move, to wash, to change her clothes.

And then, so gradually that when it became the sick metallic taste of every day I could not really believe this was happening to me, the nausea began. The too

many pictures of their friends pasted up on the Rosenfelds' kitchen wall receded as if I were seeing them
through a telescope. The dusty covers on the bed, an
old grease stain on the wall, Mary Ellen's always unfinished sketches and poems lying about the apartment,
the maddeningly shallow Russell Wright dishes—all became horribly separate, bulking, intrusive, immovable
objects like Mary Ellen herself. She could sit in her
chair as if the decision she made to sit down had cut off
all ability to stand up.

Nothing I now looked at in the Barrow Street apartment seemed to have any relation to anything else.
When I tried to write, the words broke off each other
like dry twigs. There was suddenly no light, no habit,
no naturalness to my day. I did not know who Mary
Ellen was; I felt that I was living on a sand hill surrounded by vultures and gulls who were waiting to
descend on it.

It was now early 1944; the world was burning with
war, and I was out of it, consumed with guilt. Everything was falling apart. I had a sudden horror of myself,
and left Barrow Street, wandering in a trance from hotel
to hotel, each more unreal than the last. I was as bad as
any Nazi. The Jews burned every day in Europe were
being consumed in a fire that I had helped to light. In
my daily fantasies I saved bearded old Jews from attack
in the subway, and was again a *mensch*, a son of the
people.

The more I came unstuck in these months, to fall
into a despair that seemed a right judgment on me, the
more Mary Ellen rallied to me, tried to lift me out of
my trance, to show me that I was not alone. I was not
convinced. One night, when I holed up in a miserable
hotel on West Ninety-fifth Street, she somehow managed to find me from old telephone numbers I had left

and came up to the room, embracing me and trying to fill up the total emptiness I felt in that place. There was an organized meaninglessness from the naked overhead bulb and the light glinting off the top of the cheap maple table, the snaky trail of black dust winding along the infuriatingly repetitious pattern in the linoleum floor, the German refugees timidly trying broken English phrases on the drunken Negro janitor in the hall. I had always been depressed by those densely huddled sunless upper West Side streets, the stray figures under the "NO LOITERING" signs. As I walked those streets now, I felt the city was pushing me out.

There were no apartments to be had anywhere. It was all homeless now—a series of "transient" hotels: West Side, East Side, Brooklyn Heights, the Village—surrounded by that unending wartime crowd I had seen being pushed out of Washington's Union Station, or waiting around the clock to get on a train. War-crowded New York threw back my splintered image from every store window. I could not stop walking the streets, round and round, looking for myself. It was not just my old reasons for everything, my sense of home that I missed; it was a world in which the old invisible connections still existed.

In the dead of winter I went up to Provincetown, and in the dying light, a moonless night coming on, I again walked the dunes to the Peaked Hill Bar Coast Guard station on the Atlantic, crazily looking for Natasha at the end of the American mainland. In 1940 we had often tramped this beach. There was absolutely nowhere to go now, nothing more to do. That long Sunday evening in Provincetown, I sat in a room up three straight flights of stairs in a Portuguese rooming house. Mrs. Macara's kitchen smelled of my youth. In a trance of hallucinated memory the past broke out; I could see

every uneven plastered bump of white paint on the walls
of the tenement kitchen in which I had grown up. My
ability to reenter it was total; I rejoined myself by
clutching in my notebook every sensation of the past.
Sitting in that Provincetown room overlooking one
lamplit curving street where winter fishermen huddled
past in their heavy lumber jackets, I knew that what I
remembered I could describe, and that I could describe
many things as if I had lived them. The world was more
inside me than I had imagined.

"You're so organic," Mary Ellen said to me in wonder at my sudden joy when the chance came to go to
England and to work there with the great popular education movement in the armed forces. It was to take me
some months to get on a ship, and I restlessly waited the
time out working on Blake at the Huntington Library in
California and teaching at Black Mountain College in
North Carolina. Things now improved with us as the
time came for me to leave. One night, when I quoted
Tolstoy to Mary Ellen—"God is the name of my desire"
—she grew absolutely white, and repeated it over and
over to herself. It was the most beautiful thing she had
ever heard, the truest, the most consoling. I awoke to
see her sitting cross-legged on the floor, reciting a Hindu
chant that a new friend had taught her. She made me
think of a solitary Indian on a cliff, sending up smoke
messages to the Great Spirit. In the immense Arctic
waste of our life, in the midst of the emptiness, she sat
there, a girl in Greenwich Village, sending up her
prayer.

After the war, we would see each other at Isa's parties
whenever I was back in New York. Returning from
England, I was seized by a longing to see her in what
someone told me was a new apartment. I rang her bell,
went upstairs, knocked at the door. When I told her I

was there, she seemed hesitant about admitting me, and
there seemed to be some scurrying about. As she opened
the door, a man ran into the bathroom. Mary Ellen was
sitting on a trunk, surrounded by two disorderly hills of
luggage, books, and pictures; her cats were running
around the bare floor of the apartment; her easels, her
great sketchbooks, her plants were on the floor. Obviously she had just moved in with someone; but at the
moment all was confusion, and the man himself—a
Jewish intellectual whose name I knew well—had for
some reason barricaded himself from me in the bathroom.

I sat with her and talked, as we had always talked,
about art, Rilke, Yeats, Melville. The man in the bathroom called out in a rough voice, "For God's sake, get
me some paper!" She quietly went in and brought him
what he needed. As she looked at the piles of luggage,
sketches, pictures, she said ruminatively, "Every once in
a while I seem to see the possibilities of order in it."
We both laughed, and I stood up to take my leave. Suddenly she said in a small voice, "You know, you
changed my life." I stared at her. It was the most surprising thing I had ever had from her. Changed *her*
life! She had taken the phrase, the litany, the accusation,
straight out of my heart. With this she had burned me
forever. She had burned me.

Chapter IV

JOURNEY IN WARTIME

The S.S. *Hart Crane*, a Liberty ship like a thousand others, loaded with medical stores for the Army, airplane parts, and four civilian passengers (two of them clergymen) who had somehow obtained government permission to travel in wartime, left for Liverpool in the dead of winter, 1945, off Montague Street in Brooklyn Heights. For more than twenty hours, forbidden to leave ship, to send or receive messages, waiting for us to push off and get into convoy, I stared glumly at the endless arches woven out of the up-and-down lines of metal warehouses above the piers. Just to my right was Remsen Street, where Natasha and I had lived right after our marriage. Every time I turned on deck, the frozen tumult of New York hit me in the face. Now I was as inert and incommunicado as a piece of cargo, while my past glared at me.

I had waited many months to get on a ship, usually in a succession of overcrowded railroad coaches loaded with human freight, on coaches heading West that regularly stopped on the baking plains for hours, just when our water ran out and the toilets broke down, to let through the miles and miles of freight trains crossing the country with stuff for the war. The canvas covers snapping in the wind made one long billowing curtain as the trains thundered past our line of broken-down coaches. *There* was the main action, the war, while we hangers-on sank to the bottom. Somewhere between Denver and Santa Fe we were stuck for six hours; a strangled sound came out of me as the windows became too hot to open and the broken springs under the dirty green plush upholstery, once the pride of the Santa Fe, Burlington & Topeka, nicked and prodded my rear end as I sat surrounded by screaming babies. The floor was sopped with waste from the plugged toilet. I tried to plant my mind out on the desert shimmering and broiling just beyond the window—I imagined myself entirely elsewhere, just as I had done in childhood whenever I felt I was being held against my will.

In New Mexico I tried to get into a relocation center for Japanese—many of them native-born citizens of the United States—who had been rounded up and forcibly moved from their homes on the West Coast. That late-summer afternoon in June, 1944, I was wearing a white raincoat as I went up the hill to a stockade enclosed by wire fences. In a corner, hunched over their sticks, the Japanese were playing a pitiful miniature-golf game. My white raincoat had me spotted a long way off by guards in their two lookout towers. Insanely magnified voices boomed at me all over the desert landscape, demanding my business there. I tried to talk the guards into letting me in, but I was a figure in a white raincoat, they were enormous strutting towers bulking over the desert, and I could not even make myself heard. One guard showed me his rifle and sharply told me to keep off.

I arrived in Pasadena the day the Allies landed in

France. At one end of the library and museum of Huntington, the old railroad baron, stood Neptune with his trident, at the other Diana accompanied by a hound. Inside were Gainsborough's "Blue Boy," Thomas Lawrence's "Pinkie," a Gutenberg Bible, the perfect, matchless copy of Blake's first work in illuminated printing: *For the Sexes: The Gates of Paradise:*

TO THE ACCUSER WHO IS
THE GOD OF THIS WORLD

Truly, My Satan, thou art but a Dunce,
And does not know the Garment from the Man.
Every Harlot was a Virgin once,
Nor can'st thou ever change Kate into Nan.

Tho' thou art Worship'd by the Names Divine
Of Jesus & Jehovah, thou art still
The Son of Morn in weary Night's decline,
The lost Traveller's Dream under the Hill.

A cop wielding a gun escorted me to the vaults and stood over me as I turned the great pages of *The Marriage of Heaven and Hell*, protected by some gold-thin tissue. These were the pages that Blake himself had written, lettered, drawn, and designed on copperplate, and had brought out in relief by burning with corrosive acid everything else on the plate. He had delicately and lovingly colored each quarto page. In 1783 his asking price for the whole was seven shillings sixpence. In the divine union between imagination and the true world, the spiritual world closed to ordinary perception, all these human figures, trees, roots, branches, tendrils, flowers are madly twisting around each other, are touching, winding, crossing, embracing. The world is a wedding between man and his imagination. As a man is, so he sees. As the eye is formed, such are its powers. All

separations in space, time, and perception that keep us
from the divine unity are due to a failure of mental
powers. All is within the vaulting leaping mind of man.
All deities reside within the human breast. The only real
marriage is a man to his powers of vision. The world
shall have this "infernal" Bible whether it will or no.
And what is *their* "world"? A chimera, pretense, a mun-
dane shell. It is man subtracted from himself. Vision is
the only world, world without end, the divine unity
everlasting, hallelujah!

At the moment, I was living in the country of separa-
tion. In rich, rich Pasadena rotating sprinklers untiringly
pissed on a New Yorker peculiar enough to *walk*. Nothing could be so important as being safe in your lovely
home. But in Hollywood, Clifford Odets, John Garfield,
Harold Clurman, Luther Adler, and his wife Sylvia
Sidney, veterans of the Group Theatre in the 1930s
along with veterans of many barricades, had become
moviemakers. Old rebels were at the high flood of war
prosperity and the movie business. The flood soon receded; McCarthyism was to wreck or exile many of
them in the 1950s.

No one else in the vaults of the Huntington Library,
poring over Blake's illuminated books with an armed
cop at his shoulder, lived the unreal but bracing intellectual climate of California as I did those summer days
of 1944. To go between William Blake in the vault and
the Group in Hollywood was to go about your business
in a delicious drunken haze. The great lyrics that William Blake had written, designed, lettered, and colored
on every page put me in touch with his mind as no
printed book had ever done. There were the letters of
his divine patience and human impatience, his arrogance, his sweetness, his unending intelligence, his un-
statable uniqueness. One lettered, illuminated page

could become the ideal inward world. There were special heavier emphases in the turn of a letter, in the elongated reach of a body, in a capital letter dominating a stanza that made me tremble with the nearness of his mind to his hand. There was no other poet in English so happy in his gifts and so ignored in his "failure," so religious and insurrectionary, so lyric and so profound. The volcano never subsided. FIRE FIRE FIRE. Our God disclosed Himself as Fire. The "divine vision" burns away the deceptions of the material world as corrosive acid burns away the unwanted matter on the etcher's plate. Blake himself makes every "book" as he himself makes a total world. All he lacks is the world:

> Even Milton and Shakespeare could not publish their own works.
> Mr. Blake's powers of invention very early engaged the attention of many persons of eminence and fortune; by whose means he has been regularly enabled to bring before the Public works (he is not afraid to say) of equal magnitude and consequence with the productions of any age or country. . . .

Yet that evening I sat next to Thomas Mann at a meeting of Hollywood's liberal colony. He was unbending, tight-lipped, and severe as a Prussian field marshal —English was a problem—but managed to communicate what an honor it was to be given private showings of the new Warner Brothers films. He was crazy about movies. John Garfield, whom in my youth I had known as Julie Garfinkle from East New York, looked happy as he made a strong speech, scornful of his Hollywood bosses, in behalf of Russian-American unity. Upstairs in the Huntington Library, the noiseless Remington portables tinkled from desk to desk like harpsichords. But in Beverly Hills the old troupers of *Waiting for Lefty*

and *Awake and Sing* were partying and playing pinochle with the wild glee of Jews who—for once—had
found the Promised Land as promised.

Sylvia Sidney's heart-shaped face—the face that had
regularly broken my heart in so many Warners "social"
movies of the 1930s—greeted me at the Spanish Mission door with a moneyed New Year's Eve exuberance.
The jollity from the card table was loud, and I could
barely tell my long-secret heroine of the Depression
blues, Miss Sylvia Sidney, what it was I was working on
at the famous Huntington Library. When it finally came
out as Blake, *William* Blake, Sylvia Sidney frowned in
some puzzlement, clicked her fingers to jog her memory, and called out to her husband, "Hey, Luther! Didn't
we buy something by this Blake recently?" The harmony
of the occasion was suddenly jarred. Then the big price
was remembered and the Blake drawing found.

I sat with Clifford Odets and the Irish actor Barry
Fitzgerald one Sunday afternoon on the patio of Odets's
splendid rented house overlooking a splendid Hollywood chasm between two mounds of desert, listening to
the Brahms First on his spendid Capehart—a "miracle
of modern music making" *that turned records over*.
Barry Fitzgerald, looking as peaceful and funny as he
did in his movies, was contentedly smoking his pipe, an
Irish shepherd nodding over invisible sheep. Odets's face
always tried to be a mask—he *had* begun as an actor—
but relapsed into a battlefield; in the white beams of
California sunshine burning down on us that afternoon,
every feature was spotlighted; every facet of skin worked
against every other facet of skin. There was no rest in
that face. There would be no rest for Clifford Odets in
this life, not even in Hollywood. But meanwhile there
was Brahms on an old-fashioned Sunday afternoon of
listening to the phonograph. Odets pointed a finger to

the sky and said in hushed tones, "It comes from there." He was invaded by Brahms all over his body, possessed by Brahms. He shook in public rapture, gratitude, and exaltation. He blew a kiss to the music. His glasses, swinging carelessly from his hand as he vibrated prayerfully in his chair, fell and shattered on the flagstones. As I looked down at the pieces in some concern, he haughtily explained that he had half a dozen pairs in his study.

Another Sunday the thickly opulent California scene found me being driven by Stella Adler through the Hollywood canyons. The shimmering Sunday-morning partyness of southern California was like cold white wine in the face of the hot sun. This preternaturally beautiful daughter of the Yiddish stage, still beautiful, beautiful with the same face every twenty years, was above all a presence, always on stage even when driving with the top down and the wind in her face, but driving in long foxy gray suède gloves that reached up her arms. It was all so giddy, light shining bright, a holiday ride in the canyons around Hollywood, with Stella's lacquered lipstick a brilliant gash in the middle of the Hollywood desert, that I renounced my memory of this boxed confection of a woman as the dumpy nagging Bronx housewife Bessie in Odets's *Awake and Sing* whom I had watched with awe at how oppressive a Bessie could be. Times had changed, life had changed, and more than as a change of venue. Stella's kindly modest husband Harold Clurman drove me five blocks to Musso and Frank's restaurant. You assured your status as A Figure in the Industry by arriving at the door of the restaurant in a car. Clurman was wearing a very special tie. As a director in Hollywood, he could not afford to be seen in a tie that signified anything less than "very expensive."

Even to drop into Hollywood from the Huntington

was to find myself swimming in a blue golden haze. But coming back, the loneliness was enough to make me dizzy. I reeled along the perpetually sun-bright streets dripping with sprinkler drops. The railroad tracks still passed through the town. California was brand-new, sunny, dusty. Despite the treasures of Eng. Lit. in the Huntington vaults, despite Huxley, Heifetz, Isherwood, Thomas Mann, despite the brain-damaged giant Otto Klemperer stumbling to the stage of the Hollywood Bowl to conduct the *Eroica*, it was all raw. My heart was raw. The only energy in my life came from the mind of William Blake, the perpetual reaching sweep of his illuminated and heaven-colored penmanship across the golden pages of *The Marriage of Heaven and Hell* and *The Book of Thel*.

I sat up all night in the train to San Francisco, walked up streets and down streets, made several turns around the Union League Club and the Fairmount Hotel. The town was wild with sailors chasing each other down Market Street, yelling themselves hoarse at the burlesque show. There was not a room in town to be had except in a flophouse across from City Hall. All night long I could hear bottles breaking on the stairs. In the train back to Los Angeles I was surrounded by sailors just in from the worst island fighting, showing each other Japanese swords and handfuls of Japanese teeth.

By the middle of September, I was in a train crawling around the Blue Ridge in western North Carolina. After running so long, I came to rest at Black Mountain College, where I succeeded Eric Bentley for a term. Black Mountain was an "experimental" college, just then almost without faculty and with few enough students. As the sweetly smiling Rector said before being brutally thrown out of the state for sitting too close to a Marine in a parked car, "Here we are concerned with the whole person." Black Mountain was more a "community" than a college. At the moment, it was almost anything more than it was a college, and "the whole person" did not always include the mind.

Black Mountain had been a brave intellectual venture when it had been founded in the 1930s by a rebel classical scholar, John Andrew Rice, who led a migration of other rebel scholars from fashionable Rollins College in Florida to an old YMCA hall bordering a lake in the Great Smoky Mountains. After the war, Black Mountain was to reach its highest fame and usefulness through its association with the poets Charles Olson and Robert Creeley, with Buckminster Fuller, John Cage, Merce Cunningham. In September, 1944, it had just lost that English gadfly of every academic establishment, Eric Bentley. It still boasted the Bauhaus painter and master teacher Josef Albers, the Czech conductor Heinrich Jalowetz, the German psychiatrist Erwin Strauss, the musicologist Edward Lowinsky.

These gifted refugees, some of them looking pitifully lost in the wilds of western North Carolina, were highly paternal types, masters in their fields, born to teach and with much to teach. Since many of the students seemed to be waifs, psychic and intellectual orphans, children of agitated professional families in agitated New York, Cambridge, and Chicago, the great communitarian task of learning went on all day at every meal, which the faculty helped to serve, and along every furrow of the college farm, which we were supposed to work between classes. The great man on the place was Josef Albers, who taught drawing to people who had never been known to look attentively at anything. The psychiatrist Strauss had managed to transport all the way from Munich to the Great Smoky Mountains a ponderous

German armoire and the aloof pedantries of his non-Freudian, phenomenological psychiatry.

I gave one seminar in Blake, one entirely in *Moby-Dick*, discovered that many students had never heard of Jonah, and so added a course in Old Testament characters and their metamorphoses in literature. There were so many lost sons and daughters at Black Mountain that I soon became another father-teacher always on call. Those first October days, walking back and forth between my room and my classroom-office in the beautifully light Studies Building, put up by faculty and students together, I was hypnotized by the lake on which the college was perched, the great mountains on the Carolina-Tennessee border that indeed *looked* the oldest mountains in North America. I felt myself drawing infinite draughts of mountain air, sliding into a stark purity of uninterrupted landscape.

I had never before been close to every fresh convolution of water and sky. Every morning at daybreak, walking along the lake to breakfast, I knew I was walking into winter. I could see the grass getting paler, the first spindles of frost, the stony hill at my back looking colder and stonier. Then a day of full even rain, in the middle of which I walked a red clay bog back and forth from meals to classroom. When the rain died down at twilight, I could see the mists lifting slowly from the mountains; there were huge clouds of mist shooting upward from invisible burners. I saw great black horses, let out of the stables up the road, cantering madly around the fields. Just beyond the college were barns and workshops that were still nineteenth-century provincial America—log cabin, oxen, water wheel, plow, farmers in Huck Finn straw hats. Then, wandering up a hillside one free day, I stumbled on a chain gang. The picture was complete—striped prison uniforms, legchains rattling with every blow of the ax dislodging the shale slabs, armed guards, the frightening hound howling at the stranger.

The sweetly smiling Rector was a native of the state who was trying (unsuccessfully) to get one Negro admitted to Black Mountain without seeing the place burned down in reprisal. He remembered an uncle coming back from a lynching and throwing across the table a finger he had cut off from the body. Black Mountain was surrounded by fiercest suspicion. But there were many visitors to this Utopia—artists from New York like Robert Motherwell, conscientious objectors on their way to and from the mental hospitals they served in as orderlies, vagrant idealists a decade before hippiedom who flopped on the college steps and wanted to live with us Thoreau's "life of the spirit." Lyonel Feininger, a native New Yorker who had worked in Germany until Hitler, was there one week to visit old friends from the Bauhaus. I had always loved Feininger's delicate geometry of skyscrapers and sailing ships. He turned the towers of Manhattan into a translucent city of the eye, aspiring forms in a harmony of abstractions. Like Josef Albers's "Growing," these figures never stayed put. Feininger was a quiet, slight figure in his seventies, full of the eager teaching spirit that was the rule of life at Black Mountain. He delighted me, as another fiddler for whom the height of our creaky art was the unaccompanied Bach partitas, by admitting that practicing those subtly shifting chords every morning opened up a new picture in his mind. The great solitary dances that were the Bach partitas were mysteriously satisfying figures, infinite interweavings. The mind was enchanted by the logic of perfect harmony.

Inside the college, there were constant wails of dissatisfaction from the highly charged, over-responsive students. I lived with the daily comedy, myself plus the German-mind-in-exile trying to insert a little "background" into furiously doubting American students who believed that education was all, the same education related to everything, education should go on all the time, there was nothing about a good human being that was not educable. But teachers had to do all the teaching. At Black Mountain, where there were few male students, virtually no resources, it was not always quaint to wait on your students at table, to draw fifteen dollars a month in addition to room and board. The demands of the students for constant enlightenment, information, moral sustenance, and total friendship could be frightening. The place was essentially a village with more respect for self-government than for learning, but a village cut off from North Carolina, cut off even from the Veterans' Hospital down the road, yet constantly open to every American lonely. The involvement of people with each other was feverish and distrustful. Everything was expected of a teacher. A student had exhausted his independence by coming to Black Mountain. He/she was expected to put up college buildings, to work in the fields, to "see" cleanly in the Bauhaus fashion, to respond with proper appreciation to "Batti batti" from *Don Giovanni* or the patterns in the weaving workshop, but never to discover a book or an idea by himself. Conduct required only a staunchly cooperative character. The sweetly smiling Rector used to say, "A *good* member of the community is one who works out a *good* relationship with the people in it. We are concerned with the *whole* person."

One small, driven, life-hungry girl from a small town on the Gulf Coast, embittered as she was gifted, was intoxicated by the possibilities she suddenly saw open to her as a writer. But her own intensity angered her, she

was so much alone with it. Other people would never
do right by her. She would sit in my office, glaring with
what she angrily called "my stupid foolish love for you,
you New York beast!" crouched to spring whenever I
seemed more than usually distracted. She would kick at
my door, then beat at my chest with tiny fists and denounce me for not devoting myself to her. Her attack
would at least *start* as a comic act that was meant to
show her as a "poor Florida cracker" downtrodden by
the merciless writer from New York. It would quickly
collapse into a high whining bitterness with the sound
and feel of a dentist's drill. "You *intellectual!* You
critic! You can write only about *other* people's books!"
Thin and hungry-looking, she looked as if her daily
rages were consuming her. "Isn't there enough of *me*
for *you* to love?"

There was an extreme demand for love at Black
Mountain. "A loving approach" was demanded. No
teacher living side by side with so many damaged souls
and hungry minds could satisfy it. Utopia pushed people into ecstasies of self-confrontation. We were all
marked out—by the hill people, who distrusted us, and
by ourselves for having selected ourselves for Utopia.
Utopias always end as stories; anyone who was ever at
Black Mountain would remember everything about it—
and about himself there. In that strange clearing amid
the Great Smoky Mountains, everyone's character and
history were magnified. The real question on which
everything turned was the sense of personal fate that
had led each of us to this queer assemblage. One German exile took out his feeling of persecution by relentlessly reading in everyone's handwriting "the pronounced American character weakness." The castoffs
among the students had a feverish sense of themselves,
a loneliness they studied as if they were the solar system.

Private terror was never so public anywhere else. Margaret had seen her mother jump out of a window, and had never grown an inch since. She was an elegant, funny, irresistibly poignant girl who would talk about herself, sitting in the watery autumn sunshine outside the Studies Building, both as a scientific problem and as a cosmic joke that had somehow been concentrated on her. In typical Black Mountain fashion she came to look on the texts in our seminar as therapy, a religion more providential than any religion.

Literature was nothing but wisdom literature even for my best students. At the very moment in the middle 1940s that saw the New Criticism become an academic game, every little copycat of Blackmur Tate Ransom "explicating" everything about a poem's language except what he thought of it himself, my boys and girls fastened on the most wooden lines as a guide to personal salvation. Margaret was already marked out, even at Black Mountain, by her tininess and her somnambulism. Watching her eyes widen with rapture, a crazy hope that no teacher would ever sustain, I knew that this teacher would pay for not being up to the genius he regularly praised in class. To teach at Black Mountain was to fail one's students by day and by night. There was no way even of knowing all the expectations one had aroused.

Meanwhile, out in neighboring Asheville, Thomas Wolfe's mother and sister were still in residence at the "Old Kentucky Home" on Spruce Street. I walked up to the house with an introduction from Hamilton Basso, but in their rocking chairs on the porch the Wolfes, avid for attention and expecting to be recognized, looked so flinty, leathery, and suspicious of Wolfe's many admirers already collected on the front steps that I backed off.

Wolfe's overwrought letters to "Mama" had been published the year before. The self-centered bombast ("By God, I have genius—and I shall force the inescapable fact down the throats of rats & vermin who wait the proof") was easier to understand in Asheville than it had been in New York.

There was a folk festival at the civic auditorium—it had been going on half the week—and a few of us went down to see it. Asheville was the mountain resort, the gate to the Great Smokies, the tourist and health-resort center built up by a Vanderbilt. It was full of people seeking relics of Thomas Wolfe, and seeing Mama and Sister sitting expectantly on the porch, I imagined Wolfe crying out, as he so often did in life, "Mama! For God's sake—Mama!" They were making a movie of Tom Wolfe's life—they were making a movie of *Look Homeward, Angel*—and Asheville was excited. The home town had been hysterical when the novel appeared in 1929. But collecting relics of the true sufferings and life of Thomas Wolfe had before his death in 1938 become a minor industry in the town; even Army officers stationed around Asheville collected them.

On this Saturday night Asheville filled up with soldiers and millworkers from Swannanoa and the movies let out before midnight, the men slouched in crowds in front of the leaky neon lights pouring out of the shops that featured Virginia Dare wine. There was the smell of banned whiskey among the pop bottles in the windows. The soldiers doubled up on benches in the bus station to kill time before the last bus went back to neighboring camps and the general hospital.

The folk festival was a great success, and running high that Saturday night, the last. The M.C. was a fat and boisterous little man in a white suit who never

stopped laughing and gave the impression that he was
escaping office and family. The sponsors of the show
had called out all the square-dance teams, Virginia
reelers, infant prodigies, and strumming bands from
half the valleys of Buncombe County and eastern
Tennessee, and the show had been going on for seven
hours or more in an unending din, punctured, like the
orgiastic groans of flamenco records, by the twang and
drone of guitars. Yet it was an excitement in which the
audience did not share. Once they propped up a seven-
year-old boy in a sailor suit who whined "God Bless
America" into the microphone and then "Dixie." Each
time he broke down, the audience encouraged him with
the Rebel yell. Otherwise two thousand decently
dressed people sat on with polite apathy as all evening
long fresh teams of square-dancers clattered past each
other onto the pine boards that had been built over the
first rows in the orchestra. Once the program was interrupted when the M.C., in a tone of even bigger excitement, called out that a lady from New York—from
New York City!—had come down all the way just for
this evening: to see folk. She stood up for a bow and
was briefly applauded; then the show turned into a near
jive fest. The old square dance had always had easy
ways, and its looping checkerboard matings allowed
many inner variations. But the farmers and millworkers
who made up square-dance teams and bands in Asheville had to outdo one another to rouse the tourists. The
hoopla that night lay all in the violent bidding for ap-
plause: in the bends and beat-me-daddy rhythms, which,
as any city fool could see, slyly crossed the old mountain
figures with a familiar Broadway twist. Amid the clat-
ters and screams, a couple of girls lost their shoes.

Once in the evening there came on an unexpected and
steely dance that brought to mind all the lone dignity

and inner fervor I had associated with mountain dances. It began as if it were an intrusion. A lean, middle-aged man, with the seamed face of an old carpenter and drooping black mustaches, stepped out on stage and almost shyly began a solitary jig in a far corner. Then another man came out, following tentatively after the first, and at the other end of the stage reproduced and mimicked the steps of the first. Somehow his stiff middle-class costume—dark city suit, high collar, and flashing watch chain around his middle—gave a personal accent of stepping into sudden freedom. Now another came out, and still another; old men and young boys, some in sweaters and some in shirt sleeves and suspenders; a man who might have been a high school principal, and bobbin boys from the mills.

The only link between them was the affectionate parody each performed on the other, and the weaving circle in the center of which suddenly appeared a little old woman in a shabby brown coat with a fur collar and a feather darting from her Queen Mary hat. She was bobbing away faster than any of them and laughing immensely to herself. It was a wonderful dance, I thought, most wonderful in that the men looked as if they were dancing *to* each other, while yet remaining stiff and even proudly aroused in their separate corners. The boards rang, the audience looked happy, and watching these "mountain folk" shaking off the mills and offices this gala Saturday night in Asheville, I thought with longing of the Russian-Jewish wedding dances of my childhood, when the knot had been tied, the bridal cup trodden under foot, and amidst the cries of *Mazel tov! Happy Days! Good Luck!* my tipsy and work-scarred uncles would leap out under the bridal canopy and break into those brotherly steps just before the women danced around them.

Convoy

One airplane, held by wire struts, bestrode the deck. You had to walk around the plane, under it, despite it. There it stood, its wings straining toward freedom, about to take off and so escape this tub that was to crawl inch by inch over the devouring Atlantic. The S.S. *Hart Crane* was a floating pickup truck, grim and garbagy except for the guns tended by regular Navy gunners. I was packed into the ship's tiny "hospital"—the only cabin for passengers—with three other men, sleeping in two double-deckers. A shaky column of bedpans for the Army Medical Corps, fitted hole to hole, was lined up in one corner, threatening to come down on us as the North Atlantic gales began to howl.

In that tiny hospital I spent fifteen days, sleeping most nights in my life preserver. Pipes snaked all around the ceilings and on every side of my bed. The insides of the ship had collected in that tiny airless cabin. The machinery under my feet never stopped slowly, sleepily pounding; the sound was always in my legs. Finally you wanted to spring away from it, but it crept over you like the smell of pea soup leaking from the galley. Your body became the body of the ship, and every jarring pushing pounding cold winter wind, every bucket of winter-Atlantic iron-gray water slapping against the sides sooner or later fell smack against your face.

There was a constant rumor of impending submarine attack; the crew was very nervous. Coming out of the ship's book locker, I let the heavy metal door slam, which brought out from his bunk with a scream the first mate (usually the calmest man on board), who had been torpedoed and had spent eight days in an open boat on the Pacific before being rescued.

The whirring of machinery, the constant pounding of

metal on metal never stopped. The tension started with Captain Fairbairn, who *looked* nervous the first day out, chain-smoking as he paced the deck and snapped at the crew. The first morning, the weather was calm, but soon it began to rain and snow as we went up the New England coast heading for Halifax and the rest of our convoy. Two days out, we were already fifty-three vessels in slow stately parade on the North Atlantic, plus an escort from the Canadian Navy. The S.S. *Emily Dickinson* was just ahead of us. We looked like such sitting ducks, spread out on the cold choppy ocean, that I couldn't understand how we went on, day after day, still unmolested. The long, bobbing, frighteningly slow lines of vessels in convoy looked to me like elephants massively following each other around a circus ring. How could they take their time like this? Hurry up! Hurry up, please, it's time! Time hung over the scattered debris of fifteen long days and nights in maddening delay. For safety's sake, the ships had to keep rigorously together and in line. But at sunset the sight of us spread over the ocean (with an occasional Canadian corvette running up and down like a barking sheepdog) looked piteous to me. The ships seemed more isolated at sunset. They looked easier to pick out when the last flecks from the great winter reds surrounded each ship in its bath of cold gray Atlantic water. As night fell, the ships *were* in danger of collapsing. One of the few real crises of the voyage came in a bad storm the fourth day out. Two ships collided that night, and one had to leave the convoy and make its lone way back to the nearest port.

There were endless rumors of U-boats from crew members who nevertheless seemed perfectly confident, and who never stopped eating even when they came up to you with the latest positively secret rumor that the

Dutch commodore in charge of the convoy had radioed our captain to keep a special lookout that night. After the storm, we were at last in our row; only the hospital ship trailed us.

The rumors were so mixed in with personal reminiscences of other voyages, even the voyages of other people, that it was necessary to pick your way through the stream of talk that circulated around you day and night like the ocean itself. There was no solitude on the S.S. *Hart Crane*. It was small, dense with airplane parts and medical stores, and everybody was an American who had seen the world and had much to say about everything in it. Even when I was in my bunk strapped into my life belt and trying to get on with Prescott's *The Conquest of Mexico*, I would have to listen to the Franciscan friar from Staten Island on his way to England to replace another friar. The friar was a hearty, stocky bald Friar Tuck, with great thick glasses, who chain-smoked, liked a snifter now and then, and, giggling, told dirty stories. When he lay in his bunk reading his breviary, his enormous belly rose up before him like a fence. When he was not reading his breviary, his mouth never stopped gurgling, emitting smoke, and giggling over the poor little monastic turds of what he called "my naughty stories." You could tell he was between monasteries. He would soon be shut up again, but meanwhile offered helpings out of the fine store of rye in his suitcase and would suddenly sit up in bed to chirp, "Hey, fellas, d'ja ever hear anything like this?"

In the bunk above me was the Reverend Dimmesdale, a Baptist minister from Georgia, going to France to resume Baptist missionary work among the Latin heathen. Someone with a sense of humor had planted next to a Jew, for fifteen long days and nights, two such incongruous servants of Jesus Christ. Although both had a lot to say to me—the fourth passenger, a young electronics specialist on his way to hush-hush work in England, said no more after he had announced this much, and promptly went to sleep—I noticed that the two men of God discreetly avoided conversation with each other. I could hear the Reverend Dimmesdale conjugating French verbs to himself. He was a steely-faced little man, totally devoid of personal ease in regard to any religious question. Once, hearing a member of the crew defiantly describe himself at mealtime as a "convinced atheist," he took the man by the shoulders, pushed him to the always closed, locked, barred porthole, and, pinpointing in the uncertain direction of the sky, dramatically demanded, "Who could have made all this if not a sovereign God?"

The weather seemed to change from hour to hour. Rather than go sick again in the airless cabin below, where the bedpans clanged on each other every time the *Hart Crane* stumbled forcibly in the water, I shivered on deck. There I had the distinct sensation that the world and I were entirely new, raw, open to the inhuman Atlantic. I felt numb, a glazed surface for every fresh experience to stick to me.

There was no ease on deck, crammed as it was with the airplane, the Navy guns fore and aft, the lifeboats jutting over the bulkhead. But I kept pacing in rain and sleet, sometimes standing watch with crew members just to get away from the iron lung below in which the four of us pitched from side to side to the groaning and creaking of the woodwork.

As a mere civilian, new to the perils and glories of the merchant marine, I listened a lot, I had to listen. The war was the great rich war that gave every man there his great big experience of life. The merchant marine was proud of being smarter than the dumb draftees

in the Army. There was big money to be made at sea—
"only right, when you consider the danger." An hour or
two after the evening meal, the steward's mate laid the
tables again, and the men went about devouring enormous piles of salami and cheese and hard-boiled eggs.
Sometimes they would rub their bellies as they ate to
show how lucky they were not to be in the goddamned
fucking Army, full of jerks just waiting to get themselves
killed.

The crew was jittery, but distinctly not overworked. I
was not the only one with too much time on his hands.
On the third day out, still somewhere off Cape Cod,
blues growling in from a Boston radio station, I saw us
surrounded by the fully formed convoy. Anywhere I
looked there was an unsteady line-up of ships. At this
moment Pick, the third mate, stopped to tell me that he
had "a feeling" the war was over, but that he was absolutely sure enemy submarines still on the prowl were
all around us. Looking at me, a captive forced for more
than two weeks to hear out every one of his manias, he
funneled at me in one mad stream his explanation of
who was behind U.S. society and behind the war. He
was an unstoppable opinionator, savagely in control of
anyone he collared for a little talk. Totally self-educated
and determined to educate everyone else, this large,
swarthy, pockmarked man with angry yellow hair
rolled about the ship in his sweater like a barrel that had
come loose and would run you down if you challenged
his crazy rightness on the smallest point. He had worked
on a houseboat in Florida, as a doorman in Queens, as
an accordionist in a nightclub. He explained that Jews
cannot stand rainy weather; it makes them nostalgic for Palestine. He explained that "colored" are more

liable to tuberculosis because their nostrils are narrower, thus depriving them of sufficient air. Since he was in command of lifeboat 4, which was mine if we abandoned ship, I saw myself having to listen to him forever, surrounded by the unstoppable leak of his knowledge as I looked vainly for help on the cold and clammy Atlantic.

Pick was a monster too large for the S.S. *Hart Crane*. He had too much time on his hands, too many meals to eat, too much empty space to fill with his great discovery. Americans were just puppets pulled by invisible strings. "You get the picture, of course." He put a great smear of butter on every slice of bread and every potato before attacking his meat, and loudly ordered seconds and thirds just to show that he was getting the best of life. More than any of the others, who briefly flashed on deck and in the ship's mess, and were framed in my mind as bent against the wind and water slapping at them, Pick was always on stage. The crew rushed up and down ladders, ran up signals, loudly clanked hammers at rusting machinery, yelled every mealtime at the dirt-encrusted steward's mate. In the winter murk on deck I seemed to see figure after figure as a distortion, endlessly chipping sea crust off a wheel in the midst of this suspended helplessness.

In Prescott's *Conquest of Mexico* and in the Sherlock Holmes stories I compulsively reread in my bunk as the woodwork groaned, the leading figures were whole, clear in outline, altogether there for me. Even when defeated, like the Montezuma "who felt himself rebuked by the Superior genius of his foes," they were old-fashioned persons, people as you remembered them from childhood. In Conan Doyle there was just one crime at a time, and everything else was suspended, all

England held its breath, until the Great Brain, outwardly asleep like Buddha in his total concentration on this one case, came through with a solution satisfying and *lovable*.

By contrast, the harried bundled figures rushing around me for fifteen days in downpour and wind were cutouts. But they imparted information all the time. The purser was so bored that I never saw him when he was not completing a yawn. The Army technical sergeant, security officer over the cargo, got up in the morning cursing the fucking Limeys, progressed by lunch to the fucking Russian Commies, by evening was on to that fucking Roosevelt and his whole fucking family. He never smiled, was red with anger when anyone laughed, and drummed his fingers against the pistol in his holster as he spat *fuck fuck fuck fuck*.

By the fifth day the air is bad in our cabin. The wind is howling louder and the uneasy stack of bedpans in the corner keeps falling down; there is no room to walk around. No smoking on deck after sundown. A thick black curtain between the passageway and the deck. The portholes in our room are locked solid. Mildly nauseated, belly aching, I lie propped up fore and aft in my life preserver, at rest only in the privacy of my bunk. Friar Tuck sits up in his, for some reason moved in the midst of seasickness to tell what he calls his "wicked" stories. The Reverend Dimmesdale climbs out of his berth, moves reproachfully around the Friar's high clerical tenor, then smiles to be polite. Everybody bored and jumpy by turns. I go out on deck for air. We are off the Grand Banks.

The next day I spend on the bridge, watching signals change. A Catalina patrol plane is briefly in sight. I stand part of his watch with young Ensign Fairlie, in charge of the gun crew that travels every merchant vessel. He was a math teacher in a Catskill high school, his first job, and is still so fresh-looking that he positively blushes when he recites, as if from his order book, "I take over if submarines attack." Several of the crew have traveled with him before, and tease him because he won't go near a girl when they touch port. He explains to me very solemnly, again as if reading instructions from the Navy, that he believes in fidelity to his wife. "It's lonely on a ship," he says between clenched teeth.

No joke standing watch four hours at a time in this intense cold, and Ensign Fairlie is also more solitary than the others, enclosed in this sheath of a small-town math teacher and newly married. He is a natural patriot, and so says nothing about the war. To the others it is always the "fucking" war, the "crapola" war, this "shitty" war. They are virtuosos of bitterness. Not a thing in their lives is right. Yet there is not one who does not feel that he is lifted above the rest of humanity by being an American. The power of America is their rock and their refuge. It is impossible for them to imagine the United States defeated.

New convoy joined us this afternoon. Cold steadily increasing all day. Dry, thin snow around six. Sky and water together a wet murk saying, "Get lost!" Or does it say, "*You* are lost"? Feeling like a rusty piece of machinery, left in the rain, I pop my head inside to discover that in their cabin off the saloon deck the gun crew are playing some mild slow jazz, have a spare fiddle for me. Over one bed, along with the daily schedules, someone has drawn a triangle with a heart at each corner.

One Navy gunner, a former AFL organizer, is arguing with another, who keeps saying, "Yeah? Oh, yeah? You mean yeah?"

Day after day of high winds, sea tossing us up and down without letup, but brilliant green in color. Long days of torpor, nausea, reading myself asleep over reassuring Sherlock Holmes. Decks flood in evening. In the morning, we discover a fair amount of damage from yesterday's storm. One ship in our convoy drifting about in distress. Sea soot black again. Boat number 4—*my* boat!—battered useless by last night's storm. Anyway, I won't have to be shipwrecked with the third mate. Ships in our part of the convoy "dangerously out of position." Our ship last. Only the hospital ship trails us.

First week ends today. Sea calmer; light rain. Warm. Entering the Gulf Stream. The brilliant blue-green water the other day was part of the Newfoundland Banks. Men rarely ship out twice on the same ship, remain strangers to each other the whole voyage through. A knifing reported on the S.S. *Emily Dickinson*, in line just ahead of us. Terrible to rock back and forth on this tub, day after day without letup, and then to look up and see a plane cooly winging its way to Europe a week and more ahead of us!

Quarter-moon and fog in the evening. Talked with the Navy gunners on watch and stared in disbelief at the moonlit waters of the Gulf Stream. In the bright phosphorescent triangle off starboard, the outlines of other ships in the convoy looked like the overgrown banks of the Mississippi. Before the curious mirage I seemed to be looking up and down the great river, with a hint of land just outside the bright roadstead of moonlight.

In the Gulf Stream now: warm, soggy weather. Hard to sleep, the unexpected warmth makes me itch to get this journey over with. But it is Sunday, the Reverend Dimmesdale held informal service in the dining saloon and managed to get most of us—minus, of course, Friar Tuck. The Reverend, all excited, sang us a strong sermon on the need of a purer Americanism out of more faith. After service, the young electronics man in our cabin promptly went back to sleep, waking at intervals to eat candy and to roar at another hot one from Friar Tuck. In the day, the Friar is the heartiest man among men; in the evening, he lies in his berth, under the poisonously hot lamp, reading his breviary to himself. As we were finishing supper the chief steward, Roux, of French-Canadian descent, suddenly erupted on the subject of the fucking Britist Empire. By God and by God, he yelled, that we Americans should have to bail out the fucking Limeys! He was in a convoy to Murmansk, and saw ships sink all around him, burning under the northern lights. More and more difficult to sleep, the four of us tossing and pitching in our bunks.

At ten the next morning a Canadian escort corvette rushed past us, a black signal flag at its mast. Submarines in the vicinity. Then total silence. I lay down for a minute. First depth charge: I was thrown out of the berth and ran up to the bridge. Second depth charge: the ship shook. A long wailing of ship sirens. Nobody knows anything. Then silence.

Twelfth day. Navy crew had gun practice.

Thirteenth day. Approaching St. George's Channel between Ireland and Wales, the convoy split in two, one part turning for the Channel ports; us for Liverpool. This is just where the *Lusitania* went down. More depth charges this morning. It was explained to me that the U-boats now concentrate on St. George's Channel. The Germans like to fire torpedoes at dusk, so that in the half-light there will be maximum confusion. Depth charges now every hour. Silence. As the sun went down, it took the whole prism with it into the sea; I was awed by the redness of the sky. Friar Tuck getting more and more subdued. Talked to us a little, when we were all lying awake in the dark, about a monk's life. Said he expected never to come home. Above me, the Reverend Dimmesdale practicing French verbs out loud. Asked me again today if I didn't believe in God. Who made all this, he said, if not the one and living God? Discovered that he wears a corset.

Fourteenth day. Lighthouses winking off the Welsh coast. Men boisterously relaxed, making plans for their first night out in Liverpool. Hard to sleep.

Fifteenth day. Could not sleep, so anxious to see England. Got out of my berth at four when I heard the engines stop in the River Mersey. Pitch-black in the channel, but on all sides of us great rows of lamps, a corolla of lights over black water my first sight of Europe. Waited till daybreak to get off. Birkenhead, across the Mersey, emerged on its hill. When I went down to breakfast, a young English pilot was already there, shoveling in bacon and eggs with joy on his face.

Chapter V

ENGLAND: THE LAST BATTLE

By five in the morning we were cleared and I was walking around Liverpool. Drab scrawls along the docks read "HANDS OFF GREECE." The docks were a maze of ships, cranes, muddy interior waterways, sudden yawning bomb holes that made me see Liverpool as the interior of the human body. I kept thinking of Melville arriving in Liverpool just a century before. I was dreaming it all, I could not possibly be walking English streets. But the grimness was what Melville had seen, and I stopped dreaming. "Poverty, poverty, poverty, in almost endless vistas; and want and woe staggered in arms along these miserable streets."

In a cafeteria, a frayed tired-looking priest with a sharp nose and a very thin face was finishing up his breakfast with beans. Gathering a few leftover beans on his knife, he daintily lifted it to his mouth and ate off it one bean at a time and then another with such deliberation that he seemed to be eating in slow motion. It took me a minute to realize that he was soused. Outside, the grand stony cupolas of the Victoria Board of Trade overlooked a city gashed, broken, and boarded up. The fatigue around you was like another layer of air in which you walked. Yet the spindly-looking girls in the shops, some of them still wearing head scarves and wrap-around housedresses, looking as if they had just come in from the shelter or were expecting to run back at any moment, had a birdlike cheeping courtesy that astonished me. Their measured voices kept going up and up. Cahn-I-help-you? Cahn-I-help-*you*?

In the train to London that afternoon I sat across from a brassy fashion buyer who traveled constantly between London and Liverpool. She seized clawlike at the American clothes, the American accent. She wanted to know if "your Negroes do not pay a smaller income tax in the States," they being so steadily oppressed by the likes of me and other white Americans? She was my first hint of the English obsession with America, and introduced me to the public English way of putting questions that were meant to provoke. Stubby fields and ancient farmhouses with thatched roofs glided past the train windows. In the dining car the hot gleaming teapots and scuffed glassy cups steadily sent back reflections of the fields of England while questions were regularly sent up at me. You Americans. Your America. Americans, Americans. The yawning gulf between *us* and *you*.

I had just arrived from another planet. After almost six years of war, a large part of which had been mounted against the people I was walking among, London was grimy in its daily militancy and wore the look of an old garment that had been poorly patched in many places. Everything at first glance wore the look of an emergency in which the whole population shared. Off Pall Mall the equestrian statue of Edward VII was surrounded by large wooden sheds marked "GAS CONTAMINATED MEN," "GAS CONTAMINATED WOMEN." At the entrances to the underground were sandbags and brick shields to deaden the effect of explosives. A lot of barbed wire to repel the invasion had been left over from 1940, as were the torn flapping posters that showed a friendly Bobby and the inscription "GET YOUR CHILD OUT OF LONDON" and the oddly pink and orange splotches on the walls of a bombed house that kept only a staircase, a child's play wagon, and pipes dangling in space.

"LET US GO FORWARD TOGETHER," said Churchill, scowling with firmly fixed jaw on the posters in the underground. People seemed to be on the move all day long, carrying briefcases from which a long French loaf stuck out at each end, attaché cases, knapsacks. People suddenly flopped down on the steps of ghostly white buildings in Whitehall, opened an attaché case to eat a sandwich in the street with enormous British circumspection, delicately wiped their fingers on a handkerchief, and trotted off again.

I lived in American billets just off Marble Arch underground station. Five feet away from the trains, sleeping on blankets or coats on the ground, many people were already early in the evening bedded down for the night. The luckier ones occupied three-tier iron bunks leaning against the station walls. Four and a half million houses were damaged or destroyed before the bombings ended: thousands of people slept every night in the subway stations of the West End. The authorities had tried to keep them out, but there they were, sleeping inside the round shell made by the thick deep-laid walls of the London underground and under hot round lamps. Many subway sleepers lacked homes entirely; others actually left their homes in the late afternoon to eat their dinner and to sleep in the deep shelters of the London underground—mostly elderly people, with a sprinkling of children.

There was one little old lady with glasses down her nose whom I came to know very well. Night after night that first week, I used to see her in her top bunk, primly dressed, reading the *Church Times* by the lamp in the station roof high over her head. Her head twisted out of her bunk to catch the light; one earpiece of her old-fashioned wire-frame glasses dangled. Other people took sandwiches and flasks of tea out of the ever-present British knapsack and watched their children playing follow-the-leader along the edge of the subway platform.

The blackout had been eased, they said; it was still dark enough for me. Except for the heavily shaded traffic signals at key intersections and the gigantic figures of light shakily climbing up from the mounds of anti-aircraft guns in Hyde Park, the city those freezing winter nights seemed hooded and mysteriously still. The silence was immense. The loneliness was immense. I felt shut out. "English!" I wanted to shout. "Where the hell are you, English?" I talked in the shadowy deserted streets with an Irish volunteer with the British forces who had been given compassionate leave to visit his dying father in Dublin

> Those that I fight I do not hate,
>   Those that I guard I do not love;

with a German refugee who had been wounded fighting in a battalion made up entirely of refugees. They had been refused British naturalization, but, the ex-German reported in derision, "would officially be allowed to adopt British surnames."

The night silence—between vast hollow thumps of V-2s somewhere far off—was incredible for a great city. Black windows everywhere, miles of black windows; British privacy seemed complete. I felt the immense strength of the city as a secret. There was a humming, protective web. It was definitely not the vehement power you felt in New York, everyone tearing along the street, visibly walking against the sky with impatient steps. There was a belt around you. The shielding, deadening effect of the darkness was subtle, but you knew the city was secretly on guard. Somewhere many minds were thinking for you. They were there. Amid many genteel ruins you counted on them. Even on that island, in that broken city open to more bombs and burning, its crowded faces steeled for the worst, you felt oddly safe. By a hair's-breadth, not more, this island had kept itself afloat.

In Piccadilly Circus, GIs in masses were lined up to see Judy Garland in *Meet Me in St. Louis*, trod on each other's heels as they stumbled along the pleasure circuit, flicked their Zippo lighters to have a better look at the whores waiting in a great circle for the soldiers to come up to them. My own luck in the blackout was bad. In the feeble light showing the way to Laurence Olivier in *Henry V*, I could see that the lady was smoldering with anger and, as I guessed from her dead cold eyes, would not put herself out in the slightest. I fell down the steps into the movie, and suddenly recovered my sight. The Technicolor was dazzling; I was in the golden age. The "low" characters chattered like magpies, laughed fit to burst their wine skins over the sniggering details fit for the jabber jabber jabber of common soldiers. Olivier read Shakespeare's heroic verse in his high ringing tenor as if he skated up to the break in every line and then skated back again. Olivier was the king of that golden time when wars were fought only in brilliant sunshine and even the lowest peasant in the ranks could share in His Majesty:

> I see you stand like greyhounds in the slips
> Straining upon the start. The game's afoot:
> Follow your spirit; and, upon this charge
> Cry "God for Harry, England, and Saint George!"

London that first week, everything still so violently new, unexpected, threadbare. Myra Hess, in a fur coat, playing Schubert sonatas at lunchtime in the great hall of a National Gallery without any pictures. I lifted the telephone to give a number to the billets operator. There was a smash. "Oh, dear," said the operator. "My windows have just gone." Silence. I went into her cubbyhole and discovered she had fainted. The sedate bald old civil servants in Whitehall still arrived in wing collar and bowler; the statues in the Royal Academy rooms at Burlington House were chipped but in place; the view from the bridge in St. James's Park was of a perfect set of palaces. Everything was a shaking together of traditional England and wartime England—saber-mustached proud-looking Guardsmen on Sunday clanking along the Mall with their swords on their way to service; surprisingly rosy-looking children, properly fed for the first time in their lives, playing in the dull dead alleys between the warehouse jutting on the river.

The antique iron railings around the great squares had long since been removed; the squares were supposed to look more democratic without them. By spring, George Orwell was to complain in the left-wing *Tribune*, they were being restored *in wood*. Everywhere a layer of war lay between the city and its living past: smashed churches and boarded-up store windows; splintered statues of bewigged judges and ancient public men looking a rape of the past; the clinking glassy white service dishes so much favored by the English in canteens and restaurants, usually rimmed with dirt;

planes continually overhead on their way to and from Germany; storage tanks of water at the corners and little electric arrows showing the way to "SHELTER"; the rows and rows of pale Regency houses, double columns facing each other before every door, invariably taken over by the officers and men I was to see week after week sitting behind desks in battle dress.

Those first freezing weeks, often waking up in the middle of the night to the hollow boom of a rocket landing its one-ton warhead somewhere in London, I went about collecting my material on the popular education movement among British soldiers and workers, with that everlasting cold damp on my skin and the sweet smell of soft coal spurting into the air from all the chimneys in London. Cold and rain, cold like an eel slithering in your clothes. I was cold all the way and all the time. I could see the English in their horrible basement dining rooms huddled around the grate at the far end of the room—a whole tribe in the cold Anglo-Saxon weald huddled around the fire, all hands clutching the lifesaving cup of tea. Fumes of coal dust hung on the icy London rain. Under the itchy long woolen underwear from Macy's with which I had armed myself cap-a-pie for the wars, the sweater and the heavy black waterproof bulging with the thick flashlight I carried in the blackout, I walked those first days in London gasping under the sweet gassy coal smell hanging in a bilious low sky, from time to time taking refuge in one of the snack bars over the omnipresent cracked white cup of tea.

The billets in Great Cumberland Place provided for visiting Americans were the splintered, partitioned remains of what must once have been a great town house. The houses around it were most intact, though they were soon, in one morning, to lose all their windows.

Looking away from Marble Arch and Oxford Street, the view toward Bryanston Square was tranquil, still private, sweetly old. I went to bed every night in a great bleak shell of a room, crudely whitewashed, empty except for a few army cots. The house gave off the steady suggestion that a great mailed fist had somehow gone through it and that the house had slowly shifted within itself to this blow. Little rooms had all been cut out of big rooms, were divided by cardboard partitions in which archways had been cut to lead to other rooms. The once-splendid hall had a tessellated floor in white and black that was streaked with plaster. Open wiring flew in all directions.

The manageress, Mrs. Armitage, was a brisk marvelously fresh-colored Virginia redhead married to an English officer home on compassionate leave to save the family business; her view of the "condition-of-England question" was somewhat to the right of Mr. Gradgrind's. Despite her professional heartiness, she was astonished by my interest in the opinions of "upstarts" and "the great unwashed." Dolts from the Ministry of Works had let an open sack of plaster dribble all over the once-beautiful black-and-white floor. It was only the appearance of an occasional transport officer, arriving with car and bright-cheeked chauffeur from the Woman's Army Auxiliary Corps to escort me to some camp outside of London for a "look-see," that gave her any respect for what I was doing.

The evacuation of so many women and children from the slums—the East End was a favorite target of the Luftwaffe—exposed the poor and the middle class to each other as nothing in British history had ever done. "This war took the cover off." To think that it needed a Nazi bomb to show the English to each other! The "better sort" discovered to their horror that children scratched with head lice, had skin diseases, wet their beds, shit on the floor, that their shoes lacked soles. Many fine houses in London stood empty while homeless thousands sought a night's refuge in the subways. But in country towns and villages forced to accept "hordes" from London—for an interval—there was revealed an extent of human damage that shocked the reluctant hosts as much as the dirt and proliferating skin diseases outraged them.

On a tour with O.W.I. personnel of the worst-hit parts of London, the chauffeur didn't want to stop in Whitechapel. There wasn't much to see there, only "lower-class dwellings." The bombing of the East End was savage and terrible. In one section not blitzed, the street was lined on both sides with alley houses so dark, small, and leveled together in a brown anonymous mass that I almost wept on seeing the street itself half filled, every ten yards, with shelters that took up whatever space was left. Tyne Place East—a dirtier, grimier East Side all thrown together by the bombings. The street corners scooped out by the bombing now held storage tanks of water. The houseless streets made a dead heap. Yet Liverpool Street Station was murkily beautiful in the late afternoon with its old glass roof half destroyed. The light fiercely reflected the hurrying crowds, the tea wagons, the dirt.

England had never recovered from its industrial revolution. Along the docks everything was as dark and grimy as in the first days. Iron bridges overhead between the solid tiers of warehouses, high stone walls, cobbled passageways along which ran beautiful children red-cheeked in the cold. Would they become these men with working-class caps and scarves and yellow teeth who worked in that maze of shadows?

England was a social battleground that stayed a social

battleground. The English liked class differences. They
thrived on the social drama. The German exile in the
British Museum had documented his case from classic
horrors carefully listed by English investigators. The
"drama of English society" was made up of unbelievable extremes and stolid injustices that for centuries
had inflamed, amused, galvanized English writers:

> And did the Countenance Divine
> Shine forth upon our clouded hills?
> And was Jerusalem builded here
> Among these dark Satanic Mills?

But it finally occurred to some comfortable people—
looking at the spindly, dirty bodies of the "lower
classes," listening to voices that often seemed to them
"positively the voices of animals," watching "feeding
habits" that made them retch—that "the nation was
most seriously weakened" by so many damaged people.
The war might be lost on the playing fields of Manchester, Liverpool, Glasgow.

Nowhere else in the Western world would the revelation of what one's own people looked like have come as
such a shock. But some English still did not regard
other English as people at all. My super-English landlady from Virginia was not more Tory than her husband, a major embittered by the "Labour Johnnies"
who were promising the workers "a better England"
after the war. "This war is a revolution, is it? Not where
we sit it isn't!" He was embittered by the possible collapse of the family business that had procured him his
few weeks of compassionate leave. They had me to tea
one Sunday at their "little place in the country," and
all through tea he stared at me with a haughtiness made
ridiculous by the unsuccessful Kitchener mustache

trailing around his mouth to his chin. The role-playing was intense, sometimes zany in the phrases that rolled round and round the room and bounced off the walls with the ringing sounds of self-satisfaction. Mrs. Armitage found it "totally unbelievable" that anyone in Britain should have any criticism of the "P.M." She sometimes said "Winston" not as the subway sleepers did but with the smile of someone in his set. She knew all his sayings by heart and, with a scream of laughter, reported "Winston" saying, "I don't take the view myself that we were a nation of slum dwellers before the war." "Of course," she added, "it's all been a bit of a bore since 1940." She still wore the large dinner ring in which she had in 1940 secreted a pill for use on herself, her mother, and her dog if the Germans invaded.

How sparklingly she chattered on about the great days of the blitz, her pride and happiness that Americans were doing so much for the "common cause." She talked, as I discovered many English talked, for the pleasure of talking, making beautiful English sounds, keeping open the rippling fluent surface of well-practiced English interchange. The room was suddenly made up of sharp voices bright and shiny as the gleams from the silver tea service, the chintz cushions of the sofa, the vivid print my hostess wore, the shrill double ring of the telephone, and the genteel little screams of laughter with which she addressed the telephone. At one point, all these bright noises and colors became too much for me and I asked if I could smoke. "Certainly not!" the major said, in a parade-ground voice. "Why, Geoffrey!" his wife said. "Joke, my dear fellow, joke!" roared the major. He offered strong drink. "Thank God for the booze," he said. "If Winston didn't drink himself to bed every afternoon for a badly needed rest, we'd all be lost." His wife, happy that we were getting

on so well, went on chatting as her social duty. There
was a picture on the wall of an Indian maiden. "Pocahontas," she said, smiling. Descendants of Pocahontas
turned up at every meeting of the English-Speaking
Union. She was indeed one herself, she gravely informed me.

Listening to my newfound English acquaintances in
government offices go on and on in syllables as meticu-
lously accented as verse, in voices authoritative, cor-
rectly pointed, vaguely meant to subdue, I thought of
how grumpily sluggish and undistinguished most American voices were. Here, by contrast, was a race of talkers
confidently moving over a repertoire of familiar sounds
to cajole, persuade, snub, charm, command. I could
positively hear them *using* their voices at you.

Even the many upper-class stammerers I met among
government officials and writers—people confidently
directing the flow of English opinion—did not seem in
the least impeded by their twitches, repetitions, mum-
blings, and nervous pauses. They just went on, even in
public meeting, as if everyone in the audience knew
what it was like to stammer. Might there be a bit of
distinction to it?

I was afraid for stammerers and filled in for them
every inch of the way. Attending a meeting of education
officers at the War Office where W. E. Williams, director of the Army Bureau of Current Affairs, was explaining and justifying the obligatory discussion of social
issues as part of every soldier's regular training, I was
amazed by the ease with which the officers around me
accepted Williams's horribly slow but professionally
genial recital of the "social crisis" facing England. He
stammered his way through with a smile. Williams's accent and appearance made entirely cozy his view of the
"crisis" as a "communications problem." He was a tall,

lean, benevolent-looking, vaguely literary figure from Penguin Books and the British adult-education movement who had been chosen by the War Office as an expert with a calming influence when it was decided to "go left with the troops." There had been a near mutiny after Dunkirk. Williams, a mild Socialist, was left enough to be concerned but *sound*. He warned officers that the problem was still one of morale. The hidden "damage" inflicted by unemployment and lack of education could "jeopardize the unity of the British nation in wartime." Britain could avoid becoming a second-class power by at least *listening* to its mass of discontent. Shaw and the Webbs had lamented "the waste of human life" in England. But Williams, one Fabian quoting still another Fabian, smilingly said, as if H. G. Wells had never said it, that life had become a race between education and catastrophe. The spirit of the troops was often truculent. Religion made little appeal, patriotism no appeal at all. There was neither the enthusiasm of youth nor the deliberate purpose of age. The war might soon be over, but it was still true, as Herbert Read had written in "To a Conscript of 1940," that "to fight without hope is to fight without grace."

The bitterly needed adult-education movement in England had of course begun in the lower-class unrest that followed the French Revolution. The savage neglect of the *people's* education was filled in with primitive evening classes, Sunday schools, "mechanics' institutes," and finally the Workers Education Association. All this self-help in adult education now played the role once performed by religion, but the war had aroused a social bitterness dangerous to ignore. Even during the blitz, there had been almost a million unemployed; buildings were being constructed while the wreckage of bombed buildings was left in the streets.

Dunkirk may have looked like a victory to Americans, but it was a trauma to many of the men finally taken off the beach after days in the open. Getting home without their equipment and personal effects, they felt badly used, idle, uninformed, ill-prepared for war, and despairing of a better life after the peace.

The gunners from a large Surrey unit started things. Schoolmasters and architects argued with coal miners, butchers, policemen, trade-union organizers, salesmen, solicitors, film technicians. Beginning to talk things over among themselves, they asserted and explored their long-smoldering rebelliousness more sharply in wartime than they had in the depressed thirties, when a third of the labor force was unemployed in some districts and masses of Welsh unemployed were forever straggling into London with their heartbreaking songs and pathetic banners. The discussion movement inside the Army spread to many factories, organized itself into a movement, eventually held mock parliaments in several theaters of war that spelled out the necessary rearrangement of British society. With all their principal cities under attack and the British besieged in their own homes, it was already a "people's war." But in some way never anticipated by J. B. Priestley, who had spurred the English on during the blitz with his BBC talks of a "new England," the driving demand for a new order of things went beyond his mild 1940 touching up of Mrs. Miniver and *The White Cliffs of Dover:*

> Through the fading mists there emerge the simple, kindly, humorous brave faces of the ordinary British folk—a good people, deeply religious at heart, not only when they're kneeling in our little grey country churches but also when they're toiling at their machines or sweating under loads in the threatened dockyards.

Already the future historians are fastening their gaze upon us, seeing us all in that clear and searching light of the great moments of history.

What we're all struggling and battling for. Not for some regrouping on the chessboard of money and power politics; but for new and better homes—real homes—a decent chance at last—a new life. And every woman should remember that—keep the promise locked in her heart—demand that the promise be redeemed.

These sweet sounds added to British pride and stiffened British resistance to the enemy Churchill called "the Nahsties." But what turned many in the middle class to Labour and led to Churchill's overthrow in the first postwar election was the recognition that the state was already the operative force in English life. Britain was brilliantly organized for *wartime*. The British could see it every day for themselves. The state was the direct administrator of their lives. It conscripted labor and moved it about as necessary. It trained men for the Army, sent them into battle while taking on responsibility for educating them as well. It rationed food, goods, and services; fed and housed thousands in bombed areas; organized civil defense. Yet many of these state activities and directives seemed to be accomplished through the agency of the people themselves—neighborhood committees, local units of the Fire Service, borough councils administering emergency housing and repairs, elected town administrators.

The state was identified with the most basic affairs of the average citizen. War was the only catalyst of social advance! To enlist the people all-out for war, you encouraged them to make demands on the state. Even George Orwell, who would never forget the murdering repression in the name of "Socialism" he had seen in

Catalonia, thought that the immediate establishment of *some* kind of socialized economy in England might be an incentive to fight more effectively.

None of this touched the burning sense of grievance among workers in the factories and soldiers fighting abroad or still in barracks. Their sense of injustice was irrevocable, a sacrament, a pledge of common feeling. Historic bitterness and grumbling fatalism gave the working class identity to itself, its sense of having been long marked out and put down. A long historic chain stretched out over the centuries. The gentleman Socialist W. E. Williams spoke of the "danger presented to the nation" by the damage so long permitted on England's "common folk." Williams had refused a brigadier general's commission so as to retain the soldiers' confidence in a civilian. Think of that! I heard an important official in the Ministry of Education speak of his special concern with the "dull and backward" because, "being neglected, they are the greatest danger to the state." Equality was not an English ideal to any class. I easily fell into the old passion of English Socialism, of working-class struggle and affirmation.

> England arise, the long long night is over.
> Out of your evil sleep of toil and sorrow,
> England arise, the long long day is here.

But the workers were their own people, belonged to nobody but themselves. George Orwell, who could still be seen at the left-wing *Tribune* coughing over his deadly cigarettes of the strongest shag, was sharply put down to me by a Labour Party secretary in Limehouse as "not one of us." Was Deputy Prime Minister Clement Attlee, in Parliament for Limehouse, "one of us"? He smiled carefully. English workers could be more hide-bound and exclusive than royalty. Their customs and traditions—even the rows of houses back to back—seemed dearer to some than any possible ending of the class struggle. Their separate speech, their pubs, their "low" feeding habits, their ancient bitter humor were sacred to themselves.

But this was a country in trouble and a people driven to the wall. "Browned off." "I've had it, chum." "Work and bed—might as well be dead."

"I *do* hate to keep troops waiting," said the young leftenant to another young leftenant as I arrived for my discussion meeting. Handkerchief tucked inside his sleeve, tan shirt collar positively shining, so stiffly has it been ironed, brown shoes brightly shined until they glitter yellow, shoes heavily creaking across the floor of the Nissen hut. Little blond mustache, which he lovingly pats from time to time. They have "laid on transport" for me. The car is chauffeured by a spanking-bright blond WAAC, also in stiff tan shirt and knitted tie, her cap jauntily set over one ear. Authority in England begins as a show of proper collar and tie. The blonde's army skirt is stretched tight over her neat bottom, which makes a smooth picture to present to the "ranks." They wear no collar and tie, and button their tunics to the chin.

We enter to a tremendous clatter of noisy English shoes; the sergeant's clanging tenor voice commands the men to attention. Every soldier stiffly standing is buttoned up to his Adam's apple. Row on row of symmetrically buttoned harsh woolly uniforms, short hair-cuts, hobnailed boots. Everywhere the same burly outside look, but the faces are easier and slower than American soldier faces. "Permission is given to smoke," and, sitting with conscious ease at tables or on trunks, the men hesitantly and carefully open up on "Civvy Street"—their civilian future, to be followed by "the shape of England and the world after this war is over."

Serious, grave, very deliberate men, they seem to talk against an unseen current. The leftenant with the little blond mustache, reading off from the Army Bureau of Current Affairs the ground rules governing every discussion period, cannot help sounding benevolent. Unlike Americans, the sensible British Army fashion is not to mix up men from different parts of the country. These men seem to know each other from way back, at least have associations in common. How quickly they seize each other's thoughts and guess each other out. They have the look that comes when more than five years of war have been piled on top of the mad muddling and bumbling before the war. Now, as they put it in their mild English fashion, there must be "a better lookout when all this is over."

No revolutionary abstractions here, at least not yet! "The Empire" is taken for granted, though there is no particular pride in it. They would not like to hear Comrade Orwell say, as he always does say to the indignation of his readers, that the prosperity of the English starts overseas. Unlike American soldiers, these men do not explode on schedule in order to make a point. They also think who stand and wait. They look grimly patient, stolid to the point of contempt. You simply do not put yourself forward; you do not show your hand in anything unless called upon. The silences are deeprutted. The leftenant is their little scoutmaster and they are going to wait him out.

When they open up at last, there is a deliberateness, a heaviness. Their language is overdressed; they put forward what is gravely called here "alternatives." Can the state do something *more*—nothing drastic, just "more"—for education? Every new education reform here must come down from the top. Most British children are out of school forever at fourteen, and parents don't always mind. One corporal reports that all over England local education officials—"they are the conscience of this country!"—beg employers not to hire children at thirteen but are besieged by angry parents who need their children's wages. The one university intellectual in the group, looking at me with a little smile, informs me that my "fellow countryman T. S. Eliot," now the most conservative Briton since Ethelred the Unready, has objected to the school-leaving age being raised to *fifteen*. Eliot deplores "all that 'Elegy in a Country Churchyard' nonsense."

> But Knowledge to their eyes her ample page
> Rich with the spoils of Time did ne'er unroll;
> Chill penury repress'd their noble rage,
> And froze the genial current of the soul.
>
> . . . .
>
> And read their history in a nation's eyes.

Eliot later recommended that the number of university students be cut by a third. I remembered how Emerson, speaking to the Workingmen's College in London, praised "the pathetically noble efforts of English scholars to educate their humbler brethren." But great American writers have changed. Everything about America can be such a thorn in English flesh just now. When the first prefabricated housing arrived from American factories, British authorities removed all their modern fixtures so that the many who could not get houses at all would not be too resentful. In Bristol a race riot started when American black soldiers were attacked by fellow soldiers for going out with English girls. The girls, to judge by the many scenes of grief when the black soldiers poured out of Bristol, did not seem to agree with the horror-stricken white soldiers. Even T. S. Eliot's idealization of the English "conservative tradition" is used to prove what unfeeling bastards Americans can be. And the English, in their sly way, may well be right. But even these British soldiers, asking me questions that evening on the kind of quiz program they call a "Brains Trust"—you great big powerful Brains who have actually come up from London to talk to the likes of poor *us*!—never come right out and say they hate our guts for being on top and replacing *them*. The English always give such good reasons for everything they believe and do. Putting up a show of reasonableness is a fine art here. These soldiers couldn't be more indifferent to the submerged majority under British rule in Africa or India; even the convinced Socialists say "natives," "niggers," "wogs." But any white American may be held responsible for slavery, lynching, Jim Crow. Despite all the stuff about the Tennessee Valley Authority and New Deal social legislation America dishes out here, the exclusive movie diet of Hollywood offers a truer picture. They discuss America in vague suspicious generalizations. I said "Wisconsin" at one point in the "Brains Trust" quiz, and a soldier said with amazement that he had never heard the word pronounced before. The outcry is that their education is "paltry" and that they are not prepared for proper jobs in "Civvy Street." The brutal ignorance of our decent "common folk" has not been relieved by this long, long war. A corporal who fought with the Eighth Army in Egypt fiercely asserts that Arabs are so backward, "they write from right to left and even *think* from right to left!"

The outside world is not very real to these men. At one point the leftenant explained that "Russia is a new nation, and therefore unused to statesmanship." No one laughed but me. But talking about jobs, houses, marriage, "the four-ale bar," they somehow speak for each other without the brassy American competitiveness. These men know each other, and not only because most of them left school at fourteen. They are a people. "*L'Angleterre, c'est une île.*" After almost six years of war, they have a certain look of experience shared. Yet the younger men in the Nissen hut were boys when the war began. There is a hesitation to *their* minds—not to the one university intellectual in the group—that makes me sad. "There *must* be a better lookout after all this is over."

The largest restaurant in Britain, the largest restaurant in the world, the largest restaurant of all time, was "Willow Run," the American Officers' Mess in the Grosvenor Hotel ballroom on Park Lane. It served fifteen thousand meals a day. In a great circle in the center stretched two enormous counters, behind which stood dozens of meek English girls in white aprons and caps. Round and round the vast room stretched an unending line of American officers and civilian personnel with their trays. It was like eating on the floor of Madison Square Garden in the middle of a basketball game. When you had filled up and were exited into Park Lane itself, the quietness of Hyde Park was startling: "Sheep may softly graze." Everyone in sight wore a uniform. There were Poles from their soon to be forgotten government in exile, looking brisk and irresistible to the English girls as they paraded in their black berets bearing the Polish eagle; Free French officers wearing the Cross of Lorraine on their old Maginot Line uniforms; London firemen with silver buttons; aged pensioners; American Air Force lieutenant colonels by the dozen, who had flattened the crowns of their caps and wore them negligently over one ear as if to show that they were as carefree in the air as they were on Park Lane.

Whenever a moment's warmth surprised the English climate, GIs suddenly appeared with baseball bats and hit long lazy flies to each other. Watching our countrymen at play, I met the Roths, the most hospitable American couple in Mayfair. Their hospitality was overwhelming. Joey Roth was a short, stubby, profane, manic joker with endless borscht-circuit *spritz* or fluency. He was tirelessly show business and, according to him, enjoyed a perfect happiness that you had to share at the peril of your life. He was a New York radio producer "seconded," as the English liked to say, to the Embassy as a public-relations officer. He had achieved this on the troopship taking him over by putting out a news-and-entertainment sheet that had turned his fellow soldiers cheerful and had convinced the brass that he had a genius for public relations. Now he was the only sergeant in the European Theater of Operations living with his lawfully wedded wife in a regular domicile. Susy was a darkly handsome wife with a voice capable of the most unsettling inflections; her bangs framed a face fixed in a slow social smile that told you absolutely nothing. Her voice continued to sweep over you in thrilling, throbbing special tones.

I was to become very familiar with this voice. The Roths lived all day and sometimes all night long in a whirl of friends and unending parties based on the regular flow of goodies and liquor through the U.S. Embassy. (On Oxford Street the first peaches, each carefully wrapped in cotton, were selling for three shillings apiece.) The Roths were always throwing parties. There was never a time you went up to the mews over which they lived in fashionable London that the floor was not massed with Embassy personnel, American correspondents, specialists in psychological warfare, market-research specialists in the public-opinion polls that were forever being taken of English opinion. It was difficult to talk to Joey or Susy alone, they were always so engulfed in friends eating and partying and playing The Game.

It was all like a Hollywood party of migrants to "the Coast." You could hear their shouts from the street and up the stairs as you went up—American functionaries stopping in from the big Allied radio network in Luxembourg, from the Department of Justice, from the Office of War Information newsroom in Holborn, from the Embassy, the *Satevepost* and *Time*, from the office of Strategic Services, the board of Economic Warfare, the incipient United Nations Relief and Rehabilitation Association. The parties were generally strong in psychological-warfare specialists who wrote messages to the Germans designed to persuade them to surrender. Everyone was a specialist doing something very specific and technical for the War Effort; one specialist had to be aware of another specialist's professional weight and importance at Supreme Headquarters Allied Powers, Europe. The military had it all over everybody—the lieutenant who had been a flag secretary in the Atlantic Fleet, the captain in intelligence, the classmate who by spring would be in Czechoslovakia, the Harvard literary scholar who would "liberate Buchenwald," the Air Force captain who had bombed Rumania. Ten points to the Ranger who had been with the Canadian commandos to Dieppe, twelve to the first man across the Rhine, far less to Harry Hopkins's assistant in Russia.

Joey Roth joked that he earned the Purple Heart in the battle of Grosvenor Square—the Embassy and American enclave variously called Jeepside and Eisenhower Platz—but his England was a particular achievement and he boisterously shared it with you. About the

English, as about Americans who had been decorated
for some slight wound, Joey felt that they were somehow cleverer than other people, with more resources at
their command. He once took me down to do a BBC
discussion with the historian Denis Brogan. Coming
back in the Embassy limousine, he kept shaking his head
in admiration and disbelief at Brogan's learning and
Brogan's Glaswegian disdain for those with a mite less.
Brogan interested him only as a performer who, with
a bottle of BBC's best Scotch next to the microphone,
luxuriated in a quickness of mind and range of learning that flashed like a photoelectric cell. Brogan knew
more than most Americans about families divided by
the Civil War, the early life of Franklin D. Roosevelt,
Catholic settlements on the Eastern Shore of Maryland.
As an Irishman from Glasgow, he was brilliant in abuse
of the intellectual Establishment; red-faced, he boasted
to me of having slept with more faculty wives than any
other visiting lecturer to America; and he was possessed
of total recall—especially on the sex lives of the *New
Statesman* staff, the too liberal weekly he hated even
more than he hated the powers that had deprived him
of an Oxford chair. He had a chair at Cambridge, but
he was an Oxford man, a Glasgow man, a Harvard man,
and enjoyed a sense of superiority throughout the British Isles that came out as the bitterest resentment of his
colleagues and as contempt for all reformers and radicals.

British academic stars had the gift of covering temperamental excess with stupendous learning and of im-
parting a truly impressive intellectual cockiness to their
many shifts and breakdowns of opinion. A. J. P. Taylor
went among the troops interpreting the news from week
to week. After the war Taylor explained that Hitler's

aims were just the Kaiser's all over again. But the names always before the public were England's stars, not timid ineffectual professors. They represented a tradition, a civilization, not an academic limitation. They loved confronting America as guests of America, after Joey Roth on the jump seat of the limousine quoted repartee between Jascha Heifetz and Groucho Marx. "My dear chap, you people are clearly to be the new Romans . . . while we . . . we . . . must doubtless earn our keep as the slave tutors of your household. Or is it, as Cyril Connolly says, that we are fated to be the Middle Kingdom between you and the barbarous Slav? Or may it be that we are just the last of Europe?"

Joey had his "contacts" everywhere. I sat with him through luncheons of English movie people in Wardour Street, was sent off to settlement houses in bombed-out areas to talk to bewildered urchins about Whitman, found myself walking along the old Roman wall in York and making my way through clothing factories in Leeds because there was someone "especially interesting" for me to see. And there usually was. There were more distinct and even savagely colorful personalities in any backstage British city than at the University of Chicago. I especially relished sitting with Joey at the Hotel Connaught, where he would buy martinis at four shillings a drink for the crowd waiting to hear the BBC news at six. On the wall was a mighty picture of Victoria, Queen and Empress. Under it, framed, the statement she had made to Balfour during the darkest days of the South African war:

> Please understand that there is no one depressed in this house; we are not interested in the possibilities of defeat; they do not exist.
>
> Victoria R. I.

The stately grandfather clock loudly beat the quarter-hours, and aged majestically inexpressive waiters, wearing tail coats and shirt fronts stained but still bulging with starch, tottered in bearing enormous teas. The fresh-faced young barmaid with a wicked grin would pass the martinis over her little counter, and as the great clock beat six we moved together to hear the news. The English sat there hardly twitching a muscle in their eyelids, just blinking a little at the news of still more delays in getting across the Rhine, the Americans shouting at the news of Patton's sweep across northern France, Joey machine-gunning joke-joke to keep from weeping at the pride and importance of sitting in the same room with Ambassador Winant's secretary and the P.M.'s own son-in-law.

In the Connaught, that reserve of ancient quiet pomp and power, the shrieks of Joey's writer pals were muffled by the thick warm rugs, the Victorian grandfather clock, and the cold gaze of Victoria, Queen and Empress. You saw English officialdom under glass. Those blotchy-faced carefully combed-down mandarins usually left a cigarette burning in the far corner of their mouths. How unnecessary for an Englishman to take a cigarette out of his mouth when he talked! He talked through the smoke, the smoke lay between you and him, the smoke was a fixture like the fluted white staircases spiraling out of sight in the Connaught. Peering through the smoke, you saw expert geniality, a square rocklike face, black-frame eyeglasses with the old-fashioned nosepiece you hadn't seen since you were a boy, hair that was longer in the back than you ever saw at home, and a great readiness to entertain discussion on any subject for the pleasure of entertaining discussion.

They talked as comfortably as they sat. They were very comfortable talkers. On the progress of the war and the future of the world, they shared with you their pleasure at being insiders. They *confided* in you. They lived in a world where everybody knew everybody else and where your name and place of origin were enough for an Englishman to know all about you. Once they located you on their map of the world, they laughed and talked about anything whatever as if they were sailing through the air—though in fact they heavily occupied their chairs and the fold in their black trousers kept its careful edge.

By contrast, Joey Roth seemed always to be sitting on the edge of his chair in uncertainty. Despite his violent flow of Hollywood jokes and gossip, Joey read the English as a lip-reader would. He talked to them by practicing the right things to say. Little might survive here but style, and it was English style that intimidated Joey. His whole aim as a "media specialist" and press agent for the U.S.A. was to make America lovable. So he ran around all day being funny and lovable. But somehow the English language in an official English mouth, pressing expertly now on one tone, now on another, cheerfully rejected him. No wonder that he clung to Americans in his private hours and that he remembered with whoops of joy the time when he and good old Bill Saroyan, both of them still in the Signal Corps Film and Theater Section, had written a film together in four days. Howling with laughter, each of them had taken turns dictating lines to a secretary.

In the age of Queen and Empress, the Mayfair mews where the Roths lived had been occupied by horses, carriages, a coachman; in the early spring of 1945, you went through a door that had once led into a courtyard, into three small rooms that had once been the butler's and the upstairs maids', and suddenly you were plunged into the middle of Larchmont. The expensive American domesticity was overpowering. Three thousand miles from home, the apartment was a love nest still deep in wedding presents, food, booze, a print of Picasso's "Minotaur," copies of *The Nation, The New Republic, Partisan Review,* and the latest Modern Library and New Directions books.

The Roths drowned you in hospitality. They somehow imprisoned themselves in so much party-giving. I never saw the Roths together except in a group, and the group replenished itself at such a rate that you could not make out exactly who was there. Prompting, pushing, serving, joking in the ooze and sweat of the great American party ("Fuck it, no!" he would protest when he saw someone trying to steal out at three in the morning), Joey had the look of a traffic cop out of his depth. On the one hand it was all so familiar, cozy, expected: New Yorkers in London argued fiercely whether Russia was or was not a degenerated workers' state; benign *Statevepost* correspondents described in equal detail the character of General Patton and their troubles with their wives; a sparkling Radcliffe girl who felt lost in the O.W.I. newsroom recited George Herbert to me with emotion. There would be a great feeling of release and undress. As Eisenhower liked to say when he touched back in London, we were "home."

On the other hand, why were the Roths never alone? Why, even at their parties, did they never seem to talk to each other? Once, very drunk and somehow inflamed by the mob he was usually patting, kissing, relentlessly joking with, gag after gag, Joey astonished me by cornering me in the kitchen. "C'mon and talk to me for a while. Or go in and talk to Susy for a while. Maybe you can take a message to the lady? I'm drunk and I shouldn't be telling you this, but I'm getting pretty tired of living in a crowd all the time. . . . Christ . . . this place doesn't feel like my own." He grinned. "And it sure isn't." "Why don't you chase us out?" He gave me a long, pitying look. "Don't you know?" he said solemnly. "Practically everyone else does. It's Susy. She's over me *all* the time. I can't stand it, I tell you. It's no joke when someone loves you more than you love them." Difficult as his situation appeared to be, he seemed proud of it. There was a faint smile. I thought of Gatsby saying about his house, "I keep it always full of interesting people, night and day. People who do interesting things. Interesting people."

I waited for Joey to say something more. He seemed disgruntled by his confession. It seemed vaguely irrelevant. From a corner his wife looked coolly on, her bangs like a visor from under which she stared without expression at the pack of sweating Americans. I was to see her in Paris sitting at a bar with the songwriter who became her future husband. Poor old liar Joey.

I went back to my terrible room in the American billets in Great Cumberland Place. It was very late, but there was a light in the office, and under the light was a large handsome dark-haired girl who seemed to be angrily writing a V-letter. I knew nothing about her. At times she seemed to be a girl I had seen in the officers' mess, where she would always appear as a fourth at table—a silent, large, very dark girl, her largeness somehow made up of silence.

There are strangers who keep reappearing in your life. In all the months I encountered this silently angry girl in the American quarter—Duke Street, Green Street, Grosvenor Square—I had the same sensation of having seen her before, no doubt in some other life. I was never sure who she was and that I was not confusing her with someone else. Her extraordinarily dark eyes, her gleaming blue-black hair, the orange coloring

that flashed up like the end of brightness out of her
"Spanish" face—all reminded me of someone. Yet now
that I was always seeing her in some American office at
night writing away desperately fast at what seemed to
be an unfinishable letter, she sat there with her head
bowed and turned away. Even when she was making a
deadly fourth at "Willow Run," while everyone else at
table was chatting away, even when she was sitting so
near that your knees could touch, even when you stared
hungrily at that face flaming with shyness and a body
on a grand scale in a silk print that openly pressed and
folded her like a luxurious Titian, you found yourself
trapped in her absolute silence. I would stare and stare
at her, as if to locate her *somewhere* in space. The
nearer you got and the deeper you looked, the more
that ancient sullen silence came between you. I knew,
even when I caught my breath in what came off her as
prodigious sexual warmth, that there would never be
anything else for me. I would never get past that silence.

But how extraordinary it was that I was always running into her at "Willow Run" and along all those
streets in *bon-ton* Mayfair where the American propaganda, opinion research, and propaganda services con-
gregated, and usually in some corner of a deserted office
typing away desperately and fast on endless sheets of
V-letters, tearing the letters out of the typewriter as fast
as she put them in, beating away at the letter as if only
the big office machine would get her message over fast
enough. Watching that girl typing away late at night in
every office she could get into, I thought of how often
I had run into the office near Green Park to cable Natasha for the hell of it, just to write her name and our
old address across the ocean. O love, guilt, nostalgia,
envy, armed with airplanes, walkie-talkies, cablegrams,
and secretaries, like the American news executive in

Temple Bar who dictated his letters to his wife to his live-in secretary. O Americans at the peak, dashing in and out of airplanes, mounting the skies with that hangdog look of expectancy one never saw in carefully composed English faces. It all came down in the end to one American girl sneaking into the office when the day was done to look for a typewriter, and, at home behind the machine, driving it like a racing car that sputtered with sparks, trying to say the word, that one word, that would make everything right again.

By March, only by March, when the freezing rainy cold lifted, British and American forces crossed the Rhine. "THE END OF THE WAR IS IN SIGHT." Walking down to Oxford Street for breakfast one morning, I rose into the air and every window on both sides of me broke in one glittering convulsion. A V-2 had just burst into Hyde Park. By afternoon a long queue was waiting outside a tea shop that had been hit but was still doing business. "*Their* way of showing sympathy, I suppose," Mrs. Armitage, the manageress, commented in a dry offhand manner to conceal her blazing pride in the English.

Always the queue, the crowd, the friendly spontaneous group made possible for an hour by war and its inflictions. I ate in a London community kitchen after a discussion group in an army hospital. Ambulatory patients wore horrible blue suits and red ties and, sitting alongside men groaning in bed, asked me questions about America. The American-born brigadier in charge of the hospital, hearty chap, walked in for a minute to welcome me, crisply announced, "It is a well-known fact that Negroes' minds stop working at fifteen, just ask this gentleman here," and vanished. A junior officer appealed to the men to "rally around" to the current "demob" scheme. Peace seemed to be in the air. "Amaz-

ing how we can help each other if we but try." Even
the left-winger catalyst may be "quite a valuable ally."
The patients were subdued and in their blue suits and
red ties (why *ties* in a hospital, for God's sakes) looked
like convicts out for an airing.

As usual, the children playing in the cobbled alleys
outside the community kitchen looked rosy, beautiful,
well fed. The drawn dusty Londoners at long tables up
and down the room, chewing on mushy meat pie and
rhubarb pie, showed faces arranged in vague docile
gratitude. They looked as so many older people in London now looked: wasted, cut off, and accepting it. Before the war many of them must have felt emptied like
this, but they wouldn't have shown it in this crowd. Stiff,
proper, so humble-looking. Would those shining children turn into these round-backed, white-faced adults
with the uniform bad teeth and beseeching black wire
spectacles?

By April there was a light in the pissy English heav-
ens, GIs were playing softball in Hyde Park every Sunday now, and Sunday evenings there were crowds singing hymns. Michaelmas daisies began to sprout in the
ashy soil of bombed-out houses. Posters showing this
and labeled "RENASCENCE" emerged all over London.
With a number of journalists and roving bureaucrats, I
now shared atop a circular, highly modish apartment
house in Knightsbridge a penthouse that seemed devoted
entirely to hearty sex. Since I was always traveling, I
was assigned the couch in the living room. The room
was vast but not private. It had great French windows
opening onto a balcony, and looked across a sea of
twisted chimney pots to where the candy stripes of
Westminster Cathedral stood out on the horizon like
Turkish delight.

I moved in the week F.D.R. died. I awoke one

morning to hear hymns from the radio in the kitchen and a woman screaming. In the midst of it all, the telephone in the hall was ringing with the demanding English double ring—*yip-yip! yip-yip!* I waited for it to stop, it didn't, and as I went in to answer it, a girl in her underwear ran past me and fled into a bathroom, with a diminutive Midwest professor of history, always called "the professor," hot after her. I picked up the receiver but could not hear a word, for the professor was hammering on the door and the girl was screaming back at him in a high cold cockney voice. "Enough!" she shouted. "That's enough, I tell you—! You're wacky, you bahstid, you are!" The professor still had a Band-Aid down his nose where one of his Piccadilly regulars had bitten him the night before, and the swelling veins in his fat round neck were smudged with lipstick marks; he leaned against the door, cooing to the girl in a soft drunken voice. I felt nothing but a stupefied anger at other people's passions. The war had emptied me.

On the telephone table in the hall were our tattered cut-up ration books. The hall, like the living room in which I slept, was lined with Balinese nudes and in my morning emptiness and bitterness, their breasts looked sorrowful and ill-used. On the wall someone had put a picture, cut out of *Time*, showing a Negro woman weeping and clutching her belly as the gun carriage carrying F.D.R.'s body passed down Pennsylvania Avenue. We had been orphaned without a moment's warning. The indomitable English telephone began its *yip-yip! yip-yip!* again. I seemed unable to answer it, and there came into my mind a photograph in the window of Jack Dempsey's bar and restaurant on Broadway. It showed Dempsey winning the heavyweight championship from Jess Willard in 1919. The ring was in the open, and the enormous Jess Willard looked as if he were being cut down with an ax. The young Dempsey, in a close haircut and with an exuberant scowl on his face, was circling the big stupid Willard at his pleasure and beating him to a pulp. There was blood on Willard's face and on Willard's arms, and he just stood there, splintered and gashed, like a tree waiting to be knocked down.

I had an appointment that afternoon at Faber & Faber with T. S. Eliot. At Marble Arch an anarchist was giving out "Peace Now!" leaflets by Herbert Read and Dr. Alex Comfort. A zany black with an American Indian feathered headdress was prancing up and down as he offered the crowd around his soapbox a parody of a BBC news broadcast. An unfrocked Anglican minister from Durham was preaching a brave Victorian rationalism based on the system of Herbert Spencer. A young man thundered in behalf of some old believers called the British Socialist Party, and, sputtering with anger, denounced the Labour Party's criminal sellout to the Tories.

Eliot received me with kindly vagueness. His office wall was surprisingly jammed with Harvard photographs and mementos, and so long as the conversation touched on Harvard friends, it kept flickering back to life. In his first years in England, Eliot had taught workers' evening classes for the London County Council, but such gestures were far behind him. For many years he had had to adjust his delicate and easily ravaged personality to his fame, and he wore the special face he put on in public. He might be the bishop of modern poetry, the lawgiver who had dominated the classrooms for a generation. But before me was a man easily cornered and deathly afraid of being cornered. Tall, bent, impenetrably courteous, his voice sepulchral and quivering, he seemed to be listening to every vibration in the air. The antennae he put out were like the slippage in his poems, fragment to fragment of memory, terror, and confrontation. He was a publisher sitting in his office deep in the city and his fingertips were clasped together in a gesture of listless meditation. But that altogether fastidious figure with a nose that ended in a delicate little sea shell had somehow concentrated itself into a single self-protective gesture.

He was an institution capable of great suffering. He was also a Yankee humorist, skilled in playing many parts between America and Europe. How mischievously he fitted into his English décor—he was a subtler international type than those chaste Jamesian heroes Eliot had been among the first to recognize as comic masks. Looking at Eliot, in his lounge suit, carefully constructing a personality for the public gaze, it seemed to me that James had imagined the role, Eliot now lived it. How far the Yankee imagination ranged in time as well as space—how easily an American took up any role on the English stage. Benjamin Franklin playing a rustic sage had nothing on this poker player from Missouri. America was right in that room and would never leave it. The low coffee table was piled high with *Partisan Review, Poetry, Accent*, little magazines from Iowa City, Berkeley, Madison. At one point, Roosevelt having just died, Eliot looked at me with a smile: "By the way, what's this Truman like?" "You ought to know, he comes from Missouri." Eliot laughed and recited an ancient ditty about a politician: "He would make a good mayor of St. Louis in a bad year."

That Anglicized voice had not quite completed its journey out and was capable of delicious impersonations. The tones of his voice were as expertly placed as they were in his poems; he painted pictures in my mind as he talked. The composition that he made, voice and gesture and tone, fingertips sagely pressed together, was proof to himself of his discipline. As always, I was awed by his expressive power. There was the too sepulchral, yet shaky voice in which you positively heard the grave-digger's shovel emptying its last clod upon the coffin— *Lasciate ogni speranza, voi ch'entrate!* And there was the voice I had always heard in his poetry, the voice that rose and fell with that slow-dying wide-spaced ecstasy of apprehension and regret. It was a voice with immense vibrations, shivered within itself to the memory of a bird call, a rosebush, a staircase. So many different ages of the mind followed each other on the slow hovering wheel that turned virtually without movement and without sound. And each age was a haunted image that left unimpaired and resistant the stone on which it had been sharpened. Eliot had saved himself, but just barely. The ravaged figure sat on the sea wall with one foot dangling above the water, wondering as always if he should go in. But, careful or not, he had made those exquisitely desperate cadences in which I had found the language of *my* heart. What did I care if he was now more medieval than the Pope? What did it matter that this same clerical Tory was a publisher who had just turned down George Orwell's *Animal Farm* so as not to offend our Russian ally? He impersonated a flight from emotion that could fool no one who read two lines of his verse.

> But, of course, only those who have personality and emotions
> know what it means to want to escape from these things.

He had saved himself, just barely. He had saved himself for the rest of us.

It was hot, blazing summer in London. "Double daylight time" kept the streets awash with daylight until late in the evening. We were at the rim of the world. It was the summer of our deliverance. Hitler had come and gone.

4,000,000 DEATHS AT AUSCHWITZ

The crematoria had a total capacity of 5,500,000 during the time they functioned. The Parliamentary commission, which had previously investigated conditions at Maidanek, Treblinka and other annihilation camps, describes Auschwitz as the worst in its experience.

Theses were published on the experiments performed on human beings.

Seven tons of women's hair were found ready for despatch to Germany. Human teeth, from which gold fillings had been extracted, were piled several feet high. 100,000 children's suits of clothes.

Late one Friday afternoon near the end of the war, I was waiting out the rain in the entrance to a music store. A radio was playing into the street and, standing there, I heard the first Sabbath service from Belsen. In April a British detachment had stumbled on Belsen by accident, had come upon forty thousand sick, starving, and dying prisoners. Over ten thousand corpses were stacked in piles. Belsen was the first Nazi camp to be exposed to the world, and the London *Times* correspondent began his dispatch: "It is my duty to describe something beyond the imagination of mankind." Now I heard the liberated Jewish prisoners in Belsen say the *Shema*—"Hear O Israel the Lord our God the Lord is One." Weeping in the rain, I said it with them. For a moment I was home.

The war was over. The war would never end. The night the Parliamentary Commission brought in its re-

port from Auschwitz, I was at a performance of *The
Duchess of Malfi*, with Peggy Ashcroft as the Duchess.
On stage the severed hands, strangulations, stabbings,
shriekings were such a hideous extension of the gassings,
piles of women's hair, and wrenched-out teeth reported
in the newspaper that I felt suffocated by history without end. Shaw had called Webster the laureate of Madame Tussaud's waxworks, but Shaw was a vegetarian
and did not understand that cannibalism had come
round again. Kill and kill and kill again!

> Much you had of land and rent;
> Your length in clay's now competent:
> A long war disturb'd your mind;
> Here your perfect peace is sign'd.
> Of what is 't fools make such vain keeping?
> Sin their conception, their birth weeping,
> Their life a general mist of error,
> Their death a hideous storm of terror.
>
> . . . .
> 'Tis now full tide 'tween night and day;
> End your groan, and come away.

The war was over. The war would never end. In the
middle of July I had been flown over to Paris to talk to
French professors of English about the American writing they had missed during the occupation. Liberated
France was certainly different from stodgy old Britain,
where in the coming weeks Prime Minister Attlee would
celebrate the greatest electoral victory of democratic
Socialism by saying to the cheering mass outside the
Ministry of Health: "Don't expect too much of us.
We're batting on a very sticky wicket!" France, by contrast, was in a state of revolutionary newness, had
thrown off the guilt of any possible complicity with the

enemy. It was the age of words, words, and more words. The revolutionary English managed to sound all thumbs and the French made everything new—in words. Everywhere you looked there were the colors, the slogans, the sacred memories of the Resistance. *Ici tombait Jean Lepont, agé vingt ans, mort pour la France. "Mort pour la France"!* The dead boy had bled to death right in front of the Crillon. His blood was now our blood.

Everywhere you looked there was evidence of the religious zeal the French acquired writing their own name. *La France, les Français et les Françaises . . . Le parti des fusillées!* The red, white, blue of revolutionary merriment hung over Paris in massed choruses and bands of color, shrieking *"La révolution française, le renouvellement français, la patrie!"* It was like hearing the *Eroica* for the first time. Among the French teachers I had come over to meet, there was an easiness and generosity about sharing everything at hand that I would not see again. After the first of my lectures, I shared the grassy vegetables that was all my hosts had to eat, and was solemnly presented with a cherished edition of Pascal. The heart of Paris looked like an amusement park, a great flea circus where there was nothing to buy. Emaciated-looking whores, seeming unnaturally tall, teetered by on clumsy wooden platform shoes. *Les grands boulevards* were lined with booths, stalls, and bazaars selling trinkets, lottery tickets, and running games of chance. Everywhere American soldiers, girls in white blouses and gaily colored peasant skirts riding bicycles. All the great public buildings were wrapped in flags. Le Grand Palais featured an exhibition, "HITLER'S CRIMES IN FRANCE," torture instruments, pictures of the dead and dying on the ground, the ashes of Oradour. In one of the main rooms was a large expanded photo-

graph of a corpse on the ground of a concentration
camp, his skeletal arm outstretched, Christ on His cross
again. As you left, a sign rose up before you:

> *Tous ces morts*
> *Tous ces martyrs*
> *Vous disent*
> *Souvenez vous*

Camus's underground paper *Combat*, now in the
open, every day ran the slogan "From Resistance to
Revolution." If Sisyphus was a Frenchman, he certainly
put on a good show. On the eve of Bastille Day a young
French "communard" drinking with Americans reported
that the Americans would intervene in any French revolution and yes, destroy it with flying fortresses. Before
midnight we went to a *veillée des morts pour la libéra-
tion* held at the Arc de Triomphe. Walking down the
Champs Élysées, we met some officers in a jeep and
hopped a ride. Behind us was a small group of Resistance and Army veterans following our jeep to the Arc.
It was fun until we got into the great crowd itself. Then
our jeep and our merriment were out of place, and we
slid off.

The solemnity of the thousands pouring relentlessly
into the Champs Élysées at midnight was France deify-
ing itself in secular mass. The crowd was overwhelmed
and overwhelming. It was one great rite of French self-
absolution. The survivors, like all the old collaboration-
ists, were giving themselves new life by partaking of the
dead. The largest possible flag, a tricolor with one side
draped in black, hung down the middle of the Arc. The
spotlights on it made it the fire of some ancient sacrifice.
The symbolic fire sputtered red smoky lights. All down
the great avenue, microphones in every tree cried,
"France! France! C'est à vous reconstruire la France!"

New French recruits and their girls, licking ice cream cones and petting in the privacy of the crowd, already looked too young to remember the fall of France. The top of the Arc reflected in a pearly-white light the names of Napoleon's great victories. But the Flag was the center of all. We were worshiping Flag, bathing our souls in Flag's liquid light. All heads turned to Flag. Flag gave forgiveness for France's sins as only a god can. All lights were turned on Flag, all speeches made in attendance on Flag. The watchful, subdued crowd stood uneasily within the circle of its fascination. The crowd was just an accompaniment to Flag.

At midnight the *veillée* closed with the "Marseillaise." Cannon went off at regular intervals.

At the American hotel in the Rue d'Astorg, thirty-two-year-old Albert Camus said to Sergeant Albert J. Guerard. "I love Faulkner because I too am a Southerner. I love the dust and the heat." Old, near-forgotten Jules Romains, faultless in his French literary uniform of rusty dark double-breasted suit and *Légion d'honneur* in his buttonhole, looked up at intervals at the shining proud erotic young Camus surrounded by eager literary GIs. Léon Blum, free of Vichy anti-Semites who had tried to put him away in a Nazi concentration camp for "treason," was pleading in *Le Populaire* for a "radicalism based on a respect for man. The social revolution is made necessary by the nature of capitalist development, but it will be made by man for the sake of man. What use will it be to create a new society if we allow human beings to be corrupted in the making of it?" Camus, in *Combat*, complained that "within ourselves we no longer know exactly where we are and what we want. Enthusiasm is going, and seriousness with it."

Everything was being decided with words—the beautiful words of Camus, Sartre, Emmanuel Mounier. Even the C.P posters in the subway warned in the name of our sacred dead against any halt to the purge. I went around all day in an intoxication of French rhetoric; the new books proclaimed a message of unconditional human freedom. In Camus's *L'Étranger* a man who was a stranger to all, a lumpish self-exile and murderer, gave a short surly account of his nasty little life, and the book was conclusive, radiant. Nothing could be more important that what a man owed his own consciousness. Hell was other people. Camus's hero—"the only Christ of which we are worthy"—would die for this. But within his own soul he had experienced an intoxicating flight from our usual submission to others. Camus was the true stranger to our ways.

From within this cavern of the self, human consciousness seemed to escape the confines of law, love, the vanity that in 1940 had exposed its disregard for everything except bourgeois safety and comfort. The abrupt edgy wisdom of Camus's message to his war-besotted generation was still *Resist!* It was the only message left me by my Socialist saints: Silone, Orwell, and now Camus. The writer had to take on the System— and the System seemed unlimited. Outside this intoxication of unlimited personal freedom, word-drunk Paris betrayed the voice of a secret embarrassed hysteria. "Politically" we were all crazies, mad as they come. The Nazis had erected a wall of absolute evil between ourselves and ourselves. The evil rose right up in front of our faces. The password was disgust. Having just barely dragged themselves off the German shit pile, my GI friends in Paris could talk of nothing but the death camps they had seen. One maddened lieutenant said his only interest in Germany was to get up in a plane and defecate over it. Another said that after seeing Dachau he could not look at the half-dressed whores parading Paris without seeing the naked corpses again.

But then, Paris. At eleven in the evening, the evening "gold-beaten out to ages," the old blaze in my heart, I was crossing the Pont Alexandre III. The light just ahead of the bridge was still blue, shot with milky streaks. The bronze horse on the bridge went golden. It was the wine that French painters drink, the pale blue of the Île-de-France. The war was really over.

The next day, walking in Europe at rest, Paris in the noon of summer, I am walking, swimming in the blazing hot afternoon, marching in joy down the Boulevard des Malesherbes toward my hotel off the Place St.-Augustin. Hot, brilliant, solitary: Paris asleep. There are just a few other crazies walking about in this heat. On both sides of me, the awnings over the closed and shuttered shops pull away from me in amazement. Behind me, a newspaper stand, streets thrusting diagonals. The kiosk reminds me of the armed post on the Mall in London camouflaged as a newspaper stand and able to turn its fire in any direction. But the war is over and it is midsummer hot, so hot that I drift down the street drunkenly at home with myself. Under an awning, behind a barred window, is a line of ocarinas, each squat in its shell of terra cotta. Though it is unbearably hot and the ocarinas are just little gooselike toy instruments, I am filled with great joy; I am so happy that I cannot tell my joy from the heat in the street and the sweat running in streams down my clothes. Somewhere off the Boulevard des Malesherbes there is the splash of a fountain.

I returned from Paris to find lying on my couch in the living room a pale little blonde in an English naval uniform with the markings of a petty officer. Even in bed she wore her stiff collar and a little black tie. The rest of her ended in a ragged pink petticoat. Her face was so thin and drained of color that she looked albino. As I stared at her hoping to get my couch back, she smiled at me very nicely and invited me to sit down. In the kitchen someone seemed to be conducting a loud whimpery monologue. The little naval person in my bed laughed. "Afraid my friend of the night has been causing quite a rumpus in your flat." I went into the kitchen to find a large soft-looking man in the uniform of the United Nations Relief and Rehabilitation Association shakily sipping a cup of coffee and looking up in sheepish embarrassment as the Midwest professor of history yelled, "Get that floozie out of here! *Get her out!*" "Aw, gee. Don't *take* it like that." He started to get out of his chair, weakly fell back into it, and to our amazement burst into tears. "I feel just terrible!" he shouted. He oratorically put his hand over his heart. "I shouldna done it! I am being punished enough right here!"

The girl grinned up at me as I returned to the living room. "Keeping you out of your room, aren't I? Afraid I'm not at all well." She got out of bed, still grinning— "Only decent bed I've had for the last nine days!"— and put on her trim navy skirt and solid navy shoes. "Want me to clear out, I suppose? My friend of the night promised me a cup of tea, but he seems engaged." In the kitchen the United Nations Relief and Rehabilitation Association sat in an ecstasy of remorse, ignoring her. I brought her some tea. A fixed, unbending smile seemed to be the only face she could wear. Punctilious, mischievous, she had that English look of positively enjoying a stray social meeting as a battle of wits and unveiling of pretense. Who knew what this day would bring forth? She seemed increasingly delighted with the fact that I clearly did not know how to get rid of her. Wearing her navy tricorne, she lingered over her tea in elaborate slow motion, occupied her chair with crossed legs that she did not seem able to uncross, and smiled, smiled, smiled. We were having an unexpected early-morning tea together and this was the most delightful fact in the world to her.

That English gift of putting a good public face on things, getting out of a situation! At a tinkly little chamber-music concert during a bombing raid a woman next to me had cheerfully whispered when I picked up the program she had nervously dropped, "Panic averted!" I was not surprised to see my little naval person hold up her cup in winsome plea for another, and with that same cheeky, threadbare smile, say, "Thanks, love. That's a good little love!" There was an air about her, an intactness, a way of sizing you up and eluding your own gaze, a way, above all, of protecting her own privacy—right in the middle of nowhere. She was telling stories about herself and laughing over each one. At the moment she was A.W.O.L. She had been "a little out of things, not quite myself, you know"; her husband had died in a freaky army accident crossing a makeshift bridge over the Rhine. "Drift about a lot."

She liked to be picked up, night after night. It was like being taken to a new play. You just never knew what would happen next. Americans. So funny. Always too serious about the sex thing. She made a little face. Bloody shooting gallery is what they thought it was, and her the pigeon. Afterward they got angry at *her* for being so willing. Didn't much care about it one way or the other, you know. And why was she talking to me like this? Little shrug. Didn't know where she was *now*. Didn't know where she was half the time. Floating through the time. Not much rhyme or reason to much of anything just now, was there? Just floating, love, and getting through the days and nights. So often got up in the morning, love, and didn't know where to turn. And at the moment had nothing but the clothes she stood up in.

My English tyke. My I-don't-care girl. It was her *not* caring that of course got me. She had slipped out of the race. I thought of the week at sea still ahead of me, of the large assured American girl from Public Opinion Surveys who would also be returning on the *Queen Mary*. I thought of haves and have-nots, ins and outs, winners and losers. I was a clown whose life was always being taken in hand by women. Why did this always happen to me? Maybe God was a woman after all. Certainly no one else ever had such power over me.

I was on line outside the army post office on Duke Street. The large handsome girl waiting behind me looked enough like the silently angry girl I had seen some nights at the billets, furiously writing away at one V-letter after another, the girl who never spoke to anybody but whose whole physical emanation crackled like a live wire as she sat there writing page after page to her unknown soldier.

It was not the same girl. I would know soon enough that the girl who took over was not the girl whose lonely passion had excited me. This girl, Louise, was measured, calm with the authority of someone who could make herself perfectly understood without words. She would never need words in order to make her wishes felt. My silent woman was powerful. Her power, as her next husband was to say in awe, was positively elemental. She communicated by signs and wonders, deep looks, by the flush that suddenly rushed up her face, by a whole switchboard of colors flashing signals from her skin, by the amazing luster of her brilliant black hair. She certainly did not need words much. She had decided to take me in hand, and she made this blazingly clear by such mental tuggings from her sumptuous body that a minute after I met her standing in front of the army post office in a London street I knew I had been definitely summoned. Like father, like son. It was as if she had put a card in my hand reading "Here I am." The long winter was over.

I went off with Louise, not admitting how glad I was to go. It was a warm wide-open day. The war was over. Pudgy great Churchill, the savior with brandy and cigar, had stood on the balcony of the Ministry of Health and harrumphed, "When shall the reputation and faith of this generation of English men and women fail? I say that in the long years to come not only the people of this island, but from all over the world, wherever the bird of freedom chirps in human hearts, men will look back to what we have done." London had put out the last of Hitler's fires, but large bonfires were lighting on bomb sites and in the middle of the streets.

It was certainly getting very warm. The weather was hot, positively Italian. The sunlight fell evenly on every crack in the gashed and sandbagged streets. London was putting out the last of its fires, and some stubborn ember still smolders as I remember the amazing welcome in Louise's face. That afternoon in St. James's Park the greenness of the willows burned steadily in my eyes, the gaping water tanks at the bombed-out corners were crisp with sun. My mind was beating new wings across the water in the park. And then, in the peace-astonished city, past three torches burning at noon along the river, past the broken naked rooms where a loose toy rattled against the open kitchen pipes, we walked hand in hand. It was growing still hotter. The air drummed with the sound of Lancasters flying low over

the city. Great explosions seemed to be going off somewhere very far away.

The crowd was strangely silent as it drifted slowly,
aimlessly, through the park. People looked up from
the penny chairs where they sat with great propriety,
but slouched with weariness and occasionally smiled
up from their newspapers. Even the few men in uniform who joined the crowd seemed uncertain. Fatigue
lay over the hot, sun-baked park. Everywhere people
were stretched out on crumpled newspapers. The grass
was thick with blankets, mackintoshes, wrinkled sheets
of the *Daily Express* and the *Standard*. All these bodies
flung out on the ground. Everyone open to everyone
else now. I had seen them sleeping on the subway plat-
forms those winter nights, and had just seen them in
the great bomb shelter and first-aid station at Waltham-
stow. Husbands and wives still came in every night long
after the bombings were over to sleep in separate dormitories. The war had been over for weeks, but the
women still put out hot-water bottles for the shock
cases. Lower-class England loved being one vast community bedroom. The bodies were strewn all over the
park, but kept that almighty civility.

My new friend and I sat close together, touching
and not touching. Although her head was bowed, somehow turned away, the heat coming off that warm flashing face and silky summer dress put me into a dream
of the summer ground. I was swimming, leaping, flying
in summer again, absolutely caught by the waves from
this woman's silence.

From where we sat, I could see a man who in this
sudden heat was still wearing a pullover under a rusty
tweed jacket and a mackintosh over it. He was a
meager, tensely controlled figure in the usual humdrum
black glasses with a wire nosepiece. But as he sat on

the grass with his arm around a girl, he wore his wartime shabbiness with an air. His other hand, liver-spotted, lay very near me. He should have been highly uncomfortable in all those clothes, but he did not seem to be. It was amazing what a spot of good weather could do for the English. The day was warm, everyone open to everyone else. The man in the mackintosh suddenly opened his fly, pushed up the girl's skirt, and, still wearing his glasses, still in his mackintosh, with the mackintosh over them both like a blanket, thrust himself firmly into her. Nobody seemed surprised at the sight. In the massed noisy park people delicately passed them without a word.

> A long war disturb'd your mind;
> Here your perfect peace is sign'd.
> . . . .
> 'Tis now full tide 'tween night and day;
> End your groan, and come away.

Chapter VI

NEVER HAD IT
SO GOOD

Back from the wars, and not an apartment to be had in the great rich city of New York. Landlords liked to say the city was "full." Every time I was turned away, I had an image of people after a big meal, rubbing their stomachs. A painter friend of Saul Bellow's, suddenly in the money doing covers for *Fortune*, bought a house in the country and gave me his ramshackle old studio on Pineapple Street in Brooklyn Heights.

The painter was kind, large, oracular. He went in for explanations in a deep, deep voice, a voice that seemed to rumble cosmic theories from the storm center of his belly. Even when his sentences were not fully formed, his explanations were total. The studio, which should have been in pieces, was a tribute to his handiness, his superb confidence. He was a great explainer of his friends to themselves. Bellow was to put him into the lifeboat scene near the end of *Augie March*. He is a mad scientist who has synthesized protoplasm and wants Augie to join him in further biochemical triumphs. At the moment, their ship having just been torpedoed, Augie is alone with him in the lifeboat and has to listen, listen, listen. When *Augie* came out in 1953, I roared at Bellow's growing sense of the ridiculous, of a world gone ridiculous. "Why did I always have to fall among theoreticians!" Bellow's friends were always intellectuals, and intellectuals were his favorite targets. He felt himself cursed by them, enthralled, condemned to know only people who were one part of himself. "Did you recognize the man in the lifeboat?" he proudly asked me. He was astonished, outraged that I hadn't seen the exact resemblance. "It's your old landlord Amos!" he stormed. Like Paul Goodman, Norman Mailer, Isaac Rosenfeld, and many other once old-fashioned moralists, Bellow had been through a Reichian analysis and had learned to demand his rights at all times and with all people. We had been liberated. As Bellow became famous, his sense of his great powers was affronted by the stupidity of others. It would be my function in life, like that of all critics, to disappoint him.

My landlord was soon gone, and his sweet pomposity was not what I had to live with in Pineapple Street. The many pictures he left on the walls—"my real work, not that money work I do for Luce"—were of emaciated rabbis standing behind barbed wire in Nazi camps, skeletal young maidens drooping under the contempt of Nazi guards, Jewish children with eyes like black marbles waiting their turn to the gas chambers. The pictures wore a glossy impasto thick as chicken fat, and were hideously overcolored. Even in the dark they threatened me. Yet they surrounded me with such an air of judgment—Kazin had done nothing, *we* had done nothing, but look at us!—that after a week it occurred to me to take them down. They were bad, sick pictures. In New York outrage was easy.

The studio on Pineapple Street was in a beaten-up old family house on the edge of Fulton Street and Brooklyn Bridge. The halls smelled of an old fire. I

told myself that the house dated from the days when the
burghers on Brooklyn Heights could literally see their
ships come in and in deep winter walked the ice to their
offices on Wall Street. Across the street a plaque over
the garbage cans behind the Greek greasy spoon marked
the site where on July 4, 1855, a printer who worked
only when he felt like it had himself set up in the
printing shop of the Rome Brothers the first edition of
Leaves of Grass.

Many noises rose up from a radio store on the block
and a bar-and-grill popular with sailors in from the
Navy Yard. At night, colored reflections played at my
window from the madly over-bright electric sign towering over the Hotel St. George and the lights of the
movie theater right across the street. In warm weather
the projectionist kept his door open, and I would hear
from the sound track unrelated snatches of background
music and loud arguments.

I had a lot to listen to in my two rooms on Pineapple
Street. My nextdoor neighbor, a Mr. Felippez from
Colombia, woke me every morning at five when he
started for his garage job in Bay Ridge by tramping
through the long wooden hall of his apartment on the
other side of my bedroom. Our two "apartments" on
the top floor had been crudely boxed off by a beaver-
board wall and a door that had been thickly painted
over, sealed and locked and glazed down, every chink,
to make sure that neither of us would use it. I could
hear everything that went on in Mr. Felippez's hall, and
every dark morning my day would begin with the sound
of Mr. Felippez clearing his throat, Mr. Felippez re-
lieving himself, Mr. Felippez's heavy feet passing down
the hall, mounting along the wall of my bedroom, getting louder and louder as he neared the door, and finally

crashing in my ears with a bang, carrying every thump down the wooden stairs with it.

There was nothing to do about it. I tried sleeping in my other room, but could hear him just as well. I once tried to persuade Mr. Felippez to depart for his job with a lighter tread. He smiled and smiled with many gold teeth, understood not a word, and after an enthusiastic handshake went off still smiling. The house was just a decaying hulk on the Brooklyn beach, very different from the mansion on Montague Terrace where Auden smiled, "Really, it's all as quiet here as the country!" or the beautiful old brownstone in Columbia Heights, the very perch of the greatest harbor, where Mailer would soon establish himself.

Those sleepless hours in the morning dark were difficult and beautiful. The harbor was all around me as I lay in bed listening to tugs hooting a block away. By dawn I would get up to find my painter's skylight and great north windows awash with sea light. I had coffee with Bach as I struggled with the unaccompanied partitas and then groped my way to the typewriter. I had started a loose unwieldy book about New York-at-large, based on my hypnotized walking of the city. Walking was my way of thinking, of escape into myself, of dreaming the details back. The book was all externals, buildings, loneliness, my daily battle with New York. After Mr. Filippez woke me in the early morning, I would lie there trying grimly to think the book out from the throbbings around me. I was alarmed every night I went up the usually empty steel-resounding elevator taking me to the street from the deeply dug Clark Street station. Walking past the blank back wall of the Hotel St. George, I faced the emptiness of those streets before I reached the Pineapple Street house; even the front

steps smelled as if a fire had just been put out. My
friends all lived in Manhattan and did not like to come
out. In the night I could hear vague screams and men-
acing noises; there were apparitions in the dead quiet
streets that made walking along the harbor a fearful
confrontation with shadows.

At the foot of Pineapple Street, overlooking the harbor, a promenade below the backs of the old Victorian
houses was being built. The whirligig of lower New
York and the sight of Brooklyn Bridge leaping its way
across made me think of my old neighbor Hart Crane:

> Under thy shadow by the piers I waited;
> Only in darkness is thy shadow clear . . .

Returning at night from my date with Louise in her
chic little walk-up on Fifty-fifth off Fifth, I would bar-
ricade myself in under the painter's skylight, shiver,
and try not to think of my comfy entanglement. Pineapple Street was a clutch at my old innocence, like the
book about walking New York that had everything in
it except me. Louise thought I was foolish to insist on
trudging back to Brooklyn night after night after making love in Manhattan. And it was a Manhattan that
had never been richer, smoother, more expansive. The
richness of postwar New York was part of Louise and
my visceral infatuation. The old war had barely ended,
but there was a new wartime excitement in the air as
America and Russia squared off at each other. Old
Communists could not stop lying and ex-Communists
found it unnecessary to look war prosperity in the face.
Government, protective since the New Deal, now had
an authority so overwhelming that it was hard to admit
the fear.

New York was triumphant, glossy, more disorderly

than ever, but more "artistic," the capital of the world, of the old European intellect, of action painting, action totally liberated, personal, and explosive. Harold Rosenberg, always the most penetrating and skeptical of the old New York intellectuals, was to say that action painting was the liberty of the painter to "fuck up the canvas." Where once the El had darkened cobblestoned streets, had romantic twilights for a Stieglitz, a John Sloan, an E. E. Cummings, New York was now rich in aluminum and steel buildings, buildings that resembled the massed file cabinets and coded systems they were built to hold. There were banks on every corner. The great New York light, the glare of New York, the unmatchable effrontery of New York had never been so open. It was a constant challenge just to walk up Park Avenue. The straightness of the streets—columns in a bookkeeper's account book—made you run and claw your way to your goal. There was always an immediate goal. Up and down, straight and across, numbered and ranged against each other like a balance sheet, the great midtown streets were glowing halls of power. The sharpness of outline was overwhelming. The tritest word for the city was "unbelievable." Its beauty rested on nothing but power, was dramatic, unashamed, flinging against the sky, like a circus act, one crazy "death-defying" show after another. Walking away from Louise's little apartment at Fifty-fifth or her parents' great big one at Madison and Seventieth, I found myself mentally retracing the straight lines across the avenues up and down the new buildings. Those too even lines were taking me where *they* would take me, not where I once had planned to go.

On the *Queen Mary*, loaded with returning troops, Louise seemed to be waiting for me whenever I left the enormous cabin I shared with dozens of soldiers who

did not know if they were going to be discharged or
sent to Japan. It seemed meaningless to avoid this
warmly handsome, always silent girl who had lighted on
me and aimed for love as if she were a bullet. We floated
into New York Harbor one hot August night to find
every shoreline lighted up as for a super-Christmas.
Hundreds of thousands of people were lined up on Bay
Ridge in Brooklyn, on Staten Island, on Governors
Island, on the Battery, on every inch in Jersey. Red
fireboats and tugboats blew their whistles; little fishing
boats bobbed up and down the bay with great lettered
signs: "WELCOME HOME BOYS. WELCOME HOME." Every
coil and indent of New York Harbor seemed stretched
with light that night. New York made a single exultant
beam from Sandy Hook up to Fifty-ninth Street. As
Louise and I stood on the top deck watching the great
return of Americans to America, there came from the
hundreds and hundreds of soldiers hopping up and
down around us one single scream of joy. We were
home.

But Louise was not what I had come home for; I
impatiently said good night at the pier. It was not until
weeks later that I finally took it in forever that Natasha
and I were no longer married. To my astonishment,
I found Louise waiting for me one night on the battered
steps of Pineapple Street. Then began a new life with
this handsome, attentive, calmly passionate woman—
my luxuriously silent woman—who nevertheless remained as distant as I myself was glad to be.

It was rather a businesslike affair. The calming effect
of inherited capital was a revelation. Passionately drawn
to me as Louise declared herself to be, it became clear
that she did not altogether approve of me. Part of an
illustrious German-Jewish clan, she had not the slightest
understanding of Jews still spinning in the Russian tur-

bulence. I was fascinated by—disbelieving of—her lack of all Jewish anxieties. Her college roommate had been an open anti-Semite. There were Jews for whom the Jews did not exist. There were so many silent limits to our pleasant arrangement that we seemed programmed for brilliant evenings in brilliant mid-Manhattan and lovely weekends at her parents' Connecticut farm.

The lovemaking went like clockwork, and often resembled it. Life was full of benefits. I was losing my terror and it did not occur to me that as lovers we were just trying each other out like a new purchase. We were "adjusting" in the great American style. The age of plenty rolled out before me like the softest of beds. What lovely warm evenings those were walking back from Carnegie Hall, the Russian Tea Room, the theater, our favorite Italian restaurant on Fifty-sixth. Fifth Avenue glowed as I felt her warm silky back against my palm, and the thickly carpeted steps of her walk-up had the softness of her body under my body as, just behind her and already in a trance of wanting her, I watched her run up the stairs with the key already in her hand.

Nothing now seemed so awesome, deep, close to the hidden God who burned over my childhood. My parents still lived in the same Brownsville tenement. News of the big money had not reached this house painter and this "home" dressmaker. They were as poor and isolated from America-at-large as the day they had met. They lived where they had always lived, and more and more they lived without hope. But now they were surrounded by poor blacks more than by poor Jews. Any Friday night I went back for the Sabbath meal, I hungrily sought the smallest details for the childhood I was describing—the fresh dye in the clothes piled up outside a factory off Sackman Street, the seltzer bottles trundling off the rollers as if they were rolling in from Bessarabia, Vilna, and Minsk. I was desolated by the old Jews left over in Brownsville, with their ritual wigs, their legs bent like crutches, their boarded-up storefronts, their community kitchens for the destitute, and their bitter fears of the blacks.

Brownsville was a foreign country now, a forbidden country to prospering Jews who had once lived there. It was a poison spot on the New York map even to the hundreds and thousands of blacks from the South wearily making it into the ghetto vacated by Jews. Walking back into the country of my birth, I felt separated from everything except my youth. The new mass-housing projects in Brownsville were like mass fortresses that had dropped in from Mars. Like the city housing dominating the lower East Side at the other end of the Brooklyn Bridge, they displayed not a new city but old New York invaded, here and there, by the administrative bulldozer. There were enforced settlements where once there had been neighborhoods. A sentimental Jewish librarian in the Brownsville Public Library, working with disoriented, frightened, and angry blacks "relocated" by the city into the tenements the Jews had fled, was outraged by the lack of will and fight among the new migrants being dumped into Brownsville. They should have been more "working-class," more militant. They soon were—against her.

The gifted French photographer Henri Cartier-Bresson, with whom I was to work on a book of New York scenes, was an aristocratic radical sweetly disdainful of the welfare state and the new mass-housing projects. It was old New York, the oldest New York left at both ends of Brooklyn Bridge, that gave pleasure to his genius eye as we walked the shady old wooden boardwalk down the center of the bridge.

"It breathes!" Cartier said happily about Brooklyn Bridge. "See how it breathes!" Brooklyn Bridge had been designed just after the Civil War, and the New York still left around it was old. Below the bridge on the Manhattan side was "the Swamp," center of the wholesale leather industry, and old assayers' shops, dealers in perfume and wines. John Augustus Roebling, the maker of the bridge, had planned storage space for wines in the great stone caverns where the anchorage of the bridge tied up. They now held the city's nineteenth-century files; I imagined clerks who sat there on high stools amid ancient records and blueprints and looked as if they had stolen out of old London prints. Up above, in front of eighteenth-century City Hall, was Park Row and Printing House Square, where all the great New York dailies were once published; the statue of Benjamin Franklin presented by the printers of New York, the old New York *World* building, with its green dome, and the New York *Tribune* recalled history from Horace Greeley to Joseph Pulitzer.

On both sides of the Manhattan end were factories and warehouses still recalling New York's iron age. On one of them was preserved a series of ornamental fire escapes sculptured with the figures of athletes out of the old *Police Gazette*. Above it was a gigantic dead clock, its hands forever resting at three o'clock. An age passed this way. Here New York first sank its piles in the river, always in sight of water as it began the age of plunder. The factory buildings remaining in the late 1940s, with their battered fronts and broken windows, the iron storage chambers and warehouses cut into the anchorages, were like the dirt-green scum left behind by the industrial rivers of New York as they wash against the rock.

Old New York, the bottom deposit of the commerce

that began here and moved away. The clock never moved. Over it was lettered the name of a square to which it no longer belonged. Like the tenements and clotheslines across the way on the lower East Side, like the pillars of the El still darkening the Bowery, tying up the bridge in mountains of wire and blocks of stone, they shut in a world from time. But straight ahead were the bail-bond brokers and shysters whom Cartier-Bresson photographed on the steps of the county court-house in Foley Square. He caught them with big cigar in mouth and overcoats open to show the silk lining. They comically posed for this mild-looking "tourist" with the Leica around his neck.

Cartier-Bresson's great gift was instantaneous, breath-taking lucidity. A narrow eighteenth-century alley off Wall Street suddenly presented a man sitting between two walled surfaces. This man was not pathetic, not imprisoned between two walls. But neither did he belong anywhere else. The lawyer on the steps of the Federal Court House naturally presented his big successful belly to Cartier. The old gentleman we saw on Brooklyn Heights with the homburg, goatee, and scarf perfectly draped was as right to Willow Street as the GI sitting on a fire escape under the bottom iron layers of the bridge. Cartier's genius was matter-of-fact. His light, noncommittal sympathy for the many wrecks living in the shadows of Brooklyn Bridge never swelled into any-thing more than an upper-class radical's inventory of presence after presence in a New York closed to mid-dle-class attention. His elegantly agile figure skipped along the littered streets, the Leica suddenly winging into his hands. In his English tweeds, his pleasant air of having an expensive camera to play with, he looked like an innocent, with nothing to do but use up some film. It was easy, bantering agreeableness to work with him.

Then you saw what he had come up with after a long day, and felt pressed by the social logic with which he had taken the measure of New York.

Cartier was the photographer as thinker. Stieglitz had to love what he saw, had to make it his own. Walker Evans had been pitiless, reticent in his anger and distaste without concealing anything. Cartier saw people moving, always on the run, caught up in a motion of hurry and search, but stuck on the flypaper of their own minds. There was no exaggeration, nothing set up—above all, no mockery. For all his firm left-wing logic, he did not push a theory. What counted was the city man in the city setting, the man and the street as one. He started with the human passer-by in a social world that was the other side of himself, Cartier-Bresson. This passer-by, this stranger, was what I lived with every day of my life without always seeing him. Cartier was teaching us to see him.

Cartier did not overvalue the camera or himself. In an age of camera "artists," camera wizards, Gullivers who thought they had poor old Lilliput at their mercy, he honestly saw himself as a reporter lucky enough to roam the whole world and to see the different parts of it in clear perspective. He was rich, cosmopolitan; he had an Asian wife. It was not from him that I learned he had been for three years a prisoner of war in Germany and had escaped to France, where he had organized underground photography units. The visual subject possessed him. On his relaxed evenings in an old wooden house on East Fifty-eighth Street near the cars shooting off Queensboro Bridge, he patiently painted at a modest little landscape. He worked the whole area over from every side of the rectangle, and then stared at his picture with his little smile and matter-of-fact eye.

He was soon on the wing to Egypt, Brazil, the Chi-

nese Revolution. New York to Cartier was an assignment like any·other, but it was the book of my life.
Sitting on the roof garden of the chic new building of
the Museum of Modern Art, looking straight across to
the glass-fronted pyramids rising on every side of me,
I felt myself swimming in the reflected surfaces of some
great goldfish bowl. New York was gold skin, kaleido-
scopic glass, snaky cactus on a roof garden conceived
in the image of the reproductions and posters that
framed you in. The Museum presented you, too, as an
example of correct modern taste.

Below the great avenues went up and down in ruler-
sharp order. New York was the greatest living machine.
The power it radiated was in my image of women walking Fifth Avenue in the sun; women wearing brass,
leather; women reflected in the aluminum, steel, glass,
tile they walked past. In the sharp-pointed clickety-clack
of Louise's shoes, the night-black sheen of Louise's
dress, the tiger cover of Louise's perfume and Louise's
bed, I could not distinguish voluptuous New York from
the soft sway of her figure going up the steps on Fifty-
fifth Street. She shared with her casual power something
I had always devoutly believed: New York had secret
rulers. The silent girl I had met waiting on line outside
the army post office in London now displayed the unmistakable authority that came with money. She made
decisions, arranged dinners, weekends, the Cape, passage to Italy. The less we admitted our different values,
the more she trusted to her powerful faith in herself to
iron out difficulties. Her reserve about me, even when
she seemed to be enjoying me most, was startling. It
was a shock to notice how much the rest of you could
be disapproved of by someone who regularly welcomed
you in bed. I had suddenly gone from a world in which
everyone and everything I loved seemed a more gra-

cious extension of myself to one where I felt suspended in the clear cold light of some unending detachment.

After circling around each other for two years, we got married. That night, driving to her parents' farm in Connecticut, she was so privately uncertain that for the first time in her life she drove straight into the back of another car. Limping, off we went for our honeymoon to Italy, both of us incommunicative, lonely, and excited. I had a Guggenheim and she knew the country. She was mad about Italians. For more than anything else except our son Tim, I would be grateful to her for Italy.

The Polish ship to Genoa was full of Italian Americans carrying over radios, electric appliances, cigarettes by the trunkful. There were also anti-Fascist intellectuals returning from their long American exile. Italy in the early summer of 1947 was a broken, busted country with an insanely inflated currency, bridges still missing above the rivers into which the Germans or Americans had exploded them, electric power you could never depend on from moment to moment, the obvious daily takeover of the big cities by a powerful restored Communist Party full of ecstatically credulous Italian workmen. The bus from Genoa to Florence—crammed with the first tourists in years, the corners of luggage covers on the open top beating against the back windows— whizzed past demolished railroad tracks and broken bridges, down mountain valleys, finally through Tuscan towns where leather-faced men in corduroys sat in the stony town squares before fountains framed by the immense shadows of dominating churches and palaces.

To an American writer seeing it for the first time, Italy was heaven. In Florence the lovely quiet old Albergo Berchielli on the Lungarno Acciaioli was virtually empty. When you entered from the street through the old-fashioned bead portières shielding everything inside from the sun, you fell into a cool blue lagoon made up of sepia photos of Michelangelo's David, Cellini's Perseus, the Duomo. You walked in sun, rested from sun. The city was a series of fine crystalline sensations. It was cherry season, and at every meal basins of cherries were served up swimming in cold water. Florence hushedly mirrored itself and dwelled on itself within every parlor and up ever staircase. Culture peeped everywhere through old lacework. In the little stationery shop next to the hotel, the proprietor—surrounded by still more framed photographs of the Duomo—spoke a withered Pre-Raphaelite English. He was easily affrighted by every memory of the war, and so genteel that the Anglo-American Florence of the past was all before me. I expected to see the pale, elegant figure of Henry James's Gilbert Osmond lingering in the doorway waiting for his American heiress to appear.

To the left, the Ponte Vecchio; to the right, the provisional iron structure that has replaced the Santa Trinità. The gallery that leads from the Uffizi Gallery to the Pitti Palace is broken in the middle; on both sides of the Ponte Vecchio a jagged heap of ruins, lit up under the solitary street lamp, has that crumpled, naked look of theater scenery the moment the footlights are turned off. In the daytime the ruins in Florence look incongruous—a tabloid headline in an illuminated manuscript—when you see them against the round towers and the slender cypresses, each cluster of trees supreme on its hill. The Germans were on one side of the river and the Americans on the other—hard to think of Florence being fought over on this street.

At the noon hour an old man in an old boat, moored in the middle of the Arno just below our window, is patiently, hour by hour, dredging up mud from the bottom, then just as patiently packing it away on every side of him. Across the way a boy swims off a little delta that has formed in front of his house. A scull shoots by, propelled by a young man in tights and wearing that smart beard—Dino Grandi, Italo Balbo—why did you think it was worn only by Fascist aviators and ambassadors? Just below the embankment, on the other side of the river, is the familiar whitewash slogan we saw on every wall as we came down from Genoa: "VOTE FOR THE COMMUNIST PARTY WHICH WILL GIVE YOU PEACE WORK LIBERTY."

Florence's old English community has come back—some never left—to reclaim property. "Their" lounge is an old family parlor, with the rubber plant on a lace doily over the upright piano, heavy brass-framed pictures of hunting dogs and "The Stag at Eve," old copies of the *Illustrated London News*. A withered English blonde sits in one corner, reading the *Times*, and from time to time calls across the lounge in a piercing county accent, recounting to another *inglese* her difficulties with the Italian law, "so unnecessarily complicated." In another corner an art historian with the burned-out face of Oswald Spengler; completely shaven head, rocklike Prussian military skull, burning little eyes, a fierce wide scar running across his left cheek and deep into his neck like a singed envelope. Junker face, haughty with suffering: he never looks at anyone and prowls around the lounge smoking cigarettes out of a long jeweled holder.

All signs and instructions are first in English, then in French, occasionally underwritten in Italian. The atmosphere is that of a provincial British hotel in an eternity of Sundays, though *they* "no longer come to us as they used to. They, too, are passing through difficult days." Americans, of course, are wonderful—so gay, so young, and so on; but the manager's daughter, whose English is impeccable BBC, complains with a little pout that her friends laugh at her—"my accent has become a little coarse"—since the GIs were here.

A young American writer of Italian parentage originally came here before the war to finish a medical course. Now an ex-GI and armed with the previous green passport (which may save us in the last act as Roman citizenship saved St. Paul), he gets around familiarly in American Army circles from Leghorn to Pisa and has the friendliest relations with the brass. He and the grim-faced toughie we are saddled with every time we see him are engaged in some elaborate lira-dollar game. The lira is 650 to the dollar; last week it was 900. Everybody changes money on the black market; the writer *is* a black market, and goes around Florence with great wads of sweaty tattered lire (looking like soiled Kleenex) stuffed into one of those vertical leather zipped bags that are sold at home for packing a bottle of booze into a suitcase. "It's even too dirty to wipe yourself with," he says as he holds up a fistful of lire. He plans to put into his novel on postwar Italy a long section on money—money as infected blood, money jamming every sewer, the sweaty crumpled money falling totally apart as a final joke on the Americans who come over to grab it. He chats with me under the statue of Lorenzo the Magnificent, the latest *New Yorker* in one hand and his moneybag in the other. Looking at his money blows him up like an Oklahoma Indian who has just discovered oil.

His novel will feature enemies as allies, allies as enemies. There will be a chapter on German deserters and American black soldiers hiding out together in the woods, Italians and Americans during the fighting around Florence stealing each other blind. Meanwhile "I'm piling it up so that I can write the crazy novel of this crazy period. I'm going to make enough to stake myself to a year off and vanish." Though he cannot understand why, he is clearly having the time of his life. The thing's absolutely unreal: he's way up there, in that new American world in Europe. After years of being a nobody at home, and no doubt a "wop" to the gentiles, he is now making the most of his Newark Italian, dines with generals, and patronizes the old country. Actually he does not seem to like Italians very much—says they "simply have no character," and with a certain intellectual disapproval outlines the black market to me, specifying all the ways in which the government does not govern. The whole economy now rests on illegal buying and selling. The political situation is divided between "the priests and the Commies." Personally, he assures me, he is a democratic Socialist, and rails against the surrender of the Italian Socialist Party to the Communists. But this with a bored, mocking air: what can you expect of Italians? Funny to see him among the really big American finaglers here who have come to pick up some *real* money. With all his commercial savvy and know-it-all air, he really hates Italy for being such a shambles. It has left him morally nowhere.

A painter from Odessa, exiled to Florence, drove us out to Settignano to see the Bernard Berenson villa, I Tatti. In the courtyard, which might have been the entrance to one of the retreats at which the storytellers in *The Decameron* flourished during the plague, there was a row of neat little lemon trees, each set in its black bucket with finicky care. The lemons all dropped in a plane, all exactly equal from the ground—with what

immense and induced art it was not difficult to imagine.
The elaborated niceness of the symmetry introduced
me to Berenson's mind even before I met him.

The butler seemed uncertain whether to admit us,
Berenson being away, but Leo Stein, Gertrude's brother,
came out of the library and offered to show us around.
Stein was a tall, gentle, gangling old man, seventy-five,
who looked like a Jewish Uncle Sam—rustic, nervous,
deaf, but full of talk and little wisecracks, all of them
delivered in a flat, uncompromised American twang
after forty years of Europe. It was strange to be taking
in Stein's mussed blue serge suit and hearing aid, the
knapsack over his shoulder, in Berenson's braided garden. He sounded as if he had never left Allegheny,
Pennsylvania.

The Berenson house was Tuscan "rustic" in a rebuilt
style, quietly showing off exquisite pictures Berenson
had acquired in his many deft negotiations. The house
featured one of the great private libraries of the world.
The whole thing looked like a private chapel raised to
the art connoisseur's ideal experience, where every corridor and corner had been worked to make a new altar-
piece for "B.B." to display his adoration of art. The
smallest detail revealed a man who had the means to
reject all intrusions of mere necessity. He had shaped
the whole with an inflexible exactness of taste that was
just a little chilling. Its immediate effect was not so
much to lead you to its pictures as to shame you into a
fresh realizaion of how awkward, soiled, and generally
no-account life could seem compared with art. In the
dim light of the shaded corridor a Sienese saint gazed
past me, lost in his own dream of time and interred in
an oily gloss—his face tortured with thought and good-
ness, and somehow *away*, bearing my praise and awe

with equal indifference. What golden and mysterious fish!

I noticed how jumpy Stein became when we stopped too long before certain pictures. Showing Berenson's house must have seemed a bit too much; he had been in and out of the place for years, and came daily to work in the library. I was a little surprised, knowing of his lifelong concern with painting, to hear him confess that it was not the work of art that mattered to him so much as the mind of the painter. He was very much preoccupied with every sort of psychological question and told us that he had just (at seventy-five) finished psycho-analyzing himself. The devouring interest of his life was to discover why men lie. This was a problem that touched him very deeply. He had been showing us pictures and rooms with a certain irritation, and made affectionate, mocking little digs at Berenson's expense (their rivalry is famous). Suddenly, in Berenson's study, he went off into a long discourse about psychology and the need for scientific exactness in determining character. He spoke with an uneasy intensity, as if he had been held in on this matter for a very long time, and wanted our understanding with or without our approval. It was of the greatest importance, this practice of lying; it would be a key to all sorts of crucial questions, if only he could get his hands on the solution; it was, you might say, at the center of human ambiguity. As he went on, he would look up at us every so often, pull irritably at his hearing aid, and grumble, "What? What? You think what? I can't hear you!" riding impatiently over us and his deafness for standing in his way, and rearing up against our stray comments. It was very moving in an old man, seeming to come straight from the heart: "It's important! It's the big thing! No one looks these facts in the face! Animals can't lie and human beings lie all the time!"

He was, however, very happy these days; he had got over a bad illness and was just publishing a new book of critical theory, *Appreciations: Painting, Poetry, Prose.* He talked about his writing with a mingled anxiety and enthusiasm, as if he were just starting out on his career; though very frail, he gave the appearance of a young writer speculating dreamily on all the books he was going to write. He had always suffered from being Gertrude Stein's half-noticed elder brother. She had died within the year, releasing him to get on with his career— at seventy-five. His resentment of Gertrude shone through everything he said. Talking about their childhood in Europe, when they had been trundled around by a father "who didn't think we could get any kind of decent education in America," he remembered most how Gertrude had always lorded it over him. "But you know," he said simply, "she was the kind who always took herself for granted. I never could." And one saw that she had dominated the situation when they had decided to make their lives in Europe. "She always took what she wanted! She could always talk her way into anything! Why"—discussing *their* pioneer collection of modern paintings—"she never even *liked* Picasso at first! Couldn't see him at all! *I* had to convince her. And then she caught on and got 'em for practically nothing."

After all these years, the bitterness rankled, keeping him young. How often had he been approached only as a lead to his famous sister, and this by people who hadn't the slightest knowledge of his interests? This, added to his long uncertainty about himself, lent that strangely overemphatic quality to his interest in "facts." Facts—the masculine domain of elder brothers humbly and grimly toiling away at *real* things, like aesthetics and psychology. While Gertrude, the Jewish mother of them all, took Anderson and Hemingway under her wing, and did as she pleased. She put the English language in her lap like a doll, making it babble out of her undefeatable narrowness and humor. She always took what she wanted. There was Leo Stein, at seventy-five, going back and back to the old childhood struggle. They had transferred the cultural rivalry in that ambitious family to Europe and worked it in and out of the expatriate life, making of Paris and Florence new outposts for their fierce ambition.

A few weeks after our meeting, Leo Stein suddenly died, and was laid out in front of the altar in the village church. My painter friend from Odessa couldn't get over the sight of dead Leo in front of the altar, worshippers walking around him. "He looked as if they had no other place to put him for the moment."

I had missed Berenson in Settignano, but finally caught up with him in Rome at the grand Hotel Hassler just off Trinità dei Monti. It was almost November, very cold, and he sat in a corner of the sofa with a rug over his knees, as self-consciously correct (to himself) as one of his own sentences. Eighty-two: delicate little *grand personnage* with a little white beard, frail, an old courtier in his beautiful pale-gray double-breasted suit, every inch of him engraven fine into an instrument for aesthetic responsiveness and intelligence. Self-made, self-conscious in every breath, he spoke English with such ostentatious elegance, blandly delivering himself of his words one by one, that the words might have been freshly cracked walnuts he was dropping into my hand. The famous "B.B." had turned himself into the glossiest possible work of art. How he shone before me, even

for me—every new visitor was someone to be added to
his court.

He took me in quickly, coldly, somehow fiercely.
"Your name is Russian or Hebrew and of course you
are a Jew? There seem to be so many young Jews writing in the States these days. How is that? Quite a difference from my time!" "Oh! and is there still so much
anti-Semitism in the States these days? Oh!" He listened
closely, tensely, a little suspiciously.

Just fifty years younger, I was not unrelated to this
Jew born in Lithuania in the Czarist Pale, and taken at
ten to Boston. Over the years the Butremanz ghetto
had been transformed, not so much by Berenson as
by lordly friends like Lincoln Kirstein, who once explained to me that Berenson had been "born into the
Jewish aristocracy, the old gentry." Berenson had grown
up in the Boston slums, had turned Episcopalian at
Harvard and Catholic in Italy. But once launched in
the great art world as a prime expert and authority, the
"authenticator" of Renaissance Italian paintings, being
a "Jewish aristocrat" had probably become his *carte de
visite* to the outside world, from President Eliot's Harvard to Henry James's London and Edith Wharton's
Paris. At that moment in Rome it was also a way of
getting himself out of any possible entanglements he
may have incurred by interesting himself in American
Jews. To be a "Jewish aristocrat" did not diminish one's
foreignness—this immigrant lad lived for sixty years in
Italy—but transferred it to a higher plane. There was
once a Harlem black who went South with a turban on
his head and was welcomed everywhere as a foreign
potentate.

Berenson kept up feverishly with America, took
every possible magazine and newspaper. There was even
a copy of that shabby little Rome *Daily American* on

his lap when I came in. He had remained in Italy during the war, had gone into hiding when the Germans were all over the Tuscan countryside. He solemnly affirmed that F.D.R. had alerted an American Army detachment to save him from the Nazis. Wartime hysteria in occupied Italy had also led to suspicion of Berenson as a German agent, and the renewal of his passport had been actually held up. At one point in our conversation he suddenly took the priceless green document out of his breast pocket and showed it to me with a flourish. But with all the uncertainties and suspicions that dogged Berenson because of his foreignness and the wealth he had gained from authenticating old masters to Lord Duveen's millionaire customers, he was a master at receiving visitors.

He had become an international celebrity since the war. It was fascinating to see the public elegance he gave the freezing cold hotel room we sat in, the thermos of tea, and the comforter on his knees with the Rome *Daily American* perched on it. He held up both hands to show me how the printer's ink had come off onto his extraordinarily long supple fingers; made a grimace. Thus he paid for keeping up with everything since the war. Every day he went through at least one Italian, French, Swiss, and English newspaper; took every review and magazine, even *Time*. It was all out of an intense curiosity in the political behavior of the human animal. Watching this perfectly composed picture of Olympian detachment, as finely put together as his great library, I was being asked to form a picture of him at I Tatti as Voltaire in retirement, a kind of European intelligence office—subtly remote from the pressure of events, each of which he filed away in some chamber of his apparatus for meditation.

Berenson kept coming back to Henry Miller; he had

recently discovered *Tropic of Cancer*, which amused
him in a contemptuous kind of way. He was not unfond
of this sexual rogue. He vaguely shared my admiration
for the moving long story in *Sunday After the War* that
recounts Miller's return to his parents' home. With this
thought under consideration he turned Miller into a
dreary historian of the unnecessary lower-class bleak-
ness of Brooklyn rather than the "cloacal" and confused
rebel he had just put down. He slowly and ostentatiously
pronounced "clo-a-cal" in a way that made me see all
the refuse coming up from the bottom of the Tiber and
gathering itself into the collected works of Henry Miller.
And of course I shared in the general illusion that
Kafka was a great writer? "There is a very small light of
reason burning in the world," he said portentiously.
"Mr. Kafka tries to put it out."

He had small, firm, exact judgments on everything
that crossed his path: his years, his fortune, his snob-
bery, and his taste had given him a freedom to ignore
contemporary fashions that was stimulating if hardly
satisfying. The aesthetic and upper-class world the
young Berenson had broken into remained his reference.
Picasso was a willful faker. Matisse had *once* known
how to paint, Joyce and Eliot were just obstructions on
the classic path of reason. Berenson the self-made, the
art-made, for all his talk of "life-enhancement," was
not giving a thing to the living. We had been discussing
the cultural inertia and the provincialism that become
evident after one settles into Italy, and he thought that
the decline had set in with the Risorgimento. The old
élite had surrendered its prerogatives. Why, in his first
years in Italy, the late 1880s, one could still pick up
from Roman pushcarts first editions of English eighteenth-century novels that had come straight from the
shelves of the old nobility! He found Italians now lack-

ing in individuality. It was curious to see how he went straight to fundamental themes of "style." His long romance with Italy had never included Italians—just old masters and landscape. But even Italy as he first knew it, and as he tried to keep it in I Tatti with such devotion and finesse, had had to bear a lot of jarring under the pressure of events. It is hard to possess fully everything we buy in this world.

We talked about his old college friend Santayana, who was living not far away in Rome as a guest of the Nuns of the Blue Sisters. They no longer saw each other. It was fascinating to think of those two old intellectual grandees finishing out their lives in Italy, one a Spaniard, the other a Lithuanian Jew, both formed by their early life in Boston and at Harvard. They had been together at the Boston Latin School, at Harvard, in Germany thereafter—Santayana always one year ahead, as he was one year older. Santayana the thinker was much admired by Berenson, who despite his great air was a very timid and somewhat artificial writer. It was only in talking about Santayana that he stopped seeming older and more *distingué* than anybody you had ever heard of. But they were estranged, and I did not need the oily and characteristically malicious tone Santayana took about him in his memoirs to guess that Santayana had ended the friendship.

In Santayana's eyes, Art was nothing compared with Philosophy, and a professional "expert" on Art was even more removed from Truth than a good painter. In any event, Santayana remained a Spanish absolutist in his dislike of Jews. Berenson the great artifact, a Gatsby who kept up appearances to the end, was in Santayana's eyes simply a pushing Jew. It was Berenson's genuine passion for Renaissance painting that most aroused Santayana's contempt. "Art" was just self-

indulgent, a minor activity unlike divine philosophy.
Despite Berenson at eighty-two as a frail and noble
Magnifico, the *soigné* air, the echoes of Pater and
Matthew Arnold, the great fortune built up by Berenson as the authenticator for that super salesman Duveen,
the villa I Tatti, the "Jewish aristocracy" of Lithuania,
one was compelled, after sixty years, to recall Berenson
as a young immigrant given his start by Mrs. Gardner.
As a work of art, Berenson himself was incomparable,
but there was hardly anyone left to authenticate *him*.
He said more than once that he felt a failure. In his own
eyes he was. Perhaps, like so many immigrants, he tried
too hard. "I was drawn to him," said Elizabeth Hardwick, "because he was so unhappy."

The last time I saw him, he was slowly walking with
a party of friends in front of the Villa Medici, on the
hill overlooking the Spanish Steps and much of Rome.
It was a part of his schedule every day to look at the
sunset. A young American, excited to recognize him,
walked over in a babble of enthusiasm. Berenson coldly
waved him away. "Young man! You're standing in the
way of the sunset!"

The military train took us from Florence to Udine, then
to Villach in Austria. We stopped for a night at a British
military camp, where officers in Bermuda shorts were at
ease in the blazing Alpine summer. Then appeared a
shot-up, gutted, blackened miserable piece of ex-Nazi
rolling stock full of broken windows, which looked as
if it had lugged the victims of the Master Race all over
Europe. It was an unforgettable journey up to Salzburg.
The tracks halfway to Bischofshofen gave out, the passengers climbed into trucks; standing, we bounded along
for hours before we were led into still another bombed
and blackened train, so wobbly on its tracks that as the

w.c. door slammed shut, one window fell out. A train guard with the Hitler mustache that seemed to be horribly universal in lower Austria approached me with the bitter accusation that I had the window broken and that he must in all duty present me with a bill for having the window broken.

At each station on the way to Salzburg, the stationmaster came out to salute the passing train. Flower boxes were lined up along the station platform; a fine powderly dust flashed in the air; an incessant crowd sweated heavily in leather breeches, leather jerkins, snappy local headgear with protruding tiny whisk brooms. Salzburg, the American military headquarters, was a clotted, moiling crowd scattering summer visitors to the music festival, American personnel and their Bavarian-Austrian domestic help into military compounds and American-style ice-cream parlors, homeless stateless Jews into a transient camp of their own, variously assorted DPs awaiting transport somewhere else.

At Schloss Leopoldskron, Max Reinhardt's rococo "castle"—in Mozart's time it had been the seat of the Archbishop who had done so much to keep him hungry—European students and intellectuals had gathered to advance their knowledge of America in a vast seminar organized by Harvard graduate students. The lecturers were F. O. Matthiessen, the great economist Wassily Leontief, Margaret Mead, Walt Whitman Rostow, the old anti-Fascist historian Gaetano Salvemini, just returned from his exile at Harvard. The castle Max Reinhardt had fled had been taken over by the local Gauleiter. There was a hole in the roof from a misplaced American bomb, portraits of the detestable Archbishop, porcelain stoves in the bedrooms, three Australians, the great Italian scholar Mario Praz, an ex-Luftwaffe pilot, young Frenchmen from the Maquis, an Austrian So-

cialist who had fought Franco. There were Norwegians
and Swedes, Belgians and Dutch, Finns, Greeks, Hun-
garians. A British intelligence officer listened suspiciously to my lecture on E. E. Cummings and sent in official word that we were up to something. Three Czechs
appeared—it was the summer of 1947—and Czechoslovakia, though going fast, was still itself.

There were students without a country—a young Lat-
vian DP who had been studying at Innsbruck; a White
Russian who had been brought up in Yugoslavia after
the First World War and was now neither Russian nor
Yugoslavian; a Hungarian DP who worked for the U.S.
Army in Salzburg; a Rumanian-Jewish girl whose
mother had been shot by the Germans before her eyes
and who had spent more than a year in Auschwitz.
Poland was asked to send students, but after long deliberation decided that Matthiessen's failure to include
Upton Sinclair in his reading list showed a prejudice
against Socialist literature.

The three Czechs all spoke Russian and were enthusiastic about Russia. The Nazi test pilot had had his
life saved by a German refugee, now an American
lieutenant, who warned him that the Russians were,
just then, shooting Nazi test pilots out of hand. One of
the American assistants, a navigator in the Air Force
during the war, had parachuted down somewhere near
Salzburg and had been a prisoner for weeks in the
worm-eaten barracks down the road that was now a
transient camp for Polish Jews. One Italian student,
just twenty, made me realize what the Resistance had
done for his generation. He had been born in France
and saw Italy for the first time during the war, with a
French-Italian partisan group that operated in the
North. One Spanish Republican boy came to us from
France; he had been a refugee all his life. He told me

his story on a Sunday afternoon as we walked back to
the Schloss from town after listening to Otto Klemperer
conduct Mahler at the Festspielhaus. We were walking
in the sticky white dust of Leopoldskronstrasse, making
our way between American jeeps and military cars,
wooden-faced Austrians having a Sunday walk in their
ceremonial Tyrolean jackets and dirndls. We passed a
camp for Balts who had come to Germany and Austria
during the war as forced or willing labor for the Nazis,
and were now afraid to go back to their homes in Soviet
territory. We passed a detention house for Germans and
Austrians rumored to be "minor political offenders."

My ears were still chiming from the Chinese effects
in Mahler's *Song of the Earth*. I had been thinking of
the giant Otto Klemperer, whom I had last seen in the
Hollywood Bowl, still conducting after his stroke—
shuffling and staggering his way to the podium. He was
more impressive than ever as he stood over the Vienna
Philharmonic. Klemperer the Jew was now an honored
figure. Max Reinhardt, who died in Hollywood, was
another honored figure. Yehudi Menuhin was in Salzburg playing the Beethoven Concerto under the direction of his good friend Wilhelm Furtwängler. The exquisite Festspielhaus was staging *Wozzeck* and *Dantons
Tod*. Austrians, the most enthusiastic Nazis in German-
speaking Europe, were officially a "liberated" people.
Now I was listening to stories of Spanish exile in Mexico, America, and France, looking at the unrelated
migrants walking past each other in Leopoldskronstrasse. Many of them would gladly have killed each
other right there.

In Rome I had heard the story of American Negro
deserters and Nazi deserters hiding out together in the
woods of northern Italy. I had seen old Polish Jews,
temporarily lodged in Rome, being moved on by the

Joint Distribution Committee. After playing the Beethoven Concerto with the good German Furtwängler, who had led the Berlin Philharmonic all through the Hitler period, Menuhin was bitterly upbraided outside his hotel by a group of Jewish DPs from the transient camp down the road. He had evidently been called down from his room as he was undressing; he was still in white evening vest as he stood on the steps under the light from the hotel entrance. The crowd of Jews, hardly in evening clothes, muttered at him in angry restlessness. They had collected in the street and the street was dark. Menuhin, directly in the light, was a vivid figure with his tousled blond hair, his brilliant white evening vest. He made sweet, soft, almost weeping efforts to persuade the crowd that he had done "no wrong to the Jewish people" by appearing in Salzburg with Furtwängler. "Yehudi, what are you doing here?" cried out one DP.

Who belonged in Salzburg—the natives, the homeless Jews in the DP camp who told me that they were waiting for a "contact," the bored-looking American liberators roaring past in their jeeps and shiny new Cadillacs?

F. O. Matthiessen, the star of the Salzburg Seminar, was to have a strangely personal political effect on some of our young European students. Bald, short, as neutral-looking as a clergyman, he was amazing in his sudden vehemence, his intellectual rages in front of his audience, all mixed into a deadly brew with literary and political pieties. He interested and alarmed me. This solemn and devoted literary scholar seemed wired to go off like a bomb. From the moment I heard him lecture on such uncombustible subjects as *The Portrait of a Lady* and *Four Quartets*, I awaited drama. There was always a barely smothered violence. It was merely "personal," as Gatsby said about his dream woman's marriage to another man. Matthiessen fascinated the audience of wildly assorted Europeans by the obvious urgency to himself of Eliot's Christianity. His lectures, usually genial and accommodating, carried an undercurrent of intensity that was mysteriously personal. The tension, the unforgettable fixity of his manner and voice in that seemingly mild-looking Harvard professor, became a need to bind that audience to himself, to find affinities. I have never known another teacher whose influence on students had so many harsh personal and political consequences. His suicide in 1950 was to magnify this.

Matthiessen at Salzburg movingly described his favorite Americans, James and Eliot, as the angels, the heavenly messengers of his faith in America and Christianity. But lecturing to foreign students, he transmitted himself more than he did his literary ideas. He was not a literary radical; nothing I ever heard him say showed belief in literature as an instrument of change. His taste was traditional to the point of being theological. Students did not easily understand this about him. For Matthiessen, Eliot represented Christianity, and Theodore Dreiser—a novelist about whom he wrote without conviction—American "radicalism." Matthiessen was obviously a man hungry for ideology, and he seemed to find all he needed in what European students called "the age of American literature." There was now a standard repertoire of American masterpieces. But what hushed, mystified, and spellbound Italian Socialists and German Nazis in the great hall at Leopoldskron was the lonely passion of the man. They were not familiar with the many volcanoes seething in the United States. A secretary innocently coming up to Matthiessen with a telephone message—he was lecturing—made him scream with anger.

Matthiessen moved on to the Charles University in

Prague just in time to misreport the Communist take-over of Czechoslovakia in a book of total political in-nocence, *From the Heart of Europe*. He was to turn steadily more defensive of Stalinism, and to carry vari-ous students with him. The native McCarthyites in Bos-ton expressed their jealous hatred of Harvard by steadily attacking "this professor." Early in 1950 he went to a mean hotel in Boston opposite the North Station, care-fully laid aside his Skull and Bones key from Yale, and jumped to his death. He had been catastrophically lonely since the death of his painter-friend, Russell Cheney. But he now became a "casualty of the cold war."

Matthiessen's death, not his teaching; his personal drama, not his books, made him famous. A heroic be-leaguered American radical had been driven to his death. *The Achievement of T. S. Eliot, Sarah Orne Jewett, Translation: An Elizabethan Art, American Renaissance, Henry James: The Major Phase* were books that solidified literary opinion in America within well-recognized lines. They had no interest for the larger public. In Europe, even Silone counted Matthiessen among the victims of the political wars. There was some clear derogation of literature as the half-hearted, wistful "progressivism" of this tormented man was promoted after his death. The age demanded a cause. As Harold Rosenberg said of Whittaker Chambers, "This man is not interested in politics." Politics, the confrontation of interest groups, even of the two great superstates, did not interest Matthiessen's elegists. The "progressive" camp, when it was innocently non-Communist, rejoiced in victims. The age was not severe enough and de-manded fresh martyrs.

Matthiessen at Salzburg addressed himself lastingly to certain students. He seemed to be sustained by the passionate attention and loyalty of those students, some of whom were to be with him at Prague. His idea of power was entirely moral and verbal; he did not know that students at Charles University who explained Czech politics to him had links to the secret police. Nothing in Matthiessen was so striking as his intense relationship to students—especially since lecturers at the Salzburg Seminar like Walt Whitman Rostow, describing the American economy through a pipe clenched in his teeth, talked to students without looking at them, as if they might be tolerated but never enjoyed.

Rostow was already an official type. Between lectures he sat on the grass busily writing important memos on a portable typewriter in his lap. In London during the war he had been an O.S.S. man helping to select bombing sites; he had been in the State Department and would soon return to it; he was just on his way to the European Economic Commission in Geneva; he would soon be on his way to something even more important in Washington. Yet for all his absorbed, distracted, impatient air, he managed to communicate some professional boyishness. You might have thought his a life dedicated to tennis, not power. He had not yet attained the lofty condescending style of his Johnson-Vietnam period, when he glared in disbelief at students asking for an explanation of the war. His conversation was charmingly shy.

The European students watched the American lecturers with awe. They were the audience, and we in Europe were the main event, absorbed in ourselves, in the rich, overplentiful runaway society whose every last detail we discussed with such hypnotized relevance to ourselves. In this still war-torn year of 1947, the Europeans could not help becoming aware that they were simply out of it. We *were* the main event. We were

America. Even the most timid-looking academics, simply by being part of this immense productivity, this endlessly self-fascinated society, had an immense advantage over our students. They fastened and battened on the most tormented of us, like Francis Otto Matthiessen, and could not get over their surprise that the brilliant Russian-born economist Wassily Leontief, whom in his gaiety and originality I christened the Mozart of economics, should give the main address on the American economy. Leontief's unconquerable Russian accent so infuriated one ex-Nazi, whose faultless English had been polished working for the Americans in Wiesbaden, that he asked in some futile attempt at mockery, "Is that an American accent?" "The very latest!" we cried.

To be an American was to share in this bountiful feast of money, of information, of books, of the personal chumminess that flowed from Americans at first meeting and so easily deceived Europeans into thinking this heartiness was meant as friendship. At Salzburg, Europeans and Americans were steadily proclaimed free and equal, equally open to the human strains in this little old neighborhood that led Margaret Mead, our den mother, to promote research projects into the local life as if we were in Middletown. And if American intellectuals in their unending commentary on the American scene were not enough to convince open-mouthed Europeans that America and Americans were different, there was the U.S. Army's ice-cream factory just past the great rock wall that bore the archiepiscopal coat of arms testifying to the thousand years' rule, from Salzburg, of all this Catholic country in Austria and Bavaria.

Across the street was an ice-cream parlor that featured curb service. The smart Austrian Inn was occupied by American officers and civilian personnel; the old Mirabelle club, next to the gardens, was a Red

Cross club. Salzburg was full of American signs and cars that made it look like an American shopping center. There was so much careless driving that the Army promoted a safety program. Where accidents had occurred there were markers—in English—that showed an arrow and the grim warning "DEATH STRUCK HERE . . . DRIVE CAREFULLY."

We were living in a city occupied by troops from our own country, and we had less contact with them than with the suspect natives. The young American soldiers drafted after the war's end were bored to stupefaction. I watched them sitting over rows of Coca-Cola bottles in the Red Cross club, a great empty ballroom hung with dusty paper ribbons and lined with tarnished gilt paneling. On the walls hung crude images of Mozart, Schubert, Beethoven, Richard Strauss. Every afternoon a young Austrian knocked out boogie-woogie on the grand piano, but the soldiers looked like tourists in a Paris dive waiting for something sinister to happen. Some afternoons they played bingo. The Austrian doorman wore a cap lined with spangles, discarded GI fatigues, and a moldy frock coat in which he looked as pleased as Groucho Marx. Yet there was an inconclusive look about him, as if he could never decide whether he belonged with the haves or the have-nots. Inside metallic blondes took orders for hamburgers and sundaes. They talked a functional English and smiled constantly.

The loneliness in the Red Cross club was familiar. In the moroseness of the Austrians out on the street there was bitterness and hunger. A woman came up to me crying, "I don't have enough to live on!" For the bumptious overfed new draftees in the Red Cross club, the war was already anyone else's war. They glowered with a boredom that sent out waves of decay. But American plenty in Europe meant different things to different people. An American movie company was making a film that summer in Frankfurt called *Berlin Express*. The film's press agent told *Stars & Stripes* that they were lucky to have a setting—bombed-out Frankfurt— "which would have cost Hollywood a million dollars to construct."

On the way back to the castle I would sometimes stop in at Camp Riedenburg, a transient camp for Jewish DPs. There was an official entrance to it, guarded by a militant boy who wore a brassard marked with the Star of David and would not let me in—everyone in Salzburg was suspect. I got in by climbing the fence. There was a couple named Fagelman, whom some of us were helping to get to America.

Riedenburg was another world. There were some fourteen hundred adults in it and five hundred children, half of whom had lost parents in the camps. The Nazis had vacated it to a British force; one of the buildings had a sign slipping from a nail noting that it had once been George VI Hall. The moldy shacks making up the camp lay next to the main street. At night, returning from a concert at the Mozarteum, I could see people lined up in front of the privies in the yard, moving about in rooms that looked like minute cells just above the ground.

Mr. Fagelman was the camp policeman, a dimly amiable young Polish Jew who lived in one of the better shacks of Riedenburg with his wife—who was his brother's widow—and his brother's child. Whenever visitors came in, he would grin happily and rush out to get some U.S. Army beer brewed in Salzburg. He would show us letters from his relatives in Rochester, then talk about the war. He would tell us his story; then his wife would tell us hers. It was the Holocaust Haggadah;

where one left off, the other took it up. The wife's story
was different from the husband's story, and it was the
story of the Polish Jews from 1939 to 1945. "I wish to
share with you the horrible reality that I experienced as
a Jew under Fascism.

"At six in the morning the Nazis surrounded the town
and captured approximately two thousand men, women,
children. They took them outside the city. They un-
dressed them naked. They lined them up against the
walls of a warehouse. They shot them dead. The bodies
fell into a huge burial hole. The many living yet with
the dead. Indiscriminately the Nazis poured gasoline
and set the bodies in flame. I was working as an appren-
tice in a baking shop. The Nazis walked into the shop
and asked are there any Jews present. A Christian boy
who worked with me said no, there aren't any Jews. The
boy directed me to a shabby cold attic where he locked
me in from the outside. From the attic I heard the cries
and shouts from the people in the city. Among the people killed in that crowd were my sister Sheyna and her
husband.

"We were liberated 1945 by the Americans at eight
in the evening, April 28th. Your soldiers were very nice
but did not understand why we were in 'prison.' "

Mrs. Fagelman told her story with a little smile of
self-deprecation. Perhaps I am not able to convey to you
the horror? Mrs. Fagelman lived her story over every
time she talked to me. As she stood up there in that little
room, she clutched her daughter as if she had talked
herself back into the exact moment in 1942 when the
Nazis arrived in their town.

Riedenburg was a coldly necessary stopgap for Jews
with no place to go to. Everything the Fagelmans used
had been given to them as rations after a disaster—for
so many displaced persons, so much food, living space,

light, and blankets. Everything around them reminded them of what they had gone through. They occupied the camp like people waiting for a train they are not sure will ever arrive. The American soldiers in the next street who looked after them and the Austrians walking by just outside the fence were equally strangers. They were far from hopeless. But to wait and wait for a country to go to while living in the middle of "liberated" Salzburg was intolerable, a self-contradiction.

One afternoon Mr. Fagelman took me around the camp. There was a cobbler working just inside the yard; in a corner a little old man was selling pears that he had bought in town that afternoon. In the crowd outside the administration building a white-haired old man was arguing food allotments with an American sergeant and saying in a velvety accent, "But why do we never get white bread any more? We used to get white bread!" The sergeant explained that the Army thought white bread was too expensive, but the old man did not seem to think this was a very good reason.

In one "family building" a man was sitting at a window peacefully reading the *Jewish Daily Forward* from New York; he looked like my father, returned from work on another summer evening, reading the *Jewish Daily Forward*. We looked at the tailor shop, the shoe-repair shop, and a shed in which men were dismantling a broken army truck they had picked up somewhere. In a room that was both school and orphanage there were maps of Palestine and pictures of Herzl and Chaim Nachman Bialik; little girls were walking about, tended by a young nurse.

And then we went into a long basement room. It looked like another detention camp. There were twenty-four people living in that room, including the sick. The beds were wooden slats just above the floor. There were

pails, some with uneaten food, some with garbage, next
to the wall, and little burners on which the women did
their cooking. The tables were covered with Yiddish
newspapers from New York.

In the group at the door was a woman wearing a
black dress and small gold earrings. Her face was finely
sculptured in defiance. There was so much pride in it
that her bearing made the room seem even more squalid.
Unlike her sister, who was waiting to go to America,
she would hold out for Palestine. That room had dying
people in it, and this was a woman who looked as if she
held life in her hands and didn't know where to put it.
I touched her shoulder to say goodbye. With a mocking
grin she looked at me: "*Nu?* So how do you like the way
we live?"

> *This Roman revery, which seems so sweet*
> *to us and makes us forget all the*
> *interests of active life.*
> —Stendhal

Later, when we have sailed home in midwinter to await
the baby and I am struggling with "the book on New
York," I put myself to sleep by remembering my blissful
early mornings in Rome, alone. The bountiful figure in
the next bed is more real to me as a figure in my sexual
mythology than as a wife. Sneaking out of our cottage
at the entrance to the Villa Borghese and walking down
the hill, I enter through the great gate into the Piazza
del Popolo. The inner face, made by Bernini in 1655,
reads "Felici Fausto Ingressui." Just past the obelisk in
the center, between the old sea gods on one wall and the
flowering staircase of the Pincio on the other, is the tiny
snack bar where I have my coffee.

It always works. No matter how distant Rome seems
now, and how many new threats New York offers up,

I have only to walk down that hill into the Piazza del Popolo, where every morning I see the same old woman sitting on the steps leading up to the obelisk, in order to feel a new lightness and ease, and comfortably drifting back, to fall asleep.

Daybreak in Rome. I will soon have a shower in the public *bagno*—the *principe* from whom we have rented the cottage keeps the winter's coal in the bathtub. The "people's square" is empty except for the old woman sitting on the steps leading up to the obelisk, a few tram-drivers drinking *cappucino* at the snack bar, a street sweeper brushing the ancient cobblestones with a broom of bound twigs. As the light spreads over the ancient roofs, it picks out the sculptured figure on the wall of Neptune with his trident. Patrolling the wall and watching me, a dark-faced *carabiniere* in a leather tricorne hat. There will be another Communist demonstration this morning, and he is already walking his rounds up and down just in front of Neptune and Minerva.

The cop studies me and I study Neptune and his fellow deities. Impossible to explain to the cop that all my dreams of women come dressed as Rome. I am floating in the past, surrounded by magnified bodies, bodies white and gigantic (even if they are moldering slightly), bodies stretched upon the open city of the Piazza del Popolo, bodies hovering over the great square still empty except for a few figures hurrying to work.

I walk down the Corso to the public bath. "*Buon bagno!*" cries the strapping, smiling bath attendant as she hands me a sliver of soap and the large rough towel that will soon envelop me like a toga. "*Una doccia?*" Showering early in the Rome morning, nestling in every fold of my skin the generous warmth, the steam flowing in the air, the heat in the wooden boards underfoot, feeling easy and abundant as I walk back early in the morning to where my wife is still asleep, I feel that *I* am walking in my sleep. On the Corso a green pagan figure, presiding over a fountain, is coiled like a snake and is sitting on its tail. Without disturbing itself in the least, it fixes me with a sidelong glance as I pass it. I have at last attained a perfect detachment. I am some-one else. There are mornings walking around Rome when I believe in transubstantiation. I am someone who used to live in Rome, am as happily unreal to myself as that snaky green figure on the Corso reclining on its tail. I am free to love anything in Rome. Rome is a woman more real to me than the woman I live with.

In our bedroom back at the cottage hangs a repro-duction of Leonardo's Virgin with her mother, St. Anne. The "enigmatic" Leonardo smile over the slightly open mouth dissolves me as it beckons me backward in time. So the circular staircases leading up to the Pincio and the white plaster statues of excessively mustached nine-teenth-century Italian politicians, the occasional carriage clip-clopping down the street, the Franciscan church on the Via Veneto lined with the skeletons of departed monks that Hawthorne described—everything seems to say that the present does not exist except as still another stage setting, that everything and everyone in Italy plays a role. I can actually watch myself melting into the scenery.

At siesta time I would again leave Louise asleep in our cottage to wander about in the hot afternoons. The corrugated iron shutters guarding the shop windows would come down with a bang, and I, still abroad at this hour, the hungry American pilgrim of culture, would find myself absorbed in shadows as ominous as the sharply angled streets of de Chirico. I had a not unpleasant, even picturesque sense of being alone—not lonely but certainly alone. We had come home together from England; we were married, in Italy on our honeymoon; we would soon have a son. I never lost the feeling I had that first day in London during the war. I did not know her. The controlled handsome face that responded regularly and precisely, right on the down-beat, was someone I would never know. She definitely disapproved of me. No wonder that in the mornings I would wander down the hill into the Piazza del Popolo as if in a dream. Italy worked on me so deeply that alone while living with Louise, I was open to every side of the past. But the picturesque surface was breaking up. The great patina of Italy was often false.

In the Piazzale Flaminio, Communist strikers regularly stormed against the "existing order." *Carabinieri*, much too grandly dressed for the occasion, sometimes tripped on their swords as they rushed out of their American jeeps to clobber the demonstrators. Each week I read in the overseas edition of *Time* that these strikers had torn up trolley tracks, had overturned buses, and had set fire to automobiles. Even the Rome staff of Time Inc. never knew which lordly hands back in Rockefeller Center recast their cables as ammunition in the cold war.

America was the biggest thing in Italy. *Americani* were visitors from another world. Under the showy melodramatic Italian moon shining upon the restaurants and cafés in Trastevere, crowds sat staring at crowds eating at those long lines of tables, row after row be-tween the hedges of gigantic rubber plants that marked off one café from another—an audience at the Roman play making up its own play. Wonderful to watch the long appraising stares like those of an expert judging horseflesh, with which these open-air troglodytes looked each newcomer up and down. No one missed a thing. They may have looked bored and weary with that built-in bourgeois Italian weariness, scales over their half-closed eyes as they sipped at their minuscule *espresso*. All the time in the world: they had been sitting there with that same inch of coffee, that same spoon and water carafe, since the Etruscans. But in the air the preparatory vapors of seduction; these are buds that open only at night. As soon as we walked into this lighted den, unable to keep from making the grand tour up and around the long line of tables, faint waves chattered at us. Ah, some more of the *americani*.

Louise's glossy black hair, set off by a gold-shining silk print, never ceased to astonish. "Aren't all American women blond?" Carlo Levi said to her. He panted with public desire for her. He rolled his eyes, his chest heaved so that he always fell off his barstool. Even he, the fat Roman satyr who wrote *Christ Stopped at Eboli*, had never met so deliriously exciting a woman. She had a great effect on Italians. Three whores glumly sitting together looked Louise over, conferred, looked her over again. Cigarette vendors came screeching round like a flock of gulls maddened by the smell of food off the ship's bow—old, young, sick, every age and every human condition in Italy, desperately selling cigarettes, especially counterfeit Chesterfields and Old Golds, each vendor with his stock in a little suitcase open before him like a tray.

Sigarette? . . . Nazionali . . . americani? Every five minutes new beggars appeared at the table—usually old women wearing black shawls and the look of the eternal mother of sorrows, leading little barefoot girls whose faces were gray, whose arms hung at their sides as if tired from scratching old sores. You found yourself not just responding to the situation but rewarding the performance. Under the table were more barefoot kids, in discarded GI pants and American Air Force

jackets, hunting cigarette ends and storing them carefully in little tin pails; every slavered-over butt in the
gutter would go to make new "American" cigarettes.
In the history of Italy this was the Pax Americana, or
the age of the second-hand butt.

The beggars covered the cafés and restaurants in
waves, making sure never to come up in bunches or at
too close intervals. As one beggar went from table to
table, the next stood at the hedge like an actor waiting
to go on. Despite their public indifference, the Italians
gave, every time. They were bored and after the tenth
approach exasperated, but with a shrug of shoulders or
a languid protest ("Signora! This time some mercy! You
think I'm the Bank of Italy?"), they came up with the
usual damp crumpled lira notes. The crucial test was
when some "big fork," a big eater whose face was
swollen with spaghetti, tried to look away. Hopeless.
The beggar kept turning with him and stared him down.
A left-wing faction of the Socialists tried to humiliate a
right-wing faction by listing on the wall of socialist
headquarters the beastly long list of dishes that their
opponents had consumed at lunch.

In the brilliantly humming summer night you could
hear all those Italian café dwellers talking money,
money, money, pushing at the world outside like a fly
caught in honey. In the North, triumphant Communists
were ritually drowning Fascists. I saw the picture: a
Communist partisan leader sitting on the side of a boat
solemnly keeping a condemned Fascist under the water
with his legs. It was quite a "Roman" orgy. The politically virtuous Communist did not realize how pagan,
sexy, and wild he looked with his legs on the other
man's shoulders. *Vae victis!*

The café crowd must include both victims and heroes
of Italy's struggle with Fascism, but one knows nothing.

Too many heads merely packed with antennae; poised, alert, too wise. The faces generally lack that paunchy, pasty look of overfed Americans; you can still see the bony structure on older people. The general good looks among the young are amazing. Face after face with that focused sensuality that is the personal ticket of stage people. The air is damp with sex, but you can hear sums being recited at table after table; the whole piazza is one great bourse for the black market. *Ottomilases-santa . . . quarantamilanovanta.* A fierce-looking boy rides up on a bicycle and unerringly goes straight to the American faces and clothes. Wanna buy American cigarettes—real American cigaretttes, not counterfeit? Wanna change your money, Mista? Hey, Mista? Will you for the love of God *tell* him something? You think he hasn't got the dough? Takes out a great wad of the sweaty lire. "Listen!" he says disgustedly, about to ride off, "I buy anything you got! ANYTHING!" The long wailing singsong of the cigarette vendors, as the evening drags on, becomes simply "America!"

The returning anti-Fascist exiles were not very welcome. The historian Gaetano Salvemini, at seventy-five still the peppery South Italian after his years at Harvard, as unflinching as ever in his libertarian principles, was told that he "criticizes too much." Salvemini launched himself like a torpedo at every lie and delusion in the soft corrupt body of Italian self-satisfaction, Demochristian and Communist. On the stage of the Eliseo Theatre in Rome, honored by Italian World Federalists, he bent over a table to hide his emotion when the crowd rose to welcome him home with operatic cries of *Viva Salvemini!* Then, crying *Dunque!* Let's start! he took an enormous manuscript out of his pocket and, dropping each page on the floor as he read it, proceeded to denounce all the ruling powers, right and left, American and Russian, that cooperated to keep Italians "obedient" to the many "stupidities in their past.

Salvemini was an unreconstructed man of the Enlightenment, still undiscouraged, secularist, republican. A political historian, his whole being was unbelievably dominated by austere moral principles that were the only things necessary to *all* political behavior. A democrat in a country dominated by authoritarian Catholics and Stalinists, he was too old in knowledge but actually too young in spirit to please the overheated atmosphere of "liberation." He had an abrupt, laughing, fiery way of reducing wordy issues and wordy Italians to a question of good faith. "My only rule is to behave so that I won't have to spit at myself when I shave in the morning." There was something of the small-town buffoon in Gaetano Salvemini. He liked to break up a party, especially if pompous officialdom was attending. With his polemical-looking bald head, his thick round body, his "provincial" Southern abruptness and mockery, he made the most inflamed issues personal to him and personal in attack. Before he returned to Italy, an Italo-American politician, Ferdinand Pecora, innocently solicited Salvemini's advice on "restoring Italy's image." *Pecora* means sheep, and so was pronounced "pe-cora" to make this unrecognizable. Salvemini was outraged by talk of "restoring Italy's image." He spat out in his comically raging way, "The real Fascists, Meesta Pec-o-rah, are not in Rome but in New York!" In Rome after the war Salvemini turned out to resemble nothing and no one but himself. "He criticizes too much." "He expects too much." "Perhaps he was away *too* long?"

My old hero Silone was even more deeply disliked. He had been the best-known Italian writer in exile, so it was a shock to the literati that the first Italian edition of *Fontamara* was sent over by Silone's English publisher. It was difficult to find a book of Silone's in the shops, but many writers talked against his work and scolded excited foreign visitors for loving his work— for having known it so long!

Silone, born with the century, and having spent the best part of his life in exile, was again a threat to Italian conformism. Guilt and envy had nothing to do with it. "He writes a crude Italian." It was abominable yet comic to hear *Fontamara, Bread and Wine, The Seed Beneath the Snow* knocked down for reasons of "taste" by every little literary creature. One amiable hack, who did little articles and cartoons for the Socialist press, talked as if he were reciting only the latest and most widely approved opinions as he lectured foreigners on what he called the "outside world's" absurd overestimation of Silone. This put him right in style, and gave him the only contact he had with opinion outside Italy, a country he had managed to live in throughout the Fascist period by showing how easy it was to agree with everyone around him. "*You people* cannot imagine how crudely he writes. . . ." Screwing up his shoulders with the stage-worn Latin gesture that expressed someone else's error or folly, he went on long after everyone at table had given it up as hopeless. . . . "Silone! *Per ignoranza!* Always Silone! *You people* have never heard of anyone else!"

He wrote "badly" because he was a political, not really a "man of letters." He was a member of Parliament, still an active Socialist, editor of his own political weekly. Nor did he shine in conversation, as Italians must, but seemed a "depressed and depressing character." Foreigners visiting Italy ridiculously saw Silone as a symbol of the only Italy *they* knew—the anti-Fascist exiles. Obviously only the boldest dared to defy the state —and perhaps many of the people? "But after all, it was not so bad as Hitler. You have no idea how easygoing it all was until the war and the defeats. With us, even authoritarian government was a bit of a joke."

Silone was not a "literary" writer, a deep matter in a country where "style" worked on writers like a narcotic. "My greatest pleasure," said a writer of notable intelligence, "is spending the morning polishing my paragraphs." So Silone was considered gross and, with so much of his time taken up with both inter-Socialist politics and the religious evolution evident in his later novels, a curiosity. There was still something of the Abruzzi about him—primitive, obstinate, forever solitary. As my friend Paolo Milano said, Silone was the one type Italians cannot accept—the moral dissenter. "He simply will not reduce everything to the canonical Italian level of the 'family affair.' " His Socialism was not very practical; it represented more and more a longing to get back to the human relatedness with peasants and artisans he knew in the Abruzzi. What I had loved most in Silone was his feeling for the bottom people, for those whom Tolstoy called the "dark people." But Silone, like George Orwell, had shown the intellectuals some dour ethical distrust of *them*. Betrayal from one's own people was something Silone knew a lot about. The peasant types whom sophisticated Italians condescended to were for Silone just those "who do not betray."

I wrote *Fontamara* in 1930, in Davos. Since I was alone there—a stranger with an alias to evade the efforts of the Fascist police to find me—writing became my only means of defense from despair. And since it did not appear to me that I had long to live, I wrote hurriedly, with unspeakable affliction and anxiety, to set up as best I could that village into which I put the quintessence of myself and my native heath so that I could at least die among my own people.

Sitting with Silone in a sweltering mob at the restaurant Re degli Amici—accordion players, Neapolitan blues singers, a one-man band loaded front and back with instruments and beating time to the upward and downward tilt of a rusty black derby over his eyes, wandering beggars and nuns collecting alms—Louise and I were surrounded by sociability unlimited. The King of Friends was then the haunt of all good Roman writers, Socialists, and members of the anti-Fascist "Action Party" that was just surrendering itself to the Communists. The Italian bedlam was beautiful, intellectual merriment, people calling and flirting from table to table, all one great family party. At such moments, thinking of my solitary morning walk into the Piazza del Popolo, I envied the public intimacy of these people with each other. The family motif binding Italians together seemed stronger than the personality of each one.

Even Silone looked almost happy that night, though, taking advantage of Carlo Levi's valiant efforts to speak English, he put his face in a great mass of fish, meats, and greens and remained alone with his own thoughts. Curious to watch Silone with a writer like Carlo Levi— men of the same generation formed outside the shell of Fascism and better known in other countries, both fundamental types of the writer "engaged" to action, yet so different that the extremes of the Italian character had been called on to produce them. Silone seemed entirely apart, silent with political and literary disappointments —"He has been told so often that he is a bad novelist that he is ready to believe it." But Silone was still defending firmly the deepest urgings of the oppressed among whom he grew up. After that beautiful record of an anti-Fascist's exile in his own country, *Christ Stopped at Eboli*, Levi could not decide whether he was a writer or painter or professional amorist. He was already on his way to becoming a Communist senator and was always acting it up in public, relying on his Falstaffian girth and his too hearty Italianness to keep him afloat. How he sighed and panted in public for Louise! He looked at her, looked at me. I thought he would go through his pants. It was all quicksilver, Rossini.

But the Silone I loved was to be found not in a crazy-quilt evening, not in himself, but in his work, with its scruples, its awkward tenderness, and its humor. When I lived in Italy, that work was still my background; it was one more telling of the unchanging history of the "dark people":

> The government is always against the poor, but the present government is a special kind of government. It is against the poor, but in a special way. All its strength is directed against the poor, but in a particular way.

And afterward we toiled home through the sudden cold, stopping for an *espresso*, admiring the nymphs in the Piazza del Popolo, buying a bag of chestnuts from the old woman on the corner warming herself at the fire, while in the faint light of the lamps in the Villa Borghese, just beyond Michelangelo's gates, that Roman god and emperor whose name I never learned still stood with his arm half raised, beautiful and indifferent.

Chapter VII

THE TIMES
BEING WHAT
THEY ARE

Back home, the housing shortage seemed to be a permanent fact of New York life. The best we could do, and this only because Louise knew so many Italian exiles in New York, was a gloomy sublet from Italian Jews on upper Central Park West where Central Park comes to an end and where we did, too. Our brief unreal marriage was lived with other people's furniture, pictures, other people's forks and knives, and a detailed view in our bedroom of the Lakes of Killarney that sickened me by its irrelevance. Two rooms, no doubt stuffed full of keepsakes, were firmly locked and barred. After Tim was born, there was no room with a door in which I could write. My vast shapeless account of roaming New York seemed as homeless as I did. I would prowl the streets of the upper West Side looking for "material," for I did not yet see how I could include myself.

Central Park West in the Hundreds had a great view of the Park and of the shining white fronts of Fifth Avenue across it. But you no longer entered the Park with confidence, and if the Park at most hours was no man's land, the streets stretching behind you to Broadway were more secret barbed wire. In my college days the upper West Side had always presented to me a face strained, shadowed, overcrowded. There had always been too many hills to climb, and hanging over the street too many colossal apartment houses into which the sun did not shine, too great a show of garbage pails in front of every door. But now a block away and the terminus of the Park were enemy territory. Every day I steered my way carefully, very carefully, between enclaves made up of blacks, the first Puerto Ricans, and Santo Domingans, poor whites from the South, squatters resisting removal "necessary to urban renewal," drunken supers and maddened tenants, belligerent pimps, addicts writhing like dervishes and staggering from one hydrant to another. The grimness of these bitterly ugly overcrowed streets was nothing to the anger of New York's untouchables forever slouching along the steps under the signs that said "NO LOITERING."

Broadway was a circus. The fat lady; the bearded lady; the transvestite in pink curlers who needed a shave; the hundred-and-two-year-old lady who announced in front of Zabar's "appetizing" store that she owed her perfect health to sour cream; the madwoman in carpet slippers and shopping bag who prowled up and down Broadway all day long and walked into the local pharmacy to scream, "Bestids! Criminals, all of you! Never sympathy for a person!" I saw her sitting in a phone booth marked "out of order" shouting into the mouthpiece.

The West Side as a whole was ethnic territory, foreign, "Jew land," the cheaper side of town, and the last stand of all exiles, refugees, proscribed and displaced persons. In the Park, boulders of the great rock that had once covered New York still made a trail for boys in Indian file, a springboard for boys jumping with arms outstretched and yelling, "Here I come!" New York on the upper West Side was rock all the way; rock hill and stone, up and down, no visible relief. But though I was often numbed by the way everything here came in mass, I also felt at home with so many recent arrivals. Fragments of Europe stuck to the signs over synagogues, food shops, beauty parlors. "Services Will Be Held Here by the Former Rabbi of Lvov." "Madame Slavatasky, Formerly Chief Masseuse at the Franz-Josef Sanitarium in Innsbruck." The Hungarian eye surgeon in the dusty office on the ground floor, whose wife endlessly complained of the noise made by "bad American children" playing handball against the side of the building, had found refuge in India operating on "whole villages." The autographed photograph of Einstein in the surgeon's office did not look steady on its nail and he smelled faintly of the spiced meat he had just eaten. He seemed a bit seedy for a doctor. "It is hard for my wife to keep the dust firmly out. I cannot get good hospital appointment."

As the hostile super said, and he said it often, the West Side was "Jews." Since there were many others on the West Side, it was not really a ghetto, but one foreign enclave piled on another. I did notice that non-Jews living with Jews were more likely to do so here than across town. My long Jewish memory was at home with what a patriot on the other side of town called the "West Side jackal bins." When I walked out on Broadway, I felt myself so engulfed by the furious life of the street that I had to go back and write to keep from drowning in these many lives. Nothing would release me from the burden of so much common experience; so many old European habits, hungers, complaints; so much Jewishness, blackness, clownishness, vulgarity, old age, amazement, ugliness, anxiety; so much eating, fatness, dog shit; so many soliloquies and recitations; so much anger from the mad, deprived, sick, unhappy, doped, vicious, battered, alien, powerless, afflicted. Nowhere else in New York could one see on the street, on the subway platform, in the rush hour, such public suffering. In a howling rainstorm I saw a man beating the top of a car and weeping. In the subway a man suddenly looked up from the book he was reading and shouted, "And if I *can't* pay it? If I *don't* pay it?" People walked away from him, but it was no use. I remembered from my college days on the upper West Side a blind student to whom I read Godwin's *Political Justice* the week before examinations. He had been thrown out by his family as "too much trouble." On the West Side this was not considered unusual.

In this boiling sea of foreign nations and foreign tongues, of bearded Orthodox upholsterers and tinkerers whose signs read "WE CAN FIX ANYTHING" and who occupied cellar shops on Amsterdam Avenue that had come straight from Odessa and the Old City, there stood out the Upper West Side Hebrew Relief Association. This name was not always pleasing to the Columbia professors, associates of *Commentary* and *Partisan Review*, New York *Post* editors and columnists, trade-union press agents, publishers, composers, shirt manufacturers, and psychoanalysts who were united by the unrivaled experience of Communism they had gained in their radical past and their unflinching hatred of it now. You did not have to be Jewish to be part of the Upper West Side Hebrew Relief Association. You could live in the Village or Scarsdale; there was a banker's son from Harvard who taught English at Columbia, several Irish Catholic intellectuals, and at least one Virginian who, like all the rest, had what J. Edgar Hoover would have called "a subversive record." A visiting British Kremlinologist mistook one super-hawk for a black, but there were no blacks. The Jews in the upper West Side Hebrew Relief Association were not practicing Jews, often regretted the newborn State of Israel as "nationalistic" and an unwelcome distraction from the proper business of politics. Professors and shirt manufacturers alike, they regarded themselves as a political avant-garde whose task was still to impart the lessons of the Russian Revolution. The destiny of the century now depended on oracles and Cassandras who had passed through the fires of totalitarianism, even in Brooklyn; who were an élite because they *knew*, and could not wait to educate the American people.

The Upper West Side Hebrew Relief Association included many distinguished intellectuals. All the members were more prosperous and established than their parents could have dreamed for them. They should have been as happy as larks. They knew too much to be happy. "After such knowledge, what forgiveness?" Politics had turned them mad, but no madder than many others in the forties, fifties, sixties. They just knew more. They saw the danger in Russia and were not ashamed to be obsessed. They had no forgiveness for Communists who, long before Hitler, had brought the totalitarian century into being.

And somehow there was no forgiveness for themselves, children of the thirties and of the ineradicable influence of Stalin-Hitler. Some obscure guilt weighed on them, possibly because guilt was more modish than innocence. The title of Leslie Fiedler's first book— condescending to Dean Acheson and F. Scott Fitzgerald, the Rosenbergs in the death house and poor old Hemingway—said it all for the Upper West Side Hebrew Relief Association, though at the moment Professor Fiedler was teaching in Montana: *An End to Innocence*. The film critic Robert Warshow was to write that the thing about Jews was just that they were *older*. Even the youngest members of the Upper West Side Hebrew Relief Association seemed weighed down by every fresh political shock from Lenin country. They could be uproarious about each other's characters. They were rarely light-minded. They had none of the self-dramatizing gifts that were to be found among the theatrical pros Lillian Hellman, Zero Mostel, Elia Kazan. Saul Bellow's *Seize the Day* capitalized on the anxiety that hung over the West Side like the carbon monoxide spurting straight into his hero's face from the Broadway bus. But Bellow was too detached for them and they despised the pleasures and addictions of the crowd. "Mass culture" was the opium of the boobs. It explained the failure of Socialism in America. It was sometimes called "popular culture" and could make a sociologist out of any literary intellectual.

Despite these many responsibilities, these intellectuals should have been happier than they were. The cold war and the McCarthy era needed them, raised them, publicized them. Sometimes—as in the case of *Encounter*; the Committee for Cultural Freedom; the Free Trade Union Congress, AFL, run by a former leader of the American C.P., Jay Lovestone, now stirring up strong-arm squads against French Communist unions—the government financed them. Those who had so long talked of alienation, who had proved the iron necessity of alienation, who had loved the theory of alienation and especially *their* alienation, were now with the gvernment of the United States as advisers on Communism, "experts on Communism."

The atmosphere was heavy with souped-up patriotism, and, radiating from the many disillusioned and fretful ex-radicals like a new weapon, it was also intensely religious. *All* evil was now to be attached to

Communism, no doubt because some former Communists felt their old attachment so intensely. Meanwhile throughout the country, powerless people were subjected to "loyalty hearings" because their parents had lived *near* people who took the *Daily Worker*. There were loyalty hearings in the Pentagon, loyalty hearings in factories, schools. An attendant in a New York City park toilet was dismissed because he had belonged for a few months to the Communist Party. He had broken openly with it, but his job obviously made him a security risk—he was always "underground." At the same time, scientists like Ernst Chain were refused admission to the United States; Linus Pauling was not permitted to leave the country for a Royal Society conference on his discovery of the chemical bond. The misery any of these intellectuals could see for themselves in any street of this swollen and disordered city was to be ignored. New York was having "the greatest building boom in history." Yet there was a special grievance on the part of the new patriots against "intellectuals," "scholars," "well-known personalities" whose political liberation had been slower than their own. There was malicious pleasure in the "naming" of actors, movie writers, and directors who were blacklisted but vulgarly referred to as "headline names."

One old Communist after another, one old fellow traveler after another, called because he had been "named" as a Party member or a one-time sympathizer with "Communist causes" that sometimes signified only opposition to nuclear testing, appeared to make loud public repentance before the House Committee on Un-American Activities, Senator McCarthy's Permanent Investigations Subcommittee, the Tenney Committee on Un-American Activities in California, Movie Pro-

ducers' Committees, School Board Committees, Library
Committees. He had to "come clean," make a clean
break, make loud public expression of *loyalty* to America. If he was an ex-Communist, he proved his patriotism by naming names, described his valiant struggles
inside the Communist Party for intellectual freedom,
his fervent faith in one nation under God, and so had
his hand warmly shaken by congressmen and their professional interrogators. If he was still a Communist or
did not want to go back on a Communist husband, wife,
lover, friend, he refused to admit anything, fervently
identified the Bill of Rights as his lifelong political philosophy, pleaded the Fifth Amendment, denounced
"the Committee" as a hireling of Wall Street and Hit-
lerian Fascism, identified himself with the immortal
principles of Tom Paine, Thomas Jefferson, and Abraham Lincoln. Until the wartime alliance was abruptly
switched at the outbreak of the cold war, the Communist Party U.S.A. had called itself the party of "twentieth-century Americanism."

In Milwaukee the *Progressive* magazine asked
passers-by to define Communism. Patricia Blunk, seam-
stress: "I don't have much of a definition but I think
it is someone who doesn't believe in another country's
Lord." A mail carrier: "I've been trying to find out
myself but I've never been able to get a definition." A
truck driver: "In my mind it is a guy who is working
against the government." A machinist: "I really have
not studied much on the subject. I guess it would be an
undesirable person." A clerk: "I think it is somebody
who does not believe in religion and thinks everybody
should be equal."

Every day rang out with the super-heated hatreds of
the day, end products of a history that could not be dis-

cussed, only accused or confessed. *Exposed. Smeared. Cleared. Commie. Commie Rats. Comsymp. Communistic Sympathies and Longings. Guilty by Association. Stoolies. Loyalty. Conspiracy. Anti-Anti-Communists. Knee-Jerk Liberals. Commie Jury Hits Pay Dirt. Can We Trust Our Teachers?* The Republican attorney general of Pennsylvania suspended the assistant district attorney of Allegheny County: "The issue is not whether Mrs. Matson is a Communist or ever was. The issue is whether she has Communistic sympathies and leanings as shown by her associations, her acts and her utterances." Arthur Miller was refused a passport under regulations refusing passports to "citizens *believed to be* supporting the Communist movement, whether they are members of the C.P. or not." "Let us face the facts," said Senator Robert A. Taft, "we are already in World War III." A professional anti-Communist, Ralph de Toledano, was soon to write in H. L. Mencken's old *American Mercury*, now an openly Fascist publication:

> His name, in its contradiction of symbols, adds to the bafflement: *Alger*, the almost comic personifier of the rags-to-riches story: *Hiss*, the onomatopoeia of the spitting serpent. He is the Traitor rampant in a land which by its very goodness cannot understand treason. He is the Communist.
>
> At Harvard, the coruscating genius of Felix Frankfurter lay in wait, crouched to leap at whatever ties of Christian tradition still bound Hiss to the American past of his fathers.
>
> Part of a generation sinned with Hiss, still sins with Hiss, and sits in prison with Hiss. . . . It has not learned that when a soul divests itself of God, Evil takes possession. And not having heard, not having read, and not having learned, it has earned a damnation which Reason cannot chill.

The language of hysteria was acceptable in the highest places. An alien named Ignatz Mezei was ordered excluded from the United States on the basis of evidence that the government said was too confidential for disclosure. Writing the majority five-to-four decision that an alien barred for security reasons could be held indefinitely on Ellis Island, Justice Tom Clark conceded that this might be a hardship on Mezei. But, "the times being what they are," such action might be necessary. Justice Jackson in his dissent said that Mezei seemed likely to be held for life for a cause known only to the Attorney General.

Professor Sidney Hook, in an influential polemic of the times that asked "Can Our Teachers Be Trusted?" supported the firing of supposed Communist teachers on libertarian grounds. Such centers of independent thought had no room for "a man who has sworn or pledged himself to follow a party line through thick and thin, and insofar abandoned his freedom to think, to choose and to act."

> The history of thought is to a large extent the history of human mutation and heresy. . . . I am making a plea for tolerance of all heresies within the limits of intellectual integrity and competence.
>
> This open house to integrity must not be interpreted to mean that a university or college is a community of the fey, the eccentric, or slightly mad vying with each other in exhibitionistic glee to see who can believe more impossible things at once or make the more outrageous remarks. . . .
>
> . . . We suffer from a dearth of heretics.

At a time when Hook at a public discussion of the Communist problem explained that "only a few teachers have been fired," Senator Jenner boasted that twenty or more colleges and universities in California were cooperating with state and Congressional leaders in a blacklisting program under which about a hundred members of their faculties had been removed and as many more rejected for teaching posts. . . . Some institutions hired full-time investigators, many of them former members of the F.B.I. or Army-Navy intelligence, to snoop around classrooms and the campus.

Silone had said that the next war would be between Communists and ex-Communists. In America, Leninism *did* root itself among intellectuals. Leninists with their worship of the state and their belief in authority, Leninists past or present, Leninists who remained Leninists long after they had ceased to be radicals, were at the center of the war of words. In New York many left-wing intellectuals, having just discovered that America stood for freedom and that Russian despotism was probably incurable, emerged from their proud long-standing "alienation" to lead the new ideological crusade. It shocked me to hear so gifted a writer as Delmore Schwartz fulminate crazily against Silone for being "anti-American"—Delmore was already sliding downhill—to watch the old Bolsheviks on *Partisan Review* hedge on condemning McCarthy, to read the ex-Trotskyist and now professional rightist Irving Kristol: "There is one thing that the American people know about Senator McCarthy: he, like them, is unequivocally anti-Communist. About the spokesmen for American liberalism, they feel they know no such thing."

Many old Stalinist *apparatchiks* were now serving McCarthy and other inquisitors as "experts on Communism." This they certainly were. McCarthyism was fanned by the long-frustrated Republicans. Everybody knew that it was fomented more by hatred of the New Deal than by honest fear of Soviet domination in East-

ern Europe. But political "discourse" was still dominated by the belief of the left in a "final conflict," by
Communist and ex-Communist belief in history as constant acceleration. The United States was not just to
resist Russia but, like Russia, to become a purposive
dreadnought of "History."

The terms of the attack were irrelevant to the genuine
fear of Soviet espionage. The Broadway-Hollywood
celebrities who were the favorite victims in these American purge trials were picked because they were
"names." *They* were not spies but veterans of the 1930s,
people of commonplace political reflexes who had been
frightened by Hitler and the Depression into the usual
delusion that the Soviet Union was "Socialist" and offered a way out. Professor Sidney Hook was not the
only supporter of the Communist Party in the early
1930s. Congressmen investigating "un-American activities" were ignorant hacks who saw votes in scare tactics
and exploited the political cruelty that follows every
great American war. Since unrepentant Stalinists were
incapable of telling the truth, the victims were those
who could not confess their now shameful past without
betraying others whom they still identified with themselves.

In the Moscow trials of the 1930s Stalin condemned
his old and now powerless opponents in the ruling group
of Russia not because they were disloyal to the Communist state but because they had developed secret
doubts about their old beliefs and had "divided" minds.
The American inquisitors had many an ex-Communist
in a vise; he was guilty if he affirmed Socialist ideals
that were now totally unreal, guilty in his own mind if
he "named names," guilty about the divided, secret,
hesitant figure he publicly presented before a triumphant

prosperous postwar America to which he was more reconciled than he could admit.

It seemed impossible in public to admit doubts, divisions, nuances, contradictions, hesitations, lost illusions. Orwell had described Communists as "attracted by a form of Socialism that makes mental honesty impossible." Some were stuck in the habits of a lifetime—and found that their patriotic tormentors were just as absolutist in their thinking. Communism had indeed invaded the highest places. Alger Hiss was obviously incapable of telling the whole truth about himself; the Rosenbergs in the death house wrote the crudest Party slogans to each other in the form of personal letters. Delmore Schwartz turned his many literary hatreds into political hatreds. Robert Lowell at Yaddo was to bring charges that the director, a devoted friend to many writers over the years, was a link to Soviet agents. McCarthy could hardly admit that his goal was not to eradicate Communism in America but to inflame the populace in unashamed Hitler fashion, to gain constant publicity and prominence for himself. At least half the populace believed what he said.

The demand for orthodoxy suffocated me. Almost anywhere you looked now, the lies of Stalinists and the blood lust of super-Americans yelled down everything else. Perhaps World War III *had* already begun, and Russia and America were fighting it out in time-worn slogans. The issues of the "war" were set by political doctrinaires, fanatics, pseudopatriotic careerists, super-religious reactionaries. You were with one or the other. "Politics" now meant accusation, and became such an epidemic of fear, hysteria, intimidation, confession that only old-fashioned American libertarians and democrats, brought up outside Marxism—Sidney Hook was to sneer at them as "ritualistic liberals"—seemed in this maddened atmosphere capable of defending "suspects" in government and the universities.

The ex-Communists, now usually professional enemies of all "radicalism" and "subversion," became influential missionaries to the American mind. Of course they saw no connection between their sudden celebrity and the morbid craving for an American orthodoxy, between so much consensus and the self-conscious anxious prosperity that had come in with the war; they had no objection to a permanent war economy. In this best of all possible worlds—though it did seem a bit fragile—only a specter called Communism stood between us Americans and the fulfillment of all our dreams. *Converts* to America naturally cheered America as an ideology. There was much talk of "society," by which exradicals like Trilling meant "manners," but little concern with the possibly capricious use of the power possessed by us, the most formidable power on earth. The ex-radical intellectuals were in fact total *arrivistes* and accommodating in their thinking. But they were unusually accomplished and informed, and their influence over more modest minds permitted them little sense of what was really going on at home—especially in their native streets of New York. America was at the top of the heap and there would never be another economic trauma like the 1930s. Secretary of State Acheson put it perfectly: Americans felt as if they were "present at the creation."

On my return from Europe I sometimes saw Lionel Trilling walking up Broadway. Since our 1942 meeting at *The New Republic* he had become a major influence. Although he still looked vaguely careworn and ravaged in his sensitive way, he also looked pleased with himself and life, even debonair in his homburg hat. He seemed shocked by my suggestion that we have coffee at the Bickford's on Broadway and 111th, outside of which I happened to meet him. Although he lived just a block off the Columbia campus, he looked as if he merely tolerated his environment, or could be amused by it if the occasion warranted amusement.

This was Trilling's high moment. No other critic was now so much an influence on the "liberal imagination" in America, so much a metropolitan figure and yet of the purest prestige to the derivative critics who could find an intellectual home, wanted an intellectual home, nowhere but in an English Department. From having been a problem Jew, "the first of his faith" to get a permanent post in Columbia's English Department, Trilling had become a major influence on the droves of sparkling Jews who now enlivened Columbia as if there had never been a Nicholas Murray Butler and a *numerus clausus*.

Amidst the broiling hysteria of the McCarthy period, I found comfort in some ancient American tradition of intellectual freedom among Zechariah Chafee, Henry Commager, Robert Maynard Hutchins, the genuinely conservative Hannah Arendt, and the Italian libertarian and friend of Camus, Nicola Chiaromonte. None of them had ever been deluded by Leninism. But it was the best of times for Jewish intellectuals who, as Robert Lowell said with as much truth as spite, "were unloading their European baggage." Yes, we Jews were *older*; we embodied "a school of experience." We had been stage center at all the great intellectual dramas and political traumas of this century. After "the worst episode in human history" we had just—after nineteen hundred years away from it!—declared ourself a nation again on the very soil that obsessed the Jewish liturgy. *If I forget thee, O Jerusalem.*

If I forget thee! We never forgot anything; our holy book, our book of laws and commandments, was a history book, a recital that went back so far and was repeated so fondly that the history of this people seemed magical, unreal, improbable to everyone but themselves. How could one possibly justify the return to Eretz Israel by secular, rational, "normal" reasoning? How could one explain the inordinate zeal of the Socialist Prime Minister Ben-Gurion who said of the "ingathering" of so many "exiles," "We are living in the days of the Messiah"? There was no justification for any of this except the divine wisdom to the Jews of their mad perpetuation. There was a sacredness that the Jews had made part of existence, but often understood as little as others understood *them*. The God who first disclosed himself as fire was, as usual, an impassable barrier. He could not be encompassed in words. We were, above all, creatures of culture, idolaters of words. Words were our culture; culture had to do everything. God did not seem much connected with "culture." Certainly nothing had so betrayed us as culture, humanism, the fine professions of European civilization.

No other distinguished professor of literature was so much a man of letters as Trilling, so much interested in Freud, Babel, the Kinsey Report, the E. M. Forster he made a part of our "intellectual baggage." The galley slaves of criticism in the universities were chained to eighteen sacred poems, to Brooks and Warren, to tension, ambiguity, and paradox. Trilling, with his strong sense of history and his exquisite sense of accommodation, was the most successful leader of deradicalization —which was conducted in the name of the liberal "imagination" against those who lacked it or had the wrong kind. "Radical" was not mentioned. "Communist" could be applied only to those who could not confess their past, like Alger Hiss; or those anti-Communists who had turned all the way around, like Trilling's old college acquaintance Whittaker Chambers, and could talk of nothing other than Communism.

Trilling's leadership in this "battle of ideas" was subtle, graceful, and never departed the soft culture world of "literary ideas." Like his mentor Matthew Arnold, about whom he had written his superb loving book before the war, Trilling wrote as if the only problem of society was the thinking of the "advanced intellectuals." Those in charge, and *properly* in charge, simply had wrong notions. Arnold smote the philistines: Trilling the liberals. In his America there were no workers, nobody suffering from a lack of cash; no capitalists, no corporations, no Indians, no blacks. And, on the whole, neither were there any Jews. His favorite characters were the unimaginative, misguided, generalized liberals or "educated classes." This extraordinarily accomplished son of an immigrant tailor was so passionate about England and the great world of the English nineteenth-century novel that his image of this literature turned England into a personal dream. But America? In America it was possible for a Columbia sociologist to say of this period: "In the fifties, the only perturbations, the only tensions, strains and agonies that really mattered were those which could be seen as, or inferred from, the human spirit and its ties with culture."

Perhaps Trilling's forays against the liberal "mind" were not an evasion but a form of middle-class claustrophobia. Like many less gifted and interesting ex-radicals, he was limited to New York, to his intellectual class, to friends who could never forgive themselves or anyone else for having in misguided youth trafficked with Socialism. But what raised Trilling above the dull zealots, informants, and false patriots of this agonizing period was the critic's gift for dramatizing his mind on paper. A writer of tremulous carefulness and deliberation, he nevertheless became the master of a dialectical style that expressed his underlying argument with himself. There was an intellectual tension in his essays, as in the seminars that excited the new intellectual crowd at Columbia. The old triple-named WASPS at Columbia had enforced upon him the importance of "manners" and his cherished "modulation." The new postwar intellectuals, brought up on the residue of the old radicalism and now enlisted in revising it, were fascinated by an intellectual so totally absorbed in giving full expression to his intellectual loves and revulsions. Trilling was an expressive Hamlet of the intellect who felt that the time out of joint *was* up to him to set it right. The great critic, as in Victorian times, might yet change the temper of the times by his persuasion of the "advanced intellects" around him.

Columbia's English Department, which was now metropolitan and supple, included as teachers old radical friends of Trilling, F. W. Dupee and Robert Gorham Davis; students who would be influences at large—Allen Ginsberg, Norman Podhoretz, Jason Epstein, Jack Kerouac, Steven Marcus, Robert Gottlieb, Richard Howard, John Hollander. . . . Columbia in the fifties would be the starting point of the Beats and of college bohemians who made a Greenwich Village of their own in the rooming houses and bars just off Broadway. Columbia students could easily frighten the staid members of the faculty, one of whom put his hand on his heart and said he had never seen such corrupt characters before. But these young intellectuals also knew that in

Trilling, Jacques Barzun, Mark Van Doren, Andrew Chiappe, Meyer Schapiro, Richard Hofstadter, I. I. Rabi, Mario Salvadori, John Brebner, Robert Merton, Daniel Bell they had the most emancipated *and* creative faculty in America. My old friend Hofstadter was now one of its chief luminaries. Whenever I saw him walking about in his beret or telling one of his jokes about the Japanese rabbi dismissed by his Westchester congregation, I liked to think that learning still went with our old profane New York style.

Hofstadter liked to say that he stayed at Columbia because he found it so interesting a "society." "Society" at Columbia was not the runaway society of postwar America, with its returned soldiers crowding the universities on the GI Bill, its Quonset huts for their families, its race hatreds, its urban hatreds, its somehow bracing American disorder, abrasiveness, corruption. It seemed to mean a certain intellectual contentment. Trilling's wife, Diana, writing about Allen Ginsberg and other disturbances in "The Other Night at Columbia," wrote that on her return from a reading "there was a meeting going on at home of the pleasant professional sort which, like the comfortable living room in which it usually takes place, at a certain point in a successful modern literary career confirms the writer in his sense of disciplined achievement and well-earned reward. . . . Auden, alone of the eight men in the room not dressed in a proper suit but wearing a battered old brown leather jacket . . ."

Like all of us old liberals, the Trillings lived at the edge of the abyss created in modern culture, in all our cultured minds, by the extermination of the Jews. The case of Alger Hiss seemed easier to deal with. He was a proven liar, perhaps especially to himself. And he was such an obvious case of what was wrong with liberals that he made society real to those for whom it meant liberalism gone sour.

But the faster time carried us away from it, the closer the gas came. It stole up our skin without our always knowing it. It was *total*, the inescapable crime lying across the most documented century in history. People in the millions could be considered superfluous. Lenin had first propounded this. The Jews as a people were now the most concentrated and direct example. Certainly they were not the only ones. But the abyss was at our feet because *we* believed in nothing so much as what Trilling called "the life of the mind." The life of the mind was of no use unless it addressed itself to the gas. And what then? Letters of fire had been read at Nuremberg:

> A word must be said on the decision to economize on gas. By the summer of 1944, the collapse of the Eastern front meant that the destruction of European Jewry might not be completed before the advancing Allied armies arrived. So Hungarian Jewry was killed at maximum speed—at the rate of up to ten thousand people a day. Priority was given to transports of death over trains with reinforcements and munitions needed for the Wehrmacht. Entire trainloads were marched straight to the gas chambers.
>
> The gas used—Zyklon B—causes death by internal asphyxiation, with damage to the centers or respiration, accompanied by feelings of fear, dizziness, and vomiting. In the chamber, when released, "the gas climbs gradually to the ceiling, forcing the victims to claw and trample upon one another in their struggle to reach upward. Those on the top are the last to succumb. . . . The corpses are piled one on top of another in an enormous heap. . . ."
>
> The sheer volume of gas used in the summer of 1944 depleted the gas supply. In addition, the Nazis deemed the costs excessive . . . the dosage of gas was halved

from twelve boxes to six per gassing. When the concentration of the gas is quite high, death occurs quickly. The decision to cut the dosage in half was to more than double the agony.

Life seemed far from terrible and extreme in this postwar era of expansion and prosperity when so many Jews "came into their own." But it was. We had just been ruled out of the human race, systematically annihilated on the latest scientific principles. What did our political thinkers have to say about this? The left had nothing to say, did not even include the gas in its summary view of Hitlerism as "the last decadent stage of capitalism." The right excused everything and everyone: there is evil in all of us. The great violinist Yehudi Menuhin, like many a Christian quietist, explained that "everyone is guilty." For me, no one was serious who did not fight the condemnation of a specific group that ended in its "extermination." Nothing else was serious. Murder had become the first political principle. We had to recognize the abyss on whose edge we lived.

From her first book in English, *The Origins of Totalitarianism*, Hannah Arendt was obsessed with genocide and the threat of future holocausts in an "overpopulated" world. She became vital to my life. Much as I loved her and submitted patiently to an intellectual loneliness that came out as arrogance, it was for the *direction* of her thinking that I loved her, for the personal insistencies she gained from her comprehension of the European catastrophe. She gave her friends—writers so various as Robert Lowell, Randall Jarrell, Mary McCarthy, the Jewish historian Salo Baron—intellectual courage before the moral terror the war had willed to us.

Hitler's war was the central fact in the dark shadowy

Morningside Drive apartment where she and her feisty husband, Heinrich Bluecher, now lived, taking in a boarder to make ends meet. Hannah never stopped thinking. What she thought about was uprooting in every sense: starting with the uprooting of whole peoples that had washed up on the West Side this specialist in St. Augustine, had turned her life into a voracious political inquiry. How did *it* happen? How had it all happened? How had this modern age happened? The boarder could be heard walking down the hall to the toilet. She rocked that dark flat with the flushing of the toilet; walked back to her room. Hannah paused ever so slightly in her explication of the police state. She had been brought up in a genteel upper-middle-class Jewish family in Königsberg. She had studied with Bultmann! Dibelius! Heidegger! Husserl! Jaspers! She had written her doctoral thesis at Heidelberg on Augustine's concept of love! With a little smile, she resumed her analysis of the police state. Nothing could deflect her very long from her inflexible concentration on *the* subject. Her uprooting and her need to understand from the modern age the origins of totalitarianism had become the same experience. She lived her thought, and thought dominated her life.

A time would come when her deep German conservatism, theological and classicist, made her a mightier professor than she could ever have been in Germany. It directed her to the "human condition," and away from the political terror that was the foundation of her American life. But when I met her in the late forties she was a blazing Jew, working round the clock for Jewish Cultural Reconstruction from a little office in Columbus Circle. Her job was to round up and restore to what remained of Jewish communities in Europe the libraries and religious objects stolen by the Nazis. She had been a social worker in Paris immediately after leaving Germany in 1933; she had assisted in the emigration of German Jewish children to Palestine.

A new-learned English word was "fetch." I would call her to have some coffee with me just outside her office, and she would respond in her deep voice and the barbed accent that became more German the longer she lived here, "You will fetch me? Yes?" In those days, before the sterile Coliseum took over the place, Columbus Circle was lined with shabby old United Cigar stores, suspect junk shops, run-down office buildings clearly occupied by ambulance chasers and soapless abortionists. But whenever I fetched her at the offices of Jewish Cultural Reconstruction, I was greeted by a beaming Hannah brimming over with the enthusiasm for the New World, her discovery of that new political thinker John Adams, and able genially to tolerate the late-Tammany *dreck* that was Columbus Circle. She was as arch, witty, womanly as she was acute and powerfully cultivated. When stirred by a new friend, her angular Jewish features and amazingly gruff voice melted into wistful lovingness. I was never quite sure *what* she looked like. The strong, sometimes too commanding mind went with a fiercely imploring heart. In the midst of a late-afternoon rain howling down on Columbus Circle, she talked with love about Kafka and why he was much—oh, much!—greater than Thomas Mann. I had never met a woman so reflective, yet so eager and gifted for friendship. She was entrenched in her long formal training as a philosopher, yet was glad to be an outsider, unconventional, solitary in this strange new world.

Her constant refrain was "the decisive break with tradition." There had been a tradition, and no one was more eager and willing to bestow on you, in Greek, the

prime Greek meanings of man, mind, the *polis*, the
common good. But there had been a break. Definitely,
there had been a break. Her presence on the West Side
was like Lear's on the heath. The kingdom had been
rent. Breakup was her life and everyone's life now. She
often spoke to me of her anguish at being separated
from so many old friends and associations in Germany.
With all her *intellectual* passion as well as some laconic
personal despair, she seemed to cry out a wildly urgent
need for constancy in life, every instance of life. She
was a passionate and anxious friend; from the moment
you entered her flat, she tried as it were to hold you
with old-fashioned European house offerings of candies,
candied fruits, cookies, "porto." The longer she lived
here, the more she insisted on constancy in her friends,
constancy in the world of ideas—no matter how far
back that stretched. Like her other house offering,
Greek quotations, her mind instinctively sprang to some
essential principle of life as tradition. And what happened to tradition? It broke.

Was it perhaps not in the nature of tradition to
"break"? Could any tradition go on forever? Modernity
was a tragedy because of the wrong *thinking* behind it.
Plato's myth of the cave represented the true condition
of man front and back; the world made what it is by
the forms of human perception. Marx had usurped
Plato; he had replaced the cave with "society," the inner world of our thinking by a world outside of us. The
human mind searched this vainly for a single principle
of determination and a single lever of control. Marx
was indeed right to see alienation everywhere; he had
helped to accomplish this by construing the world entirely outside himself. "Politics" had ceased to be the
public sphere, the common good; it was every man's
ambition, his blind search for his own interest. The in-

stability of society and the panic in the self-alienated
mind led to the daemonic thirst for "total domination."
The necessary fiction of all totalitarian regimes was that
terror assured "security" through total domination.
What could "total" mean but an illusion for which you
had increasingly to step up the terror? And where had
the whole terrible unraveling of our common life, of
our common *safety*, begun but in Marx's usurpation of
Plato's categories of thought?

Marx-Plato-Hegel-Heidegger-Kant-Kafka-Jaspers!
Montesquieu! Nietzsche! Duns Scotus! The great sem-
inal names were a big thing in Hannah's shelter on
Morningside Drive overlooking the sign of the Krakauer
piano factory and the bleak unenterable enemy country that was Morningside Park. The excitement of being
with her and her tempestuous, sometimes frighteningly
mental husband Heinrich Bluecher was really their belief in great thoughts, great men. The world was definitely a hierarchy, and the top of the top was always
some great thinker. Heinrich, a poor relation of the
famous Prussian military family, was a stocky, pugna-
cious, self-trained philosopher who came out of the
trenches in 1918 to make—at last!—a German revolution. The Nazis made it instead, and Heinrich left for
Paris, where he met Hannah. With his Aryan passport
and obstinate sense of justice, he returned to Germany
several times to help fugitive Jews. He had a passion
for Jews. He certainly had a passion for Hannah. They
were vehemently involved in working out a common
philosophy; and conversation with the two of them
could suddenly turn into German and open connubial
excitement in some philosophic discovery unsuspected
until that moment. Between clenched lips holding a
pipe, Heinrich growled his thought out as if he were
still on the battlefield—against wrong-headed philoso-

phers. Hannah, despite her genteel training, also talked philosophy as if she were standing up alone in a foreign land and in a foreign tongue against powerful forces of error. She confronted you with the truth; she confronted you with her friendship; she confronted Heinrich even when she joined him in the most passionate seminar I would ever witness between a man and a woman living together; she confronted the gap, the nothingness, the "extreme situation" of "modern man." Philosophy was the highest intellectual calling because it was *inescapable*, not a profession but a way of life.

The Bluechers certainly lived philosophy—not "their" philosophy but philosophy as "a thinking through of the age." Human destiny was under the armored first of politics. To sit with Hannah under the photograph of a kingly bearded bust reputed to be that of Plato was to hear that philosophy was still king. She reverted constantly to the image of the *polis*, the public realm, politics as true knowledge of the public interest. This was her protest against the unpolitical "idealism" of German intellectuals who had abstained from politics, had condescended to politics, so had opened the door to Hitler. She liked to quote Theodor Mommsen, the great German historian: "My greatest wish was to live in a free German republic, and lacking that I wrote the history of Rome." America was different. She was enchanted with the wisdom of the Federalist Papers, the political theory of John Adams, came to believe more deeply in the Founding Fathers than any July Fourth orator.

None of this touched on grimy unenterable Morningside Park across the street or the fact that the door to the Bluechers' apartment was secured by two locks *and* a pole. The sense of exile was overwhelming. In the foyer was an enormous photograph of Kafka as a student. He is awkward and funny. Of course he knows, with his famous mistrust of himself, that he *looks* awkward and funny as he poses for the photographer in Prague in derby and high choke collar, and with strained casualness rests two long bony unbearably tense fingers on the head of a dog. This is Kafka, our great and beautiful novelist, prophet, misfit. He did not live to see the Holocaust, though he guessed it and its aftermath: "Not the murderer but the victim is considered guilty." In the photograph (I do not say this to Hannah) he looks as winsome as Buster Keaton, Harry Langdon, Stan Laurel. The eternal *nebbish* with the past and future in his marvelously clear tormented mind, and nowhere to rest that mind. He is an angel of thought, condemned forever to fly the higher spheres. Hannah certainly loved the higher spheres. The presence of the Krakauer piano factory across Morningside Park never interfered with what her teacher Karl Jaspers had said, what Hegel had said, what Spinoza *should* have said. She quoted, quoted, quoted. "Nietzsche writes like a charlatan but is a philosopher; Schopenhauer writes like a philosopher but is a charlatan." The network of life was made up of the paradigmatic individuals, the great thinkers. They possessed Hannah, were the filaments of her brain. Reading modern poetry to her, I once mimicked her with E. E. Cummings:

> plato told
>
> him: he couldn't
> believe it (jesus
>
> told him; he wouldn't believe
> it)

I wouldn't have wanted her otherwise. The excitement of being with Hannah was mysterious, for it reached to foundations of thought that she accepted with a kind of awe. "I have never, since a child," she once said to me, "doubted that God exists." She had devoted herself to Augustine because of a single sentence: "Love means that I want you to be." The difference between "tradition" and the "great break" that represented current reality expressed itself for her as some ancient force of poetry, some half-remembered sublimity. All this mental idealism, fervent with the need to teach and teach, the constant injunction "to think what we are doing," produced in Americans either adulators or the bitterest enemies. Saul Bellow found it outrageous to be lectured on Faulkner—*another* novelist!—by someone from *Königsberg*. I found it comic to hear Heinrich instruct us in the meaning of marriage by way of quotations from Melville. Louise was more and more impatient with me, but Heinrich—who had nothing but Hannah—was important to Louise as our marriage crumbled away. Listening to him, her silence took on something unusually respectful. She thought him an extraordinary psychologist. Heinrich came on as an existential guide to our personal problems. He seemed to Louise a figure of exalted common sense, ready to meet life on its own terms, and not like her uselessly bookish husband. I thought him an inspired madman of sorts—she found him the most practical lawgiver for every day that she had met in years. He was the very sort of ripe, seasoned European who seemed to her a figure to rely on.

On the basis of one adverse opinion by a Harvard professor, *The Origins of Totalitarianism* was rejected by the Boston firm that had contracted for it. The editors did not bother to read it. I took the manuscript to Robert Giroux at Harcourt, Brace, who immediately recognized its quality, went through the enormous manuscript in all-night bouts of enthusiastic reading, and published it. Hannah was launched. But her insistence that Stalinism was as totalitarian as Nazism was offensive to her Marxist critics; she would not include "authoritarian" regimes like Franco Spain. Franco had allowed conflicting authorities, and did not proclaim the total domination by his party as the state.

"Totalitarian" was becoming an easy label for political intimidation of every kind. By contrast, Hannah refused the term to everything outside her own experience of the break with tradition. Totalitarianism was a phenomenon entirely new, a law unto itself. Hannah saw it Biblically as a great fall. The political structure of Nazism, as in her devastating end chapters on terror and the police, were more real to her than the social roots and strains of the German dictatorship. The relation of the Czarist state to the Leninist bureaucracy she did not examine at all. *The Origins of Totalitarianism* left its haunting and influential vibration on literary intellectuals with an overdeveloped sense of the past as *the* great tradition. It was literally about the subversion of great men and great thoughts by the social process— which Hannah saw as the social attrition and despair that turned resentment into a raging flame. The power of this resentment was something Hannah could suggest with great vividness from the Weimar experience, but there it stopped. You *saw* the German madness, but still could not account for it. When, discovering the classical wisdom of America's Founding Fathers, she firmly declared that "the pursuit of happiness" meant the pursuit of *politics*, "the public happiness," she made a European projection typical of her ceaseless instruction of her American friends.

Hannah became irresistible to Robert Lowell and Randall Jarrell. Jarrell in particular was caught up in some amazing adventure of culture in the big terrible city that Southern writers usually made a profession of despising. To be with Hannah was to learn and learn. Randall could not get enough of teaching. "I would pay to teach," he wrote. He read English poets to Hannah by the hour. He could not get enough of learning. Listening to Hannah read Goethe and Hoelderlin, he became so intoxicated that he felt he *knew* German well enough to translate Rilke, Grimm's fairy tales—eventually, even *Faust*. What attracted him to the Bluechers' house, Hannah said after his death, was that it was a house where German was spoken. "I believe my favorite country's German." He knew German by ear, by heart, by instinct—he told Hannah he was too busy translating German to learn it. He knew it as Robert Lowell knew the Greek, French, German, Russian, Italian poems he turned into reckless stunning "imitations" from other people's word-for-word translations; he knew it as poets *know* so many verbal mysteries without understanding them. Cocteau called poetry "a separate language." Randall certainly believed that poetry was separate, another country, the best country, the only country where the soul was entirely free. Hannah was shaken by Randall's insistence that poetry was the only *decency*, by the shouting intensity of a football fan that he brought to every reading of poetry and any discussion of poetry. With the beard that covered him up to the eyes, his flaming absorption in anything that absorbed him, his lovely Southern manners, and his truculent innocence, she could not account for him except as "a figure from fairyland . . . emerged from the enchanted forests in which we spent our childhood. Randall Jarrell would have been a poet if he had never written a single poem."

Randall knew better. Poetry meant so much to him

that I believe he died of not being able to reach that final place, that country, that *future*—

> *Du bist die Zukunft, grosses Morgenrot*
> *über den Ebenen der Ewigkeit*

—that he knew with his marvelous *intelligence* of poetry. I loved Randall's grasp of the poets he loved—Wordsworth, Hardy, Whitman, Eliot, Frost. I loved the wild wit and impatience with which he walked over everything and everyone to shake friends and readers with the terrible beauty of what he saw. I loved him for living and acting as if poetry should be worth a life—anyone's life, his life. Edmund Wilson was the only other writer I knew who lived so completely *in* literature. But Randall did not need so much literature in order to be a great poet; he could not fool himself. His poetry was adroit, "brilliant," put together with the greatest feeling and intelligence. It was never as moving as he was—and he was moving in a kind of passionate weakness. His cleverest essays displayed recognition by a poet studying poets better than himself; you felt he was a keen strategist studying superiors. On those below him, he spent wit and scorn ridiculing to the cruelest lengths writing that a greater poet would have ignored. Conrad Aiken protested to *The Nation* about the cruelty of Randall's reviews; Randall did not understand what had shocked Aiken.

Randall looked all shining in his glass box of poetry, surrounded on every side by *Dichtung* as a man's only way of getting into the world. His constant citations, his crying need of literature, seemed to me the last of their kind. *Verveile doch, du bist so schön!* Watching him at Hannah's, completely happy and glorying in the

profusion of her total sympathy for literature, in endless reading and quotations and invocations of the best
that has been said and thought—*if* it was said first in
German—I could see Randall lonely *outside* the classrooms of the Woman's College at Winston-Salem where
he happily taught—"I would pay to teach." Randall—
mocking, jaunty, always the university wit, masked
within his beard and behind that beard—nevertheless
pitied himself as "the poet at the supermarket." He declaimed his loneliness to a publishing-industry audience
at the National Book Awards that thought him ridiculous for saying so. The audience was right. A poet
more confident of his talent would not have needed to
raise himself at the expense of the supermarket. Randall, fighting for the true, the beautiful, the good, nobly
rushed at people who did not know what he was talking
about. He even thought himself brave and reckless for
praising Whitman to his Southern literary friends.

Randall certainly lived and died for excellence. To be
the best poet! To be the poet of a generation! When he
reviewed Robert Lowell's *Lord Weary's Castle*, his
natural piety expressed itself without limitation. The
uprush of his praise was the most perfect example in
public of Jarrell's capacity for veneration:

> I know of no poetry since Auden's that is better than
> Robert Lowell's. Everybody who reads poetry will read
> it sooner or later. . . . *Lord Weary's Castle* makes me
> feel like a rain-maker who predicts rain, and gets a
> flood which drowns everyone in the country. A few of
> these poems, I believe, will be read as long as men re-
> member English.

Lowell was another addict of Hannah's. Bellow
might find insupportable her instructing *him* about
Faulkner. When in later years Hannah's vexing book on

Eichmann and the "banality of evil" appeared, Bellow took his revenge in *Herzog:* "the canned sauerkraut of Weimar intellectuals." But Lowell, the strongest poet of my generation and given to mood swings that encouraged his gift for exaltation, responded fervently to every suggestion of her culture, her sympathy for the coming men in American poetry. As her gifts made themselves known to the "educated classes," and she emerged as her extraordinary self at Princeton, Berkeley, Chicago, was given prizes by the eagerly repentant Germans, her natural tendency to hierarchy irritated those intellectuals she put down as "little Jews." Nothing was so likely to inflame former Communists who not only were afraid of McCarthy but did not know Greek. If you were admitted into what Hannah, like Stefan George, called "the inner circle," you were obviously one of the best. As the McCarthyite epidemic grew and Hannah in public mocked ex-Communists who became heresy hunters and professional patriots, the Bluechers came to think of themselves as a lonely wagon train fighting off the redskins. Heinrich, who could not write but who talked with a conviction not often seen in American classrooms, passionately impressed his lucky students at Bard with the living presence of Abraham, Moses, Kant, Nietzsche, then described McCarthy as "the last big personal fight of my life." It was talk, it was funny, it was magnificent. The Bluechers were "unduly sensitive" to the repressive state. They had reason to be.

Wonderfully gifted Robert Lowell, whose instinct for language worked on me with the force of a jackhammer, was more exalted by Hannah's recognition of *him* than he was by her politics. I was never to understand what Lowell's politics were. His eyesight had kept him from military service, but he was a Catholic convert and positively insisted on going to jail as a conscientious objector. When I met him again at Yaddo in 1949, he was divorced from Jean Stafford and no longer a Catholic, but he sounded like Evelyn Waugh rampaging against the wartime alliance with Russia. He objected more to Russia than to the war. It was a gloomy time for me; listening to Lowell at his most blissfully high orating against Communist influences at Yaddo and boasting of the veneration in which he was held by those other illiberal great men Ezra Pound and George Santayana, made me feel worse. My "New York book" included everything in New York except me, so the book never seemed to move of its own accord. I retyped the same page over and again, stared at the bleak winter light from my bedroom window, walked aimlessly in the snow in the great estate that adjoined the Saratoga race track.

Yaddo had once been my greatest refuge and release on earth. It was the perfect escape for writers who needed solitude. Katherine Anne Porter had labored there for years over the seemingly endless voyage that finally became *Ship of Fools;* Theodore Roethke, Elizabeth Bishop, John Cheever, and many other finely tuned and overtuned American instruments had done good work there. The summer gaiety, croquet before dinner, the races in August had never meant as much to me as the perfect retreat it made for my overexcited New York soul when I wanted to be discharged from every care except a book. In winter this estate of a wealthy New York stockbroker left to writers, artists, and composers, became a thorny mysterious return to another century on the rim of the Adirondacks, a mixture of primeval woods and the genteel tradition. There were perhaps half a dozen people in residence. You lived and worked in a wooden house that could have been a farmhouse but was lined with copies of Pre-Raphaelite pictures of Dante on the Lungarno in Florence first seeing the young Beatrice, complete old-fashioned library sets on the shelves, pink-shaded lamps and crimson rugs, photographs of the stockbroker and wife, whose children had all died young. The great estate had been left to strange beings who could shut themselves up in a little room all day staring at a piece of white paper.

There was nothing to do all day but to write, after writing to walk in the woods, to walk down Union Avenue, which Henry James had thought the most beautiful street in America. Past the shut-down race track, past the little practice tracks with the low fences along which I had wandered the last summer with Natasha, watching the early-morning workouts; past the last great Victorian and Edwardian houses, now turned into Skidmore College dormitories and boarding houses for elderly Jews who still believed in a good old-fashioned spa and "taking the waters." Saratoga and Yaddo were full of ghosts. If you didn't care for so much history, the ghosts could seem jealous of your sitting in their old places. If you responded gratefully to the Victoriana hovering over your writer's prison, a few winter weeks of solitude put you chapters ahead, gave you back to yourself.

But for once I could not work at Yaddo. That winter on the edge of 1950, when nothing could still buttress the marriage, not even a little boy in the unhappy apartment on Central Park West, my book about walking New York was barren, smart, soulless. I was just not in it. Lowell and Elizabeth Hardwick were a brilliant couple, but Lowell was just a little too dazzling at the moment. He was at the top of a psychic crest down which he would slide the next season; but at this peak he talked in tongues; he was of the great company, with

Milton and Hardy and Eliot; he was wonderful and frightening. He was not just damned good, suddenly famous and deserving his fame; he was in a state of grandeur not negotiable with lesser beings. He was a Lowell; he was handsome, magnetic, rich, wild with excitement about his powers, wild over the many tributes to him from Pound, Santayana, his old friends Tate and Jarrell and Warren. Flannery O'Connor, who was also at Yaddo, seemed to be attending Lowell with rapture. All these gifted, assured, deeply traditional writers made me feel useless. No fiction writer after the war seemed to me so *deep*, so severely perfect, as Flannery. She would be our classic: I had known that from the day I discovered her stories. And at the moment I seemed unable to finish my second book; I had a wife who was no wife and to whom I was no husband. New York was political crazies and fanatics, a spiritual desert. Only the New School took me on when I wanted to teach again.

I was numb, entirely closed in, then was shocked awake by Lowell's discovery that Yaddo, too, was subversive and may once have had a secret line to the Soviet Embassy. Lowell did not seem too unhappy about the frightful discovery that the charming woman director of many years—my friend, his friend, a good friend to many writers—was secretly attempting to cut down our country. He went to the F.B.I. about it. He was as happily excited as a man can be. With his newfound authority as an American poet, he had the Yaddo trustees convened, confided to them the great things Santayana and Pound had said about *him*, and demanded that the director be dismissed.

The director was not dismissed, but we all had a terrible time waiting for the verdict to come in. Eleanor Clark and I rounded up support from many writers, composers, and artists who had worked at Yaddo over the years. But there were even more who refused to support the director because they had families, jobs, "could not take the risk." Some artists refused because they had not been given exactly the working conditions they demanded; some because they had not liked the food; some because they did not like the director's "personality." The artist under political stress was an unforgettable picture of limitless self-regard. Tocqueville had noticed that in America the individual placed so much stress on his personal enjoyment of "liberty" that he ended up surveying "a very puny object—himself." The lesser poets were not only the biggest cowards, but impossible to shut up in their boring, whining self-defense. They were concerned with Lowell's power to affect their reputations even when they had no reputations. Lowell, who would transcend the mannerism of *Lord Weary's Castle* and find a straightforward "confessional" mode perfect for his literary instinct and troubled life in an age merciless with guilt, later admitted that he had forgotten the Yaddo episode. I believed him.

The night that Tim was born, I came back from the hospital to think and think about the howling little figure with the great shock of black hair whom I had just seen in a line of howling newborn babies at Lenox Hill. I needed to hold him firmly in my mind. I dreamed that night of Louise taking Tim off and Tim in the back seat vaguely waving. In less than two years, I was to become a weekly visitor; to pick him up at school Wednesday and give him lunch Sunday; to sit with him in the playground at Ninety-sixth and Fifth watching the seesaw go up and the seesaw go down; to read comic books to him, Golden Books, and play Uncle

Wiggily on the long winter twilights; to pick him up at the school, the bus stations, the railroad station, the airport; and to deliver him after the baseball game, the game of catch, the Walt Disney movie, the occasional weekend. He was to be picked up and regularly delivered back, this precious cargo, my son Tim, this regular American feller who by seven knew down to the last decimal point the batting averages of every important player in the National League. At night, during the usual uncertain summer weeks at Wellfleet, he so raptly dreamed baseball that I could hear him saying in his sleep that he was going to bat. "I'm ready for the pitch!" he cried. "I'm ready for the pitch!"

To have a son you do not live with but take out at regular intervals is to be the perfect setup for popular daily entertainment-filled America. There is nothing to do with the little boy Wednesdays and Sundays except to entertain him. And you entertain him, sitting with wildly bored and distracted women looking you through and through and making amazing conversation with you, the only man in the playground at 2:30 in the afternoon.

A long succession of taxis to the Polo Grounds and the Yankee Stadium, the American Museum of Natural History, the Brooklyn Botanic Garden. Millions of comic books; detestable plastic *dreck* for those great American suckers parent and child; pony rides in Central Park; rowboats in Central Park Lake. One day, right in the middle of the dirty lake, screams echoing from the girls on shore, that stare: "*Other* fathers live with their sons." The seals in the Central Park Zoo jump out of the pool and right back into the pool. Seals are all slithery. Seals are surrounded by people who laugh the way people laugh when seals slither on shore out of a pool and then slither right back again. There is never anything new about these seals, not on Wednesday, not on Sunday. Nor is there ever anything new about Bimbo, the gorilla; or about the orange peels and carrot scraps on the floor of Bimbo's cage; or about the hot and disheveled polar bear frowning, pacing, leaping as he clambers up and down the rock in his stage set. Even the pony at the head of the pony cart and the kiddies lining each side of the cart look the same every Wednesday and every Sunday. So are the animal cages the same; and the animals dolorously not looking at you from their cages; and the walks between the cages; and the scattered empties; and the assorted New York strangers, derelicts, parents, vagrants, reporters, photographers, Hasidim, pushers.

What can My Lord Heart say? There is nothing to say and everything to wait for. Soon childhood has passed, no more Mickey Mouse in every corner. It is spring a dozen years later and you are playing catch in the first radiant sunshine, the ball going back and forth, back and forth, with that easy lovely motion acquired by American men as they throw a ball to each other for hours at a time with the ready, eager, assured motion known only to men who love baseball. The game between father and son is deadly serious at times. The hard ball gets thrown harder and harder, and when you pitch to him at bat he sometimes smashes the ball in a line drive right at your face.

The Wednesdays were the same; the zoo especially was the same. But the successive acts are rapid, and the howling infant with the towering mass of black hair is a lean, handsome, careful young man, who sometimes stares at you to say that something dropped out of *his* life forever and that *you* may not fill the gap. The years rush on and on, moving from baseball to "politics." The ball thrown at you with a hard smashing curve now demonstrates the infallibility of People's China, the oppressiveness of "Amerika." Every conversation looses the political avalanche of our century; unlooses every other hard-won tie; unlooses zeal, political righteousness, and intellectual contempt. He and his classmates throw themselves with the force of their bodies against a building, throw themselves into the black schools in Cambridge, calling the children of the oppressed "out into the struggle." The curve ball he throws at me grows still harder every year, more derisive, certainly more difficult to catch. The man at whom he throws it seems with each new political argument more and more removed from *me*. But as Tim says with a grin, "We are all the children of those who were radical in their youth."

The years will rush on even faster. But at the moment it is the winter of 1950, it is freezing in New York, and I am frozen with grief and longing. Tim is a little boy not two years old staring at me from behind a glass door as, finally, the silence between Louise and me ends in one last, unforgettable shout and I am out, leaving the little boy behind the glass door.

It is freezing in Washington, too. McCarthy is snarling at a witness—reducing his history, our history, my history, to shit. Arthur Miller will soon be saying to the McCarthy inquisitor: "This is now sixteen years ago. That is half a lifetime away. . . ."

The inquisitor Arens, the good American Vishinsky: "Can you tell us who was there when you walked into the room?"

"Mr. Chairman, I understand the philosophy behind this question and I want you to understand mine. . . . I could not use the name of another person and bring trouble on him."

McCarthy to President James Conant of Harvard: "I

must say that when you have been a Communist, when you have been a member of a conspiracy, there is no presumption that you have reformed."

The American *government* was beyond criticism. At one point Senator McCarthy asserted that the "U.S. State Department was helping finance some newspapers that were *highly critical* of President Eisenhower, Secretary of State John Foster Dulles and the Wisconsin Republican Senator himself."

No doubt the times had much to do with our attrition. F. O. Matthiessen jumped to his death. More important to me, George Orwell died in the same year; the tribune of my generation, the clear beautiful voice of the old radical conscience was gone. During the negotiations for the divorce (it was five years since we had met on line in front of the U.S. Army post office in London), the great news of the hour was that Truman had finally dismissed MacArthur. As we waited to see the lawyer and were making conversation, Louise said, "The kids in the office are real mad at Truman."

Chapter VIII

THE NEW LIFE

The wildly ranging book on all of New York I could not manage while I was married to Louise came unstuck when I found myself back in the painter's studio on Pineapple Street, Brooklyn Heights. I was finally able to write *A Walker in the City.* Under the skylight in the bedroom, still surrounded by the unlosable smell of old smoke in the hall, I saw that a few pages on "The Old Neighborhood" in the middle of the book, which I had dreamily tossed off in the middle of my struggles with the city as something alien to me, became the real book on growing up in New York that I had wanted to write without knowing that I did.

I was close to my book now, close to myself, at home with New York. The harbor was all around me. I would lie in bed listening to the tugs hooting; I would wake up to find my painter's great north windows awash with foggy sea light. At night, walking across the promenade below Columbia Heights with its full view of the harbor, I would spend hours looking at the squat illuminated ferryboats bobbing up and down across the smooth dark of the upper bay rimmed by stark single lines of light in the dark skyscrapers of

downtown Manhattan. The ships that tied up at the
piers just in front of me, ships with one lonely light in
the rigging, were charged with the same amazing detail.
Everything I now looked at, from Stieglitz's "The
Steerage" over my desk to the raw water-stained wall
of my bedroom on which hung a reproduction of Cézanne's "Boy with the Red Vest," was amazingly close,
microscopically clear. At Black Mountain, Lyonel Feininger, an amateur mountain climber up and down Bach's
unaccompanied violin partitas, had noted the importance of Bach to forms in painting. Each day, I began
my struggle to set down the streets, shapes, odors that
made up my vision of the city by playing Bach, listening
to Bach, remembering Bach. The distinctness of each
note in the broken chord, the moving line of ancient
dance rhythms—all gave me mysterious nearness to my
material. Cézanne's boy had a red vest. The redness of
that vest and the body in that vest taught me passionate
attention. In Stieglitz's "The Steerage" the "immigrant
woman" in the foreground whom I had long imagined
as my mother, draped in the large towel over her head
and shoulders that had always concealed her face and
purpose from me, now united the different faces and
bodies on the bottom deck with their thoughts. The boy
I remembered in *A Walker in the City* was a necessary
fiction, he was so virtuous. He became a walking pilgrim, quick to sniff the New York ozone as the many
exciting worlds of which literature is made. He was a
manikin on which I could hang my discovery that I
could put into words life, my life, certain decisive moments of life remembered. The city was the stage of that
life. Every day I went prowling and sniffing in a delirium
of sensations that came into my mind as whole sentences. Glistening monads of imagery amazed my sleep.
The city before my eyes in 1950 lifted me back into an-

other city; one level of being swept me into another. Still haunted by the first morning light, and my father the painter in his spattered overalls shouldering down the long dark hall to the front door of our old tenement, I walked down the smoke-smelling fire-threatening stairs of this kooky house on Pineapple Street. The open street. Urban removal and burial are everywhere. This house will not last another three months, and I have returned from the dead to tell you what a neighborhood was once like.

In the half-light, the fresh and early-morning dark, a few workmen are walking to subways and buses, each of them occupying a great space in the empty street. That still resentful intactness in the bodies of workmen and women who go to work so early, an angry sense of their own energy—we are a first offering. Clacking down the street, they look strangely magnified, like everything else I look at too intently these days.

I go about these Brooklyn streets that were mockingly named after fruits—Pineapple, Cranberry, Orange— and turning in to Fulton Street, where the rows of low red houses (soon to be demolished) look like Edward Hopper's "Sunday Morning" and still have that just barely triumphant American loneliness, I go along Fulton toward Brooklyn Bridge and the harbor, past the cobbled streets, the boarded-up saloons, the pool parlor, the old-fashioned German bakery with the wrecker's ball poised over it; past the straight lines of garbage pails rattling cover to cover in the wind, the sailors' missions and the greasy flophouses whose lights never go off; past the little stores darkened by gray muslin curtains that are the evangelical chapels of the Puerto Ricans and the Mexicans in the neighborhood; past the usual drunk of some sixty years, with a gray stubble and

vomit over his coat, sitting on a Fulton Street doorstep
waiting for the bars to open.

In the strange light of this first hour the city looks
loosely stitched together, its cracks and seams sickly
vivid in the half-light like an untended wound. What
has not been torn down is waiting to be torn down. The
drunks lie in the noble alleys of old stables like the
casualties of New York battle. This is the downward
slope of the waterfront; nobody gives a damn; booze
hangs in the air like rancid syrup. I go past withered
old frame houses where movie posters have been plastered along the broken doors; past gaping stone-littered
yards, taking up the same trail every block of flophouses
and saloons; past the same old wooden tenements with
all their windows knocked out, or indifferently gashed
and splintered by the industrial crossfire around them.
All this part of Fulton Street, leading down to the docks
and towers of Brooklyn Bridge, is the hard outside rim
of Brooklyn Heights—the sailors' landing where Hart
Crane looked for rough trade:

> Under thy shadow by the piers I waited;
> Only in darkness is thy shadow clear.
> The City's fiery parcels all undone,
> Already snow submerges an iron year. . . .

Country of the shivering, the Salvation Army's delight.
It is all stony and hard in the half-light, hard as the
great rocks on which Brooklyn Bridge is raised. A bleed-
ing man is holding his hand to his eyes.

But what I see when I return to my book is a woman
in a housedress sitting at an open window on Sutter and
Chester looking down at boys slamming a black little
handball, hard as stone, against the brick wall of our
tenement. The connections are fierce. From the ball in

the mitt to the mitt in the hand to the slam of the ball
against the wall, up to the eyes and breasts of the woman
in the housedress at the window, the connection is
fierce. But her son can never "satisfy" or console her.
No man, least of all the lonely house painter in the spattered overalls happy to get out of the house at the crack
of dawn, can ever come near her cosmic loneliness. It
took all the packed-up fear of Russia to produce the
daily fear that the likes of *us* will never change anything. So when she sits at that open window I perform
for her, and when I sit here getting happier with each
new page I still perform for her.

There were suddenly lots of girls, girls more plentiful,
passionate, and proficient than I could have imagined
in my old-fashioned youth. The new spirit at large in
the city was woman, woman emancipated, woman de-
sirous and alive—but woman psychologized and forever psychologizing, "life-enhancing" and positive, and
telling you how to face the future with your little boy.
The all-put-together woman—woman constructed from
Simone de Beauvoir, Mary McCarthy, Karen Horney,
Melanie Klein; woman free in bed and dynamic life instructor out of it—was something new in my experience.
I had stumbled upon a revolution. Women found the
much-married man not without promise, but definitely
in need of guidance. One by one they cheerfully made
their way to far-out Pineapple Street, cheerfully climbed
my rickety stairs, looked around my wild and picturesque habitation with a sigh. After stretching themselves
on the bed and satisfying themselves on me as if I were
a bedpost, one after another told me that I knew
nothing about women, that I was running away from
life. I would never find true happiness by myself, and
was undependable.

Sex was suddenly so laden with ideas that I was initiated, over and over, into one school of wisdom after another. A great many authors were quoted to me in the course of an afternoon. I was struck with the surprising practicality of literature; Mary McCarthy and Simone de Beauvoir and Melanie Klein seemed to know how to live, how to teach a woman how to live, how to teach a woman to teach a man how to live. For these women there was no idle pleasure in mere words; even a stray line from Yeats which one woman professor quoted sounded like Karen Horney.

There seemed to be as much cultural authority in the bedroom as there was in the classroom under the wings of the New Criticism. Even on all fours, one woman had so many psychiatric models in her mind as she talked and talked that I was shocked by her relative inattention to the physical pleasure she was demonstrating at the same time. When it was over, and we were both in bathrobes drinking tea, she went on so firmly analyzing my character that I had to listen for her to feel like herself. Women everywhere were now alive to bursting with their newfound discovery of themselves as emancipated daughters and wives. They were all for life over sorrow, for joy over anxiety and death. They were freshly programmed for freedom, ideologized for perfect happiness. The life force in women was didactic, insistent, voluble. An obvious misfit at marriage, I needed shaping up, fitting out, restructuring.

Beth came into my life as a decided relief from so much instruction. A blond young novelist who had just won a literary contest with her first book, she was funny, giddy, saucy, as full of gags as a stand-up comic, pleasure-loving, endlessly pleased by martinis—a fond careless girl to pal around with. She made it clear from the outset that in spirit she belonged to the twenties, with her great love Scott Fitzgerald, and not to the gloomy ex-leftists of *Partisan Review*, where, except for Saul Bellow, Delmore Schwartz in his rare moments of geniality, and Harold Rosenberg, she felt smothered by a vindictiveness that took out on young writers the bitterness felt for Stalin. Beth seemed as offhand, wisecracking, and consciously a rebel as only a rabbi's daughter could be. "You have never met anyone remotely like me!" It amused her to be dated by homosexual psychoanalysts who, in pairs, took her out on the town. Her old college pals were show business, the impresarios of struggling little opera companies, the librettists of Broadway musicals. She knew all the words of all the best songs of all the hit shows from the glorious twenties. Nothing about Beth's easy ways made me happier to attend her scenes and songs from the great Broadway shows and to feel that she was just as confident in her life as she was in her plans as a novelist. She would soon be going off to France on a Fulbright.

As "the Walker" neared conclusion, Beth went over each line. We worked over the book in bars where every drinker sat carefully apart from every other drinker; you could not easily tell a friendly or flirtatious interest from the animal stare with which people took your measure as you sipped, gestured to the bartender, made conversation with your partner. We finally took the manuscript to old-fashioned cafeterias on Lexington Avenue smelling of newly washed floors and hot soup. They were the only real New York cafés, indulgent to people sitting all afternoon over a cup of coffee; were full of New York solitaries who obstinately sat and dreamed the hours away despite the fluorescent lights overhead that buzzed and burned like x-rays and the explosive fall, scream, and clatter of trays, metal knives, and spoons on the too-bright hospital white of the counters.

The laughing, charmingly giddy honey-colored youngster with pencil poised over my scarred pages was obviously a girl of many parts. She was a grammarian as well as a comic; she wept over Handel but, in the phrase of the day, wanted to stay loose. There was a lightness to our days and dates together; we swept past many invisible floors of air. In Key West, the end of that year, she stood with one leg charmingly poised in air like the herons we so much admired and told me she was going on to France; so I went over on the boat with her. It was not always clear who was Scott and who was Zelda; but we were the Fitzgeralds living it up in another postwar period of easy travel, the money to be extracted from a magazine at the last possible moment. In a series of movie reels we went through France and Italy loaded down with two typewriters and quantities of luggage maneuvered in and out of compartments that were already overloaded with passengers, baggage up to the ceiling in every rack, standees in the aisles. The sight of us dragging and being dragged by so much luggage brought derisive shouts of "Americans! Damned Americans!"

The days filled up and filled up, the days rushed past; we had been picked up by life and were happy. In our two rooms in the Rue de la Harpe, an Arab street overlooking the Boul' Mich', we felt favored by friendly gods. Louis Aragon was writing every week in *L'Humanité* that Americans were propagating germ warfare in Korea. But we were singing in the Paris street as we stumbled back from a student restaurant off the Place

Odéon. A workman leaning drunkenly against a wall cried out, "You're lucky to be able to sing!"

We were lucky to see inside the Lascaux Cave before it was closed, lucky to walk past two lines of smoking torches into that belly of the Ice Age. Inside the cave wildly colored horses and bison reared into a future the naked cavemen could not have imagined. Now we could not imagine those paleolithic men with bloody arms and color-smeared fingers returned from the hunt to line up *from memory* these animal faces. I was trying to grasp the staggering procession on these walls, but the paintings were already in such danger from the air and smoke and crowds pushing you along that you were given little time to look into this dark pit and abyss of time.

We were lucky, lucky; though there was so much anticipation to every day, so much living fast, so much drinking and writing and talk of writing, every day like the first cold shuddering minutely displacing taste of a martini, we were in Latin Europe and this Europe was our past. Jews are a Mediterranean people. We were lapping it all up, counting up the cities, wolfing down a Europe being served up just then especially for Americans who had only to look and look, eat and drink, as they reeled with happiness through Europe's golden summer. In a square peasant courtyard framed by poplars, geese staggered in single file; in Aix, farmers in leggings came into town to drink at each other, their caps, triangular French faces, and toothbrush mustaches identical as they glowered and mumbled at each other over their cards and wine. And it was all picture, as remote from us as the argument in a Paris café; the storybook paintings on the walls of the Rijksmuseum in Amsterdam; the tiniest of medieval towers along the Arno in Pisa; the beaming maid in Salzburg bringing in jugs of steaming coffee and hot milk as I hid under the coverlet in Beth's bed.

"UNSERE IST EINE OPTISCHE ZEIT" said the great banner in Cologne over the proud exhibition along the Rhine of sparklingly bright, ultra-precise German telescopes, microscopes, and camera goods. Ours certainly is a "visual period." The Rhine sparkles between ruins. I am at last in *their* country. And what do I find as a visiting professor of "American civilization" in still-ruined Cologne, this Cologne of ashes and cinders? Ostentatious manners! The "land of consideration" beyond all possible bourgeois yearnings! Civility absolute! The smiling deference from every pore that one truly "cultured" German simply delights in showing another cultured German! All Germans of the "educated classes"—and how would a *Gastprofessor für Amerikanistik* know any others?—seem to address each other in a Henry James drawing room. *Bitte, bitte, bitte schön!* If you please, and pretty please. A mother in the trolley car was screaming because a man, "as a joke," had just taken away her son's ball. "I lost my house, too!" she said. A woman coldly watching her: "It is clear that she doesn't have much culture." The maid with the starched bow over her behind scraped and bent and bowed every time she approached our table. She said "please" when she set a plate down and "please thank you sir" when she took it up. *Guten Morgen, Herr Professor, Dear Professor!* My boiled egg was handed in at breakfast as if it were a Kimberley diamond and I a rajah. Amid so many scrapings, bendings, and bowings, I looked up to see Hannah Arendt at a party in her honor. She had just received a great literary prize. Hannah was wreathed in smiles, and all possible compliments chirped around her like birds. I had had no idea that Germans were so genteel. A Keats specialist at the university who had me to tea looked vaguely horrified and lifted a disdainful finger as he explained that talk of concentration camps was "vulgar."

Hannah and I silently walked through the ruins of old Cologne. "Don't think! Look!" said Wittgenstein. I was looking. Cologne's many churches were full of gaping arches, pillars irrationally left standing against streets of rubble, houses sheared down the front and one great big German void behind the front. Rebuilt Cologne was shiny, neon-lighted, and looked as cheap as an Amsterdam Avenue housing project. The pale "American-style" buildings rose above the ruins like the pink skin grafted into the faces of so many wounded soldiers. The push for *Lebensraum* inside flattened Cologne was ferocious. In Ehrenfeld, hundreds of people still lived in air-raid shelters. A young doctor who visited in the poorest quarter found one family living underground in a cellar made out of old airplane parts. "The automobiles in Cologne live better than many people. The garages of the new-rich have windows; the people underground have none."

The war was on every street: in the green Wehrmacht jackets of the trolley-car conductors; in the skeleton wearing a helmet and warning me against the perils of *Marxismus* from the front page of the ultra-nationalist *Stahlhelm*; even in the idiot fat caryatids left nakedly standing and left over from the brown city mansions of Wilhelmine Germany. As usual, they were holding up nothing at all. Block after block after block, the same squashed houses with their insides open to the street. Block after block after block, the loose mounds of brick blowing up the same yellow dust. Near my room at the far end of town, the whole outside wall of a house caved in one night in 1943 or 1944 or 1945, slid halfway down the street. The house was still there, just about to topple, its old girders twisting out from under it. The great black mass of broken wall looked as if the pavement itself had reared up in fright.

On every street Hannah and I walked, there were the blind wearing the three-dotted yellow armband to alert passers-by; young men wearing the black glove over the stump of a hand. "Our Army surgeons rarely tried to save limbs. They just cut and cut." The ashen streets were full of faces so burned and blasted that the inserts of new skin imparted a falsely babyish and pleading look.

Solemn people; only the children laughed. A sudden clap of sound when a child ran after her dog. Hannah walked through Cologne's ruins in silence with pursed mouth, but made a face when we passed the miserable little movie house on the Zulpicherstrasse in front of which a large poster showed John Garfield advancing on a blonde with a gun. Next week, Roy Rogers. A tension was building up. We were in Germany, obsessed by the murderers, but seeing everything from different worlds. When Beth arrived from Paris, there was a bitterness that was mercilessly to show up each of us in relation to the other. As a foreigner in Cologne, I was to register myself with the city authorities. The message came through my sticky blond assistant, variously referred to as "Dr. Caligari" and "the Himmler of American Studies." He was the former Nazi test pilot whose life had been saved by a German-born lieutenant in the U.S. Army.

My assistant knew Gothic, Church Latin, Anglo-Saxon, spoke English perfectly, was a specialist in *Amerikanistik*, but could not "understand why one poem is better than another." His eyes were close set, his expression always watchful, absorbed, somber. His way of getting through the day with me was routinely to ask questions in a surly disbelieving way that reminded me of a hostile dog coming around at regular intervals. It cheered me in my German exile to frustrate his excessive sense of hierarchy. My office was in a contemptible stucco building on the outskirts of the university, a building that also housed the Criminological Institute. Anyone wishing to visit the institute had to sound the bell at the front door. My office was on the ground floor, so I usually went to the door to let in a student wishing to see me or to learn criminology. "Dr. Caligari" was outraged by the unseemliness of my getting up for a student. Putting on his best smile for me, he would carefully explain that certain visitors to the Criminological Institute could pose a danger to the library—perhaps even to me, the honored *Gastprofessor* —and that "even irrespective of this," the same honored *Gastprofessor* could not help seeming to lower himself if he interrupted his important work to rise from his desk, go to the front door, open the door for a student.

In passing on to me "the absolute regulation" that I had officially to register my presence in Cologne with the civil authorities, my assistant, as always in his obedient life, was drearily doing his duty. I refused, his face fell, and he stared at me sullenly. "You understand that this is an official request and must be obeyed? Why should you as an honored visitor in Cologne not obey the regulations pertaining to temporary visitors to the Federal Republic?" Looking him over as he expressed amazement, disbelief, and some final recognition that strange forces were working in me about Germany, I knew what would unsettle him at the moment and I said it: "Enough Jews have 'reported' to the civic authorities in Germany."

When Beth joined me, Hannah was nettled by our

uneasiness in Germany and by the new bond this made between us. My blond "golden girl" with her fantasies out of Scott and Zelda of reliving the twenties, and my eager pal and drinking companion on every wild impromptu excursion in France and Italy, seemed to be terrified by being in Germany at all, and clung to me against the dreary rubble and fiery self-destruction of Hitler Germany. No matter what they said, we were in Germany and we were *Ostjuden* in Germany. Hitler dominated her dreams. She was a fantastic dreamer, woke up every morning exhausted by the three-volume novel she had dreamed during the night. One night she even woke me to demand an apology for something I had said in a dream. Her dreams in Germany were all too understandably full of demons and goblins out of the Black Forest. Her sudden utter *homelessness* made me realize for the first time how thin the 1920s were, how much she was ever ready to be annihilated. The nights were for dreams, the mornings for despair. And somehow all this added to my fascination with her and her totally unpredictable flow of temperament. She was right: I had never met anyone remotely resembling her. You never knew where you were. The moment at the peak of the moment, the flash, the wild merriment, then the sudden expulsion, made up a daily drama of Heaven and Hell, utter despair and quick salvation, that took over my life. It was uninterruptable by anything else, so voracious and continuous a drama that I felt sucked into it, day after day, out of fascination, out of imitation, out of amazement at the unadmitted *ecstasy* of so much emotion.

But we were in Germany, in Germany suddenly with Hannah Arendt, and we had a different Germany in mind. Her sudden triumphs as a returned Jew and expert on Hitlerism—she was being awarded every prize in sight—made her flash out at both of us. "Little one," she said to Beth, "don't be afraid, little one!" She still spoke of "little Jews." That "*little*" sounded even worse in Germany than it did in New York. Yet Hannah had opened her first lecture in Germany: "I am a German Jew driven from my homeland by the Nazis." The students applauded her vociferously. My students also applauded *me* vociferously. Every time I walked in to give my lecture and heard the students greeting me with German enthusiasm—madly pounding the floor—I had to remind myself that in their peculiar way they were welcoming me.

The war was over. The war was not to be mentioned. Not a word was said by my students about the war. They were busy getting ahead on the magic road of *Amerikanistik*, and with determination that had made their elders the despair of everyone else but other Germans, they spoke and wrote the American language with ease, sparkle, and even humor. It was impossible to dislike any one of my particular students, they were so fond of the American texts I loved most. In their youth, their ease, their amazed laughter when I ignored protocol and met them for conferences and oral exams in the local coffeehouse, they were like other nineteen-year-olds in Minneapolis, Cambridge, Washington Square. *The war did not exist*. History as it pushed along just removed the past. Young Catholic Rhinelanders, with their surprising attachment to France and Italy, their disconcerting formal "niceness," were somehow above the war, out of it completely. In their own minds they represented freedom from history. The ruins meant a new start. An obsessed grieving Jew in Germany was supposed to put out a lifeline to them lecturing four times a week on the American writers he loved. Looking at my eager boys and girls, remembering 1914-1918 tales

of German poets and intellectuals who had died with
pocket editions of *Leaves of Grass* in their uniforms, I
heard myself falling into the usual dream of America
as Emerson, Thoreau, Whitman, Mark Twain, and so
on. The sight of a pink-cheeked German student saying
out loud to himself E. E. Cummings's

> i sing of Olaf glad and big
> whose warmest heart recoiled at war:
> . . . .
> *"I will not kiss your f.ing flag"*

cheered me up immensely—even when it turned out
that it was not the poem that interested him so much as
the happy subversive shock he gave himself by quoting
"fuck" and "shit" against the heavily proper background of Cologne University. Newborn little post-
Nazi democrat in your American incubator! You are a
test democrat as "Dr. Caligari" was a test pilot!

The infernal correctness, the heavy good manners of
returned ex-officers, poured over us like heavy German
whipped cream. Would *mein Herr* betray that he had
recently been a steady killer? Were they just a little
afraid of each other? At a conference of "American-
ists" I watched unbelievingly as the local American
"adviser for education," a soft stout amiable dean of
education from Kentucky, sat at the head of the table
with an oily young German openly interpreting every
sentence into his ear. I seemed to see a proconsul sent
out from Rome to conquered Tunis or London, sitting
in the imperial box at the local games, while a syco-
phantic native filled him in.

Such proper people, such bustling importance, such
heavy good will. Only their students seemed to ruffle
the war generation. A hearty rosily fat education minister of the Bonn government, wearing a red rose in the

buttonhole of his beautiful tweed suit and absolutely shining with pleasure in the importance of his existence, grew white with anger as he listened to tales of unheard-of-slackness among university students. Looking for a moment like one of those Wilhelmine caryatids in downtown Cologne proudly holding up a building that was no longer there, he fixed his jaw with top-sergeant grimness as he came out with: "German students must learn . . . to . . . *work!*"

One weekend Beth and I went down the Rhine to Basel and got married. We were to celebrate at a great Fulbright conference held at Cambridge University. Hearing that I was about to leave, a city official coldly asked to use my dollars to make us both some money on the black market. To persuade me, he made a show of inviting me to dinner. It was my last week in Cologne, I had seen all the Roman pillars and wine presses left from the foundation of Cologne by the Emperor Claudius in A.D. 50, and the official was an imperious rogue and in such a tightly controlled rage that I was curious to see how and when the great German façade would lift.

I hit my shins as I stumbled through totally bombed-out streets and arrived to hear my host with his candy-box smile apologize for ten minutes that his lady was ill. Although dinner would be sandwiches, there would be more than enough to drink. Also on hand was a famous economist whose English poured as comfortably as the wine. There was so much wine that after a while the Germans lapsed into German and had an argument about the fighting on the Russian front. They had both been officers and, it turned out, had heard considerable shooting of civilians by the S.S. The house filled with night, the wine flowed madly, and when I finally managed to escape my poisonously cordial host, the distinguished economist, seeing how their conversation had enraged me, insisted on following me. The house was surrounded by ruins, and I walked fast through one set of ruins only to get barricaded behind another. With the slow-motion friendliness of a drunk, my dinner companion was determined to explain everything to me about everything. He took my arm and with unbearable cordiality led me into a beer hall. In Salzburg the local peasants reeling back from the *Weinhaus* with their excited German shepherds literally howled with a high falsetto screech in the back of their throats. In Cologne the beer drinkers who had outlasted all the other beer drinkers sat glued in their chairs, white-faced and unsmiling under their rusty lawnmower haircuts, as they stared at the stranger who in a Cologne beer hall, late at night, was listening to a former lieutenant colonel on the Russian front.

The economist was a clever man, a good man. "I am even an ancient Social Democrat." He couldn't bear to see me leaving Germany without some further conversation on *the* topic. "Yes, we heard them shooting, but we were regular army and had nothing to do with it." Nobody I met or saw or taught had had anything to do with anything. The humanitarian doctor who visited in the "poorer quarter" had spent the war in Switzerland. My landlady's husband had been in England. The distinguished economist had heard other people shooting.

In the dark Cologne night, amid so many ruins, I got myself back to our room.

By the waters of Cologne, there we sat down, yea, we wept, when we remembered Zion.

It was already light and there was light through the

night as we took the midnight train from Cologne for the Dutch port and the ferry to England. Chinks of light emerged through the night-long milky fog, widened and widened as the train rushed down the great lowland plain to the sea. Soon all these chinks of light became one broad beam of choppy water. We were in England, with its chipped white crockery and the obsequious folderol with which all waiters, porters, and taxi-drivers lifted their voices to sing "thank you, oh we do thank you very much indeed," for the privilege of serving you.

In Cologne the windows of every food shop bulged with overflow. In dear beautiful Cambridge—more beautiful than ever, shining with postwar paint and polish as if the withered masters with striped pants and decayed teeth were expecting a royal visit instead of Fulbright Americans lecturing to British dons—the nutriment was vague. But the manners were still a triumph over any possible adversary, especially American. The substance was thin, but the manner had survived the war; it might not survive the peace.

We were easily cowed, but the "lower orders" were still obstinately pro-American. The opening night of the Fulbright conference—a splendid gathering at King's College in one of the most beautiful rooms on earth, all golden wainscot and sweet-polished oak—Alan Pryce-Jones, the young brilliant editor of the *Times Literary Supplement* ("Welsh, but it seems a coming man"), delivered with his most beautiful and winning smile a demolishing of all things American that left me numb with admiration. It had taken centuries for a mere Welshman to acquire such cool Norman insolence, but he had acquired it. The performance, the public British performance! Pryce-Jones, comfortably reading his paper as if he were chatting, hands in his pockets, serene in the light of many gracious candles, was hard to get hold of and to pin down. But his intention was as public as his beautiful smile. He was speaking for the classical world against its barbarian invaders. Cambridge had to suffer some American instruction, but there would be a few barbs to send us off.

The smile, the charm, the perfect coolness of Pryce-Jones's silky insults were to remain with me like those fabled instructions from the Foreign Office: "Never apologize and never explain." I was impressed with the thought and calculation that had gone into this bravura performance, the ritual show of superiority that had amused me during the war. Some of our audience, British dons, were not. Four solemnly waited on me the next morning and insisted that I deliver a "refutation of the sod's remarks." "Why is this so important to *you?*" I asked. "Man!" growled a lantern-jawed surly scholar who looked a cross between Ichabod Crane and Abraham Lincoln. "We're Scotch-Irish! We made your country!"

It was the first golden summer of our married life, and we were in Cambridge. Behind the colleges, where I went once to inquire about my missing laundry, you saw the other race. The leanness here was not distinguished, as with dear E. M. Forster, who popped in from time to time like an adoptable rabbit, lovably muttering, "My name's E. M. Forster." "Yes, yes," we said fondly, "we know." "Your countryman Trilling has made me famous!" The people in the college laundry and storage room had eaten very different food. The bodies of the washer-women were bent in indecipherable shapes. Behind the beautiful lawns, the beautiful river, the most beautiful chapel in Christendom, there were kitchens *and* bedrooms heavily hung with drying laundry and smelling of fish. On the kitchen tables lined with oily stained newspaper stood the ever-ready bottles of A-1 Sauce and the chipped dirt-lined crockery.

The road to King's College Chapel still led through Wigan Pier. England had sacrificed everything to the war. And did anybody care? "Socialism" now looked to me like the last sacrament, and the Labour Party just the largest of the dissenting churches. Even in office, it would always be the "opposition." It was the disarming carelessness and *nichevo* at the bottom of English life that now disarmed me. The inefficiency was stupendous. A roof developed a great leak; the rain fell steadily, but not always into the pails along our bedroom floor. There was such a long drunken conference of workmen in front of our door that it seemed more sensible to continue the conference in the nearest pub than to attempt to fix the leak. And why not and who cared? Our days seemed an accompaniment to good English ale, bitters, stout, Scotch, gin, Pimm's Cup. The English were the greatest talkers on earth, whether alone or in pairs. To start or to join a good conversation, you just needed a glass; the more something flowed into the glass, the more there showed the brilliance, the gamesmanship, and the crevices inside the scholarly English mind.

The younger son of a duke, secretary of the Cambridge Communist Party, was passing out leaflets attacking the American presence in Cambridge and Korea and a nearby air base. The young dons, all too sober, were feverishly taking notes and trying to follow Denis Brogan's mind, which at eleven in the morning was sparkling with all possible American facts and issues as easily as it was sparkling with Scotch. They were proud of Brogan's learning but bored by his cool contemptuous *Realpolitik*. He was an academic wonder, not a historical thinker. England boasted great Scots scholars as once it had produced great Scots explorers and sailors. But "Great" Britain did not exist for these young dons, who after four, five, six years in the Army, were trying to inch their way up the rickety English ladder. They looked on America with fascinated dislike, chartered and weighed every morsel in the eternal record: England's neglect of its own people.

The record was there, as in the days when Marx had irritated his boils sitting in the British Museum over reports from factory inspectors. The English documentation of English injustice, oppression, exploitation was the first story of the industrial revolution and had furnished the gospel of socialism everywhere. It had helped to fuel revolution in Russia, Latin America, China. But in England? In England the young dons felt than England was "out of it." The welfare state assured many comforts, but little excitement. The war, not the National Health Service, was their finest hour. The English still got a secret thrill from dressing up, playing parts, putting each other down. The Labour Party had accomplished a revolution of sorts, but it was not one to lift a foreign heart. Air Marshall Lord Tedder, Denis Brogan, Alan Pryce-Jones, the college porter and the college butler, the angry Scotch Irishman from Manchester who looked like his American cousin Abraham Lincoln —all took their accustomed places on stage around the young Queen and the senile Churchill, talked about a monster called America, but icily looking each other over, thought mostly of getting a hoist up England's greasy pole.

That midsummer in the early 1950s, canoeing to Grantchester with Henry Commager, who as back paddle pretended that we were stealing up on our enemy and exuberantly shouted instructions to keep up our "swift

and silent Indian stroke," roaming Cambridge around
the ghosts of Milton, Newton, Wordsworth, Darwin,
Tennyson, it seemed to some of us lucky Americans
that we had the best of all possible worlds. All thoughts
of crisis seemed inopportune. The beauty of Cambridge
that summer was made up of ease, warmth, drink, and
the unending company that floated us into parties that
were all the more enjoyable for being such jokes by
the English themselves on the roles they had played so
long. Sir Charles Darwin, master of Trinity, received
his guests in front of a portrait of his celebrated grandfather before sending them out to the garden party.
The mummery was perfect. It was an English pageant.
Sir Charles looked like his grandfather behind him, and
grunted at his American guests with a slow smile just
right for the master of Trinity. The beautifully inscribed
cards of invitation, the flowered dresses and enormous
hats in the garden made nonsense of "England teetering
on the brink." But there was a touch of Jeeves inter-
rupting the performance of *Heartbreak House* obviously
being performed by the second-string players from the
D'Oyly Carte Company. Conference members from the
red-brick universities had not been invited, and two
Oxford dons who turned up explained that they were
Marxist-Leninists. But English inertia and self-love
overcame them. Looking around the garden party, I
saw how Americans, in all their personal disorder, were
natural agents of change. They represented so much
unsettlement that they saw nothing ahead of themselves
but more and more of the same. They wanted! We
wanted! How much we wanted! The English had made
a revolution, but seemed stoical about it. All the free
eyeglasses and crutches from the National Health Service (a modest payment would soon be required)

could not restore the élan of war's common danger. "Then we were really together."

Back in America the table was full, very full. And watching McCarthy on television as I sat with Mark Van Doren at a Columbia bar—McCarthy was snarling, spitting, spewing at the Army, at the Secretary of the Army, at Eisenhower, at a miserable fellow-traveling dentist from New Jersey—I also knew that some things on that overflowing American table were poisoned. Mark Van Doren himself had only recently had his picture included in *Life*'s rogues' gallery of American leftists. Row on row, filling two whole pages, were the condemned Albert Einstein, the curly-headed ingenuous Norman Mailer (who had not yet discovered that he was Norman Mailer), the arch fellow traveler Henry Wallace, the inevitable Corliss Lamont and Charles Chaplin, Thomas Mann, Jo Davidson, the indubitable "Comsymps" Lillian Hellman and Donald Ogden Stewart, together with the young Leonard Bernstein, Arthur Miller, Vito Marcantonio, Adam Clayton Powell, assorted writers, artists, teachers.

So this was the "American Century"? Luce's war propaganda had borne some hideous fruit. Mark Van Doren's books on English literature would soon be removed from a New Jersey college library because of *charges* that he had "been connected with Communist-front organizations and had expressed sympathy for the Hollywood writers convicted of contempt of Congress in refusing to say whether they were Communists."

That was funny and terrible. With his peculiar spare look of nobility, with that grave, deep voice that made me think of Emerson declaiming sonorous periods in his famous platform voice, with a love of eloquence

and a habit of eloquence that had made Van Doren
the perfect teacher of a winter afternoon in Philosophy
Hall—after his lectures on Virgil-Dante-Milton we followed him home to Bleecker Street on the Seventh
Avenue local so as to continue a conversation that
ranged from Homer to Hart Crane—Van Doren in the
1950s was still a noble American presence. The word
was central, the Van Doren voice hugged the words,
saying them in love for the old America. You could
never forget, with Van Dorens, that they came from
Hope, Illinois. "Six great horses of Spain, set free after
his death by De Soto's men, ran West and restored to
America the wild race lost there some thousands of
years ago."

> If I were there in other time,
> Between the proper sky and stream;
> If I were there and saw the six
> Abandoned manes, and ran along.
> I could sing the fetlock song
> That now is chilled within a dream.

And there on the screen, enveloped in a mist of
smoke and beer, was the Grand Inquisitor of un-American thoughts, smiling, grimacing, talking fast, fast, fast.
The nose was prominent, the voice curiously muffled,
slurred. We did not know then what a boozer he was
and that he would die of acute hepatitis when his liver
failed. He talked fast not in the excitement of talk but
as if to slip something over. The strangest thing about
McCarthy was how distracted he looked for all his
belligerence. His mind was clearly not on the immediate
suspect. There was that solid block of face, that balding
face that looked as if he were trying to keep his features
in line, and there were those roaming, spent, madly
shifting eyes.

Mark Van Doren looked at Joe McCarthy with a smile concerned, timid, ironic. The teacher looked at the Inquisitor. Mark was used to instructing people; he looked wise and his voice was wise in its crinkly comforting bass. He had been teaching since the First World War, and he still believed in wisdom. He now looked at McCarthy as if he would have liked to teach *him*. There was that old Midwestern, obstinate public school faith that America was great. "The worst the student, the more joy in teaching him." In the haze of student smoke, cheap beer, and worse jokes, Mark was still noble, still the teacher.

That hot, dry summer Rachel was born in Northampton, there was the stillness every day that fascinated me in Emily Dickinson:

> Was like the Stillness in the Air—
> Between the Heaves of Storm—

The empty, hot-still Smith College campus was overgrown with dusty trees; I could feel myself getting drunk on that profusion of green. Every morning I reeled around Paradise Pond and the campus; every morning I could see two retired spinster professors, lean Spartan types in sensible shoes, snortingly taking their constitutional. You would never see *them* holding hands as you did the English professor and his old Harvard classmate of the 1920s, lonely souls, one married, who were already withered last leaves of New England rectitude—though often persecuted and blackmailed. With their terror of the morals squad they did not know that sexual revolution was at hand, "liberation from fear" about to invigorate the land. Amid the few bouncy college girls left, forever in shorts and red knee socks on their way to and from the playing fields, amid the bicycle wheels forever turning, turning on the beautiful college paths, I was touched by the sight of a few ancient men and women still committed to valiant sexual rebellion.

But of course it was summer many years ago, and the place was nearly empty, and full of ghosts. There was the ghost in Amherst, where I would soon be teaching, of that genius squirrel Dickinson, darting among the trees and throwing out pellets of paper with great poems on them. "But no man shall see my face." And here in Northampton, eight years before her suicide in London, there was already a kind of ghost who was Smith '55, the college's most brilliant literary graduate in years, winner of all its prizes, straight-A girl all the way, who concealed her wrath and small hysterical genius by looking the typical WASP on campus.

She was the last in line waiting to get admission to another asinine "creative writing" class. All the girls seemed to be blondes in camel's-hair coats, the required uniform when the Connecticut Valley began to shiver, and *their* stories moved on a patter of smooth English and were thoroughly phony. When I requested one girl to read a Hemingway short story as an antidote to her obvious lack of worldly knowledge, she disdainfully shook her pretty curls and pronounced Hemingway "afraid of sex." The last girl in line looked like all the others. When she handed over some pages, I had grown so wary that I began to skim, then became suspicious. The writing was so coolly professional that I scented plagiarism, and said with some bitterness, "These could be published in ———— and ————." "I know," said the girl, "they've already taken them." I read them carefully and turned back to the top sheet to learn her name. "Sylvia Plath." "If you can write like this, why the dickens do you need 'creative writing'?" "I'm lonesome here, and want to talk to you."

The class met alternately at our apartment overlooking Paradise Pond and in a gloomy building dating back to the Gilded Age. One afternoon when the winter dark was settling over the campus by three, as was usual in the Connecticut Valley, a piercing scream came down to my classroom from the floor above. The girls went on with their reading of each other's work as if *I* were hearing voices. The scream was repeated, to the same indifference around me. A teacher up above, famous for practicing his unpublished novel on his students, had them act out the more agitated scenes from his book. One of them required a scream. The scream had been heard many times in the course of a Smith girl's four years, and by now had become as much part of the college as camel's-hair coats and the fact that the professor's novel remained unpublished.

Sylvia never said a word when the others enthusiastically read their work. When we met at home, she was the first to clear the dishes after coffee. She was certainly a "regular girl," full of smiles. Despite her lonesome need to "talk" at our few lunches in a spaghetti joint on Green Street, she was guarded to an extreme. I knew nothing about her and never expected to know anything. Sylvia, the blond smiling favorite of her teachers, had nothing to do with the writing machine whose products she nonchalantly presented me every week without interest, and which I read, without being stirred in the least, as one might listen to hours of court music by a human metronome. I saw only bleakly skillful stories. As a poet she would not become alive and frightening until she faced her fascination with her own death.

She had tried suicide and had been discovered under

a porch just in time. Her manner was "perfect," as Smith College liked to say; the things she indifferently turned out for me were also "perfect." There was not a line, not a thought, not a word that the magazine business would have changed. Sometimes, when she seemed tremulous and on the brink of saying something unusual, I wondered again at the cool professional sheen to anything she wrote. She had tried suicide; she had notoriously been tried, tested, and honored, over and over—their pet achievement—by the nervous English Department. But the words came to my desk any Tuesday at four as if she could write in her sleep.

I saw her only once more after my Smith College year; she had returned from her fellowship in Cambridge, she was living in Northampton with her husband, Ted Hughes; she was now a young instructor at Smith and she hated it and "*them*." From being the proud boast and great love of the English Department she had become just another overworked and overlooked junior instructor; she could not wait to get away. But on the surface she was a cheery young newlywed, studying the latest cookbook, and eager to give a good dinner to her old teacher, to whom she owed nothing whatever. At dinner we talked, we prattled, and the dark Yorkshire poet, her ferociously talented and surly husband, listened with contemptuous patience to her woe in teaching at Smith and my woe in teaching at Amherst.

Suddenly Beth and I were alone in Amherst with a new baby, a ridiculous excessive Victorian house, caught in a state of isolation personal and official that could be traced in large part to the intellectual dictatorship exercised by the opinionated Head of English. Amherst was big on "teaching," not private learning and dissident opinions. Students were a captive audience of

The Method, as so many American students were to be of one critical Method after another. Several good writers had departed the English Department without being able to persuade the Head and his sycophants that there might be several ways of respecting precision in the use of English words. The gospel at Amherst was semantics, strictly enforced on all freshmen and section men who spouted Hayakawa as dutifully as they wore tweed coats or paraded funny hats on the college paths when it rained. The bible was Hayakawa's *Language in Thought and Action*. If there was a "real world" anywhere, it consisted of words, not things. Although John McCloy and other makers of the New Europe were Amherst trustees and powers, and the leading trustee was John Foster Dulles's law partner, there was no real world outside Amherst.

The Head put it succinctly in one of his rare articles —showing college boys what to think was much more satisfying to a man who each week wrote private letters by the score but seemed to find most books just mistaken. Attacking Daniel Defoe and other nincompoops for describing the outside world as if there *were* an outside world, the Head explained that reality exists only in our consciousness and that Defoe and such vulgar realists had "the world upside down."

To counterweight this influence, I had been hired by President Cole, with the blessing of Robert Frost, who was still the poet in residence, the Frost in residence. The president and Frost felt helpless. I was the humanist they brought to Amherst to oppose the gimcrackery that occupied the head of the Head and who had the English Department in his head.

The Head wrote me a letter in English 1 style that carefully read: "This is an expression of my pleasure in learning that you are coming to teach at Amherst," then excluded me from the English Department. I could see why he never wrote anything but letters. He seemed to exist on a level of personal authority. There was nothing between us but war. The Head had over the years successfully indoctrinated his students, many of whom were now alumni and possible donors, to believe that the function of a teacher was to teach his little system. The captive students were put through exercises and demonstrations designed to show that their usual perceptions were untrustworthy, that they had known *nothing* about the right discrimination of words until they came to English 1, and that they were to write with a labored accuracy not different from the labor of all the other students around them. Life was a wholly aesthetic matter, as non-writers were indoctrinating American students in the fifties. Literature was too serious to be left to writers.

Frost, though he was always in evidence, was absorbed in himself and was still teasingly attaching himself to admirers and possible biographers. He already had an official biographer, Lawrance Thompson, but did not seem to believe that one would be enough. He cultivated me as he did so many other critics and literary scholars. There could never be enough essays in tribute, possible books about him. To Lawrance Thompson's disgust, Frost was still flirting, flattering, tempting, negotiating. He always seemed on the point of instigating some new campaign in tribute to him from one of the many college audiences he regularly visited to "say" his poems—audiences without which this extraordinary poet and despot could not live.

Frost was visibly a creature of immense talent, subtlety, force, pride, remorse, and anguish. Unlike the Head and the sycophants—one of whom had been trying for years to finish a book proving that "*Jane Eyre* is a failure"—Frost had emotions as well as genius; he was open to America, to everything in its past and to everything in *his* past; he was open to sorrow, and determined to express it all. He had taught himself *something* about literature; which is all that even the greatest writers can learn. According to the Head, Amherst had to teach its boys everything. Everything meant that since every artist lives by his private consciousness the objective world is totally dependent on the private. The "real" world, as one embittered graduate of English 1 put it when he revolted against the Amherst of the fifties by becoming a political terrorist at Stanford, was at Amherst "merely perceptual, being was mere consciousness of consciousness. Symbols were on a higher level of existence than objects. And since all these beliefs were far beyond the ken of ordinary people, our instructors' relationships to us was that of priest to initiates. The first lesson was that our teachers were brilliant, that they were in possession of some great mystery, and they were to lure us into this inner sanctum with sly looks, bizarre questions, a thousand little suggestive ironies, cryptic comments on our papers, and, very occasionally, a dramatic physical act in the classroom."

One of the dramas was for the instructor to enter his classroom through a window instead of a door; another was to draw up a map of the local area and naggingly reject the students' definition of "symbol," "map," "here." My own students, confined to American Literature and the European Novel in Translation, had certainly learned how to get literature down to a science. One term paper presented graphs of the action in Hemingway's *Across the River and Into the Trees*:

Graph X shows every reference made by Hemingway to *wind* in *Across the River*. Graph Z shows the number and distribution of *wind* references in Thoreau's *Walden*. There is no "plot graph," as there is no plot in *Walden*. The reason for including this graph is one of Control. The purpose of this paper is to show the abnormally high incidence of wind images in Hemingway's book and their unusual use.

"Control" was a big word at Amherst. The function of criticism was to control literature through canons officially present in *all* literature. The function of teaching was to control the minds of students. As "people from New York," a form of cultural disapproval easier to apply to us than "Jews," Beth and I argued so openly with ourselves and anybody else that we were not satisfactory examples of "control." Another, oddly enough, was Robert Frost. Bulking physically as well as by reputation over the easily cowed audience in Johnson Chapel, Frost was a fascinatingly direct and *ruthlessly* troubled man. He had "everything"—every official prize, a citation from Congress on his seventy-fifth birthday, adulation on every campus, sales that made him the envy of most novelists. But swollen physically and with everything in his life unforgotten and unforgiven, he bulked over the smug and discreet like a great bear—whom they had to feed with unexhausted attention and praise lest he fall on them snarling.

Eighty years old when I met him, as full of honors as a field marshal, he was *the* poet of backward-looking America as well as the mocking master of the most unexpected pause and twist in a single line. But other writers were always *wrong*—"intemperate," vaguely "European," still expatriate in thought, lopsided, Bolshie, boobs about the great enduring good of American life. This "most American" of poets, the idol of Senator Robert Taft, was a raging battlefield of ambition, competitiveness, guilt. Although "Robert Frost" was a compelling phrase everywhere in academe, Amherst was something special for Frost. He had come in 1917, the first poet in residence on an American campus, summoned by the remarkable libertarian president and educational pioneer, Alexander Meiklejohn. He had survived Meiklejohn and several successive presidents, and was now the Jupiter of the Connecticut Valley. If American poetry was a contest, which of course the leading contestants thought it was, Frost was certainly the big winner. Without being happy. What did he want? What more did he want? Dickinson in that shut-up house on Main Street had had little enough but her bedroom to work in. Whitman pleaded in old age that he was too crippled to get around on foot and had obtained money from Mark Twain for a horse and buggy. The money was for his tomb.

Frost wanted his tomb in the form of the biggest and most adulatory biography, and I knew why. He could not bear the life he had lived. That tomb would have to be made in some English Department. Where else? No wonder that the official biographer Lawrance Thompson, who had put many years into his scheduled three volumes, came to feel that Frost was *his* death warrant. He died before the great work was completed, but managed with respectful slyness to document Frost's raging character fully. Frost was "revealed" to be not John Greenleaf Whittier but yet another destructive American ego.

My image of Frost was gained in the small hours of the night. The great thing for me was how this ponderous, bulking, swollen man—swollen as much with fame ("I have to keep them out of my wastepaper baskets, god damn them!") as with age—lived on his earliest memories, his fears, and the agony of remembering his wife. With so much eating him away, he should have consumed himself instead of growing larger, thicker, more self-assertive.

Going to bed was a problem for him; he had always put off going to bed as long as possible. As a farmer, he had stayed in bed mornings and groaningly at noon had made his way to the barn to milk his cows. But at eighty, with a body more and more unmanageable, he was afraid he might die in his sleep. After dinner at our house on Woodside Avenue—where a little Cinzano vermouth, which he claimed never to have encountered before, apparently set him up for a night's excited talking—I would walk him to his room at the Lord Jeffery Inn. He would then insist on walking me back; I would have to walk him back still again.

In the dark Amherst night we worked our way past the football stadium, the shaky bridge, and the mud everywhere under foot. Frost never seemed to notice anything, least of all my shivering yawns, in the rambling, fiercely resentful trance into which he fell when he talked about his mother taking the body of his father from San Francisco to New England, the aborted term at Dartmouth, his "second try at education" that one unfinished time at Harvard. His soul was crowded with ghosts. His life was unrelieved. Despite all the fame and the "baby critics" in the universities explicating him for dear life, his life at two in the morning, trudging through Amherst, was still a cry for appreciation, an effort to throw off a curse. So it had been when he was alone with his family on the New Hampshire farm his grandfather had given him and he was trying to eke out not a living but a life by writing poetry. He, too, had been left behind in old New England, like the surly farmers and their maddened wives.

About this time it was announced that a radar signal had bounced off the moon. Frost's startling personal expressiveness, bulking into the silence of the night like his body in old age, reminded me of that radar beep in outer space. His wife had died twenty years before, and he kept circling around her name, their difficult family life, his fears that all Frosts were somehow off balance. His father had beaten him like a madman.

A very old, enlarged, slowly moving man, he defended every particle of existence left to him and remembered every grief with a kind of rage. The subtlety and hardness of his thinking had always struck me most in the company of professors who were always concessive, watchful, neutral, and subdued. Those nineteenth-century men who dominated the twentieth by having grown up with that ancient ferocious self-assertion! Edmund Wilson would travel by taxi from Wellfleet to his friends all over the Eastern seaboard. He once visited me in Amherst, resting himself on the porch like a squire out of Gogol, and suggested we slip into the registrar's office at Amherst to look up the grades of his grandfather Thaddeus.

Frost was also from this species, where people were harder, more intelligent, and not afraid to suffer. He had the wary physical repulsion of other temperaments that often comes with very powerful imaginative capacity. He was just the opposite of the dutiful scholars and teachers with whom he spent much of his time; he was by no means prepared to consider an opinion because it had been published. His own critical thinking was original, speculative, of course fiercely practical, based on what he had worked out in defense of his creative mission as a poet seeking to catch the spoken language. Younger poets he noticed when they evaded the test of skill, lacked dramatic tone and "sparkle."

He especially disliked writers who slipped into "radical" postures. He liked to say that this was "defeatism" calling itself utopian. There was a wild show of strength he was always putting forth, even when there was no occasion for proclaiming it, even when he was just fending off fawning questions. Why had he repeated the last line of "Stopping by Woods on a Snowy Evening"?

> And miles to go before I sleep,
> And miles to go before I sleep.

"Because I couldn't think of another!" "Strength" was his test of a man and opinions. Strength he obviously struggled for more than anything else. "Strength" became a big American blob in the universe-at-large. It was a tribute to the old America that had apparently been destroyed by Franklin D. Roosevelt's cowardly, cringing, wasteful social legislation. This was before President Kennedy took him up and Frost discovered that he was a Democrat.

He could not stop talking. He could not stop talking about *them*, early enemies: he could not stop talking about his great friend the English poet Edward Thomas, killed in 1917. He kept coming back to Ezra Pound, now in St. Elizabeth's, as he had first seen him in London. Frost was not drowning, far from it, but his whole life certainly passed in review as he dragged me through the first springtime mud. He was holding on to life sentence by sentence. The wonderful thing about these much-recited yet still pent-up memories was the spell they put on him as he "spoke" them. He was saying the same thing in his letters and even in his public talks in Johnson Chapel. But walking with me, the transitions in his night thought were hauntingly spaced and somehow as stoical, lean, bitten off the edge of the soul as they are in his best early poems. There he describes over and over the conflict waged by his savage loneliness and harsh will. There is fright in the background: his "moral" balance is threatened. The "pastoral" and "regular American" Frost was real, but it was not what his docile audience thought. Frost wrote some great poems, in the classic stoic American way, out of a struggle with the nothingness that surrounds the hard-won human order.

One morning he summoned me to his room at the Lord Jeffrey Inn and triumphantly waved a new poem at me, which as usual—he hated a desk—he had been writing on a board in his lap. "It's called 'Kitty Hawk' and I'll bet you can't guess what it's about!" "The Wright brothers?" "Knew you would say that! It's about a girl I chased down there in 1893!" The "girl" was his future wife Elinor, who had run away from him when they were high school sweethearts.

He did not tell me that. Nor did he say it clearly in the poem, which became too whimsical a monologue in the sterile sagelike style of old age. What had impressed me in great pieces like *The Hill Wife* was the man and woman story, marriage as a Greek tragedy of will against will. There had been a forty-year battle between the Frosts. A son had committed suicide. A daughter had gone Fascist, and could be so vicious about Jews that Frost, taking Beth to tea on Green Street in Northampton, said he was afraid to have her meet his daughter.

Suddenly Amherst became a disaster area for Beth and me. The place drove her crazy; the smug professional domesticity of the fifties—*Küche, Kirche, Kinder*—made her feel that a woman writer was unwanted. Her unceasing complaint was that she had no place there. I was certainly isolated in Amherst by the Head and his sycophants; Beth became frantic. My self-made girl was suddenly lost. There was a torture in her soul that I could come near only by accepting a guilt I did not feel. I felt foolish. I had been deluded to think that we could settle down, find "peace" in a small college town where the furnace man said "you people from New York" and professors carefully put down in a notebook every quarter they spent for gas. A college official said of a well-known Amherst historian: "For a Pole from the Valley he's done surprisingly well." A dean's wife counseled us not to talk too long with an interesting new instructor and his wife: "It's not wise to cultivate young people. They may not get tenure."

Summers in Wellfleet, I heard Edmund Wilson say that in his dreams he often rewrote a book he had been reading before falling asleep. Critics were correctors by nature, and I certainly *attempted* some correction of Beth's character. I could not believe that she was totally desperate, shipwrecked in Amherst, unable to write. But I was equally fascinated by the way she turned me into a character. I was firmly lodged in her mind, contracted by her closeness of observation. It was like being married to Saul Bellow. As Bellow was to say, never had people observed each other so pitilessly. The style among novelists, perhaps especially among Jews revolting against the long tyranny of the family, was the mocking sharpness of observations. I, as a critic, thought Beth's character malleable, like a sentence in a typescript. She, as a novelist, found my character fixed; in her mind I was already in type.

The change from the wisecracking funny party girl to the prisoner of Amherst, as she felt herself to be, aroused all our possible fury with each other. Amherst, snug within its confident domesticity, watched us with a sly laugh. We fought like the cornered Jews we were,

attacked each other's lives top to bottom. We were full
of rage, the self-generating drama of two writers with
very different minds. She was suddenly tough in a new
style I had not kept up with. It was vaguely the Augie
March, slam-bang, swashbuckling expressiveness we
both admired in Bellow, but which Beth seemed to live.
Even when we got happily swished and threw dishes
out the kitchen window—only to find them all unbroken
when the snows cleared—I was shocked by the satisfied
violence with which she proclaimed an end to our marriage. I was a "three-time loser," which was obviously
true. I heard it with relief. There was no doubt about
it. I was not good at this marriage business. I looked
forward to lonely freedom.

Instead, we went back to New York and were intoxicated by the freedom and range of our city. New York
seemed fabulous to us. We could not get over our luck
in being able to live there again. In the first flush of
return, we felt like Rachel. Driving into New York, I
cautioned Rachel to sit down. She had been standing on
the back seat and waving to passing cars. "I can't!" she
said. "I feel married to everybody!"

My last day at Amherst was the last time I saw Frost.
It was the spring of 1958 in the president's house; he
was sitting back in a large armchair, smugly telling all
and sundry how *he*, Robert Frost alone, had succeeded
in getting Ezra Pound out of St. Elizabeth's Hospital
in Washington. He disliked Pound, he disliked him
more than ever, but he had done it. "Archie couldn't
do it!" he boasted. "Hemingway couldn't do it!" But
he had gone straight to Eisenhower's Attorney General,
Herbert Brownell, and Brownell had been impressed
by his avowal that Ezra Pound was not a danger to the
United States. Pound's Fascist broadcasts—views not

unfamiliar in Frost's own family—seemed to Frost just the marks of an exaggerated and disordered personality. Although he hadn't seen Pound in many years, he still felt troubled and threatened by Pound's "excessiveness." "Excessive" was perhaps not the exact word for Pound spewing out mad hatred against Roosevelt, Churchill, democracy, and the Jews, but no one questioned Frost that day or said a word back to him. Getting Pound out of the loony bin was his triumph. As a dogged old-line Republican conservative and friend of Sherman Adams, he had been able to go to Eisenhower's Attorney General, he had put order to what had been disorder, he had helped close the case. Eisenhower had declined to receive him one day when he visited Sherman Adams at the White House, but that was all right. *He* had now done it all.

Frost was proud of what he had done for Pound precisely because he disliked him. He had disciplined his feelings against Pound; in a sense he had given a lesson to Pound, whether Pound knew it or not.

"I did it," he said in pride and exhaustion. "I went right in there, to the office of the *Attorney General*, and I talked to him." He made a face. "That Ezra," he said.

Chapter IX

GROWING UP
IN THE
SIXTIES

In a stained old Panama hat, the long white dress shirt that he wore everywhere—"I have only one way of dressing"—brown Bermuda shorts that bulged with his capacious middle, and carrying a handsome straight gold-topped cane that had long been in his family, Edmund Wilson, having been driven there by his wife, Elena, now walked slowly, with some difficulty, along the edge of the great ocean beach at Wellfleet on Cape Cod. Finished with his long daily stint, he was now ready to look at Nature and have a talk.

The beach was full of interesting and notable people to talk to. There, on any August afternoon in the mid-1960s, could be seen Arthur and Marian Schlesinger, Gilbert Seldes, Allen Tate and Isabella Gardner, Edwin and Veniette O'Connor, Richard and Beatrice Hofstadter, Robert and Betty Jean Lifton, Irving and Arien Howe, Harry and Elena Levin, Daniel and Janet Aaron. At times there could also be seen Stuart and Suzanne Hughes, Jason and Barbara Epstein, Philip and Maggie Roth, Marcel and Constance Breuer. Once there was a view of Svetlana, daughter of Stalin, accompanied by the Georgian writer Paul Chavchavadze, whose wife was a Romanoff and who herself often modestly made her way to the South Wellfleet post office to receive letters from her cousins in Buckingham Palace. It was said that Svetlana and Mrs. Chavchavadze had even compared notes on what it was like to live in the Kremlin.

On the beach sat television producers, government and U.N. advisers from the social scientists and psychohistorians, professors by the dozen—people all definitely "in." There was so much important, authoritative writing going on in Wellfleet that one professor's wife, trying to hush the neighborhood children, put her head out the window and said pleadingly to the children, "The professor is writing a book review. I'm sure all your fathers and mothers have reviews to write, too!" The children of another writer, left to themselves on the beach, were playing a game with a ball devised by the witty novelist Edwin O'Connor. It was called "Schlesinger," and consisted of trying to knock over a beer can propped up on a little sand hill. If you failed the number of times there were letters in "Schlesinger," you had to pay a forfeit thought up at the last moment by O'Connor, which usually consisted in walking around some of the lesser discussion groups on the beach and mocking the Hungarian psychoanalyst and the graphic designer from Yale.

O'Connor enjoyed joshing "the heavy intellectual set"—there were so few other novelists about. But making fun of Schlesinger was not making fun of Jack Kennedy and the New Frontier. O'Connor could not have been prouder of his fellow Irishman; no one else on that beach mourned him so sincerely and was still enjoying the 1960s so much. In his first days in Wellfleet, Ed O'Connor had gone about on a bicycle. *The Last Hurrah*, a sucessful comic novel of the last great Irish politico in Boston, had made him rich. He now had a beautifully severe avant-garde house in the Wellfleet woods built for him by a haughty Russian-born architect who never arrived on the beach without two enormous, restive, threatening German shepherds that frightened everyone around while his master, who had an icy Oxford accent and the majesty of a Diaghilev, could be heard knocking down everyone else's political universe. From time to time he was an advanced liberal.

Wellfleet, just a few miles from where Provincetown spreads over the tip of the Cape, was not as famous for writers and rebellions as Provincetown. It had no rebellions and no rebels. Its first notable summer folk were architects and designers from the Bauhaus; its next, psychoanalysts. By now it was distinctly, as the pretentious consort of a famous historian put it, *la plage des intellectuels*. It was indeed. By now there seemed to be a book for every day of American history. The universities and the mass media had joined in incessantly producing still more documentation of "just what makes us tick" and "our American heritage." Nothing "American" was alien to the incessant cultural analysts and psycho-historians, many of them of recent immigrant stock, who each summer in Wellfleet held seminars and read papers at each other, endlessly fascinated by the wealth of material to which they felt happily related by their newfound status as academic authorities and advisers to government.

Edmund Wilson, who lived in Wellfleet the year round, hated it in summer and called it "the fucking Riviera." Oddly, Wilson was one of the few "old radicals" in Wellfleet, along with his friend Charlie Walker, the old Greek scholar and labor historian. I had first seen Wilson in Provincetown in 1940; he was carefully bicycling to the Portuguese bakery. He bought his

crazily rambling house in Wellfleet before the main
Cape highway, Route 6, had been laid out near his door.
That was long before *la plage des intellectuels* in Wellfleet had become a continuation of Cambridge, New
Haven, the Institute for Advanced Study, and the executive assistants' wing of the White House. When I
had met Wilson in 1942, he was married to Mary Mc-
Carthy and already isolated from fashionable opinion
by his obstinate isolationism. I had met him again, in
London at the end of the war, at the great party given
for him by the Ministry of Information when he was on
his way to Italy and Greece as a roving correspondent
for *The New Yorker*. He was still against the war, still
bitterly suspicious of the English. True to his own
British delight in being difficult, he turned a cold face
to the many writers who had come to pay him homage
and amazed me by his appeal: "We must stick together
against these Limeys."

Wilson's arrival on the Wellfleet beach regularly
caused a stir. A distinct mental avidity and nervous unrest fixed itself around his bulky antique figure. He was
so definitely not of this time, of these younger people,
this academic set. The sight of him in his Panama hat
and well-filled Bermuda shorts, the cane propped up in
the sand like a sword in declaration of war, instantly
brought out in me the mingled anxiety and laughter that
I used to feel watching Laurel and Hardy about to cross
a precipice. There was so much mischief, disdain, and
intellectual solemnity wrapped up behind that getup,
that high painfully distinct voice, that lonely proud face.
His immense authority for everyone on this beach—
especially among the literary professors, who explained
to their classes that Wilson was not "really a critic at
all"—was clearly at odds with the too elegant cane, the
stains so carefully preserved on the Panama hat, the

absurdly formal long white shirt sometimes flopping
over the bulky stomach in the Bermuda shorts. He was
a "character." The improbably loud high voice—like no
other voice you would ever hear, it seemed such a deliberate effort—launched into a "topic" before the man
had even sat down. It amused and amazed as much as
it intimidated. He asserted himself just by making his
stage entrance onto what Thoreau, walking down here
from Provincetown in all weathers, had in awe called
"the great beach."

The ocean rolled and thundered. The sand shone.
The cliffs of stark dunes overhead, green grass and tiny
twisted shrub pine against the gold sand, gleamed with
wild rosebushes. Our happiest times were here, at the
edge of the land, the ocean, the dunes. The beach was
a great body, and on this beach we were bodies again.
Beyond "Joan's beach," where a wartime army hut had
been moved as a summer cottage for a lady from New
York and her painter boyfriend, still stretched the out-
ermost Cape, forever beating in your ears from the
ocean, the emptiness of that long wild ocean beach
where you could still contentedly walk, make love, and
skinny-dip.

But "Joan's beach" was a riot. The great beach was
replaced every afternoon by the great society. Each
year Joan's weathered old beach hut sank more abjectly
into the sand while around it rose the mercilessly stylized avant-garde house of a wealthy Leninist from
Philadelphia. A leathery old man with a shaven head
and showing off a powerful chest, a man who looked
just as photographically virile as the old Picasso, walked
with emphatic strides to the "nudies' beach." In the
great clown tradition of the good old American sum-
mertime, pliant young girls in striped tank suits and
Huck Finn country straw hats sat in the lotus position

practicing Yoga. The ocean gamboled, young men dived into rollers and then hopped up and down in the water waiting for a wave to carry them back to shore. Down the beach couples lay about open, free, and friendly as if they had just made the happiest love. Red Japanese kites with long tails bobbled up and down wheeled by the screams of the children on the cliffs.

In the midst of all this Edmund Wilson was hoarsely at the center of everyone's attention, sometimes forced against his will into the usual gossip and polemic. He sat without ease; he scooped up a handful of sand and let it drift slowly through his half-clenched fist as people running out of the water gathered around him only to run back into the water. So many staring, giggling, and deadly scrutinizers, guessing that he was "someone," made him nervous, but he unhappily sat on, unable to make his escape. So he talked. He talked as if he were reluctant to talk but too stubborn to stop. He talked as if talking were a physical difficulty forced upon him by a disagreeable world. But it was one he had learned to use for his own purposes, and even with cunning, in short, shy, killing observations. Then, looking as if he had just heard himself for the first time, he would throw his head back in a loud whinnying laugh.

He talked about what he was reading and writing. He talked, as he wrote, from current preoccupations only. His talk was as formal as his writing. He invariably led off with a topic. He had been reading this new thing of Sartre's, and had to say that the fellow was not as big a windbag as he had been led to believe. He liked the man's big French radical schemes. This Allegro man and his brazen but not uninteresting guesses on the mysterious principles and practices of the Essenes. An irritable rejoinder to Gilbert Seldes, who had been telling a story about getting tight with T. S. Eliot in the twenties. Gilbert had the date wrong. A new book about our animal aggressive tradition. Everything the new young anthropologists were telling him he had known from Darwin. He was still a nineteenth-century mechanist and materialist: "We must simply get along without religion." As for T. S. Eliot, he had the story in his notebook *and* the exact date. Had you by any chance looked into Swinburne's novels? The amusing structure of the Hungarian language, which he was just then learning? "My dear boy," he had greeted me on the beach the week before, "have I given you my lecture on Hungarian? No? Then sit down and listen." There was also this new book on magic. He was very proud of his magician's lore and often set out to do tricks that did not always succeed. He was too distracted. At Rachel's birthday party one summer, he came with his equipment and disappeared into the lean-to searching for newspapers he said he needed for his act. Time passed, no Edmund. We looked in and found him absorbedly reading one of the newspapers.

Everything alive to him was alive as words, had to find its exact finicky representation in every single trace of his experience and of his reading. Much of the day and often late into the night, he sat in his great big study in the old house just off Route 6. He sat there with the stuffed owl that he hated, with the sets of Scott and Dickens that had come down to him from Wilsons and Kimballs and Mathers like the gold-topped cane and the family pictures he could never stop studying. Just outside the study was the great Delphin set of the Latin and Greek classics in their heavy striped bindings. Inside the study were the books he used for each book, like the many-volumed Michelet he had needed for *To the Finland Station*.

There were several desks in that study, and he moved

from one to the other as he worked now on one book, now on another. He wrote always by hand, in his elegant and peremptory script, and there were as many projects going on at once as in a Renaissance painter's workshop. Everything in the household revolved around his day's work and the regimen needed to accomplish it. He had his own record player in that room, his own bathroom just a few steps down from his study, his own bedroom when he wanted it in this separate suite of rooms. Out on Route 6 cars screeched on their way to and from Provincetown, the pleasure place; girls with streaming hair bicycled past in halters and shorts. But inside the study that was deep inside the house off the main highway, Edmund Wilson—protected by his tall beautiful European wife, Elena—sat writing at one desk or another, reading in one language or another, eagerly waiting for Elena to bring the mail back so that he could get still more reading matter and letters to answer.

He lived to read and write. Each new language—after the Latin, Greek, French, and Italian he had learned at school, the Russian, German, and Hebrew he had acquired mostly by himself, the Hungarian he was now so proud of, the Yiddish he typically attempted from grammars after he had learned the Hebrew alphabet—was a "love affair," he once said to me, with some subtle new syntax to love. He laughed at academic specialists with their proprietary talk of "my field"—more usually, in modern American, "my area." One of his favorite antagonists was a scholar who was always pressing him to read Cervantes. (Spanish, for some reason, never interested Wilson.) "Elena and I have been attempting *Don Quixote*," he once calculatedly told him, "and I have to admit that we find it just a mite

dull." The other turned pale and stood up shaking:
"Harvard thinks differently!"

Yet what Wilson wrote dealt so much with the plight
of personality, his fascination with his own family, his
need to involve himself with other people, that one
could see in his every sentence the extraordinary effort
he put out, by words alone, to free himself from bookish
solitude. Life was one elaborately constructed sentence
after another, and he had been sentenced to the sentence.

The formality of sentence structure even on the
beach, like the aloofness of his manner when you were
drinking and gossiping with him in his own house, was
like nothing any of us would ever see again. Ponderously shy, abrupt, exact, and exacting, he was matter-
of-fact in a style of old-fashioned American hardness.
He could be massive, unyielding on the smallest matters.
Why did I always feel that I had to shout in order to
reach him? There was that famous distraction, the great
bald dome thinking away, arranging its sentences, even
as he talked to you. But of course he made no easy
splash of talk to swim in, as the rest of us did at the
many cocktail parties. To depart from the question he
had set was to find yourself addressing questions to the
air.

He was tyrannically correct with himself and offi-
ciously correct about everybody else. The correct word,
the unquestioned historical detail were professional
matters. Competence was the only right relation to
others. He worked from fragments and études in his
notebook; short flights were the natural span of his intellectual imagination. But he had also absorbed from
his passion for grammar (and no doubt his long solitude; he was an only child, with a deaf mother and a

neurasthenic father) some un-American patience and thoroughness. He knew nothing else so well as how to make a book. He made books out of his intellectual satires against intellectuals, out of the light verse he sent his friends at Christmas, out of his *New Yorker* book reviews, out of his hatred of Robert Moses's high-handed urban renewal, out of his compassion for Indians, out of his typical belief (based on early holidays there) that Canada represented a better, uncorrupted version of his now too big and too powerful country, out of his aversion to the endless bookkeeping forced on American taxpayers by the Internal Revenue Service. This somehow turned into a book against the cold war.

Wilson made books out of virtually everything that crossed his mind. But certain subjects (especially American, nineteenth-century, related to the Civil War and the Gilded Age) never just *crossed* that mind. They stayed there, decade after decade, to be used as articles after they had first been sketched in his notebook-journal. Then they got rewritten for his books and would be rewritten again for new editions of these books. What he knew he knew; what he read he remembered; what he had seen of San Diego or Jerusalem or Odessa stayed with him forever. No one else I knew had so much patience with his own writing, his own impressions, the stories he told and retold from notebook to article to book to the next meeting in his living room. He could recast his own writing—and yours—with the same air of easily inhabiting the world by words alone. No one else I know had the same impulse to correct and rewrite everybody else. He once returned from lunch to *The New Yorker*, saw on someone else's table a proof of my review of his book *The Shores of Light*, and calmly changed a date in it.

He could be hilarious in his retentiveness, his obstinacy, his intense personal relation to any book or subject that he liked very much or disliked very much. Discussing *The Scarlet letter* (a book that as a literary modernist he easily disliked because it belonged to the American schoolroom or too much to his own past: on his mother's side he was descended from Mathers), he was angrily asked by a young professor of American Studies, "May I ask when you last read the book?" "Nineteen fifteen," Wilson said breezily.

Later, relaxed on the beach after the crowd had gone to a cocktail party at a psycho-historian's (it was to begin as a memorial service on the anniversary of Hiroshima, and one could see trailing up from the beach a procession of shoeless intellectuals, the ladies in fashionable white outfits, carrying candles), Wilson was rosy with Scotch and full of his special belief in conspiracies. Getting liberated as crowd, bottle, and day dwindled, he said, with the caustic smile he reserved for anxiously Americanized and patriotic Jewish intellectuals, "Bobby Kennedy knows who *really* killed his brother—and is not telling." "Edmund, you're going overboard, the way you did in that preface!" He learned back on his sand hill with perfect confidence. "My dear boy, you mustn't discount my legal background."

My legal background! He meant Edmund Wilson, Sr., one of the best lawyers of his day in New Jersey, at one time attorney general of the state and, though a Republican, invited by Woodrow Wilson to join his Cabinet in 1913. Edmund, Jr., seemed to trace his own tics, quirks, and obsessions to his father, who was a passionate admirer of Lincoln the lawyer. (The tragedy of Lincoln runs through *Patriotic Gore* as the tragedy of the superior man in America.) The father identified with Lincoln the melancholic. Though a lawyer for the Pennsylvania Railroad and able to give his less finicky relatives advice about the stock market, Wilson, Sr., would not buy a share of stock. He regarded stock transactions as a form of gambling. Like many brilliant men of his generation, he thought his own life a forfeit to the big-business spirit of America. He became a "nervous invalid," a total hypochondriac; his professional career yielded to his concern with his own symptoms. His wife, a heartier type, not "intellectual," went deaf under the strain of her husband's breakdown.

Edmund Wilson knew he was "odd," and was always looking into his ancestry for the sources of his own obsessions as well as the intellectual interests plainly derived from the many preachers, lawyers, doctors behind him. He wrote about his parents and grandparents: "The fact was that I knew almost nobody else. I knew they had their doubts about me, and that in order to prove myself I should have to show that a writer could become a successful professional." T. S. Matthews, who had known Wilson on *The New Republic*, liked to say that Wilson's parents had once bought him a baseball suit—but that he had gone on reading even after he had put on the suit. As a writer, he had indeed proved himself thirty years before with *Axel's Castle*. But despite his many books since and his long record of production, he had become with increasing insistence a kind of self-proclaimed outsider to the "America I see depicted in *Life* magazine." He liked in the 1960s to say, in the sight of so many "sophisticated" academicians, that "old fogyism" was creeping in. He now made a point of stating—boasting?—of how little money he had accumulated. Thanks to his worrisome income-tax case, he was in financial trouble virtually to the very end of his life in 1972. *The Cold War and the Income Tax* was, however, a bit of political afterthought when he was nailed by the government for neglecting to pay his taxes. He was just too distracted even to sign the returns that his wife prepared for them. But when the government attached much of his income and heavily fined him, it became a point of defiance with him, as against the swollen crazily prosperous sixties, *not* to have amassed much money and to be, in the good old American style, "agin the government." My friend Peter Shaw wrote that in the sixties every typical product of America (including the student rebellion) "lacked modesty of scale." Edmund Wilson was certainly not "modest"; but he did enjoy being out of scale with the rest of the country.

At several periods in his life, he noted in his journal, he had felt impelled to write protests against various officials of the United States government; he first wrote one as a sergeant in the A.E.F. Medical Corps. As if he were now one of his own forebears, he lived in two "old-fashioned country towns," Wellfleet, Massachusetts, and Talcottville, New York; he depended on a small income from one of his few relatives who had gone into business; he did not drive a car or use a typewriter; he did not teach, give lectures, join honorary societies that asked to honor him. When he at last accepted the Emerson-Thoreau medal of the American Academy of Arts and Sciences, he explained that he must refuse to make a speech and insisted on reading his translation of Pushkin's *The Bronze Horseman*. When he accepted the MacDowell medal, he terrified the chairman by rolling the medal between his palms to show that he could make it disappear.

He would not play the game. Every year he became ceremonially more difficult, seemingly more perverse, more alienated from what President Johnson called "the Great Society," from the endless American sociability, from the "successful career" that American writers strive for as thirstily as professors and oil executives. Of course he had authority, and how proudly he could use it. To ward off the many people who want something from a "name," he had a postcard printed up on which it was noted (with a check against the appropriate box) that Edmund Wilson does not read manuscripts for strangers; does not write articles or books to order; does not write forewords or introductions; does not make statements for publicity purposes; does not do any kind of editorial work, judge literary contests, give interviews, broadcast or appear on television; does not answer questionnaires, contribute to or take part in symposiums. And so on!

As the contrast deepened each year between Wilson and the "America I see depicted in *Life* magazine," his concern with right words and standards seemed to become more intense, his irritation with sloppiness and misuse even more pronounced, his sense of his own intellectual honor loftier and yet more anguished. The old radical was becoming the old curmudgeon.

Behind Wilson's ever more pressing urge to make order of his life by words, behind the obsessive journal-keeper feeding on the one book he never had to give up writing—a day as its own subject, its only expressive task—there was some patrician belief that through style everything, even in his disordered country, would yet fall into place. He had always been a fussy corrector of everything he read. Now the authority derived from his sound education, from his many books and almost "bewildering" interests, from being *Edmund Wilson*, became as necessary as the articulation of the bones to the movement of the body. This insistence on "correctness" —as of a judge or minister or national leader in the days when a few solitary geniuses molded American culture—became basic to the sense of his role in American life. Let the young and the newer stocks have their pretentious social science theories and academic careers and ridiculous "New Criticism"! He was the last American man of letters, the great anachronism—and not without mischief.

Wilson now depended on "style" in an aristocratic-political sense more familiar to English universities and the House of Commons than to American intellectuals. He seemed to read the young writers with more attention than they read themselves, and loved to point out to a writer his misuse of a word and some error in detail. "Trotsky was killed not with a pickax but with an ice ax. You made the same mistake in your last book." Sometimes the pressure to write well was so grinding that, as one noticed when the notebooks began to be published, there was not a picture seen but just the effort to make one. Writers his too concrete mind could not grasp—Blake, Kafka—he dismissed with a wave of his hand. What he understood he understood.

There was a kind of political majesty to all this. Behind the pressing personal urge to correctness, I saw the moral significance of "right words" to Wilson's class—the professional gentry of lawyers, preachers, educators, scientists, which from the time of New England's clerical oligarchs had remained the sustaining class of American intellectual life. Despite all these eager beavers from the newer stocks, the few figures with the most unquestioned influence still represented— and often in the person of Edmund Wilson himself— the old American clerisy. These were still the policymakers, while imitative critics spoke haughtily of "irrelevant texture" in Shakespeare. Was the intellect in America to be banished to the new mass universities? The true thinkers were the policymakers behind the scenes who, no matter how many billions heaped up by the older robber barons they gave out as heads of the great foundations, were as detached as Henry Adams from the unctuous propaganda of American business.

Wilson thus seemed the one man of letters in the American tradition who still represented the traditional American caste of professional diplomats like George Kennan, judges like Oliver Wendell Holmes and Learned Hand, scholars who were lawgivers like Noah Webster. No wonder that *Patriotic Gore*, our American Plutarch, ended on Justice Holmes, as it began with Harriet Beecher Stowe and that most superior intellect, Abraham Lincoln. Such men and women were "the capable," as Sinclair Lewis (a doctor's son) had admiringly called the lonely doctors, philosophic lawyers, and scientists who in his work resist the bitch goddess that William James (another doctor) had called American success. Though business ruled the roost and money was more important to everybody, it was "the capable," who came from a long tradition of professional concern, who still kept up for others the standards Edmund Wilson grew up with.

The chief expression all this took was the bitter polemic he wrote in 1962 to preface the long-delayed *Patriotic Gore*. It had taken him fifteen years to put the book together from a lifetime of reading and absorption in the literature of the Civil War. In the summer of 1962 his bitterness against the American state took the form of a preface that was really an effort to deny the love of the American past and his belief in American moral heroism that made the book itself so moving.

Like so much else in his work, *Patriotic Gore* also took off from family history. One of his earliest memories seems to have been of the original two-volume set of General Grant's memoirs, published by Mark Twain (and sold by subscription to all good Americans) as a service to the strange man who had crushed the South but as President had proved a disaster both to the nation and to himself. After leaving the White House he went bankrupt, was cheated of his own money, and dying of cancer, he undertook the *Personal Memoirs* at Mark Twain's urging in order to provide for his family.

Wilson, so deep in "all that Civil War stuff" that the enchanted reader could not help following him at every turn of the great narrative, nevertheless opened his book with a preface that read as if composed to drive off anyone still holding the illusion that the Civil War was historically necessary. As if the title (from "Maryland, My Maryland") were not surly and sarcastic enough, Wilson compared the Northern "refusal to grant the South its independence" (certainly an unhistorical way of putting it) to the Soviet suppression in 1956 of the Hungarian revolt. The history of the United States was nothing but a big-power drive. The United States had been an aggressor against the Indians, against the Mexicans, against the South. "The institution of slavery, which the Northern states had by this time got rid of, thus supplied the militant Union North with the rabble-rousing moral issue which is necessary in every modern war to make the conflict appear as a melodrama. . . . The North's determination to preserve the Union was simply the form that the power drive now took. . . .

"I am trying," Wilson claimed, "to remove the whole subject from the plane of morality and to give an objective account of the expansion of the United States." This was hardly Wilson's forte. The value of his book, of course, lay in its intense biographical method. Wilson was no more at ease in "objective" history than he was in removing any subject "from the plane of morality." His main text, so assiduous in tracing every detail of character and intelligence in his main figures, was full of the most obvious gratitude for what they had contributed to the eradication of slavery and the preservation of the country. But on and on Wilson went in his preface, ticking off Pearl Harbor as Roosevelt's doing ("... it has been argued, to me quite convincingly, that this act was foreseen by our government and—in order to make our antagonists strike the first blow— deliberately not forestalled at a time when a Japanese delegation was attempting to negotiate peace"), ticking off Hiroshima, ticking off our postwar belligerence toward Russia, ticking off our preparations for bacteriological and biological warfare. The United States, it seemed, had obstructed Castro's Socialist revolution, thus forcing him to seek support from the Communists. (Castro was himself to give the lie to this in acknowledging his long Communist background.) But Wilson was in such a state about any and all wars fought by the United States that he was wild enough to write that though Jews had strong reasons for fighting Hitler, it was wrong of them to support the war, since "the extermination of six million Jews was already very far advanced by the time the United States took action."

Wilson then excused the Southern resistance to the civil-rights movement on the ground that Southerners "have never entirely recognized the authority of the Washington government." This was as mistaken in fact as it was foolish in theory. The South was the most militaristic section of the country and had been enthusiastic for war against Spain in 1898, against Germany in 1917, Korea in 1950. Southerners in the 1840s had led the attack against Mexico and had wanted to annex Cuba. Lincoln had said over and over what the North knew to be the simple truth: it was the South's attempt to foist the slave system on the free territories that led to the Civil War.

Wilson's bitterness on the subject of America's "power drive" of course represented the despair of many Americans as their government vainly attempted to "contain" the whole world against Communism. The government since 1941 had become too autonomous and powerful. But Wilson, very much like Thoreau in his own passionate political essays against the American state, made no effort to prove his case; he just helped himself out with caustic images taken from his reading on the power drives of animals. There was little in that preface one could deal with as historical evidence. It was a series of defiant assertions in the old American style: government is not to be trusted! Many younger Americans were soon to feel this, but they had radical solutions for still *more* government, Leninist style, that Wilson laughed at.

A question naturally emerged. Why, if Wilson felt bitter about the Civil War and about American history in general, should he want to spend fifteen years on this book? To which the only possible answer was another question. Why, if he *said* he felt that way about the Civil War, should he have written such an extraordinary book around it?

For *Patriotic Gore* is a great book. It was the greatest single performance of Wilson's unique career as a man of letters (and contained in passing the most profound considerations on literature in America I had ever read). It made the passion that went into the war, and into the disillusion that followed it, more affecting than any other contemporary book on this greatest of national American experiences. It had in particular a fullness of historical atmosphere, a sensitivity to the great personages of the vital writers and leaders, that made the reader see Mrs. Stowe, Lincoln, Grant, Sherman, and the others as commanding figures in a great

American epic. Though Abraham Lincoln "examined the mechanical devices that were brought to him in the years of his Presidency and is reported to have understood them, he does not seem to have been much impressed by the development of machinery in America or even much interested in it." Grant, dying of cancer of the throat, dictated his *Personal Memoirs* until it became impossible to use his voice. "Humiliated, bankrupt and voiceless, on the very threshold of death, sleepless at night and sitting up in a chair as if he were still in the field and could not risk losing touch with developments, he relived his old campaigns."

There, in the heroes, the writers, the sensitive consciences, the faithful diarists of the conflict, was Edmund Wilson's own story. There was no real social history in this book of studies in the literature of the Civil War, no grasp of the real social issues and movements behind the war and nineteenth-century America. History to the "old radical" was still, as it had been to Emerson, biography.

As the sixties darkened into war, and he became increasingly ill, his sense of himself, of his necessary authority, became more pronounced and more tragic. At a party in Ed O'Connor's house in the Wellfleet woods, Wilson, drunk and defiant, said, laughing, that the F.B.I. would be suspicious of him. "I've been married four times!" As he stumbled out of the party and down the stairs, the consort of the famous historian who was so proud of knowing exactly who was who on *la plage des intellectuels* said throatily, "Really, shouldn't someone look after the poor old man?"

At the moment we were all looking very well after ourselves. Round and round we rode the great carrousel of American literature, American money-getting, American fame. Some of us were getting nearer than others to grabbing the gold ring that beamed at us every time we went round again. Ed O'Connor, with his money from *The Last Hurrah*, awoke one day to find himself with a Porsche, the house in the Wellfleet woods, a magnificent town house in Boston, and the friendship of the Kennedys in nearby Hyannis, nearby Boston, friendly Washington. Ed's newfound wealth was somehow also *our* treasure. Everyone basked in it.

The blowy shifting dunes of the great beach, where Ed and I walked every golden heady summer of the early 1960s, had been his patrol ground as a lonely Coast Guardsman during the war. It amused him to compare his walks then and now; his early life as a beggarly radio announcer before the war and his overflowingly happy, wealthy life now. O'Connor still had a radio announcer's voice, could mimic all the Wellfleet characters, and told his stories with professional charm. His practiced voice played on you. The easy flow that he had developed as a radio announcer was now the total geniality of the wealthy host—a host who neither smoked nor drank, was until 1962 a confirmed Irish bachelor, a fiercely old-fashioned Catholic surrounded by Jews against whose "lack of religion" he grumbled, but who were among his closest friends.

Another Boston Irishman was in the White House. And in this happy go-ahead best-sellerdom that had suddenly come upon him, Ed O'Connor shone and gleamed like a new car. The young on the Wellfleet beach doted on him, chalked "VISIT THE HOME OF THE STARS" on his brand-new driveway; there was one great summer birthday party when Beth presented him with a money belt. Ed gave his best performance as the Scrooge in charge of the pay toilets that someday were sure to desecrate "our beach," suddenly threatened by the government's damnable creation of a National Seashore.

The woods back of the O'Connor house that birthday party were suddenly full of White House detail in incongruous business suits as Arthur Schlesinger and Richard Goodwin, released from academic constraints and just in from the Kennedy compound at Hyannis, gamboled and gossiped. Ed O'Connor, the Irish ascetic and non-drinker, quietly served more and more drinks to lissome girls in bikinis. Young men in rustic beards sat cross-legged on the floor humming and strumming folk rock to their own guitars. There was a cocktail-party sense of everybody's ability to move fluently anywhere. Power from Washington seemed to be stored up in the cells of Kennedy's executive assistants and advisers even on a weekend romp in Wellfleet among their old colleagues from Harvard, M.I.T., and the Institute for Advanced Study.

With his heavy, wearily pitted face Richard Goodwin radiated shrewdness in the midst of relaxation. The councilors to the Prince seemed to themselves to be in unforeseen but abundant relation to power. Things were done for you; travel to any part of the earth instantly and beautifully arranged; your opinion gravely solicited on the best way to foster the economic development of Latin America and on what subtle shifts might yet be expected among the hard-liners in the Kremlin. Above all, *you* were now "Society," the only true upper crust, those in the know.

Their rich, lean, handsome chief and war hero had fulfilled more than his own ambition; he raised with him intellectual prodigies whose glamour had been confined to academe. He radiated like the sun. He was not just the center every day now of everybody's attention, rich, and the President, shining with the light of kings; he was at the center of everything and everybody, and could give you—as the councilors were always quick to tell you—the inside dope on de Gaulle, Khrushchev, Macmillan. The councilors identified with the Prince, with his youth and handsomeness; with the style of conscious impudence that the Kennedy sons learned from their father, so that you could not always tell whether a Kennedy was his father or his father's son. They were proud of his sophisticated and agile wife; proud that he had so many girls; proud of travel arrangements typed out on White House notepaper; proud, without knowing too much about it, of the thirteen million the campaign had cost.

But proudest of all were they of the "scholarly atmosphere around the White House." After all, they were scholars; that was their usefulness. It was more than a privilege; it was an education to be at the beck and call of a President with this inside mastery of the whole throbbing social machine. Even as a candidate, Kennedy had excited the usually hardened Washington observer, Richard Rovere: "The easy way in which he disposes of the question of Church and State . . . suggests that the organization of society is the one thing that really engages his interest." Such a contrast, as Kennedy himself pointed out to visitors, wih the Eisenhowers' many television sets, so important to *those* dowdy people that they ran wires down a wall to the nearest outlet.

Intellect was in touch with power. The councilors brought back news about talks with their chief about Disraeli, an interesting review in the latest *New Statesman*. His favorite book was Lord David Cecil's *Melbourne!* He could speculate, so rare in a politician, about the fate of power in American lives. As he was grinningly objective about himself, his father's old Neanderthal opinions, his father's wonder-making fortune, so he was "cool"—that great ideal of the period—facing the many world crises that were known first to the President.

The President knew, and through his councilors you knew, that Chiang's "people" wanted a war. They presented him at lunch with the most beautiful and delicate vase, and all they wanted in return was a little war! Khrushchev, visiting a great farm in the Middle West, had been given figures that turned out to be inflated, and Khrushchev had used this to score off Kennedy. Power was great but strangely frail when you least expected it—as at the Bay of Pigs. Power included some secret essential, it was at the mercy of some larger reason, but this would not be admitted on the surface. In some way power remained an illusion of power. The more pressure you applied to your claim, the more it took on the fatalism of old Celtic tales. There were ancient spirits or wizards who promised you a treasure and would deliver; but the treasure itself could not be depended on. Ah, but a Gael could be sad for all his power and laughter.

Meanwhile, however, the hard-pressed people of this suffering earth cried out for change, a modicum of hope. Goodwin drew up large-scale reforms for Latin America, presented them to Kennedy with the warning that big business would oppose them. Kennedy, great man, smiled and told him not to worry. The famous Kennedy toughness would support burning social change as well as our "posture" vis-à-vis our "adversary." Goodwin was as confident about changing many things as was *Life* when it announced in the first summer of the new administration:

It is apparent to the editors of *Life* that the national goals of our country can be stated in these two propositions: (1) Win The Cold War (2) Create a Better America. Can a magazine presume to say that it will help win the Cold War, help create a better America? It cannot presume otherwise.

Everything was suddenly possible because intellect was in charge. The Kennedy administration in its happy dizzy first year was a social occasion from which certain overearnest advisers like Professor Henry Kissinger were finally excluded as not being "entertaining" enough. It was important to be entertaining, nimble, quick; it was most important to entertain possibility in all things. Intellect was in charge. Over and again I was told by the professors in the White House not only how much Kennedy read, but how *quickly*. There was a driving claim all day long on History to be made, History to be recorded. The field was open at last to the informed and brainy. What I did not learn from the councilors was that Kennedy, with his patchy education and the snubs he had suffered at Harvard as rich Joe Kennedy's son, resented intellectuals as much as he used them.

In Wellfleet I had just finished "The President and Other Intellectuals" for the *American Scholar* issue on the new administration when Arthur Schlesinger called me from the White House to extend the President's invitation to lunch. In my essay I described the admiration between the President and writers so different as Robert Frost and Norman Mailer; went on to Kennedy's executive need of scholars and intellectual "experts." I brazenly, on the basis of reading and interviews with many Kennedy observers, doubted his seeming freedom from the conventional wisdom, but not his quickness, his overwhelming interest in journalism, his

concern with History as something to be made. The key
to Kennedy's character was one I thought I knew all
too well: the need to remodel himself, to recreate himself, to fit himself to the endless demands behind which
gleamed the immense stakes available in American life.

Reading Kennedy's books and current pronouncements had impressed me less with Kennedy as "intellectual" than working for him had impressed his councilors. I told Schlesinger that my essay would displease
the President, and suggested that Schlesinger read it
before I accepted the invitation to the White House.
Schlesinger laughed but read it his next weekend at
Wellfleet. As we walked up and down the beach, shivering in the sudden wind that had come off the water, he
praised my observations, corrected some facts, supplied
more information, and assured me that there was nothing in it to embarrass him with the President.

It was August, 1961; Kennedy had been in office for
seven months. Despite the Bay of Pigs, the rising tensions with Russia, the uprush of black protest in the
South, the ferocity of American "conservatives," the
bloom was still on the rose. His eyes were curiously
bloodshot, but he looked so fresh and easy in the White
House that he carried you along with him. He was full of
gossip about the great; literary items he grinningly liked
for their titles, like Irwin Shaw's "The Girls in Their
Summer Dresses." He mused that success in America
was always in personal terms, and so became ultimately
unsatisfying, while in Russia the individual achievement
was swallowed by the group. He talked personalities
around the globe, from de Gaulle to Ilya Ehrenburg.
What struck me most was not the easy, bantering knowledge and the well-reported aggressiveness; it was the way
he shifted from arrogant authority to a wistful need for a
more confident learning than he possessed. He, too, was

a personality under construction—rare in a politician, but one explanation of his openness to all impressions and his need to charm. He was still "making himself," responding to the many demands on his character. The political ideas were something else. He was a "tough pragmatist," and turned everybody else around him into one.

He wanted very much to be liked. I was astonished by how much he put himself out for me, how willingly he disclosed himself and his smallest resentments. He now had a great contempt for *Time*—once his journalistic ideal—whose "foreign editors get their great knowledge on the train between Greenwich and New York." He was intellectually concessive to scholars and historians, to the leading novelists of the moment. But he was obviously fascinated by personality and by what he called "brain power" as the clue to a man's importance. The volume of cultural envy and resentment amazed me in a politician so glamorous and, at that moment in the Western world, positively supreme. Was I the only luncheon guest who wondered over so much intellectual chic? Was there no one at those White House dinner parties who questioned his pretensions? Yet I could see why so many President-watchers were fascinated with his style. He regarded himself—and his domestic emotions—as a dramatic event. He recounted André Malraux's visit with the same excited ability to cover every personal detail that he admired in writers—and applied to his own life and marriage. Malraux's two sons had died in an automobile accident. The man was amazing in his stoicism. Then Kennedy said, with husbandly sharpness, "Malraux sure went for Jackie. So naturally Malraux is now Jackie's favorite novelist."

The once-golden cloud over an American President certainly covered this President those first months in

the White House. There was a dazzle to Washington
that I ascribed to Kennedy himself—to ambition, not his
ties with "intellect." I went back to the Willard, added
to my already written piece some appreciative notes on
Kennedy as a personal force in all our lives, and un-
mindfully waited for the *American Scholar* to appear
in the fall.

It appeared and Kennedy was outraged. Despite reports of choler from William Styron and other literary
friends of the President, I had not anticipated just how
furious a President could be made by a literary critic in
the *American Scholar*. The article produced a fan letter
from Professor Henry Kissinger, obviously still smart-
ing at not being "entertaining" enough for Kennedy.
Only when Schlesinger's *A Thousand Days* appeared in
1965 did I also realize that my article had so irritated
Kennedy that Schlesinger promptly forgot that he had
gone over my article with me in Wellfleet. *A Thousand
Days* held me up for ridicule as still another "New York
intellectual" ignorant of the necessities of power. "As
for Kennedy, he was very funny about Kazin's essay
when it appeared in the *American Scholar*. 'We wined
him and dined him,' he said, 'and talked about Hemingway and Dreiser with him, and I later told Jackie what
a good time she missed, and then he went away and
wrote that piece!' "

In the exuberance of the New Frontier in 1961—then
the maelstrom of the sixties—nothing could have mattered less than my uninformed and obstinate suspicion
of power. Like my old friend Hofstadter, who never
saw an American President and would not have gone
out of his way to see one, I was afraid of so much power
in the hands of one man. Henry Adams, who was
mesmerized by the power given to politicians he de-

spised, said he was content to be a "stable companion to Statesmen." Hofstadter did not much care where Kennedy's stable was. He was a historian of American society, American hopes, and American paranoia, not a councilor to the Prince.

We were all innocents, even the councilors. Power beyond reason created a lasting irrationality. Kennedy's hideous death, turning the promise and the secret corruption of the thousand days into the century's most famous murder mystery, uncovered enough to intimate that the mystery was the government's secret doings and might never be revealed. Government ruled, not "Society." Kennedy's assassination, followed so soon by Johnson's war and Nixon's war, Johnson's folly and Nixon's lying, made one wonder if Kennedy's early promise had been based on anything but his extinguishable charm, irony, deftness. "Camelot" became a sneer, an emptiness. Had anything been there except so personal a sense of power? The refugee physicist Leo Szilard had alerted Einstein to reach Roosevelt with the news that an atomic bomb was feasible. Leo Szilard in the early 1960s haunted Washington, constantly pressed the Kennedy administration on the dangers of nuclear war, and was termed insane by one executive assistant. How official these once-sardonic university wits became! As Vietnam slowly heated up, Goodwin assured Beth: "It's the little wars that stop the big wars." "History" in the making, "History" in the writing, had been everything to Kennedy and his entourage. History now waited for historians to see beyond so vain a sense of history.

But the truth was already in. You could say anything about power except how intoxicating it was. The old war had certainly made us tough, and the cold war made us tougher. The power could be glimpsed in the rows of gleaming jet planes on every great airfield; in the proud glint of the great new glass-walled office buildings on Third Avenue, Park, Sixth that looked like file cabinets, steel desks, Xerox machines, coding systems; in the new look of women as they went into the labor force and recognized themselves in the technological vortex as a constituency, not appendages to the kitchen. We were flying, floating in air, streaming, living it up under extended wings. There was a runaway feel to "society," to our lives; to the mingled hope and terror, the sudden wild sexual freedom and man-woman battle that Mailer caught better than anyone else—and acted out, in respect for constant confrontation.

In 1943 poor Isaac Rosenfeld, dead by the 1950s, had sat in his orgone box looking for a message, for the Messiah, for the perfect freedom and happiness that would come to him as unprecedented sexual power— from the spheres. He hoped to get in touch with the hidden energies of this universe. But Isaac lived and died alone; too soon for the age of Mailer. Mailer, Bellow, Goodman had all been delivered by Reichian analysis to be bold, defiant of convention and body armature. But Goodman's homosexual loneliness had saved him from "bourgeois convention." Long before a mob took this over as if it had nothing to believe in but homosexuality, he had fondly believed that to be singular and lonely was genius. Bellow had "broken through" with *Augie March*, but despite his natural caution, his brilliantly self-centered novels described the sexual impatience of the rising Jewish middle class. Lowell, redeemed by suffering from his overdeveloped early style, found his true self and his best material in the irreducible self he portrayed in *Life Studies* wandering about Boston sanitariums.

But no one else caught so well as Mailer the hidden public temper that would now flash out, from Washington to Greenwich Village, as a sexual riot that praised itself as radical politics. Mailer's genius was to know the real grittiness and obscenity of American life, which he had learned in the Army, a bantamweight Jew from Brooklyn up against rednecks who could take seriously only someone who would fight them. Unlike Bellow, Goodman, Lowell, Mailer really knew—and rejoiced in—what Trilling would sadly have called the "underside" of American life. He knew that what intellectuals now wanted was what Washington wanted: to break out; to show muscle; to "confront" and confront again; *not to be intimidated*. Mailer went public, as no other writer of the period did, with the new revelation that it was really all a question of playing the right role. What he did not need to speak and what his audience welcomed most was his antagonism to secret government, to the wealth and power of which he was naturally suspicious even when their sexual self-expression fascinated him. You did not have to be so talented as Mailer to be tough; but if you were tough you could now think yourself talented. Middle-class hedonists eventually shocked Mailer by adopting sex not even as honest lust but as the latest advice. The itch to break out was everywhere now.

What would not subside after the "protest movement" did was the inflamed sexual language and bravado that supported the new painters and writers when you could see nothing but the triumph of surface. "I have to paint large so as to keep it intimate," said Mark Rothko. "Action painting, like the new atomic physics," said an admiring critic, "has the power to release trapped energy, to set great forces at work at liberty for good and evil." "I paint the unconscious," said Jackson

Pollock. "I am nature." There was indeed no "modesty of scale," as the young historian sourly commented after the sixties were over. And especially was there no privacy. Everything was public, visible, explosive, "*strong*." Was it just the confident new American middle class flexing its muscles, showing off? Did "protest" come only from those who had the power to defy authority? On my way to Tuskegee to lecture one week, I saw blacks meekly walking the sides of the highway, students still so shy that no one told me and I did not know until I had come home that the lights in New York had all gone out one night. In New York, Mailer was writing that "the ambition of a writer like myself is to become consecutively more disruptive, more dangerous, and more powerful." I had learned early to believe in Mailer's prophetic instinct. He was *the* writer of the big American change after 1945. The instinct was surer on American life, where he could be uncanny in sniffing out the secret policemen, the power brokers, the biggest money, than on himself, who was understandably fascinated by what he most urgently suspected. Like Fitzgerald, he used himself and used himself; the contradictions were his life. Unlike Fitzgerald, he could not make himself the believable fantasy he was in life. He was so insatiably *mental* about everything that he became his ideas, his heroes. Oddly, he was too reflective to be content with fiction. Despite his genius for publicity, he could lose himself completely in his favorite abstractions. His political instinct was brilliant, but he was always looking for political concepts that would not hold very long. Once, giving me lunch at the Plaza, he got so caught up preaching sex as freedom and power, denouncing the repression of sex as the prime cause of "cancer," that he did not notice the fashion show put on in the Oak Room and the models dipping and swaying around our table.

Beth and I soon lived a full New York life crowded with love and anger, ambition and cultural war. The book-crammed walls of our apartment high over the Hudson seemed to rock with the violence between the generations. We could not seem to agree on anything except Rachel, not even on the obvious necessity of making a clean break with this excessive attention to each other. Novelist and critic, artist and mere intellectual, we were playing out a cultural drama, a literary passion play, in which issue succeeded issue. There was the ineradicable Germanism of Hannah Arendt, the latest literary recipe just imported from Paris by Susan Sontag, the new leftist chic of the "New York Review of the Vietnam War," and what Beth at the most profound juncture of night and morning, when she woke up as angry as when she had gone to bed, roundly declared to be the indifference to fiction, and especially woman's fiction, by the literary Establishment.

She fascinated me, she alarmed me, she constantly tempted me to think that there was still something I could do to appease her, some magic word that would bring back the love-mad young girl I had first met. I was hopelessly one self. Beth the novelist included so many selves, dreamed so many stories, that I was never sure which one I was in. I was amazed by the fluency of mood, of character, of her dreams. Like the novelists she most admired, she seemed to be made up of some invisible writing that nevertheless dominated her, shifted with the balance as it tumbled around her. She was easily turned on, and off; was possessed by what possessed her at any single moment. I was awed. Bellow said when I published a sketch of him over the years, "I'm not used to other people running the picture gallery." There was in Beth a mixture of the novelist's narcissism and infernal shrewdness about others, an irresolution about herself but a psychic's intuition about other people that made me expect, in the most awful moments, that a different Beth would turn up in a minute.

So there was always, from hour to hour, a new wife to look forward to. After a bad fight steeped in alcohol, there would be in the middle of the morning tearing impatient lovemaking; followed by a deep fall into a silence and sadness I could never reach. Life was full anytime we were together—of homecoming and bitterness, excitement and peril, wild joy and the most deathly loneliness inside the same apartment. What a New York riot! What a two-person drama leading to and from the elevator; among the many drinks, the throwing of books and papers, the curses; all the old Jewish nightmares of annihilation being played out at the bar of the Russian Tea Room, while waiting on line to see the very latest French movie on Third Avenue, in restaurant after restaurant where the food, left uneaten, seemed to look up at us in shame.

We made quite a show—perfect scrappers—and I understood her resentment all too well. I was a critic, forever perched on the judgment seat, of whose hearty unending approval she could never feel confident. I was confident that I could read the mind behind a book and that there was some perfect mind—but that was in another country. This naturally ran against Beth's belief that a critic's job was to provide total support and no criticism of anything whatsoever.

Although I lived by this battle, my love and support were certainly imperfect. I could not handle so demanding a literary ambition rooted in panic, anger, fear of annihilation. I was losing faith in my own power to love. Our marriage seemed to be a Jewish autobiography, not a marriage of minds. Our fears were identical and repetitive—our fears kept me coming home. As Beth said, we were each other's family. To which I silently added: each other's *old* family.

Family! The dismemberment and torture of the Jewish family was a too familiar fear in our house. The farther we got away from the Holocaust in time, the more it took up residence right on New York's West Side. The giddier our travels, drinking, our love and dismay, the more suddenly a trapdoor seemed to open into bottomless fear. This we had in common; this we knew: for Jews the war had never ended. The posthumous Sylvia Plath, "Lady Lazarus," stunned us by the knowledge she had of this. Her ferocity had been hidden by her perfect impersonation at Smith of a scholarship girl playing nice. But she had guessed the truth; to face this truth was already to die a little. "What the person out of Belsen . . . wants . . . is the knowledge that somebody else has been there, and knows the *worst*."

The Holocaust would not go away, and so could be denied. The more "Jewish" we became, the more we were open to the new horror: *the past did not exist unless you had lived it yourself*. There was no historical memory if you chose not to have one. The buoyant, the storm-laden, the tumultuously revolutionary sixties filled up the present. The pleasure principle mocked the "atavistic" Jewish demand for a sign from one's fellow men.

At a painter's smart dinner party in the East Nineties, two visiting Indian diplomats explained, with a little smile, that the Holocaust had never occurred. It was all propaganda. Beth became furious. A prominent Jewish publishing executive was annoyed. She had spoiled the dinner party.

Our own battle went on and on. It was as if neither could conquer the past but had to find it in the other, to liberate itself through the other. The drama soon palled. The marital discord that had seemed central, all-consuming, because it was fixed in monogamy—that essential furniture of the good life—now plainly seemed a piece of middle-class indulgence. The young en masse suddenly became revolutionaries against all fixed things. They were terrible, outrageous; they were outside of literature; they were even anti-literature. But since they were our children, children of the new middle class, they were perfectly equipped and ready to dynamite us.

The sons were out to get their fathers—especially if the fathers had been "radicals" during a certain ancient Depression. Although I was as much a target to my own son as my old friends were to *their* sons, I had a secret sympathy with the sons in general. It was spring, the sons were bursting out in France, England, Italy, *Germany*, and students were sitting on the windowsills of the Columbia buildings on Broadway, laughing and singing in the sunshine. Carnival time. At the beginning. The students certainly looked freer and more joyous than Irving Howe, Dwight Macdonald, Stephen Spender, and other "old revolutionists" at the inevitable panel meeting held by the middle-aged to tell the young what to think. The students, at the beginning, certainly looked different from the booted-and-spurred horse cop in Sam Browne belt and hooded shades who contemptuously barred my way to a telephone in the coffee shop that his "special operations squad" had taken over. A Columbia professor, an "old Socialist" and hence by no means in easy sympathy with the strike, burst into tears when he saw the cops dragging students into the paddy wagon. The students did not mind the paddy wagon, far from it; but they especially relished the sight of "old Socialists" in tears.

The sons were attacking the fathers where we lived. They attacked our attachment to libraries; to books uselessly piled on more books; to our fondest belief that violence had nothing proper to do with sex and sex nothing to do with politics. America needed thinking, said Professor Richard Hofstadter in the Cathedral of St. John the Divine at Columbia's 1968 commencement. (The campus was too bloody-minded to accommodate the usual ceremony.) It needed the humanities; it needed learning, civility, understanding, not angry mindless platitudes. And besides, hinted Hofstadter, some of us, even *us*, used to be radical as well. Had we changed so much? he pleaded. Cannot you recognize that the America we suffered for in the thirties is yours?

But America has changed, Tim responded scornfully to me when, that tumultuous spring of 1968, I met him at Widener. Twenty years old; army fatigues, of course; the sweeping mustache; an impatiently loving, slightly pitying expression. The young were no longer waiting to be noticed. They were on stage! And as for "Amerika," it is not and never was what you timid old Social Democrats thought it was. Hofstadter and I were what Blake called horses of instruction; the sons were tigers of wrath. Blake said that the tigers were wiser in their wrath than the horses of instruction. For we had "made it"; had turned into an Establishment; were compliant intellectuals who lent comfort to the same old system *just* by our being liberal, moderate—"*wise.*"

Was all this joyous *brio* "revolution"? Playacting? Publicity? Spring? The son corrected the father, who could use correction. But was there more to this than the social self-confidence of the Ivy League up against demoralized old profs who never quite knew what the young meant, or if they meant anything more than to show up old profs? There was a fine Oedipal aggressiveness which, for one son painfully identifying with his immigrant father, shocked like a sudden visit from outer space. A yippie flyer of the period became almost as dear to me as the slogan put up by students, in Paris —"*L'imagination au pouvoir!*"

> . . . disobey your parents; burn your money; you know life is a dream and all our institutions are man-made illusions effective because you take the dream for reality. . . . Break down the family, church, nation, city, economy; turn life into an art form, a theater of the soul and a theater of the future; the revolutionary is the only artist.
>
> What's needed is a generation of people who are freaky, crazy, irrational, sexy, angry, irreligious, childish and mad; people who burn draft cards, burn high school and college degrees, people who say "to hell with your goals!" people who lure the youth with music, pot and acid; people who redefine the normal; people who break with the status-role-title-consumer game; people who have nothing material to lose but their flesh. . . .
>
> The white youth of America have more in common with Indians plundered than they do with their own parents. Burn their houses down, and you will be free. . . .

As it happened, at the moment the entrance hall of Widener was lined with showcases bearing ancient Hebrew grammars and exhibiting THREE CENTURIES OF HEBREW AT HARVARD. I rejoiced in the yellowing pages; the alphabet that always reminded Edmund Wilson of how far these letters had traveled; the letter ע , the *'ayin* that I could never encounter without seeing my mother's young face; the Hebrew letters into which the

Jews transcribed the German, Spanish, Greek, Arabic they spoke in different countries. These Hebrew letters surrounded me as the deepest part of my History.

Tim was also my History. He was on the run, had no time to look at the frayed and yellowing pages showing THREE CENTURIES OF HEBREW AT HARVARD. Real life, his moment, the great moment of his generation were all outside. Before the Center for International Studies, a pent-up crowd of protesting students was demonstrating as if it were not a Harvard building but the infamous Pentagon itself. I looked at my son with love and wonder—young, brilliantly alive with the confidence of a generation that would "tear down the war machine," he was enveloped in a mass of comrades and duplicates, seemed never to be alone. I thought of myself climbing the long weary hill every day, year after year, from the 137th Street IRT station to the City College. Tim and friends seemed to be "carrying out" an attack on unemployment, racism, persecution that I had shared all my life, that I never felt more than during the Vietnam war. Yet we laughed at our own uselessness when Irving Howe, Muriel Rukeyser, and I went to see Vice-President Humphrey about the war. "Why don't you talk to *him?*" Humphrey said bitterly.

No more "mere" protest. This was action! Everything that blazing spring was clear to the young—just a little too simple, perhaps; trembling on the brink of violence; already engulfed in political delusion—as Tim and his friends saw all justice and truth in the Vietcong, ran through the school halls in the poorest parts of Cambridge "calling out oppressed youth," who, baffled but no doubt grateful to get out of school for the day, perhaps disappeared instead of marching on the State House and the local draft board.

But of course it was "oppressed youth" who were

getting sent over to save Vietnam for democracy. In the
cities of "Amerika" young people were chalking on the
walls *"God Is Not Dead, We Are"* and, without a
doubt, driving wild that already crazy war President
who called himself "the head of the free world":

> Hey, hey, hey, L.B.J.,
> How many kids did you kill today?

And all those *new* councilors to the new Prince! Rostow,
owl-glassed, with his sheaf of position papers, briefing
papers, scenarios, and game plans, was photographed
by *Life* leaning against a column on the White House
porch as he waited to see The Boss. No doubt Rostow
said to Johnson what he said to me at the University of
Texas in the last paroxysm of the war: "I'll tell you how
we can still win this." That military genius and perfect
Southerner General Westmoreland, who looked as if no
thought ever passed through his mind that he alone had
ever thought of:

> I know that the passing of a loved one is one of life's
> most tragic moments, but sincerely hope that you will
> find some measure of comfort in knowing that your son
> served his Nation with honor.
>
> His devoted service was in the finest traditions of
> American soldiers who on other battlefields and in other
> times of national peril have given the priceless gift of
> life to safeguard the blessings of freedom for their loved
> ones and for future generations. In Vietnam today brave
> Americans are defending the rights of men to choose
> their own destiny and to live in dignity and freedom.
>
> All members of the United States Army join in
> sharing your burden of grief.
>
>   Sincerely,
>   s/ W. C. Westmoreland
>   General, United States Army
>   Chief of Staff

For Tim there was a straight line of words, of radical will, an intoxication of militancy perfectly matched and opposed by Walt Whitman Rostow, by the big-bellied plumbers and construction workers who now made a point of wearing on their hard hats decaled American flags and on their work shirts still another American flag. The most heavily unionized workers, the good ethnics who put their bodies on the line, had become the spearhead of American jingoism against the effete intellectuals, the pampered college brats. It was a class matter, all right. The workers wanted the war; wanted bigger defense budgets and the jobs that came with them, wanted (said they wanted) to keep strong "family life and tradition." As I went past Columbia during the strike, a taxi-driver screamed at the "longhairs" picketing alma mater, "You fucking rich sonofabitches! I never had a chance to go to no college! I had to work!"

And covered himself with the flag. The fire engines screaming their way down Amsterdam Avenue with flags flying looked as if they were going into battle. The cops wore flag pins *and* miniature flags on their uniforms. Cars flew flags from their radio aerials and carried bumper stickers of the American flag:

THESE COLORS DO NOT RUN
AMERICA! LOVE IT OR LEAVE IT
THE PEACE SYMBOL ⊗ IS THE FOOTPRINT OF A COWARD

The great battle of advertisements in America—Hertz versus Avis, Palmolive versus Ivory—was repeated now in the furious opposition of old ladies wearing the American flag in rhinestones glaring at peaceniks in jeans and desert boots; in "pigs" versus "Reds" and "Comsmps"; in "Washington" against "Hanoi." At the Democrats' convention in 1968, the great orgasm of extreme right and extreme left, Tim and his friends, sleeping on floors, were raided and beaten by Chicago cops who had carefully concealed their name plates and, while hitting them, righteously condemned them for the shit the young people's dogs had left in a corner.

Some academicians were most "with it," in the excitement of getting away from their everlasting "programs in criticism." The Modern Language Association, weary of literature, elected as its president a mediocre literary ideologist whose slogan was "To Hell with Culture" and who advised his followers: "Smear the Walls of Lincoln Center with Shit." No "modesty of scale" showed itself in the pretentiousness of Philharmonic Hall; in Boston's John Hancock skyscraper, where the glass panels were always getting sucked out by the building's self-generated winds; in the moral idiocy of the academic critic who taught his students to perform "an imaginative confrontation with the text" but tacitly defended the Nazified Hell's Angels who murdered young Meredith Hunter at the hysterical Rolling Stones rock festival at Altamont.

The stylish academic critics had long had American students at their mercy. Having indoctrinated the young in the proper literary *attitudes*, in certain necessary "perspectives on literature," they found that the radicalized young were now in charge of *their* thinking. Now it was the teachers who were being indoctrinated by their students; teachers ran after the angries and the mother-fuckers and the revolutionary student brigade and *venceremos* in a vain effort to catch up with the young. The Performing *Self*, as one critic put it, succeeded what an old New Critic had called the Critical Performance. "Performance," the great American ego trip, was as important on the campus as in bed. Many a documentary journalist of the period, not as prophetic and honestly radical as Mailer, now made himself exactly equal to the event. Nothing was more common in the sixties than the radical apocalypse served up in girlie magazines to businessmen who were still more satisfied with their "rewards" than not, but who liked a suggestion of something politically wicked as they liked in the centerpiece the flash of pubic hair.

The American system rolled with the punches, absorbed every criticism, and somehow rewarded the most aggressive critic. "The "performers" were made happy by the publicity; the writers were intoxicated by their superiority to the befuddled masses in whose behalf they were openly defying the hateful system. Bellow, growing conservative and more and more contemptuous of the "wasteland intellectuals" (who were his life, his material, his favorite point of departure), indignantly insisted that "they" wanted to see blood run in the streets. This was not true. Like Bellow, they, too, wanted their moment of glory, but, having nothing in particular to say, had to act it out. There was a reception for the Chicago Six or Seven or Eight at a rich woman's house in New York. Abbie Hoffman, like a young star in *Hair*, arrived in the dirtiest possible T-shirt, jeans cut off at the knee, and then proceeded to take them off, looking at the ladies in furs with the expectancy of a TV star looking for the "go" light on the camera. "Better living through chemistry!" he said, laughing, when some Weathermen blew themselves up concocting a bomb on West Eleventh Street. Publicity ruled. Publicity *was* the public. Nobody could resist the media. Nothing could keep the cameraman from walking into any meeting, up to any stage. The age of endless "exposure" mockingly absorbed every defiance. Tim and his friends in Cambridge became favorites of the cameramen and reporters, and were often asked to hold a certain pose, to make a particular face. The radi-

calized academics, at their great big revolutionary out-
burst in New York, put up flyers and posters around
the Americana Hotel:

WE DEMAND AN END TO AMERICA'S WAR ON VIETNAM
           TO PROFESSIONAL IRRELEVANCE
JOIN US IN BUILDING
           A HUMANE PROFESSION IN A HUMANE NATION
           A FREE UNIVERSITY IN A FREE SOCIETY
LET'S PUT HUMANITY BACK IN THE HUMANITIES

When the foot-weary security men (retired waiters and
post-office workers) were ordered by the hotel manage-
ment to take the posters down, they were attacked as
"Fascist goons." Meanwhile, the president of the University of California was saying: "The university has
become a prime instrument of national purpose. . . .
What the railroads did for the second half of the nineteenth and the automobile for the first half of this century, the knowledge industry may do for the second
half of this century; that is, to serve as the focal point
for national growth. And the university is at the center
of the knowledge process."

Dear Professor Kazin:
    I am (or I was, until about a year and a half ago) a
graduate student in English at the University of ———.
I've been in New York for two weeks, trying to tell someone (anyone) that the country is going to collapse, probably sometime this summer and certainly by the end of
the year. But no one will listen. Two years ago, in a class
on American literature in the twenties, I saw through
the styles of the twenties and the sixties to the pattern
that correlates them and realized that a process was being
repeated, that the final event in the process must be the
collapse of the system. That another collapse would be
fatal. Huge and apparently unrelated bodies of informa-

tion—from history, philosophy, theology, sociology, literature, learning theory, linguistics, logic—began to click suddenly into place to reveal their relationship to each other and the pattern behind them. When all the data was integrated, the pattern was complete . . . a precise description of beauty.

The test of a theory is the number of facts it correlates and explains. . . . This one correlates them all; once someone recognizes this, it will gain a momentum of its own. Until then I will run into the system's inherent resistance to new ideas. I have been bucking it for two years and I am growing desperate. Since I realized that the collapse is inevitable, I have followed the process with an ever-increasing precision. We have reached the brink of chaos, and still no one has listened, not even for half an hour.

Meanwhile the great American *state*, as opposed to this vast Jell-O-like *society*, pursued the mirage of victory and "peace with honor." The war went on and on; went on television every night, regular as clockwork. Every night, right on your own home movie screen, you could see flamethrowers bursting into bunkers; American ships firing into a jungle as they floated down a river; "choppers" dizzily whirling up into the sky, pouncing down onto the ground with a flashing retardation like the slowing of a wheel made up entirely of knife blades.

I am an onlooker; there are now millions of onlookers at ringside, and no doubt the time is getting short for some of them, too. The war is outside me. "Before each scene," said Henry James, I "wish really to get *into* the picture, to cross, as it were, the threshold of the frame." Beads of fire; starbursts of light that hit me like sound. I am unresigned to this performance night after night. Here is a shot, on the front page of the *Times*, of the Saigon police chief Loan, with rolled-up sleeves and a revolver in his hand, about to shoot a captured "V.C." wearing a sports shirt. *The photographer is as close as the "executioner."* The shirt stripes on the man being shot are just as clear as the grimace, anguish, contortion, shock, and horror in his face, an inch away from the revolver about to blast his head. Screaming with pain, tearing off their clothes, Vietnamese children are fleeing a "misdirected" bombardment of napalm. The eye runs quickly over these items of someone else's pain, the daily score of someone else being shot, mauled, gassed, penetrated, burned, concussed, bombarded.

The war is an interruption between drinks and dinner on the six-o'clock news; between dinner and bed on the eleven-o'clock news. The onlooker, grateful that his son is not in a foxhole, his daughter not one of the girls who are running screaming on the highway tearing their clothes off after that "misdirected" napalm attack, thinks out his writing and teaching schedule for the morrow as he goes to bed. And in bed, even in the starburst of making love, he definitely feels that time is getting short, shorter. The nausea of this war is eating him away. A loneliness in the world, a loneliness of repetition with this world, a loneliness that cannot, should not be appeased.

Watching the war, death steals into my soul on faint, almost imperceptible wings. It does not feel like the flashing, whirring, flashing knife blades on top of the chopper in Vietnam. Here in New York it comes on little cat's feet. In the street a raised Hispanic voice somehow as compact and measured as a voice imprisoned on tape cries aloud. Imprisoned by the walls of my bedroom and a real crazy New York moon shinning right at me, I try to make out the words, the sense. I should like to discover the claim someone is making of his self-enclosed trouble. The high sharp parrot voice in the street says the same thing over and over, but I cannot make out the words. Just another cry in he street from someone sounding off; and listening to nothing in particular.

Chapter X

WORDS

My mother, a Russian-Jewish immigrant who never learned English, died the year I briefly visited Russia to perform cultural exchange. All the while I was in Russia—eighteen days that weighed on me like centuries, and that reminded me of a Soviet poet's admission that in "fifty years of the Revolution we have lived five hundred"—I kept thinking of the old woman dying in America as a young girl in Russia.

"I haven't dreamed like this since I was a girl," she said to me every day as the cancer widened. She had been almost proud of her old "inability to dream." To dream was a luxury denied to my mother, who respected her own anxiety and constant labor as if they were the Jewish religion. She even slept with her fists clenched, her face set. DO NOT TAKE A MOMENT'S REST. RUN, DO, WORK, AND KEEP YOUR OWN GOOD IN MIND. My mother had made a point of not enjoying her sleep. She had not "indulged" herself at night any more than she had ever "given in" during the day.

But now, as the disease struck, removed her from everything but the disease, she dreamed all the time. "I can't stop dreaming," she said with a certain pride as she made one last effort to get out of bed, muttering, "I must stop wasting time." For months and months before the Saturday night I saw her die, she dreamed of Russia; talked brokenly of Russia; recalled a Russia she had never wanted to recall before. She pressed me to accept the invitation to Russia. "Perhaps they will let you visit my old village?" The dogged heavyset woman, who in her last years was bent, stooped, arthritic, hobbling about under mysterious ancestral chains, turned into a skeleton exuding some sweet flowery smell of decay. But in sight of death she dreamed; then amazed me by gaspingly making some peace with herself.

The first person to enter the plane when it landed in Moscow was a soldier with a rifle. We had to make our way past this rigid figure to the committee from the Union of Soviet Writers waiting with interpreters, merry quips, and sly put-downs to welcome us. Carl Sandburg had shuddered to think of sharing his vast audience with us, and with his guitar was making his way through Russia alone. The repartee that erupted between the writers' bossman Alexei Surkov and myself suddenly became so barbed that there was no chance for the editor who was our senior man to deliver his prepared speech. As we drove to Moscow through sheets of rain, the editor lamented that he had meant to tell the Russians that he had been attacked during the McCarthy period as "the Red Brahmin from Beacon Hill." The dark rain somehow made great wide-bellied Russia even more overpowering than I had expected it to be. I felt lost in this immensity; the highway stretched ahead forever with no other cars on it. The enormous superhotel just opened for "foreigners of the first rank," as one Russian smirked, was a colossus outside and in, with glazed glossy floors and long lines of crystal white chandeliers hanging row after row overhead like so many bulging refrigerators about to burst. On every floor enormous ladies sat behind tables, coldly scrutinizing you as you came up to get the key to your room. No need to state the room number, they already knew it. The room itself was framed with harmless landscapes of the famously sweet Russian countryside. But when you finally were disgorged through the hotel door onto the vast tumultuously packed Moscow street and the many-laned boulevard, nothing could have immediately appeared more distinct yet less accommodating than the crowds pouring past the statute of Mayakovsky and the supercolossal government buildings.

It was all another world, but familiar with things I must have seen in a previous existence: hotel rooms and lobbies smelling of furniture polish; severe and Spartan figures from the "intellectual world" silently expressing disapproval under half-shut eyelids; large woman bodies like square dumplings crammed into leafy Russian blouses over pink slips, gold proudly flashing from their teeth; old women in aprons and white headcloths forever sweeping the streets, sweeping them as clean as can be, sweeping every path in the park clean of every leaf with witches' twig brooms, sweeping around every Russian standing on an outdoor scale to get himself weighed, sweeping around elderly men wearing rumpled Panama hats as they sit on park benches reading Cervantes, Stendhal, Mark Twain. That stoic wary look of people not just walking by—oh, no!—but living in a society where social practice is consistent with Marxist theory and everyone must be consistent with everyone else.

Meeting Soviet officialdom, what, strangely, is most familiar is that pompous propriety in offices; that schoolmaster Russian exactness and straightforward

seriousness. Our *delegatsia*, irritating to the Russians by
its lack of world-famous names ("Where is your Hemingway, whose sixtieth birthday we have celebrated—
your great progressive dramatists and friend of people's
democracies Lillian Hellman?"), shocks by its levity,
its refusal to visit agricultural fairs, its loud internecine
disagreements, its drinking vodka as cocktail without
necessary support in stomach of *zakuski*. How can I
tell the Foreign Commission of the Union of Soviet
Writers as it receives us in what was once Tolstoy's town
house that the statute in the courtyard of Lev Nikolaye-
vich himself so moves me that as we go inside to be
orated at by writers' bossman Alexei Surkov I can
barely look at the pictures behind him of good and
tried Comrades Anna Seghers, Martin Anderson Nexo,
Pablo Neruda, Louis Aragon?

Surkov sits with Soviet seriousness behind the—of
course—green-clothed table and informs of the power-
breadth extent of literature in the great country which
covers "easily" one-sixth of the world's land surface.
Did we know that in the Soviet Union is produced literature in some sixty languages? "Golly! Sixty languages!"
exclaims the editor in our delegation. Is probably even
more, replies Surkov with quiet pride. Did we know,
do we know, can we possibly *not* have known that fur-
thermore and in addition there exist thousands of magazines, of worthwhile books copies in hundreds of thousands? Of famous classics international literature millions of readers? So great is the demand that never are
we printing enough! Take poetry! The demand for
poetry is indescribable, the Russian love for poetry
traditional; people wait all night outside the many book-
shops to snap up the whole edition the minute it is coming out.

Communist words wore out for me a long time ago.

"Worker." "Imperialism." "Class enemy." "People's Democracy." "Progressive." Now Surkov is wearing me out as his mighty voice, his great Russian wind instrument of a voice, fills the room with literary statistics. We are listening to still another commercial, recorded so long ago and so empty that I am fascinated by the sharply inquisitive looks we are getting from Surkov's sidekicks, who detect I am not properly respectful and who have obviously never seen anything resembling this *delegatsia* outside American movies.

And which Soviet literary personalities do we wish to see? When I say Pasternak, Surkov leans over to a colleague and grins: "Now it's out in the open!" He turns me down. "Between Pasternak and ourselves there is, you might say, a state of peaceful coexistence." Slight mimicry of official language is permitted on occasion. At the puppet show the M.C. barked: "Liquidate the piano!" But to pay us back for our interest in Pasternak, Surkov laughingly describes the abstract art at the American exhibition in Sokolniki Park. At the entrance is the sculptured figure of a woman. Is this bizarre female perhaps a representation of the American woman? Laughs heartily. He will now imitate for us an American avant-garde painter at work. Closes his eyes, wildly throws imaginary paint about. Grins. What's more, the psychiatrists who recommended that Ezra Pound be kept in a mental hospital, not jail, did so because they were all Fascists!

Life is this enormous communal present tense in which we are building Socialism. The past exists only when it is rewritten. The past has so often been misplaced, amended, omitted, put on trial, not to say "liquidated," that I was delighted to hear from one of the many young Jews who served as our interpreters— "just call me Georgie"—that it was now officially established that many of the old Bolsheviks shot by Stalin in the terrible thirties were actually not guilty as charged and were in fact being posthumously rehabilitated.

"Of course the trials were phonies," says Georgie, in perfect American. He impersonates an American so well that he boasts of sneaking into Intourist hotels to confuse Yankee visitors. Georgie's father was killed in the great slaughter of the Red Army before Kiev when Stalin forbade retreat. But "the Old Man" was still Georgie's hero—"How we wept when he died!" Georgie knows and does not know the past. There is a stone marked "Kamenev" among the honored dead buried in the Kremlin wall. The old Bolshevik Lev Kamenev was shot after the first big purge trial, in 1936. "Kamenev *here?*" I exclaim. "This is another Kamenev!" Georgie says hurriedly.

The present scene overwhelms in its many tensions. Walking back to my hotel late one night after a party given by an American diplomat who deeply admired the Russian patience, stoicism, "the readiness to sacrifice, so unlike us," I walked into blinding arc lights outside some foreign embassies. It was one in the morning, but in front of each embassy armed policemen were patrolling as if war had broken out. My host had recently gone to a famous Moscow hospital for a minor operation. Wide awake under slight anesthetic, he had nowhere to look but at an operation being performed right next to him on a man's hand.

So much effort, resolution, obstinate hope, and accustomed suffering were in the life stories, the war stories, the new films, the terrible patriotic plays that I found myself caught by the throat, loving the woman guide Natalia for her stories of her husband's imprisonment, hating the other guide, Olga, for her obvious lies. But you could be sure of nothing, especially not of your

first impressions. Alexei Surkov lied to me that he had
been present both in Petrograd and Moscow when the
Bolsheviks seized power. You could tell by his face that
he was serving up still another commercial. Surkov was
a famous government toady who was to say to Mandelstam's widow that "Pasternak's novel is no good because its hero, Dr. Zhivago, has no right to make any
judgments about our way of life—'we' had not given
him this right."

But how was I to know whether that dear girl Natalia
—another of our many young Jewish interpreters—was
telling the truth or not when she dryly summarized the
tribulations of her physicist husband, locked up because
of "lapses" in a Russian-Japanese translation machine
he had invented?

Natalia appeared to be the most controlled and intelligent of our Russian "helpers." She had perfected
her easy English assisting at the Soviet Embassy in
India. She had translated "many Graham Greenes" into
Russian. She was with us in Moscow; with us in Tashkent, Kiev; with me in the Red Arrow express to Leningrad; with us at the airport when after eighteen
crowded, increasingly ominous days we finally entered
the Sabena plane for London. She seemed to be with
me in particular as we tiptoed through Lenin's austere
rooms in the Smolny Institute, Bolshevik H.Q. in 1917,
and gazed at the portraits on the wall of the Revolutionary Military Committee, which had organized the actual
insurrection against the Winter Palace. Natalia and I
were on such easy terms that I was not afraid to ask her
why a certain Trotsky was now missing from the Military Committee he had actually led and she was not
afraid to whisper back, "Why don't you ask them what
happened to him?"

Natalia accompanied me to the Hermitage on the

great day there were brought up from the cellars the French Impressionists (and a few Post-Impressionists) collected in Paris by Russian merchants before 1914. Leninist-Stalinist commissars of art had ruled them bourgeois degenerate art unsuitable to hang in the great museum with the famous Rembrandts. Many of these paintings had not been seen in a public place since the Revolution. Monet, Degas, Cézanne were on the floor propped up against the sofas. Some young American museum curators, who knew the full extent of these collections, kept pushing the Hermitage staff to bring up more and still more paintings. They named each work they wanted to see. The astonished Russians astonished themselves even more by meekly going back to storage rooms for more once-"degenerate" works.

The circular room in which we sat was shot with disks of light as if flaming out from some second sun; I was amazed by Natalia's indifference to these fabulous paintings. The young American curators' knowledge and enthusiasm irritated her. I went up to the great windows and looked out at the great square, dominated by an arch at the far end, down which the Bolsheviks had rushed to attack the Winter Palace. The Hermitage seemed attached to the Winter Palace. I was looking out at the first great battlefield of the Revolution. But the paintings propped up against the sofas were more authentic revolutions to me than Revolution Square.

If this had been a movie, the sound track would have imitated rifle fire, revolutionary marches, military commands, cries of the dying and the exultant. Instead, American museum curators were exclaiming over the fresh colors of French paintings that had not seen the light of day for perhaps fifty years. Guards were hopping from one foot to the other, nervously watching over the national treasures. Natalia was scowling. Returning

to the Victorian hotel, amazingly full of plaster effigies
of the gods on Mount Olympus, Natalia bitterly described her feelings of suffocation in Russia. She came
into my room with me and made a solid straightforward
Russian declaration of love for me. I was still six feet
away from her when Georgie just walked into my room
without knocking, as if by prearrangement. Had I been
set up?

I would never know. The Russians were great at
mocking petty things about themselves, but pompously
explained to you the major things about America. The
weather report was a military secret; there was no telephone book available in Moscow, Leningrad, Kiev;
from Tashkent we were not allowed to travel to Samark-
and. Atomic explosion in the area? Falling meteors?
Political crisis in Uzbekistan? There was just one hotel
in Samarkand and it was booked solid, but no one told
us that until we went home. Happily mooning about in
a corner of the Sverdlovsk airport, bothering nobody, a
drunk perfectly vertical was loudly castigated by Georgie for the shame he brought on the Soviet Union in the
sight of foreigners. Very correct people, so consistent
with themselves and the state that it could be funny. A
delegation of Uzbek writers, standing in a straight line
like so many acrobats waiting to go on, joyfully announced that the works of our great Ernest Hemingway
had been translated into Uzbek, then asked which
Uzbek writers had been published in English. When we
confessed we didn't know and weren't sure that *any*
Uzbek writers were available in English, the little chairman cried out "Is that *fair?*"

"Cultural exchange" was a catch-as-catch-can-affair
debate with Konstantin Simonov and Ilya Ehrenburg;
with the watchdog of literary orthodoxy Alexander

Chakovsky; with translators and professors of American literature who in public sounded like "organs of state security" and in private laughed at themselves and at me for taking them seriously. Why, in my lecture on American writing, had I bothered with such ambiguous and possibly sinister figures as William Faulkner, Robert Lowell, Norman Mailer, Saul Bellow, and omitted Theodore Dreiser's masterwork of social criticism *Tragic America?* The great science novelist Mitchell Wilson? The "progressive" dramatists Lillian Hellman and Arthur Miller? It was all the more difficult to take seriously the public vehemence of the fine novelist Leonid Leonov when he signaled to us which was the friendly guide who was reporting on us to higher authority. After an impassioned "reply to your lecture," when the virtuous indignation with my views was passed on from one auditor to another, I was told "it's all for public show" and received, at second hand, polite regret from Hemingway's best-known translator that he had been unable to intervene.

I was much too involved to be a good cultural ambassador. True "cultural exchange" consisted in endless toasts to peace and friendship between our two great nations; in not even *thinking* about the proscribed Pasternak the night we dined in Peredelkino right across from Pasternak's house; in not remembering the fate of Babel and Mandelstam, or the slaughtered Yiddish actor Mikhoels, the Yiddish writers Bergelson, Feffer, Markisch, Kvitka; in not being able to say a word to the poet and editor of the "liberal" journal *Novy Mir*, Alexander Tvardovsky, about his fight to publish Solzhenitsyn's *One Day in the Life of Ivan Denisovich*; in listening gratefully to Ilya Ehrenburg as he received us for tea in his splendid country house and explained everything except why he was the only survivor of the committee of famous Russian Jews commanded to gain international support when Hitler invaded.

There were so many questions I wanted to address to Ehrenburg's wrinkled, clever, haughty, sad face. How comes it, Ilya Grigorievich, that so rich and famous a writer, reputed to own a Rembrandt, surrounded in his country house by Picassos and Braques, has so few teeth? Is it true that under Stalin you joined in the attack on "rootless cosmopolitans"? Why in talking to us do you make so many references to your popularity with Soviet readers, evidenced by the "bushels of letters" they send you? Why is it necessary for you, who fled the Revolution and returned to Russia only in 1940, to triumph over other writers by establishing your friendship with Picasso, your love of painting, your essays in homage to Stendhal and Chekhov?

"Mother Russia," as they say, has finally rehabilitated Ilya Ehrenburg in his own eyes; I don't believe it. He looks uneasy, yet is more boastful than any other Soviet writer I have met. In youth he wandered over Russia as a tramp; lived long in Paris after the Revolution; at one time thought of becoming a Benedictine monk; then worked his way back during the Spanish Civil War by writing flaming articles for *Izvestia* from the front. He returned to Russia on the brink of war to become Stalin's favorite correspondent, then played a role (what role?—nobody will say exactly what) when Stalin openly turned on Jews, framed and shot twenty-four of the most prominent Jews in the Soviet Union.

A leading Soviet writer and "literary personality," Ehrenburg has not moved any levers in Russian history. He has not changed anyone's mind about anything. Perhaps he will be remembered only as one who had the ability to survive. Unlike Babel and Mandelstam and how many profoundly talented victims, he has just been borne along by Mother Russia, Mother Volga, on the flat broad back of the incessant present. Russians have horribly been carried along by time, space, and revolution. They have suffered history, but few in Russia have made history except the soulless "engineers of humanity" at the very top. And a few writers and rebels whose work will live as long as the Russian language itself, but who themselves have also been borne along the great-bellied river, carried like an insignificant spar of wood into the incessant Russian present, the devouring present.

"Russian history has been, one might put it, peculiarly tragic," began the novelist Leonid Leonov, then shook his head and went on to other matters. "I should have liked to talk to you about Dostoevsky. I have, you might say, a *special* interest in Dostoevsky. . . . Anyway, now that you have visited us, we are to visit you! See you in America!"

I have done my act. In this reactionary land I have lectured and expostulated in behalf of *The Sound and the Fury, The Great Gatsby*, "Sunday Morning," "The Love Song of J. Alfred Prufrock," and so on. Now at the airport, waiting to board the Belgian plane that actually has copies of *Time*, the *Observer, Le Monde, Die Welt*, I am struck by the fierce looks being directed to me by the young poet who in a wide-brimmed fedora looks as if he has stepped out of a Warner Brothers movie of the 1930s. Next year, when the Soviet literary delegation makes its exchange visit, this poet will undoubtedly hint to us that the fat, gushingly friendly Jewish girl interpreter accompanying them everywhere is a police tail. He will melodramatically change the topic every time fat, smiling Olga comes into the room. But at the moment, seeing us off at the Moscow airport,

he is a coldly correct frowning official who plainly dis-
approves of all the useless disputes I have started in the
Soviet homeland. And he is right. I am an embarrassing
cultural ambassador, I am the son of Russian Jews.

I embarrass. Jews embarrass. No reference may be
made to the millions who fled Czarism for the New
World, to the Jews who believed in nothing so much as
the Revolution and died at its hands; to Trotsky, Joffe,
Kamenev, Radek, and on and on; to the Jews slaughtered during the war in Minsk, Kiev, Kharkov; to the old
Jews still wandering about the great Russian land who
have never recovered from the hatred of Jews directed
by both Stalin and Hitler. Why are Jews so superfluous
here? Mikoyan: "We have our own cadres now."
Khrushchev: "They are all individualists and all intellectuals. They want to talk about everything, they want
to discuss everything, they want to debate everything—
and they come to totally different conclusions!"

In Tashkent, coming out of the local park of "culture
and rest," I fell in with an aged Yiddish-speaking couple who had left Odessa just ahead of the Nazis. The
man had been blinded by a machine-gun bullet from
a Nazi plane shooting up evacuation ships crossing the
Black Sea; the wife led him about. My cocky Jewish
guide Georgie, who refused to introduce me or to talk
to them, was infuriated that the three of us were talking
Yiddish in the hot Uzbek street. The old man put his
arms around me and, mumbling Hebrew blessings and
weeping, went on with trembling voice to recount everything that had happened to him and his wife during the
war, after the war. Suddenly Georgie pulled at my
sleeve and asked me to return to the car where my fellow Americans were impatiently waiting to return to
the hotel. I went to the car, discovered that everybody
was asleep, and returned to the conversation. Georgie

pulled at my sleeve again. Would I please terminate the
interview? My presence was most urgently requested
back at the car. I waved him aside, went on listening to
the old couple, then found Georgie actually trying to
pull me away. The blind old man became more and
more disturbed, took his wife's hand, and in the glaring
sunlit street they stood behind an old sentry post at the
entrance to the park, trying to escape notice. I took my
place in the car.

My mother had assured me when I called her from London that she was "better, getting better." But as if she
had been holding off death until I returned, she looked
up at me, nodded, and turned her face to the wall. A
photograph of Herzl, all beard and glossy frock coat,
had appeared over her head. She never spoke again.
Months passed. We watched over a skeleton, had to
stop the nurse from idiotically forcing food down her
mouth. The body's collapse was total; she had long since
departed in spirit, but her loud struggling gasp filled the
room. The breathing pushed at me fiercely, pushed, and
I was caught up in its lonely unconscious bellow.

Saturday night. My father and mother had started off
married life in a furnished room on a Saturday night.
She had gone to a grocery on Orchard Street to get food
for them, and had returned to find him weeping. Saturday night, forty-seven years of silent marriage later, he
sat stupefied in another room as I watched her die. Her
gasps rose out of her like fish struggling to reach the
surface of a tank; they drummed so loud in my ears
that I could not credit them to this skeletal face and
annihilated body. Louder and louder she gasped; rhythmic pounding breaths; up, up, up, up. Suddenly it all
stopped. She stopped.

Two hours later they carried her out in a green sack.

I dreamed of Indian fakirs walking barefoot on burning coals. At the grave there was a huddle of old immigrant Jews in black overcoats. A rabbi hired for the day, who had never seen her and had a lisp, told us, as they lowered her into one of the twin holes my father had bought from the Workmen's Circle thirty years before, that she had been mother and grandmother, and excellent in both departments. My wonderful Aunt Nechama, almost the last of the old Jewish anarchists, called on my father and me in the expected ritual way, studied me carefully, and slowly came out with it. "You have just been to Russia!" "Yes, dear." "So tell us." "Tell you what?" "*Do* they or don't they have true Socialism there?"

Standing on a low brick parapet in a divided Jerusalem crisscrossed with barbed wire, entangled in barbed wire, Beth and I could look down at the blue circles painted on the Arab houses to ward off the evil eye and across to where the dry furrowed Judean hills bounded and leaped before us. The Bible had said it—the Bible was true—I was seeing the Bible with my own eyes. "As the mountains are round about Jerusalem, so the Lord is round about his people."

The Jewish God could have been born only in these empty desert places. My Old Man, my God, the one and only Father. He spoke to Moses in fire; He moved in fire; perhaps saw Himself as fire. When did the religion of the Jews lose its elemental fire, the Jews their martial strength and ancient stoniness? When it became the weepy religion of powerlessness in their exile. In this stony landscape and glaring light one lives the old savageries again. The Jewish God could have been conceived and maintained only in the desert and on these heights. It is an eternal defense position.

But looking away from these flaring hills, what a jumble and clutter of churches, domes, minarets, rooftops; walls snaking in and out of each other; fortifications, battlements, archways, enclosures, gates, alleys, caves, tank barriers, sandbags, caverns, shops dug out of stone. The border is everywhere in Jerusalem; gun emplacements and signs: "STOP! DANGER!" The sun shines on all this Jerusalem limestone, crowding the eye still further. In divided crisscrossed Jerusalem we have to make our way from one Jewish street to another over rooftops, to walk through the top floor of one building connected with another. We are closed in by the heaped pieces of this historical jigsaw puzzle; just to move you have to walk along the cracks. The exhilaration of being in "a free Jewish country" comes with a sense of imprisonment. There is a tightness in the belly; barbed wire, broken stone, sand smelling of dung.

Only the Jews, with their "mystic bonds of memory," who in their minds and their daily prayers never left the land of Israel, could after nineteen hundred years have planned a mass return to this country. But caught up in this tremendous longing to redeem the past, you are also imprisoned in this effort of will. Every inch Jews occupy in this land has been bought with blood or treasure, blood *and* treasure.

The past rises up. The aunt who was afraid to flee the Nazis—"Maybe it is God's will?"—and was shot on her doorstep, has three daughters whom I have met for the first time in a town named Gate of Hope. When I sit with them on their little whitewashed balcony, we laughingly enumerate all the journeys that have brought us together here. And the prevailing theme—this is 1960—is of confidence in "the outside world" and of normality. We are normal and everything here is normal. The Canadian taxi-driver who drove us out here roars at us that he will get us to settle in Israel. His tone plainly says: "*I* am at home and *I* am normal. *I* am the most normal taxi-driver in Israel, and Israel is the only place for normal people."

The "outside" world will do right because it is "*guilty*"? Nevertheless, only with the endless duplication of persecution and extermination, of incessant justification and explanation, finally of armed struggle against the massed forces of their surrounding world, have the Jews been able to gain this precarious foothold, enveloped in this snaky border, this barbed wire, this imminent sense of danger, the eternally looming catastrophe. There is no ease in Zion. There is never any safe homecoming for Jews. The overpowering sense of effort, of strain, of will can be more haunting here than in the ghettos to which we were driven. On some days the *newness* in Jerusalem reminds me of a stage set. The shiny museum has been presented by Helena Rubinstein; the Hebrew University has been presented one building after another, one stone after another, by one or another South African or English millionaire. Even the painstaking gardens and actual dirt sticking to old Palestine and the Arab hovels below can seem a flamboyant example of what the Jews can do "in their own land."

"When are you coming to join us?" asks Yigael Yadin. "When are you bringing your children?" The famous archaeologist, the chief of staff during the 1948 "war of liberation," son of the great scholar who during the war obtained the Dead Sea Scrolls for Israel, asks such questions comfortably and even a bit arrogantly. He is at home in Israel. He will soon be at home in every crevice of Masada as he directs the excavation atop the great rock where the last Jewish zealots killed each other off rather than fall into Roman hands. He will soon bring back the last material souvenirs of Bar-Kokhba's revolt against Romans. *We* are connected here but are certainly not at home here. The argument gets loud and heavy, stretches long past midnight. "Will you shut up and let us go to sleep!" a neighbor yells from the house across the way. Though we laugh at our own excessive Jewish heat, the argument is just another instance to us of Zionist contempt for Jewish life elsewhere in the world.

By 1967, with the famous six-days victory in hand and Jerusalem "reunited," this contempt had vanished. Triumph brought with it the greatest possible anxiety. Never before had there been so keen a sense of common fate. The Israelis had "discovered" that they were alone in the world. When the news, signaled by the beep-beep-beep, came on the radio, my cousins and their children all stood at attention, as if waiting to hear their fate.

I arrived in Israel nagged by the feeling that I had an appointment to meet someone as yet unknown to me. As the plane's wheels hit the ground, people burst out singing the popular chant "*Hevenuu Shalom Aleichem. Shá-lom! Shá-lom!*" "We have brought you peace. Peace! Peace!" The plane, of course, arrived on a Friday just before sundown, with night falling fast and the Sabbath just about to lay *its* peace on us. I seemed to myself to be in a raging hurry. There was something or someone I had come a desperately long way to meet. I rushed into the Tel Aviv Hilton and found it strangely silent, empty elevators going up and down. A young porter smilingly took my bag, but, as if in a Kafka tale, forgot it in one elevator and led me into another, he was too full of his recent war experience. "I, too, have helped to liberate Jerusalem." I rushed from elevator to elevator looking for my bag. Suddenly there the battered thing was, traveling up and down the majestic elevator by itself. It was now clear that I had to get myself to Jerusalem while I could still see the craggy mountain landscapes.

The roads were lined with soldiers waiting for a lift, and the taxi-driver, explaining that they have to hitch-hike to and from a base, happily stopped for two sweaty corporals who climbed in with their little Uzi machine guns and fell asleep. The driver works every night all through the night. A Rumanian, he forced his way into Palestine during the war, lost a brother on a ship trying to run the British blockade, lived on a few cents a day as a laborer in the orange groves, finally joined the British Army and fought in North Africa and France. A subdued little middle-aged man, very quiet and mea-sured in his manner, he drove like a person who got his only joy driving a night taxi up the hills to Jerusalem. In his low voice, he spoke of "our state," "our effort." Like many Yiddish speakers who came from Eastern Europe when they were past their youth, he spoke of the shapers and makers of the state (and of his sabra sons in the Army) with some awe at what "they" could do. "They're something, I tell you," he said in awe about "our leaders." "Altogether serious people. When they make a state, it's a state. When they make an army, it's an army. They don't play around. The Arabs thought maybe we were going to play tennis?" Then sadly: "I hear they lost as much as fifteen thousand men. No re-joicing for us. And peace it's not either. For the first time it's the victors who plead for peace."

Across the street from the King David Hotel, on the stone steps and railings of the YMCA, some boy and girl soldiers were kidding around. Their sabra Hebrew is fast, the syllables bitten off, not declaimed in a sing-song before the Ark; Hebrew is their language, Israel their country, Jerusalem their capital. "Jews under forty have never heard of the Protocols of Zion." On that street, a few hundred yards away from the windmill that marks the first Jewish dwelling constructed outside the walls of the Old City a century ago, music-box chimes were being softly microphoned into the fragrant gardens. Greenwich Villagey–looking boy soldiers, in hippie beards and camouflage pants, were flirting with girl soldiers who in their neat outfits looked delicious. It was all incredibly, bountifully peaceful. The street was almost dark now, and in the fragrant dark people were slowly walking with that light step in empty streets that I remember of Friday night in childhood.

The next morning a poet who was "sort of a military governor for a few days" of Ramallah, a Jordanian town north of Jerusalem, took me along when he went to call on an Arab family whose car, "liberated" by Israeli soldiers, he had restored to them. The traffic out of Jerusalem this Saturday morning was hot and heavy; everybody in Israel wants to see the Old City—closed to Jews since 1948—and they want to see the occupied parts of Jordan, where white flags fly from every house and where the arches put up by King Hussein across the highway no longer show the royal insignia. After military policemen passed us through, the traffic eased up, and we drove along in full view of the wild, hilly stony Jerusalem landscape, between identical new suburban houses built out of the light-colored stone that gives "Jerusalem the Golden" all the same color. Ramallah was packed with Israeli soldiers who seemed to be passing very familiarly up and down the streets. By the time we pulled up at our destination, a house right on the highway, our party was full of Israeli writers still in uniform, and Dutch and Scandinavian well-wishers. The owners, an architect and his wife in their sixties, re-

ceived us with highly charged courtesy. They thanked
the poet-"military governor" for returning their car,
quietly added that the radio was missing from the car
plus a bracelet and some trinkets from the house, and
when the poet expressed his dismay, informed him that
all the car radios in the neighborhood had been lifted
by the Israeli occupiers.

Somehow this led to Nasser's radio speeches, a subject grimly on Israeli minds. When the war broke out,
the Egyptian radio repeatedly affirmed, "Jews, we are
coming to kill all of you. We are going to exterminate
you." Still, everything was going swimmingly until the
lady of the house, smoothly diffident in manner, said,
"It appears the Egyptians lost as they did because their
generals are traitors." The Israelis were stunned, but
the poet quickly shifted into a passionate plea for Arab-
Israeli cooperation. His hosts listened impassively when
he explained in a voice choked with emotion that Israelis were not to be feared. Why, wherever there are
two Jews there are three political parties. And there had
not been a single instance of 'an Israeli soldier raping
an Arab woman. "*Pas une femme violée—pas une!*"
Whether this reassured our hosts, they didn't say. They
did say that they were from Jaffa (now Yafo, a Tel
Aviv suburb), an Arab town before 1948.

Back in Jerusalem this Sabbath I went, at last, to the
Wall. Outside the walls of the Old City I found myself
engulfed in Israelis, Arabs, tourists, pilgrims by the
thousands staring at each other. The old barriers were
down and a mass of Jews and Arabs seemed to be walking *at* each other, around each other, jostling each
other, and avoiding each other. Nearing the Wall, I
found myself caught up in a great procession of heavily
Orthodox Jews. A little blond boy in full Hasidic re-
galia—knee breeches, white stockings, with pious side-

curls falling down his cheeks, screamed "Pagan!" at a tourist aiming a camera on him—on the Lord's Day!

The steady tramp of the Orthodox raised a lot of dust. By the time I got my first sight of the Wall, at the back of a large cleared area, the crowd made a powerful mass in those war-shocked streets. The Wall rises up at the end of this long vista now, where in the old pictures it formed a narrow courtyard. The official explanation is that everything in the area was razed so that large crowds could move freely. There was a lot of hard fighting here, and the area was of course full of damaged houses. After the 1948 fighting, all Jews disappeared from the Old City and all *their* houses disappeared. When they recovered the Mount of Olives, holiest of Jewish burying places, the Israelis discovered that tombstones had been used as latrine covers. Jerusalem is "not negotiable." "What's this?" Ben-Gurion shouted when he saw that the old street sign in Arabic and English was still hanging there. A soldier knocked the sign down with the butt of his rifle.

At the Wall, as in an Orthodox synagogue, the women were dutifully praying in one section and the men in another—praying like mad, bowing repeatedly, rocking in the ecstatic movement of the worshiper's body that is to unite him firmly to God. A thoroughly anonymous man, beardless and wearing a sweat-stained old Panama hat, was saying thanksgiving prayers, to the reiterated cries of "Amen" and "Hallelujah" from the formidably bearded Hasidim behind him, in long white stockings and knee breeches, caftans and great round fur hats. One man would take the Torah out of the Ark, and others would immediately gather around him to kiss the coverings. Beardless men in sports shirts and the Hasidim in their seventeenth-century Polish costumes, with full beards and sidecurls, were all joyously standing together. We were all there. The line-up was real.

At El Arish on the Mediterranean, on our way to the Suez Canal, I sat in a grove of palm trees looking at the clear, shining, blue-green water. Everywhere were shoes that had been thrown off by the Egyptians so they could run faster. As we toiled to the Canal through the Sinai desert with a busload of correspondents and photographers, a mild-looking little Israeli colonel hitching a ride to his encampment bitterly observed the enthusiasm with which the photographers shot every blackened, burned-out tank and truck. From the Gaza Strip to the Canal you could see hundreds on hundreds of shot-up, burned-out Egyptian vehicles. It was not difficult to picture soldiers on fire and screaming. One photographer, coming back with shots of still another burned-out tank, announced triumphantly that he had seen a body in it. The little colonel said with scorn, "May I say one word? You have seen what we can destroy. May I ask you please to notice what also we can build?"

That night at the Canal, camped with a small army of reporters on the spacious grounds of an Arab villa, I laughed at how far I had come in my longing to see the great world. I was resting on a cousin's greasy, muddy army sleeping bag lined with old bloodstains, and I was fighting off midges. There was no way of getting off the grounds; the Israelis had clamped a curfew on the town. A couple of yards away a Swedish correspondent was guardedly sipping at his private bottle of Scotch. Three leggy beautiful models from *Elle* were entwined with the French journalists who had thoughtfully brought them along. In Gaza the sight of these models had greatly excited young Arab men in pajamas, who, walking hand in hand through the streets, had broken off from each other to chase the girls. The midges kept biting. It was impossible to sleep; pistols were fired into the air to keep off curious Egyptian urchins. As soon as the long night broke and there was light to see by, the Israeli officer began busily to shave.

The Canal, the border, a shed just along the Canal with Arab schoolbooks left behind in the deserted town of El Qantara. The shed had been broken open and loose pages of the schoolbooks drifted in the wind. Wild-mustached Israeli soldiers were sitting on dining-room chairs in the main street of El Qantara laughing over an enormous framed photograph of Nasser they had found in one of the houses. Across the Canal, Egyptian soldiers could be seen darting from behind sandy boulders and darting back in again; I felt like an interloper in outer space.

Later, on a tour of the West Bank of the Jordan, we came to the Allenby Bridge, which was crumpled without being knocked out. On the Israeli side, army engineers had built a solid wooden boardwalk across; the twisted loosened girders of the original bridge had been left just as they were at war's end. On the other side of the bridge sat enclaves of Arab families who had just made their way over. Some fifty people had flopped amid their clothes, furniture, even their kitchen ranges and refrigerators, which the *women* unbelievably carried over, dragging everything over the twisted girders. I watched the scene through army binoculars: the people squatting out there were waiting for buses to pick them up, but no buses had shown up; it was a grim sight. Off in the distance, on the veranda of a house, sat a group of Jordanian Army officers looking at *us* through binoculars. When I asked how long they might be sitting there like that in an empty field, my driver cried out, "Don't forget how many refugees *we've* had!"

On the way over he had been telling me how his father, a tombstone maker on the Mount of Olives, had been murdered by his Arab assistants. The young Israeli guard overlooking the bridge, an ingenuous-looking blond boy, irritably asked the driver if I was a Jew. Told that I was, he grinned broadly: "Then you're okay!"

Yussele Rosensaft, a Polish Jew, claimed to have escaped from Auschwitz; he ended up in Belsen. He remained in Belsen after the liberation, married a former prisoner, had a son born there. In New York, rich and transformed as in a fairy tale, he collected modern paintings by the carload. But his only interest in life was the memory of the Holocaust. He located the survivors of Belsen in Canada, Australia, the United States, France, England, Israel, West Germany. Paying for everything—"I am obsessed with Jews and their future" —he organized the Belsen Survivors; searched out and published novels, poems, and memoirs of the Holocaust; enlisted Elie Wiesel, Saul Bellow, George Steiner, and other writers to support this effort.

I went over to his sumptuous apartment at Madison and Seventieth to learn more about the Belsen Survivors. Rosensaft was downstairs in the lobby, feistily questioning the doorman about an expected package. Short, stocky, a fighter in every gesture, he bustlingly took me upstairs. As we entered the apartment, he went around the room lighting up a mad museum of Chagalls. There were so many pictures on every wall that the effect was of stumbling drunk up to a movie screen and not being able to escape it.

Rosensaft sat at one end of a long yellow silk sofa, his wife at the other. The vast unoccupied amount of yellow silk between them certainly showed off the sofa.

The wife wore a sleeveless dress. The blue concentration-camp number on the inside of her arm just above her wrist seemed longer than others I had seen; there may have been more than one number.

We were having a most genteel tea, little cakes on paper doilies, the tea served in porcelain so fragile that under the stress of the talk the cup seemed about to break in my hand. Rosensaft talked at me as if I had walked into the middle of a story he had been telling with increasing fury night and day. He said that the French government insisted on reburying in a separate plot the French who died at Belsen. Since this meant digging up everyone else, the Belsen Survivors were resisting the French.

Trying to manage my tea and the little cake precariously balanced on my knee, I listened in a stupor to Rosensaft's ferocious account of the legal efforts being made to oppose the French government. I did not fully take in all the details. I did not know what to believe. He seemed to believe it all. Impatiently bouncing up and down in his corner of the yellow silk sofa, he could not stop scalding me with his outrage. Every muscle pulsed in his face as he talked in a torrent of inimitable scornful Yiddish laden with the details of Belsen. He throbbed with indignation. Above his head a procession of sylphs and bearded fiddlers floated over the roofs of the *shtetl*, dream after dream by Chagall.

Rosensaft, too pent-up to sit there any longer, hurried me around more pictures hung with the same mad profusion in every other room of his apartment; he hurried me into his limousine, replete with chauffeur. In the midst of the rush-hour traffic on Park Avenue, he described the last days in Belsen. On April 15, 1945, a British detachment in the north of Germany stumbled on this deeply hidden camp to find typhus raging; forty thousand sick, starving, dying prisoners; thirteen thousand corpses stacked on the ground.

Rosensaft complained that everything was falling apart. The world no longer knew, was simply not interested. He had never expected, when Belsen was liberated, that the postwar period would be so chaotic. "I need some good news!" he cried. "Give me some good news!"

On the twenty-fifth anniversary of the liberation, Rosensaft flew us to Belsen, then to Israel to sweeten the pill. Rain was falling as we trudged up the clean, well-kept road from the "museum" at the entrance to the four-sided memorial stone where we said *Kaddish*.

EARTH HIDE NOT THE BLOOD SHED ON THEE
BY THE MURDEROUS NAZIS

Belsen was just a cemetery now, a clean and seemly German park, a park of mass graves. It was an astoundingly small place. Within this quarter of a mile had been packed in fifty-eight thousand people, to say nothing of the unburied corpses. The S.S. had its quarters in "new" Belsen, farther off. Stone after stone read: HERE LIE FOUR THOUSAND . . . THREE THOUSAND . . . Here and there were stray little memorial stones to individuals; no graves. A huge wall facing us had memorial inscriptions in every European language. A large cross had been put up by the French government. Next to me in the procession was a handsome blonde, perfectly coiffed and beautifully dressed. She had a number on the inside of her arm. She had gone back to live in Germany, but smiled at the perfect German orderliness and cleanliness of Belsen, 1970. "You should have seen it in 1945 when the end was near. The guards ran around like mad, not knowing how to get rid of the corpses. In their panic they went crazy, more vicious than before."

In the light-colored pretty dining room of the splendid hotel in Hanover, the writers told joke after joke as the white wine gushed into our glasses. Our hands were shaking. Rosensaft in Israel, greeting us expansively in Herzlia at a hotel on the sea, was genial to the point of bursting. There were speeches at the dinner in the garden; a great dinner and more speeches in Jerusalem, where Prime Minister Golda Meir paid tribute to the Belsen Survivors and crisply ended, "Believe me, friends, we shall overcome." (Rosensaft was to die bankrupt in a few years, his pictures confiscated to pay his debts. His shaky fortune was not altogether real. What there was had gone to "my Jews.") Saul Bellow, on the other side of my table, was laughingly translating the Prime Minister's Yiddish into the left ear of the girl accompanying him. Wiesel spoke at length in English, remembered arriving in Auschwitz shortly after his bar mitzvah, with his prayer book, new prayer shawl, and suddenly realizing what was about to engulf him.

Everything Wiesel said was pitched high, stabbed you and was meant to stab you with the impossibility of finding words for Jewish martyrdom. The Bible psalmist had cried aloud in despair that he could not find the word—the deep, deep word forever lacking to human speech—that would convey the bounty of God. This was still the tradition. God cannot be uttered; He cannot be imagined; He cannot even be spelled. The Jewish word strives after a reality that is spirit, that can never adequately express our debt to God, our awe, our love, and our fear. So Wiesel spoke not only of the Holocaust but of the impossibility of expressing it. Like God, the final solution was somehow beyond us. The other nations had forgotten it; the survivors themselves were an embarrassment. Couldn't we all see that the survivors were now an embarrassment? If the survivors weren't there, it would be so much easier for the others.

Wiesel's speech went higher and higher. It was a survivor's soliloquy, a litany, a rhythm, a *Kaddish*. There was no word that might say an end to anguish. He spoke mysteriously, orphically, of "laughter" as the ultimate response. The audience listened humbly, in total respect, as he teetered on the edge of incommunicable profundities. But it was also rhetorical, hysterical, a writer's public performance without irony. And looking at Bellow bored by the flood of words, I thought of the poor Jews we had grown up with who found an irony in language itself. Even their beloved Yiddish could never do justice to *their* struggle for existence. I felt the residual cruelty of the Holocaust. The Jews could not state their case without seeming to overstate it. The world was getting tired of our complaint.

A book by a Northwestern University professor says that the Nazi extermination of European Jews was nothing more than a Zionist-inspired myth. The book, *The Fabrication of a Hoax*, argues that there was no German policy of Jewish extermination and that millions of European Jews were not deliberately slain in Nazi concentration camps. He contends many of them died of disease and starvation or were "deported to the East."

Assertions of a Jewish holocaust, he says, were contrived by Zionist leaders to promote sympathy for a Jewish homeland in Palestine.

"O Word, Thou Word That I Lack!"

The Coney Island Hospital was so crowded that a line of beds stretched down a corridor. In one of the beds lay a tiny old man with the elaborate, overhanging mustache of a Greco-Turkish wrestler. His egg-shaped head was so bare that every light fixture in the ceiling seemed to reflect silvery bars and circles on his skull.

His face was calm, even contemptuous, as he lay there in a kind of stupor, mysteriously crying "Hey! . . . Hey!" at regular intervals, and always in the same inhuman voice, like identical bleeps off a radar screen.

My eighty-two-year-old father was in a nearby bed. He had had a heart attack as he was preparing to go South, had been taken to the hospital's intensive-care unit and, suffering a stroke in the hospital, he now lay almost speechless. He stared up at me from more than his usual solitude. Every time I went down the corridor to visit my father, I noticed that the bald old man with the too virile mustache had thrown off his coverings, had pushed up his canvas sack of a hospital gown to expose himself and so get some attention from the busy, rushed, often frantic hospital attendants. It was not the tender loving care he may have been looking for. A harried nurse, hysterically running down the corridor waving a syringe, looked down at the old man and cried, "Nick! You dope! Cut it out!" In one swift contemptuous motion she managed to pull the sheet down past his knobby knees and to indicate that his nakedness was as interesting to her as the contents of a bedpan.

My father could not be moved. His few broken sentences were hard to understand. I stood at his bedside, watching his tongue flap helplessly in his mouth. It seemed to me that some accusation was being made.

> Some are born to sweet delight
> Some are born to sweet delight
> Some are born to endless night

My father had never altogether learned English, he had been seriously deaf for years; he was eighty-two, confused in speech, and almost too frightened to speak. Unable to produce even the signature he was once so proud of having learned, he hopelessly mixed the letters up, and slapped his head with vexation and shame.

He stared at me and I stared at him. Father and son can accomplish an eerie and terrifying similarity. I felt I could see every burst and broken fiber in his brain. At regular intervals came from the corridor Nick's bleating, unnerving, regular, and repeated cry "Hey! . . . Hey!" I could not just stand there looking down at my father. We looked exactly alike, and I was shocked to see in the mirror the face I had seen on him when I was twenty. I walked into the corridor with some strangled desire to stop these unceasing cries. I would have liked my father, poor dying old man, poor as the day he had come to America, to yell out like the little bald wrestler with the powerful mustache.

The days passed. Nick's repetitious bleats and regularly exposed genitals seemed to blend in with the constant shrilling of telephones, the squeak of rubber wheels bearing a patient to and from the operating room, the cheerful rustle of a nurse's breasts in her nylon uniform, the heaviness of red-faced visitors in overcoats, fur hats, and boots, carrying overladen shopping bags as they stamped into the hospital from the witheringly cold winter streets. Nick had become as indistinguishable a fixture of the hospital as its metal furniture. He was part of the corridor. I often saw him uncovered, and no one paying him the slightest attention.

Standing by the grave, I shakenly say *Kaddish*. My proudest memory of my father is that when I was a boy and stood with him on Sunday mornings as he waited in the crowd of house painters on Pitkin Avenue to be tapped for a new job, he would shyly but with unmis-

takable delight introduce me around as his *Kaddish*.
"Meet my *Kaddish*." Meet the son and heir who will
see me to the grave and say the last prayer over me.

> Blessed and praised, glorified and exalted, extolled and
> honored, adored and lauded be the name of the Holy
> One, blessed be he, beyond all the blessings and hymns,
> praises and consolations that are ever spoken in the
> world.

I mangle the ancient awesome text that has not a word
about death in it, ashamed before the few of us left
(and a straggle from the Brotherhood of Painters and
Decorators) that I read the words so badly. But looking around me I feel amused pride. Never in his life
did my father have so many people in attendance on
him. This could have been quite a moment for him
who for the greater part of his life, but especially in the
long tediousness of his old age, was so easy to over-
look that it used to drive me wild to hear even young
people call him "Charlie."

That Gedaliah became "Charlie" is less surprising
than the fact that in the last months of his life my
father's childhood exposure to Hebrew prayers caught
up with him without his knowing it. He developed
aphasia; his speech became more and more broken. In
the Orthodox old-age home and hospital in which the
old Socialist finally found refuge and died after being
dismissed from hospital after hospital as hopeless, incurable, "too far gone to respond to treatment," old
immigrant Jews like himself, already disturbed by his
inability to make himself clear, listened with astonishment to the repetition of an invocation from the first
prayer said by children upon awakening in the morning,
a prayer long buried in my father's mind:

"*Lefonecho* . . . Before Thy Face I render thanks to Thee, Everlasting King, who has mercifully restored my soul within me; thy faithfulness is great."

Strangely he repeated this over and over, mixed it into every English phrase. As I walked into his room, he would cry out, "So how is everything. *Lefonecho? Lefonecho*, when will I be getting out of here, *Lefonecho?*"

It was, said the old men around him, peculiar. He was peculiar. No one had ever heard anything like it. Even in his final illness, he was not like other men. What was this unconscious, unnatural repetition of "Before Thy Face" doing in the mouth of an old Socialist and trade unionist who could never be dragged to synagogue and who would pronounce himself "emancipated" with a complacency that made me wince. My father was almost too self-centered to be interested in God, and he was no Hebrew scholar. But after so many millenniums, the Jewish God might have turned humorist. There was certainly a terrible joke somewhere. At the end of my father's life, classic deference to the Almighty, the Master of the Universe, the Father of All Mercy, our Lord and our God and our Shield, surfaced in one blood-loosed portion of my father's brain. "Before Thy Face!" "Before Thy Face!" In his mechanical repetition of these words my father suddenly made me think of those zealous worshipers before the Wall in Jerusalem who, like wound-up dolls, rapidly, unceasingly bow to Him at each phrase as they say their prayers. But my father's *Lefonecho* . . . *Lefonecho* . . . *Lefonecho* had no meaning for him. It was just another symptom, the final peculiarity in the life of this always peculiar man, my father, about whom I never heard a word of praise from anyone close to him, not even a word of indulgence except from doctors, nurses, hospital supervisors. "What are we to do with him?" "Where are we to send him?"

In his last, drawn-out, maddening incapacity, when he could not speak clearly, he finally became incontinent, thus infuriating the other old men around him who had never been able to draw him into their pinochle games and conversation. It was this impatience with him even among sick old Jews like himself that troubled me most. He had never been like other Jewish fathers, and he was certainly not like them now. Not friendly, not "regular," he sat grimly alone, not talking to his roommates. I excused him to them, explained that his unfortunate malady made normal talk impossible. But he had always been a great man for walking about instead of talking, for walking alone. Even after his stroke, which affected only his speech, he constantly paced the corridor outside his room, would stand near the elevators as if determined to make his way to the entrance hall below and past the guard at the door. He needed to feel himself near an exit. As he sat beside the television set without looking at it, muttering words that became mysterious torn-up sounds, holding me to him because those sounds kept promising to become words, he would point at the window and cry brokenly, "Out! What is the use of this? Out!"

He had always been a great man for making an exit quickly, silently, disapprovingly. Before his stroke it would excite him to meet me for lunch in front of the Forty-second Street Library—I inevitably found him pacing the Fifth Avenue steps when I, in my turn, arrived early. But he never initiated a conversation. He would shyly, ungivingly answer my questions about his week when I forced conversation on him. For the many years before his death when he was deaf, and so incompetently handled his deafness that he seemed altogether walled into the silence and fixity, it required a special effort on my part to break through. "See anybody this week?" "Who should I see? Who calls me up?" He left most people indifferent and condescending. "Hey, Charlie, how are ya, Charlie? Whaddya say, Charlie? That's good!" Though he exasperated me because, ridiculously, I still expected my father to be a father, he could reduce me to such helpless love that I walked away from every hospital he was in—there were four in six months—muttering all the rage against his life, fortune, the world that I never saw *him* express until it was too late to make himself understood. On the day of his admission to the Orthodox home, knowing he would never walk out of it, he threw the infuriatingly overladen lunch tray against the wall.

After my mother's death I had prevailed upon him to move to a little hotel near the seafront in Brighton Beach. I noticed as we pulled up to the door that in his nervousness he had separated the different parts of his hearing aid. He had lost an essential little disk. It was not in the car, it was not in the street, but as I reproached him for his awkwardness and felt the old humiliation of stooping in the gutter for something essential to putting my old man together, he took in all my impatience and began to weep. Bitterly, accusingly, in one of the few moments of direct concentrated feeling I ever had from him, he cried out, "You have never loved me!"

His last year was terrible. Since he could not speak clearly, could walk but was unable to go anywhere except the corridors, the incapacity peculiar to his life was always before my eyes. "I can't do it!" he growled after I had walked him to the john. "I can't do it!" He looked straight at me with silent bitter eyes. He did not even, like the most pious Jews, have a God to rail against.

Edmund Wilson was lonely in Wellfleet the year round, and he was afraid of dying. He surrendered to us his magnificently desolate Audubon print of two long-haired squirrels, each alone on its tree and looking as apprehensive as only a squirrel can even when it has cornered some food against the evening. He could not, he said, endure those squirrels any longer. They reminded him too much of himself. He fortified himself by writing, as indefatigable journal keepers do. "After all, the center of the world *is* my mind."

Death was the antagonist that his obstinate nineteenth-century materialism could not defeat. It would give him no help. His Grandfather Thaddeus's old Presbyterianism was no help. Was it possible that Jews had an answer? The question was as delightful to me as Edmund's writing that he had lost himself in four thousand years of Jewish history and could not get out. One of his favorite maxims in his lonely Wellfleet winters was *Hazak Hazak Vinithazak*, addressed by Orthodox Jews in synagogue as they come to the end of the year's prescribed reading. "Be Strong, Be Strong, and Let Us Strengthen One Another!" In Hebrew letters, this is engraved on his tombstone in the Wellfleet cemetery.

In Manhattan's West Eighties, where I live, there is nothing to write about but people. "Nature" hardly exists, and the architecture, when it is not simply eccentric, can be seen from the street as representing nothing but the calculation of how much money can be squeezed each month out of these cubicles.

This too human landscape can be suffocating but is interesting to write about. On peeling benches lining the traffic island down the middle of Broadway, very old-looking women, who cannot be as old as they look and who are hideously made up, sit tensely and somehow angrily taking in a little sunshine. They are frequently impeded in this by drunks drooling and sprawling over them as they sip from bottles decorously contained in paper bags; by junkies who are reeling but determined to make conversation; by the transvestites wearing falsies and pink curlers who have neglected to shave. There is also a pair of identical sandwich men who duplicate each other's knife-like nose, knobby chin, and eyes. Although they do not wear disguises of any kind, they look like masked thieves about to pounce. The crudely handwritten placards they wear (one on his front, the other on his back) denounce the C.I.A. for killing John Kennedy and the nameless conspirators who have seized our government and are poisoning all the breakfast cereal. All day long outside the Baptist Church a ruddy totally smooth-looking bald man proclaims the Authorized King James Version of the Bible to be the only one acceptable to God. From time to time, however, he can be seen going through the subway cars screaming at young men and boys: "Be a man! Get a haircut!"

The fast-aging ladies trying to soak in a little sunshine can often be heard saying to each other that New York is not what it used to be. The "dregs of the city," as one old lady calls them, seem to take a special pleasure in tormenting old ladies. There are many heated discussions about the right to these benches. There are many human explosions. "New York is just a failure," I read in a literary weekly. There are certainly many failures on these streets. The professor of Russian, my own Pnin, no longer teaches at the City University and sits all day on one of the benches in the middle of Broadway shaking his head over the many drunks. The mad-woman of Broadway, who still prowls the street in house slippers and always carries a shopping bag, is indomitable and never seems any older as she wanders into Zabar's, screams "Bestids, all of you!" at the people in ski clothes lined up before the lox counter. She still can be seen in the drugstore talking into a telephone marked "out of order."

Meanwhile the unending charge of traffic on Broadway emits many gases, which mingle with the odors of oiling, frying, and broiling from the many hamburger joints and delicatessens. The ladies who came over with concentration-camp numbers on their arms are often now buxom blondes in mink coats. The venerable and capacious apartment houses on Riverside Drive and West End Avenue, famous for having room enough for our many books and pictures, are full of doctors, editors, lawyers, actors, museum curators, writers, and psychoanalysts who every morning run after taxis, battle each other for taxis, to take them to their offices across town. On the east side of Broadway, leading past Amsterdam and Columbus, in winter last month's snow is still frozen solid, garbage is piled up, you cannot take your car out of the garage without narrowly missing a trail of broken glass, and the steps of the ratty tenements are lined any morning and afternoon with black strangers, strangers who obviously have nothing to do.

Life is charged, busy, tense. People complain with witty bitterness about the scruffy whores in leathery hot pants who are still at their posts at eight in the morning, when the private-school buses pull up at the door. They worry about the children who have to come back alone in the winter dark. The man following Rachel across the park was perhaps not after her at all. The irritable violence in the air leads to constant

alarms, some false. This is not the South Bronx, "A
JUNGLE STALKED BY FEAR, SEIZED BY RAGE"—where
merchants conduct business in their stores from behind
bulletproof glass and where packs of wild dogs pick
through rubble and roam the streets, sometimes attacking residents. Nor is this Brownsville, my old *shtetl*,
which the other day settled on my doorstep.

Returning from a weekend in East Hampton, I was
already pressed on every nerve end by being able to do
no better than a double park behind a moving van that
had picked the exact moment of my return to unload
seven rooms of furniture into our usual mob scene of
a West Side apartment house. I squeezed myself like a
safecracker along the cars at the curb to unload my own
car. And suddenly heard an insanely magnified voice
screaming through a bullhorn, "Brownsville slumlord!"

Since I saw many evictions from the Brownsville
tenement in which I spent my first twenty years, I felt
much confused by the manic reversal on West End
Avenue as I watched half a dozen young black women
with placards denouncing the cheerful songwriter in the
penthouse whose father left him two tenement houses
in that once prime and promising American ghetto,
"Brunzvil." A young Jew with a bullhorn, who looked
exactly like pictures of Trotsky in 1905, was leading
his followers in a rhythmic chant: "Ostrofsky is a slumlord! We refuse to pay any more rent to Ostrofsky the
slumlord! Brownsville demands decent living conditions! We protest!"

The Puerto Rican elevator men looked on without
malice and without comprehension. The passers-by
managed, with that inimitable New York look of angry
self-occupation, to walk past the demonstration as if
the blacks from Brownsville were shouting from a distant planet. All went on as usual—the psychiatrist and

museum curators in our building fought each other for taxis, the transvestites in their pink hair-rollers defiantly made eyes at glum unseeing laundry drivers, the kooky twins held up their crudely lettered pieces of cardboard. And I, staggering in under my "portable" electric typewriter, cartons of books and papers, and the certain knowledge that I would soon get a ticket and had probably left the key in the ignition, recognized that I was being welcomed back in style as the moving men, transporting their loads past me, hoarsely announced that I was in their way.

The songwriter in the penthouse, an amateur scholar of American theology who has edited an up-to-the-minute anthology called *Jonathan Edwards on Hellfire*, teases me on the change in our lives since we departed what is *now* the most undesirable of all living spaces since the Black Hole of Calcutta. In my time Brownsville was remote. It was certainly not the center of anything. But it was once a great Jewish family, and there were people there, the purest of old Jewish believers in the past, in the future, in God, in the redemption of Eretz Israel by hard toil on the land according to Tolstoyan principles (and hand in hand with our Arab neighbors), whom forty years later I talk to in my dreams as if whatever happened since I left them need not have happened.

When the Mayor of New York took some touring mayors down to see Brownsville, the Mayor of Boston called it "the first tangible sign of the collapse of our civilization." My co-religionist in the penthouse ("the *upstairsike*," my mother would have called him) has sharpened his New York wit on Calvinist theology. He likes, in our occasional encounters in the elevator, to entertain me in deadpan fashion with new chapters in the rollicking saga of what it is like to be bequeathed a tenement in Brownsville. He can never collect his rents without a covey of police to guard him, is ready to abandon the property. There are a lot of fires.

WOMAN SAYS SHE
SET 2,000 FIRES
SUSPECT IN BROOKLYN TELLS MARSHALS OF
12-YEAR TOTAL

A 23-year-old Brooklyn woman arrested early Monday after she was seen running from a vacant Brownsville building that was on fire has allegedly admitted setting two to four fires every week for the last 12 years, or a total of more than 2,000 fires.

The woman, Priscilla Haynes of 419 Blake Avenue, in the Brownsville section, assertedly told fire marshals that she "liked to see the flames," and got a thrill from watching fire equipment rolling up to a burning building.

The woman allegedly said that she would wander about the Brownsville section in the vicinity of her home looking for vacant buildings. Then, she was reported to have said, after selecting empty dwellings or tenements, she would return to them at night, start a fire, then watch from nearby as the firemen fought the blaze.

During acute depression and periods of romantic difficulty, Miss Haynes was quoted as having told the marshals, she would set eight or nine fires a day to relieve her despondency.

"She said that fires were the third biggest thing in her life," Marshal O'Connor said. "First she said there was her mother, then her brother, then fires."

I went down to Brownsville to write about a native's return, or "The Depression Revisited," but soon lost heart. The place looks worse than the East End of London after the blitz. Apparently the roofs are regularly set on fire; the tops of the old tenements, built of

New York's usual cheap apartment-house brown brick, are charred, blackened, fire-streaked. When I walked down Sutter Avenue for the first time in twenty years, I was horrified by the look of rusted blood down so many windows, the mounds of garbage heaped in a continuing line down the *middle* of the avenue, the long line of empty boarded-up storefronts, and the dead angry silence in front of the stoops on the street where I spent so much of my boyhood playing catchball off the steps—on a street still named Herzl.

The place overcame even Richard Moore, a militant Black Panther leader in from Oakland to rally the oppressed masses. "I have never seen people live like this." On one occasion a dog crept in front of Moore's slowly moving car and simply refused to move.

Meanwhile there is the other New York, the capital of words, the chosen city that is even more splendid, chic, glittery, and excessive now than when I dreamed of entering it—the New York of the great museums, of Madison Avenue galleries on sparkling Saturday afternoons in the fall, of Fifth Avenue in the glow of lunchtime and the cocktail hour. The more the city seems to hang by a nail—the more we approach "the last days of New York"—the wittier and more knowing the commentary. We are the best historians of our own death. Because it isn't a death for the culture industry, the television event, the ballet, the opera, the new movie houses on Third Avenue, the newspapers that tell you how to live, what to think, where to shop; for the sexy shops and caressing little restaurants—the New York that is still most enchanting at dusk, when all the lights seem to go on at once, when the spurt of release that comes at the cocktail hour creates one more vibration in the excited exiting from those lighted skyscrapers of so many clever men, so many stirringly liberated women.

Between classes, I sit in the library high up on this college building on Park and Sixty-ninth. I go over "Sailing to Byzantium" with a shy black girl from the West Indies who has a lisp. Who said this is no country for old men? I have traveled the whole route and now sit, in this beautiful bedlam and chaos, helping my student trace the lines in Yeats, one after another, as if she were deciphering some ancient ruin in the desert. I feel I am dreaming aloud as I look at the rooftops, at the sky, at the massed white skyline of New York. The view just across the rooftops is as charged as the indented black words on the white page. The mass and pressure of the bulging skyline are wild. New York is wild and Yeats is wild. How wonderful and funny it can be, this late October afternoon, to be going over Yeats word for word and line by line against the screech of millions all over this city. Even in its "last days," the secret of New York is raw power, mass and volume, money and power.

Across the river in Jersey a great fire is burning on the piers. The sky is maddened. From the party high over Lincoln Center, looking down on the plaza that from this distance looks more serene than it really is, in the midst of a rumble with a psychoanalyst about the "neurotic guilt of survivors," you can see the great fire raging, truly raging, on several Weehawken piers. Blaze was always my word for joy. Fire has haunted my life and I talk to my dead in my dreams—our dead—like those epic heroes who in the other world talked to *their* dead separated by a screen of fire. O Lord who made Himself known as fire, where are you? "Return, O Lord,

Have Pity On Thy Servants!" Sweet loves! Absent friends! Mama, Papa! *Where* are you? The people arguing about movie reviews, Lina Wertmüller, the "neurotic guilt of survivors," have their backs to the fire. It takes some effort to call their attention to it. But as they finally turn around and see it, a new party excitement takes over in the face of that blazing insistency over Jersey. The sky is all red, crazy-red. People reach out, feel each other hungrily. The sky over our heads has been loosened at last. I want to love again. I want my God back. I will never give up until it is too late to expect you.

INDEX

About the Author

Alfred Kazin's book *On Native Grounds* changed the entire direction of current and retrospective literary criticism in this country. He has written numerous other books of criticism, and has been editor of many collections and critical studies. He has taught at Harvard, the University of California, Smith, Black Mountain College, the University of Minnesota, the City University of New York, and other universities here and abroad. He is at work on a major new book, *The American Procession*, about American writers of the nineteenth century.